3rd Workshop on Representation Learning for NLP 2018

Held at ACL 2018

Melbourne, Australia
20 July 2018

ISBN: 978-1-5108-6717-8

ACL 2018

Representation Learning for NLP

Proceedings of the Third Workshop

July 20, 2018
Melbourne, Australia

Introduction

The ACL 2018 Workshop on Representation Learning for NLP (RepL4NLP) takes place on Friday, July 20, 2018 in Melbourne, Australia, immediately following the 56th Annual Meeting of the Association for Computational Linguistics (ACL). The workshop is generously sponsored by Facebook, Salesforce, ASAPP, DeepMind, Microsoft Research, and Naver.

Repl4NLP is organised by Isabelle Augenstein, Kris Cao, He He, Felix Hill, Spandana Gella, Jamie Kiros, Hongyuan Mei and Dipendra Misra, and advised by Kyunghyun Cho, Edward Grefenstette, Karl Moritz Hermann and Laura Rimell.

The 3rd Workshop on Representation Learning for NLP aims to continue the success of the 1st Workshop on Representation Learning for NLP, which received about 50 submissions and over 250 attendees and was the second most attended collocated event at ACL 2016 in Berlin, Germany after WMT; and the 2nd Workshop on Representation Learning for NLP at ACL 2017 in Vancouver, Canada.

The workshop has a focus on vector space models of meaning, compositionality, and the application of deep neural networks and spectral methods to NLP. It provides a forum for discussing recent advances on these topics, as well as future research directions in linguistically motivated vector-based models in NLP.

Organizers:

Isabelle Augenstein, University of Copenhagen
Kris Cao, University of Cambridge
He He, Stanford University
Felix Hill, DeepMind
Spandana Gella, University of Edinburgh
Jamie Kiros, University of Toronto
Hongyuan Mei, Johns Hopkins University
Dipendra Misra, Cornell University

Senior Advisors:

Kyunghyun Cho, NYU and FAIR
Edward Grefenstette, DeepMind
Karl Moritz Hermann, DeepMind
Laura Rimell, DeepMind

Program Committee:

Eneko Agirre, University of the Basque Country
Yoav Artzi, Cornell University
Mohit Bansal, UNC Chapel Hill
Meriem Beloucif, HKUST
Jonathan Berant, Tel-Aviv
Johannes Bjerva, University of Copenhagen
Jan Buys, Oxford University
Xilun Chen, Cornell University
Eunsol Choi, University of Washington
Heeyoul Choi, Handong Global University
Junyoung Chung, University of Montreal
Manuel Ciosici, Aarhus University
Stephen Clark, DeepMind
Marco Damonte, University of Edinburgh
Desmond Elliot, University of Edinburgh
Katrin Erk, University of Texas
Orhan Firat, Middle East Technical University
Lucie Flekova, Amazon Research
Kevin Gimpel, TTI-Chicago
Caglar Gulcehre, University of Montreal
Gholamreza Haffari, Monash University
Mohit Iyyer, AI2
Katharina Kann, LMU
Arzoo Katiyar, Cornell University
Miryam de Lhoneux, Uppsala University
Tegan Maharaj, Polytechnique Montreal
Ana Marasovic, Heidelberg, University
Yishu Miao, Oxford University
Todor Mihaylov, Heidelberg University

Pasquale Minervini, UCL
Nikita Nangia, NYU
Shashi Narayan, University of Edinburgh
Thien Huu Nguyen, NYU
Robert Östling, Stockholm University
Alexander Panchenko, University of Hamburg
Matthew Peters, AI2
Barbara Plank, University of Groningen
Marek Rei, University of Cambridge
Roi Reichart, Technion
Alan Ritter, Ohio State University
Diarmuid Ó Séaghdha, Apple
Holger Schwenk, Facebook Research
Tianze Shi, Cornell University
Vered Shwartz, Bar-Ilan University
Ashudeep Singh, Cornell University
Richard Socher, Salesforce
Mark Steedman, University of Edinburgh
Karl Stratos, Columbia University
Sam Thomson, CMU
Ivan Titov, University of Edinburgh
Shubham Toshniwal, TTIC
Andreas Vlachos, Sheffield
Pontus Stenetorp, UCL
Anders Søgaard, University of Copenhagen
Jörg Tiedemann, University of Helsinki
Chris Quirk, Microsoft Research
Lyle Ungar, University of Pennsylvania
Eva Maria Vecchi, University of Cambridge
Dirk Weissenborn, German Research Center for AI
Tsung-Hsien Wen, University of Cambridge
Yi Yang, Bloomberg LP
Helen Yannakoudakis, University of Cambridge

Invited Speaker:

Yejin Choi, University of Washington
Trevor Cohn, University of Melbourne
Margaret Mitchell, Google Research
Yoav Goldberg, Bar Ilan University

Table of Contents

Workshop Program

Friday, July 20, 2018

09:30–09:45 *Welcome and Opening Remarks*

09:45–14:45 **Keynote Session**

09:45–10:30 *Invited Talk 1*
Yejin Choi

10:30–11:00 *Coffee Break*

11:00–11:45 *Invited Talk 2*
Trevor Cohn

11:45–12:30 *Invited Talk 3*
Margaret Mitchell

12:30–14:00 *Lunch*

14:00–14:45 *Invited Talk 4*
Yoav Goldberg

14:45–15:00 **Outstanding Papers Spotlight Presentations**

15:00–16:30   Poster Session (including Coffee Break from 15:30-16:00) + Drinks Reception

Corpus Specificity in LSA and Word2vec: The Role of Out-of-Domain Documents
Edgar Altszyler, Mariano Sigman and Diego Fernandez Slezak

Hierarchical Convolutional Attention Networks for Text Classification
Shang Gao, Arvind Ramanathan and Georgia Tourassi

Extrofitting: Enriching Word Representation and its Vector Space with Semantic Lexicons
Hwiyeol Jo and Stanley Jungkyu Choi

Chat Discrimination for Intelligent Conversational Agents with a Hybrid CNN-LMTGRU Network
Dennis Singh Moirangthem and Minho Lee

Text Completion using Context-Integrated Dependency Parsing
Amr Rekaby Salama, Özge Alacam and Wolfgang Menzel

Quantum-Inspired Complex Word Embedding
Qiuchi Li, Sagar Uprety, Benyou Wang and Dawei Song

Natural Language Inference with Definition Embedding Considering Context On the Fly
Kosuke Nishida, Kyosuke Nishida, Hisako Asano and Junji Tomita

Comparison of Representations of Named Entities for Document Classification
Lidia Pivovarova and Roman Yangarber

Speeding up Context-based Sentence Representation Learning with Non-autoregressive Convolutional Decoding
Shuai Tang, Hailin Jin, Chen Fang, Zhaowen Wang and Virginia de Sa

Connecting Supervised and Unsupervised Sentence Embeddings
Gil Levi

A Hybrid Learning Scheme for Chinese Word Embedding
Weiguo Sheng and Weiguo Sheng

LSTMs Exploit Linguistic Attributes of Data
Nelson F. Liu, Omer Levy, Roy Schwartz, Chenhao Tan and Noah A. Smith

Learning Distributional Token Representations from Visual Features
Samuel Broscheit

Jointly Embedding Entities and Text with Distant Supervision
Denis Newman-Griffis, Albert M. Lai and Eric Fosler-Lussier

A Sequence-to-Sequence Model for Semantic Role Labeling
Angel Daza and Anette Frank

*Predicting Concreteness and Imageability of Words Within and Across Languages
via Word Embeddings*
Nikola Ljubešić, Darja Fišer and Anita Peti-Stantić

16:30–17:30   Panel Discussion

17:30–17:40   *Closing Remarks + Best Paper Awards Announcement*

Corpus specificity in LSA and word2vec: the role of out-of-domain documents

Edgar Altszyler
UBA, FCEyN, DC.
ICC, UBA-CONICET
ealtszyler@dc.uba.ar

Mariano Sigman
U. Torcuato Di Tella - CONICET.
msigman@utdt.edu

Diego Fernández Slezak
UBA, FCEyN, DC,
ICC, UBA-CONICET
dfslezak@dc.uba.ar

Abstract

Despite the popularity of word embeddings, the precise way by which they acquire semantic relations between words remain unclear. In the present article, we investigate whether LSA and word2vec capacity to identify relevant semantic relations increases with corpus size. One intuitive hypothesis is that the capacity to identify relevant associations should increase as the amount of data increases. However, if corpus size grows in topics which are not specific to the domain of interest, signal to noise ratio may weaken. Here we investigate the effect of corpus specificity and size in word-embeddings, and for this, we study two ways for progressive elimination of documents: the elimination of random documents vs. the elimination of documents unrelated to a specific task. We show that word2vec can take advantage of all the documents, obtaining its best performance when it is trained with the whole corpus. On the contrary, the specialization (removal of out-of-domain documents) of the training corpus, accompanied by a decrease of dimensionality, can increase LSA word-representation quality while speeding up the processing time. From a cognitive-modeling point of view, we point out that LSA's word-knowledge acquisitions may not be efficiently exploiting higher-order co-occurrences and global relations, whereas word2vec does.

1 Introduction

The main idea behind corpus-based semantic representation is that words with similar meanings resentation is that words with similar meanings tend to occur in similar contexts (Harris, 1954). This proposition is called *distributional hypothesis* and provides a practical framework to understand and compute the semantic relationship between words. Based in the *distributional hypothesis*, Latent Semantic Analysis (LSA) (Deerwester et al., 1990; Landauer and Dumais, 1997; Hu et al., 2007) and word2vec (Mikolov et al., 2013a,b), are one of the most important methods for word meaning representation, which describes each word in a vectorial space, where words with similar meanings are located close to each other.

Word embeddings have been applied in a wide variety of areas such as information retrieval (Deerwester et al., 1990), psychiatry (Altszyler et al., 2018; Carrillo et al., 2018), treatment optimization(Corcoran et al., 2018), literature (Diuk et al., 2012) and cognitive sciences (Landauer and Dumais, 1997; Denhière and Lemaire, 2004; Lemaire and Denhi, 2004; Diuk et al., 2012).

LSA takes as input a training Corpus formed by a collection of documents. Then a word by document co-occurrence matrix is constructed, which contains the distribution of occurrence of the different words along the documents. Then, usually, a mathematical transformation is applied to reduce the weight of uninformative high-frequency words in the words-documents matrix (Dumais, 1991). Finally, a linear dimensionality reduction is implemented by a truncated *Singular Value Decomposition*, SVD, which projects every word in a subspace of a predefined number of dimensions, k. The success of LSA in capturing the latent meaning of words comes from this low-dimensional mapping. This representation improvement can be explained as a consequence of the elimination of the noisiest dimensions (Turney and Pantel, 2010).

Word2vec consists of two neural network models, Continuous Bag of Words (CBOW) and Skip-gram. To train the models, a sliding window is

1

Proceedings of the 3rd Workshop on Representation Learning for NLP, pages 1–10
Melbourne, Australia, July 20, 2018. ©2018 Association for Computational Linguistics

moved along the corpus. In the CBOW scheme, in each step, the neural network is trained to predict the center word (the word in the center of the window based) given the context words (the other words in the window). While in the skip-gram scheme, the model is trained to predict the context words based on the central word. In the present paper, we use the skip-gram, which has produced better performance in Mikolov et al. (2013b).

Despite the development of new word representation methods, LSA is still intensively used and has been shown that produce better performances than word2vec methods in small to medium size training corpus (Altszyler et al., 2017).

1.1 Training Corpus Size and Specificity in Word-embeddings

Over the last years, great effort has been devoted to understanding how to choose the right parameter settings for different tasks (Quesada, 2011; Dumais, 2003; Landauer and Dumais, 1997; Lapesa and Evert, 2014; Bradford, 2008; Nakov et al., 2003; Baroni et al., 2014). However, considerably lesser attention has been given to study how different corpus used as input for training may affect the performance. Here we ask a simple question on the property of the corpus: is there a monotonic relation between corpus size and the performance? More precisely, what happens if the topic of additional documents differs from the topics in the specific task? Previous studies have surprisingly shown some contradictory results on this simple question.

On the one hand, in the foundational work, Landauer and Dumais (1997) compare the word-knowledge acquisition between LSA and that of children's. This acquisition process may be produced by 1) direct learning, enhancing the incorporation of new words by reading texts that explicitly contain them; or 2) indirect learning, enhancing the incorporation of new words by reading texts that do not contain them. To do that, they evaluate LSA semantic representation trained with different size corpus in multiple-choice synonym questions extracted from the TOEFL exam. This test consists of 80 multiple-choice questions, in which its requested to identify the synonym of a word between 4 options. In order to train the LSA, Landauer and Dumais used the TASA corpus (Zeno et al., 1995).

Landauer and Dumais (1997) randomly replaced exam-words in the corpus with non-sense words and varied the number of corpus' documents selecting nested sub-samples of the total corpus. They concluded that LSA improves its performance on the exam both when training with documents with exam-words and without them. However, as could be expected, they observed a greater effect when training with exam-words. It is worth mentioning that the replacement of exam-words with non-sense words may create incorrect documents, thus, making the algorithm acquire word-knowledge from documents which should have an exam-word but do not. In the Results section, we will study this indirect word acquisition in the TOEFL test without using non-sense words.

Along the same line, Lemaire and Denhiere (2006) studied the effect of high-order co-occurrences in LSA semantic similarity, which goes further in the study of Landauer's indirect word acquisition.

In their work, Lemaire and Denhiere (2006) measure how the similarity between 28 pairs of words (such as bee/honey and buy/shop) changes when a 400-dimensions LSA is trained with a growing number of paragraphs. Furthermore, they identify for this task the marginal contribution of the first, second and third order of co-occurrence as the number of paragraphs is increased. In this experiment, they found that not only does the first order of co-occurrence contribute to the semantic closeness of the word pairs, but also the second and the third order promote an increment on pairs similarity. It is worth noting that Landauer's indirect word acquisition can be understood in terms of paragraphs without either of the words in a pair, and containing a third or more order co-occurrence link.

So, the conclusion from Lemaire and Denhiere (2006) and Landauer and Dumais (1997) studies suggest that increasing corpus size results in a gain, even if this increase is in topics which are unrelated for the relevant semantic directions which are pertinent for the task.

However, a different conclusion seems to result from other sets of studies. Stone et al. (2006) have studied the effect of Corpus size and specificity in a document similarity rating task. They found that training LSA with smaller subcorpus selected for the specific task domain maintains or even improves LSA performance. This corresponds to the intuition of noise filtering, when removing information from irrelevant dimensions results in improvements of performance.

In addition, Olde et al. (2002) have studied the effect of selecting specific subcorpus in an automatic exam evaluation task. They created several subcorpus from a Physics corpus, progressively discarding documents unrelated to the specific questions. Their results showed small differences in the performance between the LSA trained with original corpus and the LSA trained with the more specific subcorpus.

It is well known that the number of LSA dimensions (k) is a key parameter to be duly adjusted in order to eliminate the noisiest dimensions (Landauer and Dumais, 1997; Turney and Pantel, 2010). Excessively high k values may not eliminate enough noisy dimensions, while excessively low k values may not have enough dimensions to generate a proper representation. In this context, we hypothesize that when out-of-domain documents are discarded, the number of dimensions needed to represent the data should be lower, thus, k must be decreased.

Regarding word2vec, Cardellino and Alemany (2017) and Dusserre and Padró (2017) have shown that word2vec trained with a specific corpus can produce better performance in semantic tasks than when it is trained with a bigger and general corpus. Despite these works point out the relevance of domain-specific corpora, they do not study the specificity in isolation, as they compare corpus from different sources.

In this article, we set to investigate the effect of the specificity and size of training corpus in word-embeddings, and how this interacts with the number of dimensions. To measure the semantic representations quality we have used two different tasks: the TOEFL exam, and a categorization test. The corpus evaluation method consists in the comparison between two ways of progressive elimination of documents: the elimination of random documents vs the elimination of out-of-domain documents (unrelated to the specific task). In addition, we have varied k within a wide range of values.

As we show, LSA's dimensionality plays a key role in the LSA representation when the corpus analysis is made. In particular, we observe that both, discarding out-of-domain documents and decreasing the number of dimensions produces an increase in the algorithm performance. In one of the two tasks, discarding out-of-domain documents without the decrease of k results in the complete opposite behavior, showing a strong performance reduction. On the other hand, word2vec shows in all cases a performance reduction when discarding out-of-domain, which suggests an exploitation of higher-order word co-occurrences.

Our contribution in understanding the effect of out-of-domain documents in word-embeddings knowledge acquisitions is valuable from two different perspectives:

- From an operational point of view: we show that LSA's performance can be enhanced when: (1) its training corpus is *cleaned* from out-of-domain documents, and (2) a reduction of LSA's dimensions number is applied. Furthermore, the reduction of both the corpus size and the number of dimensions tend to speed up the processing time. On the other hand, word2vec can take advantage of all the documents, obtaining its best performance when it is trained with the whole corpus.

- From a cognitive modeling point of view: we point out that LSA's word-knowledge acquisition does not take advantage of indirect learning, while word2vec does. This throws light upon models capabilities and limitations in modeling human cognitive tasks, such as: human word-learning (Landauer and Dumais, 1997; Lemaire and Denhiere, 2006; Landauer, 2007), semantic memory (Denhière and Lemaire, 2004; Kintsch and Mangalath, 2011; Landauer, 2007) and words classification (Laham, 1997).

2 Methods

We used TASA corpus (Zeno et al., 1995) in all experiments. TASA is a commonly used linguistic corpus consisting of more than 37 thousand educational texts from USA K12 curriculum. We word-tokenized each document, discarding punctuation marks, numbers, and symbols. Then, we transformed each word to lowercase and eliminated stopwords, using the stoplist in NLTK Python package (Bird et al., 2009). TASA corpus contains more than 5 million words in its cleaned version.

In each experiment, the training corpus size was changed by discarding documents in two different ways:

- *Random documents discarding:* The desired number of documents (n) contained in the subcorpus is preselected. Then, documents are randomly eliminated from the original corpus until there are exactly n documents. If any of the test words (i.e. words that appear in the specific task) does not appear at least once in the remaining corpus, one document is randomly replaced with one of the discarded documents that contains the missing word.

- *Out-of-domain documents discarding:* The desired number of documents (n) contained in the subcorpus is preselected. Then, only documents with no test words are eliminated from the original corpus until there are exactly n documents. Here, n must be greater than or equal to the number of documents that contain at least one of the test words.

Both, LSA and Skip-gram word-embeddings were generated with Gensim Python library (Řehůřek and Sojka, 2010). In LSA implementation, a Log-Entropy transformation was applied before the truncated Singular Value Decomposition. In Skip-gram implementation, we discarded tokens with frequency higher than 10^{-3}, and we set the window size and negative sampling parameters to 15 (which were found to be maximal in two semantic tasks over TASA corpus (Altszyler et al., 2017)). In all cases, word-embeddings dimensions values were varied to study its dependency.

The semantic similarity (S) of two words was calculated using the cosine similarity measure between their respective vectorial representation ($\mathbf{v_1}, \mathbf{v_2}$),

$$S(\mathbf{v_1}, \mathbf{v_2}) = cos(\mathbf{v_1}, \mathbf{v_2}) = \frac{\mathbf{v_1} \cdot \mathbf{v_2}}{\|\mathbf{v_1}\| \cdot \|\mathbf{v_2}\|} \qquad (1)$$

The semantic distances between two words $d(\mathbf{v_1}, \mathbf{v_2})$ is calculated as 1 minus the semantic similarity ($d(\mathbf{v_1}, \mathbf{v_2}) = 1 - S(\mathbf{v_1}, \mathbf{v_2})$).

Word-embeddings knowledge acquisition was tested in two different tasks: a semantic categorization test and the TOEFL test.

2.1 Semantic categorization test

In this test we measured the capabilities of the model to represent the semantic categories used by Patel et al. (1997) (such as drinks, countries, tools and clothes). The test is composed of 53 categories with 10 words each. In order to measure how well the word i is grouped vis-à-vis the other words in its semantic category we used the Silhouette Coefficients, $s(i)$ (Rousseeuw, 1987),

$$s(i) = \frac{b(i) - a(i)}{\max\{a(i), b(i)\}}, \qquad (2)$$

where $a(i)$ is the mean distance of word i with all other words within the same category, and $b(i)$ is the minimum mean distance of word i to any words within another category (i.e. the mean distance to the neighboring category). In other words, Silhouette Coefficients measure how close is a word to its own category words compared to the closeness to neighboring words. The Silhouette Score is computed as the mean value of all Silhouette Coefficients. The score takes values between -1 and 1, higher values reporting localized categories with larger distances between categories, representing better clustering.

The high number of test words (530) and the high frequency of some of them leaves only a few documents with no test words. This makes varied corpus size range in the *out-of-domain documents discarding* very small. To avoid this, we tested only on the 10 least frequent categories. The frequency of a question is measured as the number of documents in which at least one word from this category appears.

2.2 TOEFL test

The TOEFL test was introduced by Landauer and Dumais (1997) to evaluate the quality of semantic representations. This test consists of 80 multiple-choice questions, in which it is requested to identify the synonym of a target word between 4 options. For example: *select the most semantically similar to "enormously" between this words: "tremendously", "appropriately", "uniquely" and "decidedly"*. The performance of this test was measured by the percentage of correct responses.

Again, The high number of test words (400) and the high frequency of some of them leaves few documents with no test words. So we performed the test only on the 20 least frequent questions in order to have out-of-domain documents to discard.

3 Results

3.1 Semantic categorization Test

In Figure 1 we show the LSA (top panel) and word2vec (bottom panel) categorization performance with both documents discarding methods.

For each corpus size and document discarding method, we took 10 subcorpus samples (in total we consider 90 subcorpus + the complete corpus). In each corpus/subcorpus, we trained LSA and word2vec with a wide range of dimension values, using in each case the dimension that produces the best mean performance.

In both cases, performance decreases when documents are randomly discarded (orange dashed lines). However, LSA and word2vec have different behavior in the out-of-domain document discarding method (blue solid lines). While LSA produces better scores with increasing specificity, the word2vec performance decreases in the same situation.

LSA's maximum performance is obtained using 20 dimensions and removing all out-of-domain documents in the training corpus. While, when all the corpus is used the best number of dimensions is 100. These results show that performance for a specific task may be increased by "cleaning" the training corpus of out-of-domain documents. But, in order to enhance the performance, the elimination of out-of-domain documents should be accompanied by a decrease of the number of LSA dimensions. For example, fixing the number of dimensions to 100 the performance result in a reduction of 55%. We also point out that this technical subtlety has not been taken into account in previous results that reported the presence of indirect learning in LSA (Landauer and Dumais, 1997; Lemaire and Denhiere, 2006).

Figure 2 shows the results disaggregated by number of dimensions. It can be seen that in all cases the performance decreases when documents are randomly discarded (bottom panels). However, in the case of LSA, the dependency with the number of out-of-domain documents varied with the number of dimensions (top left panel). In the cases of 300, 500 and 1000 dimensions, the performance decreases when out-of-domain documents are eliminated. In contrast, we obtain the opposite behavior in the cases of 5, 10, 20 dimensions, in which the elimination of out-of-domain documents increases LSA's categorization performance.

Consider the case when k is fixed in the value that maximizes the performance with the entire corpus (around $k = 100$). When the corpus is "cleaned" of out-of-domain documents, the remaining corpus will have not only fewer documents, but also less topic diversity among texts. Thus, the number of dimensions (k) needed to generate a proper semantic representation should be reduced. As k is fixed in high values, LSA may not eliminate enough noisy dimensions, leading to a decrease in the performance. This effect becomes

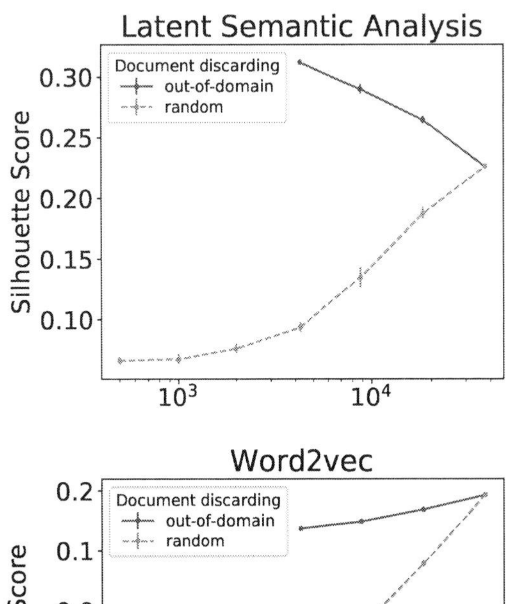

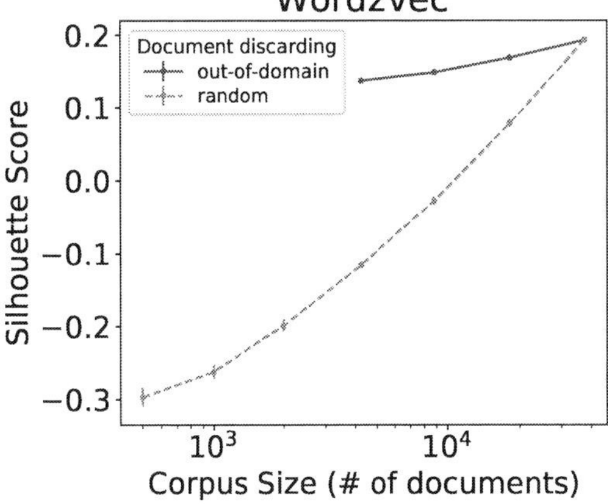

Figure 1: Semantic categorization test analysis. Silhouette Score vs corpus size for with both documents discarding methods: *random document discarding* (orange dashed lines) and *out-of-domain documents discarding* (blue solid lines). The shown Silhouette Score values and their error bars are, respectively, the mean values and the standard error of the mean of 10 samples. In most of the dots, the error bars are not visible, this is because their length is smaller than the dot size. The dimension was varied among {5, 10, 20, 50, 100, 300, 500, 1000} for LSA and among {5, 10, 20, 50, 100, 300, 500} for word2vec. Due to the high computational effort, in the case of word2vec we avoid using 1000 dimensions.

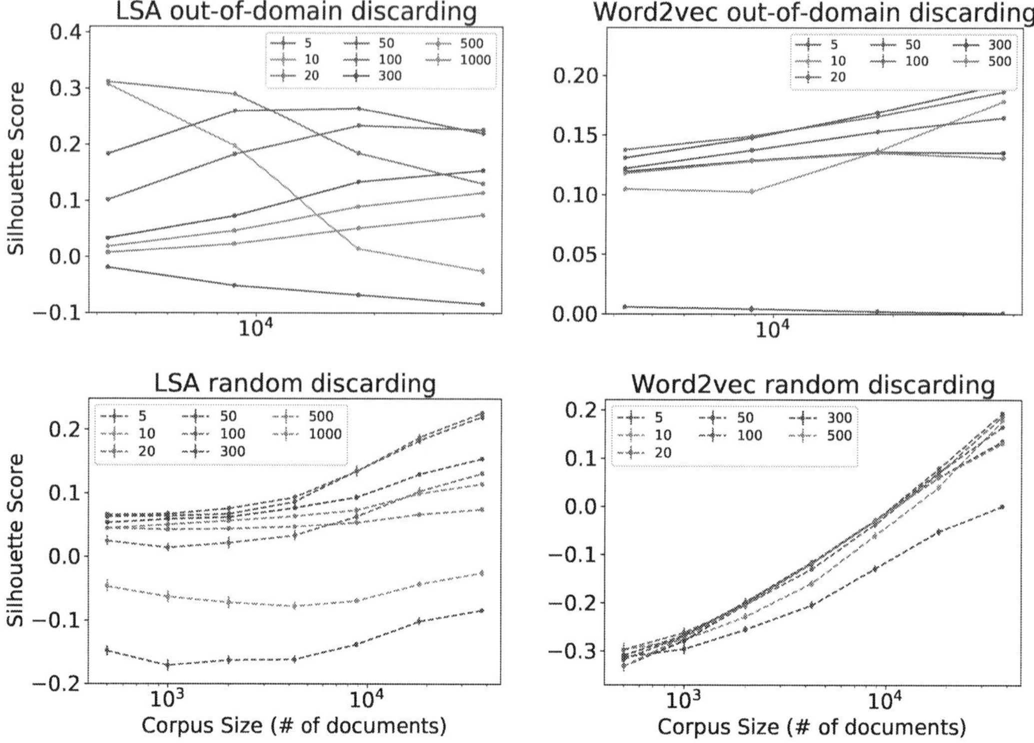

Figure 2: Semantic categorization test analysis disaggregated by number of dimensions. Categorization performance (Silhouette Score) vs corpus size, by number of dimensions. Both document variation methods are shown: *out-of-domain documents discarding* (top panels) and *random document discarding* (bottom panels). The shown scores values and their error bars are, respectively, the mean values and the standard error of the mean of 10 samples.

larger when the selected k is high, as it can be seen for $k = 300, 500, 1000$. On the other hand, consider the case when k is fixed in the value that maximizes the performance with the "cleaned" corpus (around $k = 20$). The presence of out-of-domain documents in the complete corpus increase the topic diversity. As k is fixed in low values, the LSA will not have enough dimensions to represent all the intrinsic complexity of the whole corpus. So, when the corpus is "cleaned" of out-of-domain documents, the performance should increase.

On the other hand, in the case of word2vec, the performance decrease, with almost all dimension values, when out-of-domain documents are eliminated. Moreover, the discarding of out-of-domain documents do not require a considerable decrease of the number of dimensions. These findings supports the idea that individual dimensions of word2vec do not encode *latent* semantic domains, however, more analysis must be done in these direction (see Baroni et al. (2014) discussion).

3.2 TOEFL Test

In Figure 3 we show the TOEFL correct answer fraction vs the corpus size. We varied the corpus size by both methods: the *out-of-domain documents discarding* and the *Random document discarding*. As in the categorization test procedure, a wide range of dimension values where tested, using in each case the dimension that produces the best mean performance.

In both models, performance decreases when documents are randomly discarded (orange dashed lines in figure 3). For LSA, the elimination of out-of-domain documents does not produce a significant performance variation, which shows that LSA can not take advantage of out-of-domain document. This results are in contradiction with Landauer and Dumais (1997) observation of indirect

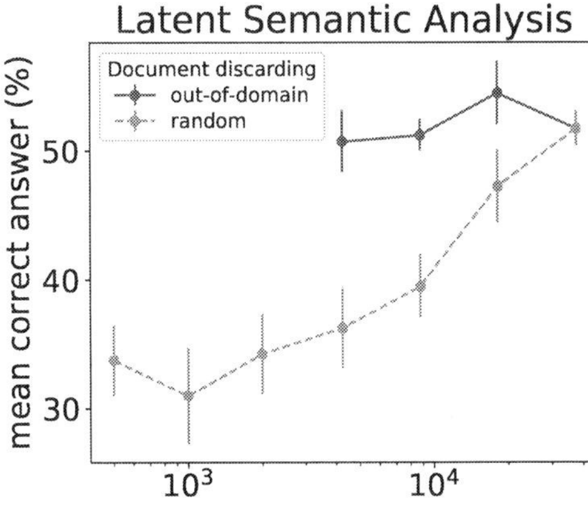

Latent Semantic Analysis

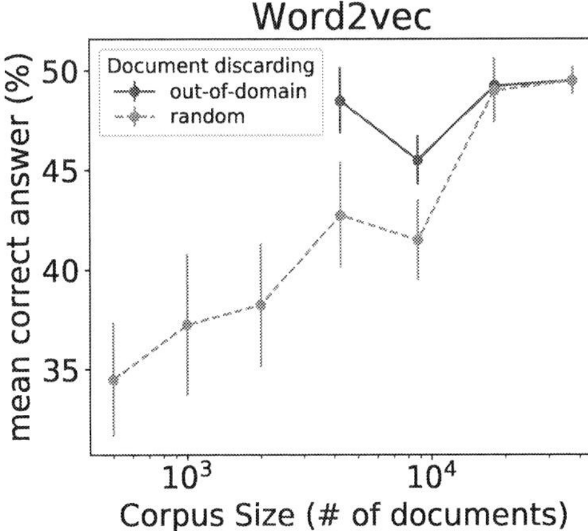

Word2vec

Figure 3: TOEFL test analysis. Correct answer percentage vs corpus size with both document variation methods: *Random document discarding* (orange dashed lines) and the *out-of-domain documents discarding* (blue solid lines). The shown Silhouette Score values and their error bars are,respectively, the mean values and the standard error of the mean of 10 samples. The dimension was varied among {5, 10, 20, 50, 100, 300, 500, 1000} for LSA and among {5, 10, 20, 50, 100, 300, 500} for word2vec. Due to the high computational effort, in the case of word2vec we avoid using 1000 dimensions.

learning. We believe that this difference is due to the lack of adjustment in the number of dimensions. On the other hand, word2vec has the same behaviour as in the categorization test. The performance when the out-of-domain documents are discarded show a small downward trend (not significant, with p-val=0.31 in a two-sided Kolmogorov-Smirnov test), but not as pronounced as in *random*

document discard method. Unlike the categorization test, the performance measure in the TOEFL Test present a high variability (see Figure 4). This observation is consistent with the large fluctuations shown in Landauer and Dumais (1997). Despite this, we consider relevant to use this test in order to be able to compare with Landauer and Dumais (1997) results.

4   Conclusion and Discussion

Despite the popularity of word-embeddings in several semantic representation task, the way by which they acquire new semantic relations between words is unclear. In particular, for the case of LSA there are two opposite visions about the effect of incorporating out-of-domain documents. From one point of view, training LSA with a specific subcorpus, *cleaned* of documents unrelated to the specific task increases the performance (Stone et al., 2006). From the other point of view, the presence of unrelated documents improves the representations. The second view point is supported by the conception that the SVD in LSA can capture high-order co-occurrence words relations (Landauer and Dumais, 1997; Lemaire and Denhiere, 2006; Turney and Pantel, 2010). Based on this, LSA is used as a plausible model of human semantic memory given that it can capture indirect relations (high-order word co-occurrences).

In the present article we studied the effect of out-of-domain documents in LSA and word2vec semantic representations construction. We compared two ways of progressive elimination of documents: the elimination of random documents vs the elimination of out-of-domain documents. The semantic representations quality was measured in two different tasks: a semantic categorization test and a TOEFL exam. Additionally, we have varied a large range of word-embedding dimensions (k).

We have shown that word2vec can take advantage of all the documents, obtaining its best performance when it is trained with the whole corpus. On the contrary, LSA's word-representation quality increases with a specialization of the training corpus (removal of out-of-domain document) accompanied by a decrease of k. Furthermore, we have shown that the specialization without the decrease of k can produce a strong performance reduction. Thus, we point out the need to vary k when the corpus size dependency is studied. From a cognitive modeling point of view, we

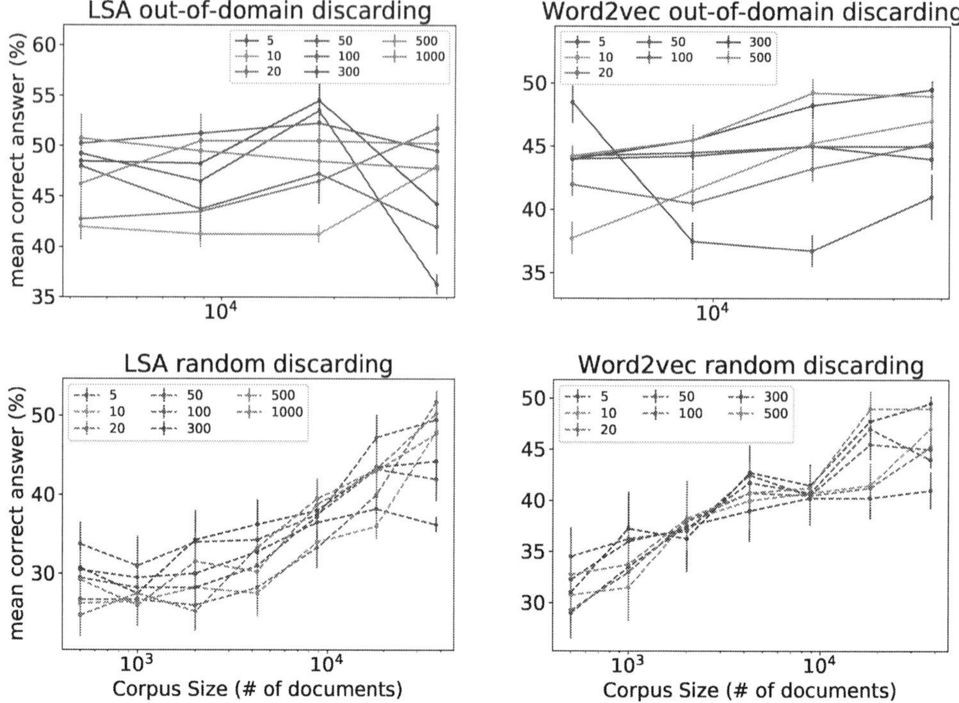

Figure 4: TOEFL test analysis disaggregated by number of dimensions. Correct answer percentage vs corpus size, by number of dimensions. Both document variation methods are shown: *out-of-domain documents discarding* (top panels) and *random document discarding* (bottom panels). The shown scores values and their error bars are, respectively, the mean values and the standard error of the mean of 10 samples.

point out that LSA's word-knowledge acquisitions does not take advantage of indirect learning (high-order word co-occurrences), while word2vec does. This throws light upon word-embeddings capabilities and limitations in modeling human cognitive tasks, such as: human word-learning (Landauer and Dumais, 1997; Lemaire and Denhiere, 2006; Landauer, 2007), semantic memory (Denhière and Lemaire, 2004; Kintsch and Mangalath, 2011; Landauer, 2007) and words classification (Laham, 1997).

Acknowledgments

This research was supported by Consejo Nacional de Investigaciones Cientficas y Tcni-cas (CON-ICET), Universidad de Buenos Aires, and Agencia Nacional de Promocin Cientfica y Tecnolgica. We also want to thank LSA and NLP Research Labs, University of Colorado at Boulder for shearing access to the TOEFL word set.

References

Edgar Altszyler, Ariel Berenstein, David Milne, Rafael A. Calvo, and Diego Fernandez Slezak. 2018. Using contextual information for automatic triage of posts in a peer-support forum. In *Proceedings of the Fifth Workshop on Computational Linguistics and Clinical Psychology: From Linguistic Signal to Clinical Reality*.

Edgar Altszyler, Sidarta Ribeiro, Mariano Sigman, and Diego Fernández Slezak. 2017. The interpretation of dream meaning: Resolving ambiguity using latent semantic analysis in a small corpus of text. *Consciousness and Cognition* https://doi.org/10.1016/j.concog.2017.09.004.

Marco Baroni, Georgiana Dinu, and Germán Kruszewski. 2014. Don't count, predict! a systematic comparison of context-counting vs. context-predicting semantic vectors. In *ACL (1)*. pages 238–247.

Steven Bird, Ewan Klein, and Edward Loper. 2009. *Natural language processing with Python.* " O'Reilly Media, Inc.".

Roger B. Bradford. 2008. An empirical study of required dimensionality for large-scale latent semantic indexing applications. *Proceedings of the 17th ACM, CIKM* pages 153–162. https://doi.org/10.1145/1458082.1458105.

Cristian Cardellino and Laura Alonso Alemany. 2017. Disjoint semi-supervised spanish verb sense disambiguation using word embeddings. In *ASAI, Simposio Argentino de Inteligencia Artificial*.

Facundo Carrillo, Mariano Sigman, Diego Fernández Slezak, Philip Ashton, Lily Fitzgerald, Jack Stroud, David J Nutt, and Robin L Carhart-Harris. 2018. Natural speech algorithm applied to baseline interview data can predict which patients will respond to psilocybin for treatment-resistant depression. *Journal of Affective Disorders* 230:84–86.

Cheryl M Corcoran, Facundo Carrillo, Diego Fernández-Slezak, Gillinder Bedi, Casimir Klim, Daniel C Javitt, Carrie E Bearden, and Guillermo A Cecchi. 2018. Prediction of psychosis across protocols and risk cohorts using automated language analysis. *World Psychiatry* 17(1):67–75.

Scott Deerwester, Susan T Dumais, Thomas Landauer, George Furnas, and Richard. Harshman. 1990. Indexing by latent semantic analysis. *JAsIs* 41(6).

G Denhière and B Lemaire. 2004. A Computational Model of Children's Semantic Memory. *Proc 26 thAnnual Meeting of the Cognitive Science Society* pages 297–302.

Carlos G. Diuk, D. Fernandez Slezak, I. Raskovsky, M. Sigman, and G. a. Cecchi. 2012. A quantitative philology of introspection. *Frontiers in Integrative Neuroscience* 6(September):1–12. https://doi.org/10.3389/fnint.2012.00080.

Susan Dumais. 1991. Improving the retrieval of information from external sources. *Behavior Research Methods, Instruments, & Computers* 23(2):229–236. https://doi.org/10.3758/BF03203370.

Susan Dumais. 2003. Data-driven approaches to information access. *Cognitive Science* 27(3):491 – 524. https://doi.org/http://dx.doi.org/10.1016/S0364-0213(03)00013-2.

Emmanuelle Dusserre and Muntsa Padró. 2017. Bigger does not mean better! we prefer specificity. In *IWCS 201712th International Conference on Computational SemanticsShort papers*.

Z. Harris. 1954. Word Distributional structure 23(10):146162.

X Hu, Z Cai, P Wiemer-Hastings, a Graesser, and D McNamara. 2007. Strengths, limitations, and extensions of LSA. *Handbook of Latent Semantic Analysis* pages 401–426. https://doi.org/10.1164/rccm.201012-2079ED.

Walter Kintsch and Praful Mangalath. 2011. The construction of meaning. *Topics in Cognitive Science* 3(2):346–370. https://doi.org/10.1111/j.1756-8765.2010.01107.x.

D Laham. 1997. Latent Semantic Analysis approaches to categorization. *Proceedings of the 19th annual conference of the Cognitive Science Society* (1984):979.

Thomas K Landauer. 2007. Lsa as a theory of meaning. *Handbook of latent semantic analysis* pages 3–34.

Thomas K. Landauer and Susan T. Dumais. 1997. A solution to Plato's problem: The latent semantic analysis theory of acquisition, induction, and representation of knowledge. *Psychological Review* 104(2):211–240. https://doi.org/10.1037/0033-295X.104.2.211.

Gabriella Lapesa and Stefan Evert. 2014. A large scale evaluation of distributional semantic models: Parameters, interactions and model selection. *Transactions of the Association for Computational Linguistics* 2:531–545.

Benoît Lemaire and Guy Denhi. 2004. Incremental Construction of an Associative Network from a Corpus. *26th Annual Meeting of the Cognitive Science Society* pages 825–830.

Benoit Lemaire and Guy Denhiere. 2006. Effects of High-Order Co-occurrences on Word Semantic Similarity. *Current psychology letters* 1(18):1–12.

Tomas Mikolov, Kai Chen, Greg Corrado, and Jeffrey Dean. 2013a. Distributed Representations of Words and Phrases and their Compositionality. *Nips* pages 1–9. https://doi.org/10.1162/jmlr.2003.3.4-5.951.

Tomas Mikolov, Greg Corrado, Kai Chen, and Jeffrey Dean. 2013b. Efficient Estimation of Word Representations in Vector Space. *Proceedings of the International Conference on Learning Representations (ICLR 2013)* pages 1–12. https://doi.org/10.1162/153244303322533223.

Preslav Nakov, Elena Valchanova, and Galia Angelova. 2003. Towards a Deeper Understanding of the LSA Performance. *Proceedings of Recent Advances in Natural Language Processing* 2(2):311–318.

Brent A Olde, Donald R Franceschetti, Ashish Karnavat, Arthur C Graesser, and Tutoring Research Group. 2002. The right stuff: do you need to sanitize your corpus when using latent semantic analysis? *Proceedings of the 24th annual meeting of the cognitive science society* .

Malti Patel, John A. Bullinaria, and Joseph P Levy. 1997. Extracting semantic representations from large text corpora. *Proceedings of the 4th Neural Computation and Psychology Workshop* pages 199–212.

J. Quesada. 2011. *Creating your own LSA space*, Erlbaum, chapter 1.

Radim Řehůřek and Petr Sojka. 2010. Software Framework for Topic Modelling with Large Corpora. In *Proceedings of the LREC 2010 Workshop on New Challenges for NLP Frameworks*. ELRA, Valletta, Malta, pages 45–50. http://is.muni.cz/publication/884893/en.

Peter J. Rousseeuw. 1987. Silhouettes: A graphical aid to the interpretation and validation of cluster analysis. *Journal of Computational and Applied Mathematics* 20:53–65. https://doi.org/10.1016/0377-0427(87)90125-7.

Benjamin P Stone, Simon J Dennis, Peter J Kwantes, Drdc Toronto, and Sheppard Ave W. 2006. A Systematic Comparison of Semantic Models on Human Similarity Rating Data : The Effectiveness of Subspacing pages 1813–1818.

Peter D. Turney and Patrick Pantel. 2010. From frequency to meaning: Vector space models of semantics. *Journal of Artificial Intelligence Research* 37:141–188. https://doi.org/10.1613/jair.2934.

S. Zeno, S. Ivens, and R.and Duvvuri R. Millard. 1995. *The educator's word frequency guide*. Brewster.

Hierarchical Convolutional Attention Networks for Text Classification

Shang Gao, Arvind Ramanathan, and **Georgia Tourassi**
{gaos, ramanathana, tourassig}@ornl.gov
Computational Science and Engineering Division
Oak Ridge National Laboratory
Oak Ridge, TN, USA

Abstract

Recent work in machine translation has demonstrated that self-attention mechanisms can be used in place of recurrent neural networks to increase training speed without sacrificing model accuracy. We propose combining this approach with the benefits of convolutional filters and a hierarchical structure to create a document classification model that is both highly accurate and fast to train – we name our method Hierarchical Convolutional Attention Networks. We demonstrate the effectiveness of this architecture by surpassing the accuracy of the current state-of-the-art on several classification tasks while being twice as fast to train.

1 Introduction

Text classification is an important research area in natural language processing (NLP). Traditional text classification approaches utilize features generated from vector space models such as bag-of-words or term frequency-inverse document frequency (TF-IDF) (Sebastiani, 2005). More recently, deep learning approaches have been shown to outperform traditional approaches based on vector space models (Zhang et al., 2015; Tang et al., 2014). These newer deep learning approaches typically rely on architectures based off convolutional neural networks (CNNs) or recurrent neural networks (RNNs) (Young et al., 2017).

RNNs, which are designed to learn patterns over sequential data, have been successfully applied towards various NLP tasks (Liu et al., 2016; Irsoy and Cardie, 2014; Cho et al., 2014). In NLP, RNNs typically process one word at a time and learn features based on complex sequences of words. While RNNs are capable of capturing linguistic patterns useful for NLP tasks, especially over long segments of text, they can be slow to train compared to other deep learning architectures – in order to calculate the gradients associated with any given word in a sequence, an RNN must backpropogate through all previous words in that sequence, resulting in backpropogation functions far more complex than those in feedforward or convolutional architectures.

CNNs, traditionally used for computer vision, have also been applied to NLP tasks with notable success (Zeng et al., 2014; Dos Santos and Gatti, 2014; Wang et al., 2012). Unlike RNNs, which learn patterns across an entire sequence of text, CNNs use a sliding window that examines only a few words/characters at a time. Thus, CNNs learn features based on the most salient combinations of X words/characters where X is determined by the window size used; unlike RNNs, CNNs are less capable of capturing linguistic features across long distances. Despite this shortcoming, CNNs can often be as effective as RNNs in many basic NLP tasks (Yin et al., 2017). Furthermore, CNNs are generally faster to train than RNNs.

In this paper, we introduce Hierarchical Convolutional Attention Networks (HCANs), an architecture based off self-attention that can capture linguistic relationships over long sequences like RNNs while still being fast to train like CNNs. HCANs can achieve accuracy that surpasses the current state-of-the-art on several classification tasks while being twice as fast to train.

2 Related Work

In 2014, Kim (2014) proposed one of the first CNNs for text classification. Kim's CNN used three parallel convolutional layers; these process a sentence using a sliding window that examines three, four, and five words at a time. The three

Proceedings of the 3rd Workshop on Representation Learning for NLP, pages 11–23
Melbourne, Australia, July 20, 2018. ©2018 Association for Computational Linguistics

convolutions then feed into a maxpool across the entire sentence, which selects the most potent features in each convolution and concatenates them into a single feature vector. Finally, the selected features are fed into a dense softmax layer for classification. Due to its simplicity and strong performance in many tasks, Kim's CNN architecture is still commonly used today in many text classification tasks (Qiu et al., 2017; Gehrmann et al., 2017).

One shortcoming of Kim's CNN approach is that it cannot find linguistic patterns beyond a fixed window size, which may harm performance for complex NLP tasks. Attempts have been made to mitigate this issue by increasing the CNN depth and using local maxpooling to increase the receptive field (Conneau et al., 2017). However, Le et al. (2017) showed that increasing CNN depth helps the performance of character-level CNNs but not word-level CNNs. They further demonstrated that a shallow word-level CNN similar to Kim's proposed structure can outperform much deeper and more complex CNN architectures on a wide range of text classification tasks.

The current state-of-the-art in text classification are Hierarchical Attention Networks (HANs), developed by Yang et al. (2016). Whereas the previous approaches mentioned are all based on CNNs, HANs utilize RNNs. HANs use a hierarchical structure in which each hierarchy uses the same architecture – a bidirectional RNN with gated recurrent units (GRUs) (Chung et al., 2014), followed by an attention mechanism that creates a weighted sum of the RNN outputs at each timestep. The HAN processes documents by first breaking a long document into its sentence components, then processing each sentence individually before processing the entire document. By breaking a document into smaller, more manageable chunks, the HAN can better locate and extract critical information useful for classification. This approach surpassed the performance of all previous approaches across several text classification tasks. However, compared to CNN-based approaches, HANs are much slower to train because they utilize RNNs.

In 2017, Vaswani et al. (2017) created a deep learning model for machine translation based entirely on self-attention mechanisms (Cheng et al., 2016; Lin et al., 2017; Paulus et al., 2017). Traditionally, CNN or RNN layers are used to extract meaningful features from words or images;

attention is applied afterwards to the output of the CNN or RNN layers to help the network focus on features that are most salient (Luong et al., 2015; Xu et al., 2015; Hermann et al., 2015). However, Vaswani showed that self-attention could be applied directly on raw word embeddings to extract important relations and apply meaningful transformations on words. Like RNNs, this attention-based approach can capture relationships over long distances; unlike RNNs, this approach utilizes a feedforward architecture and is much faster to train. Vaswani achieved state-of-the-art results in machine translation using 10x-100x fewer trainable parameters than previous state-of-the-art models.

We hypothesize that a similar self-attention-based architecture can achieve both fast and accurate performance in text classification tasks. In the following section, we show how we adapt the attention-based architecture developed by Vaswani for machine translation into an effective approach for text classification.

3 Hierarchical Convolutional Attention Network

The overall structure of our HCAN is shown in Figure 1. The components and structure of our HCAN are described in greater detail in the following subsections.

3.1 Scaled Dot Product Attention

Suppose we have a sequence of word embeddings $E^{input} \in \mathbb{R}^{l \times d}$, where l is the length of the sequence, d is the embedding dimension, and e_i^{input} is the i-th word embedding in the sequence.

Self-attention, sometimes referred to as intra-attention, compares each entry e_i^{input} to every entry e_i^{input} in that same sequence; this allows for the discovery of relationships between entries in the sequence. Self-attention outputs a new sequence $E^{output} \in \mathbb{R}^{l \times d}$ in which each entry e_i^{output} is a weighted average of all entries e_i^{input} in the input sequence. Each entry e_i^{output} should contain within it the most pertinent information to that entry from all entries in the input sequence e_i^{input}.

$$\text{Attention}(Q, K, V) = \text{softmax}(\frac{QK^T}{\sqrt{d}})V \quad (1)$$

Scaled-dot-product attention (Figure 2, Equation 1) is a type of self-attention developed by Vaswani et al. that was shown to work well

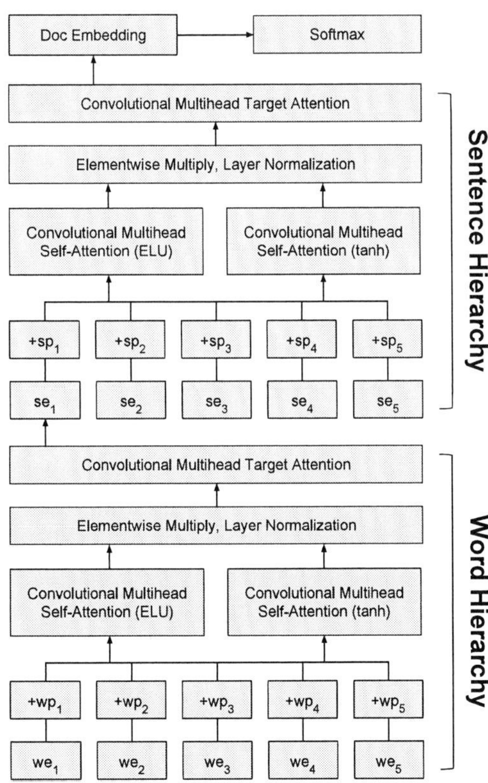

Figure 1: Architecture for our Hierarchical Convolutional Attention Network (HCAN).

in machine translation. Scaled-dot-product attention utilizes three word embedding matrices – the 'query' embeddings $Q \in \mathbb{R}^{l \times d}$, the 'key' embeddings $K \in \mathbb{R}^{l \times d}$, and the 'value' embeddings $V \in \mathbb{R}^{l \times d}$.

In the most basic implementation of self-attention, Q, K, and V can all be substituted by the same sequence of word embeddings $E^{input} \in \mathbb{R}^{l \times d}$. Q and K are used to create a weight matrix QK^T based on the similarity of entries in the sequence. Vaswani et al. found that scaling this weight matrix by a factor of $\sqrt{d}$ yields better performance for higher-dimensional word embeddings. Once this weight matrix is scaled and normalized, it is multiplied with V to create a new output sequence $E^{output} \in \mathbb{R}^{l \times d}$ in which each entry e_i^{output} is a weighted average of all entries e_i^{input} in the input sequence.

3.2 Convolutional Feature Extraction

Rather than use the same E^{input} for Q, K, and V, we can use a function to extract different features

from E^{input} for each of the Q, K, and V embeddings. This allows for more expressive comparison between entries in a sequence; for example, certain features may be useful when comparing Q and K but may not be necessary when creating the output sequence from V. For our feature extractor function, we use a 1D convolution with d filter maps and a window size of three words, which provides more context for each center word when extracting important features (Equation 2).

$$Q = \text{ELU}(\text{Conv1D}(E, W^q) + b^q)$$
$$K = \text{ELU}(\text{Conv1D}(E, W^k) + b^k) \qquad (2)$$
$$V = \text{ELU}(\text{Conv1D}(E, W^v) + b^v)$$

In the equation above, $\text{Conv1D}(A, B)$ is a 1D convolution operation with A as the input as B as the filter, $\{Q, K, V, E\} \in \mathbb{R}^{l \times d}$, $\{W^q, W^k, W^v\} \in \mathbb{R}^{3 \times d \times d}$, and $\{b^q, b^k, b^v\} \in \mathbb{R}^d$.

We found exponential linear units (ELUs) (Clevert et al., 2016) to perform better than rectified linear units (ReLUs) and other activation functions. Unlike ReLUs, ELUs can output negative values, which allows for more complex interactions between the Q and K embeddings when calculating word weights – each word can be assigned a large range of both positive and negative values before being sent into the softmax function.

3.3 Convolutional Multihead Self-Attention

For each entry in the output sequence, scaled dot product attention calculates a set of weights that is used to create a weighted average; the same weights are applied across all d dimensions of the V embeddings. To expand the capabilities of scaled dot product attention, Vaswani et al. introduced multihead attention. Rather than using a single attention function across all d dimensions of the embeddings, multihead attention uses h parallel attention functions, each of which attends to a different portion of the embedding dimension. This allows different portions of the embeddings to be combined using different weights so that the final output sequence can be constructed from a more expressive combination. Vaswani demonstrated that multihead attention performs better than regular scaled dot product attention for machine translation.

$$\text{MultiHead}(Q, K, V) = [head_1, ..., head_h]$$
$$\text{where } head_i = \text{Attention}(Q_i, K_i, V_i) \qquad (3)$$

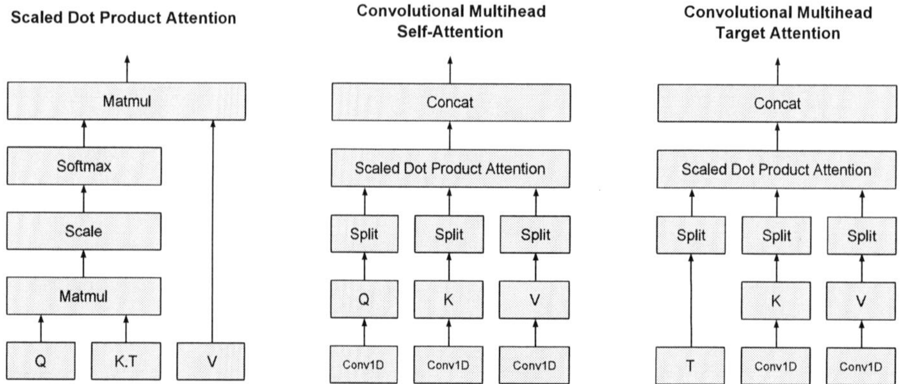

Figure 2: Scaled dot product attention, convolutional multihead self-attention, and convolutional multihead target attention.

Our implementation convolutional multihead self-attention (Figure 2, Equation 3) is based on the multihead attention developed by Vaswani. After using convolution to generate the Q, K, and V embeddings, we split each of the Q, K, and V embeddings into h sub-embeddings such that $\{Q_i, K_i, V_i\} \in \mathbb{R}^{l \times d/h}$. Each triplet of sub-embeddings is then fed into their own scaled dot product attention function. The final output is the concatenation of the outputs $head_i \in \mathbb{R}^{l \times d/h}$ from the individual scaled dot product attention functions to form an output sequence $E^{output} \in \mathbb{R}^{l \times d}$.

3.4 Capturing Complex Word Relationships

In general, attention mechanisms are designed to produce a weighted average of an input sequence. Unfortunately, when trying to capture the overall content within a linguistic sequence, a weighted average may not be sufficient. Two examples of this are negation and scaling. In negation, a word sequence such as 'was not the case' may reverse the meaning of words in another part the sequence (i.e. multiply those embeddings by -1). Similarly in scaling, a word sequence such as 'to a high degree' may increase the polarity of another part of the sequence (i.e. multiply those embeddings by some positive value). Attention mechanisms, which only create weighted averages, are not designed to capture these interactions.

To better capture these types of linguistic interactions, we test the effectiveness of using two convolutional multihead self-attentions in parallel and performing elementwise multiplication on the outputs (Figure 1, Equation 4). This allows the

network to capture more complex interactions between elements in the sequence and expands the expressiveness of the final output beyond that of a simple weighted average.

$$
\begin{aligned}
\text{Parallel}(E) = {} & \text{MultiHead}(Q^a, K^a, V^a) \\
& \odot \text{MultiHead}(Q^b, K^b, V^b) \\
\text{where } Q^a = {} & \text{ELU}(\text{Conv1D}(E, W^{qa}) + b^{qa}) \\
K^a = {} & \text{ELU}(\text{Conv1D}(E, W^{ka}) + b^{ka}) \\
V^a = {} & \text{ELU}(\text{Conv1D}(E, W^{va}) + b^{va}) \\
Q^b = {} & \text{ELU}(\text{Conv1D}(E, W^{qb}) + b^{qb}) \\
K^b = {} & \text{ELU}(\text{Conv1D}(E, W^{kb}) + b^{kb}) \\
V^b = {} & \text{tanh}(\text{Conv1D}(E, W^{vb}) + b^{vb})
\end{aligned}
$$

$$(4)$$

Because tanh outputs a value between -1 and 1, it is used to generate the V embeddings for the second self-attention to prevent the final output from becoming too small or large after multiplying the outputs from the two self-attention mechanisms.

3.5 Convolutional Multihead Target-Attention

The output of our convolutional multihead self-attention is a new output sequence $E^{output} \in \mathbb{R}^{l \times d}$ in which l is based on the length of the input sequence. For classification purposes, we require that each sequence regardless of its length be represented by a single fixed-length vector $V \in \mathbb{R}^{1 \times d}$. We therefore introduce convolutional multihead target-attention, which utilizes the concepts from multihead convolutional self-attention but operates like the traditional attention mechanism that is used on the outputs of a RNN.

$$\text{Target}(E) = \text{MultiHead}(T, K, V)$$
$$\text{where } K = \text{ELU}(\text{Conv1D}(E, W^k) + b^k) \quad (5)$$
$$V = \text{ELU}(\text{Conv1D}(E, W^v) + b^v)$$

In convolutional multihead target-attention (Figure 2, Equation 5), instead of comparing the entries in a sequence $E^{input} \in \mathbb{R}^{l \times d}$ to each other, we compare them to a learnable target vector $T \in \mathbb{R}^{1 \times d}$ that represents the most critical information to look for given a specific task – the content in this vector is learned through backpropogation based on the task at hand. The output is a single weighted average $E^{output} \in \mathbb{R}^{1 \times d}$ that captures the most critical content across the sequence. This final output vector may then be fed into a softmax and used for classification purposes.

3.6 Positional Embeddings

RNN-based approaches for text processing can inherently account for word order when extracting features. However, feedforward and convolution-based approaches such as our implementation of convolutional multihead self-attention do not have this capability. One way to address this problem is by adding positional embeddings $P \in \mathbb{R}^{l \times d}$ (Gehring et al., 2017; dos Santos et al., 2015). Positional embeddings are vector representations of the absolute position of an entry in a sequence. These are added directly to each word/sentence embedding in the input sequence before the sequence is fed into the convolutional multihead self-attention. We use randomly initialized embeddings that are learned during training; we found that these provide a slight boost toward classification accuracy.

3.7 Hierarchical Structure

In their work on HANs, Yang et al. attained state-of-the-art performance by utilizing a hierarchical structure that first breaks up documents into sentences. The lower hierarchy reads in word embeddings from a given sentence and outputs a sentence embedding representing the content within that sentence, and the upper hierarchy reads in the sentence embeddings created from the lower hierarchy and outputs a document embedding representing the content of the entire document; this document embedding is then used for classification. In our experiments, we test the effectiveness of our HCAN with and without this hierarchical structure. We expect that, like with RNNs, self-attention has difficulty capturing meaningful semantic relationships over very long sequences with too many entries; using a hierarchical structure to break down long sequences into more manageable chunks mitigates this issue.

Each hierarchy in our HCAN consists of two parallel convolutional multihead self-attentions followed by a convolutional multihead target attention (Figure 1). Positional embeddings are added to the inputs of each hierarchy to allow the network to identify relationships based on word/sentence positions. We tried increasing the depth within each hierarchy by using multiple layers of self-attentions but found that this did not improve model accuracy.

3.8 Regularization

To regularize our network, we apply dropout of 0.1 on the normalized attention weights (produced by scaling QK^T by $\sqrt{d}$ and then applying softmax) within every scaled dot product attention. Furthermore, we apply dropout of 0.1 on the word and sentence embeddings after the positional embeddings have been added, which has been shown to be effective in other NLP applications (Peng et al., 2015).

We also apply layer normalization (Ba et al., 2016) after the elementwise multiplication of the two parallel convolutional multihead self-attentions (Figure 1). This not only applies a regularization effect, but also speeds up the rate of convergence. Layer normalization is used instead of batch normalization because layer normalization is still effective with very small batch sizes.

4 Experiments

4.1 Datasets

We evaluate the performance of the HCAN on four classification tasks using three datasets (Table 1).

The Yelp reviews dataset [1] consists of over 4.7 million Yelp reviews of various businesses collected over 12 metropolitan areas. For our task, we use only reviews from 2016 (approximately 1 million reviews) and try to predict the rating 1-5.

The Amazon reviews dataset (McAuley and Leskovec, 2013) consists of 83.68 million Amazon product reviews from different product categories spanning May 1996 to July 2014. For

---

[1] https://www.yelp.com/dataset

Table 1: Dataset Descriptions

Dataset	Classes	Documents	Vocabulary	Task Description
Yelp Reviews 2016	5	1,033,037	72,880	Sentiment Analysis
Amazon Reviews Sentiment	5	500,000	67,802	Sentiment Analysis
Amazon Reviews Category	10	500,000	67,802	Topic Classification
Pubmed	8	800,000	182,167	Topic Classification

our evaluation, we selected 10 popular categories and extracted 50,000 randomly selected reviews from each: books, electronics, clothing, home and kitchen, sports and outdoors, health, video games, tools, pet supplies, and food. We use this dataset for two separate classification tasks – sentiment analysis (1-5) and product classification.

The Pubmed dataset [2] consists of more than 26 million citations, abstracts, and other metadata from biomedical literature dating back to 1964. For our experiments, we use Pubmed abstracts associated with 8 common medical subject heading (MeSH) labels: metabolism, physiology, genetics, chemistry, pathology, surgery, psychology, and diagnosis. We only use abstracts that are associated with a single label, yielding a final selection of 800,000 abstracts, 100,000 for each label.

4.2 Baselines and Hyperparameters

As a baseline, we test the performance of two traditional machine learning classifiers that do not utilize deep learning: Naive Bayes (NB) and logistic regression (LR). For logistic regression, we use L1 regularization with a penalty strength of 1.0.

We also compare the performance of our HCAN to that of two other deep learning models. First, we test a word-level shallow-and-wide CNN using an architecture similar to that developed by Kim (2014) for sentence classification. We use three parallel convolution layers with 3-, 4-, and 5-word windows, all with 100 feature maps. These feed into a temporal maxpool across the entire document and the result is concatenated. We apply 50% dropout on the concatenated vector and feed this vector into a softmax classifier. This simple architecture has been shown to outperform many deeper and more complex CNN-based models (Le et al., 2017).

We also test the performance of HANs (Yang et al., 2016), which are the current state-of-the-art. For our HAN, we use the same optimized hyperparameters as those used by Yang – each hierarchy

is composed of a bi-directional GRU with 50 units and an attention mechanism with a hidden layer of 200 neurons.

For the HCAN, we tuned the hyperparameters on the Yelp 2013 dataset. We tuned the attention embedding size d and the number of attention heads h used in our scaled dot-product attention. We use embedding size 512 and 8 heads for our final implementation.

4.3 Setup Details

For each dataset, we lowercase all characters and remove non-alphanumerics other than periods, exclamation marks, and questions marks (used to split documents into sentences). For the traditional machine learning approaches that utilize TFIDF features, we generate unigrams and bigrams with a minimum document frequency of 5. For deep learning models that utilize word embeddings, we train Word2Vec embeddings using a minimum word frequency of 5 and a dimension size of 512.

The deep learning models are all trained on a single document at a time with no batching. This configuration allows for variable length input so that long documents do not need to be cut short and short documents do not need to be padded. All models are trained using the Adam optimizer (Kingma and Ba, 2015) with learning rate 2E-5, beta1 0.9, and beta2 0.99.

We split each dataset into train, validation, and test sets using stratified 80/10/10 splitting. The TFIDF-based models are fitted on the train sets and evaluated on the test sets. The deep learning models are trained on the train set, and every 50,000 documents we evaluate on the validation set until the model converges. We save the model parameters with the highest validation accuracy and use those parameters to evaluate on the test set.

4.4 Results

The results of our experiments are displayed in Table 2. For each deep learning model, we record the final test accuracy, average time to train on a single

---

[2] https://www.ncbi.nlm.nih.gov/pubmed/

Table 2: Test set accuracy, mean training time for a single document, and total training time on each task

Classifier	Yelp 2016	Amazon Sentiment	Amazon Category	Pubmed
Naive Bayes	63.12	61.66	88.14	75.81
	–, 1.8s	–, 0.8s	–, 1.3s	–, 4.2s
Logistic Regression	71.31	67.57	88.69	78.57
	–, 306s	–, 101s	–, 173s	–, 463s
Word shallow-and-wide CNN	74.44	70.75	88.20	78.15
	17ms, 9hr	15ms, 5hr	15ms, 5hr	35ms, 22hr
Hierarchical Attention Network	76.30	72.56	89.68	79.89
	96ms, 67hr	97ms, 35hr	113ms, 37hr	167ms, 110hr
Conv Attention Network	75.01	71.24	89.27	79.21
(One Self-Attention, Maxpool)	19ms, 13hr	19ms, 8hr	19ms, 8hr	38ms, 25hr
Conv Attention Network	75.17	71.45	89.35	79.70
(One Self-Attention, Target Attention)	21ms, 14hr	21ms, 9hr	21ms, 9hr	39ms, 26hr
Conv Attention Network	75.21	71.45	89.41	79.86
(Two Self-Attentions, Maxpool)	23ms, 15hr	22ms, 9hr	22ms, 9hr	41ms, 27hr
Conv Attention Network	75.25	71.78	89.71	79.95
(Two Self-Attentions, Target Attention)	25ms, 17hr	24ms, 10hr	24ms, 10hr	43ms, 29hr
Hiearchical Conv Attention Network	75.00	71.09	88.85	79.31
(One Self-Attention, Maxpool)	24ms, 16hr	23ms, 9hr	23ms, 9hr	42ms, 28hr
Hierarchical Conv Attention Network	75.75	72.33	89.55	79.91
(One Self-Attention, Target Attention)	34ms, 23hr	29ms, 12hr	29ms, 12hr	47ms, 31hr
Hiearchical Conv Attention Network	75.54	72.43	89.34	80.09
(Two Self-Attentions, Maxpool)	31ms, 21hr	31ms, 13hr	31ms, 13hr	50ms, 33hr
Hierarchical Conv Attention Network	**76.51**	**72.85**	**89.89**	**80.13**
(Two Self-Attentions, Target Attention)	49ms, 32hr	38ms, 16hr	38ms, 16hr	53ms, 35hr

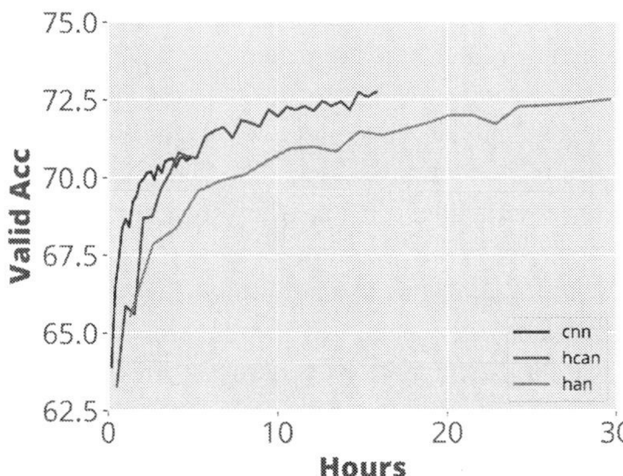

Figure 3: Validation accuracy vs time on Amazon sentiment analysis task.

document, and total time to converge. For timing, all models were trained on a single NVIDIA TITAN X GPU.

In all four tasks, the HCAN achieves the highest test accuracy. Furthermore, HCANs process documents and converge more than twice as fast as the HAN (Figure 3). Within the HCAN, using a hierarchical structure achieves better accuracy than not using a hierarchical structure, using two parallel self-attentions achieves better accuracy than using a single self-attention, and using target attention outperforms using maxpool, especially when using a hierarchical structure.

We note that the difference in accuracy between the deep learning approaches and traditional machine learning approaches is greater in the sentiment classification tasks than in the topic classification tasks. We expect that this is because sentiment classification requires more semantic nuance, which can be difficult to capture via TFIDF features. On the other hand, topic classification may require the presence of only a few specific words to indicate a specific topic.

5 Discussion

Based on our results, we see that the two best performing architectures are the HCAN and the HAN. Unlike the shallow-and-wide CNN,

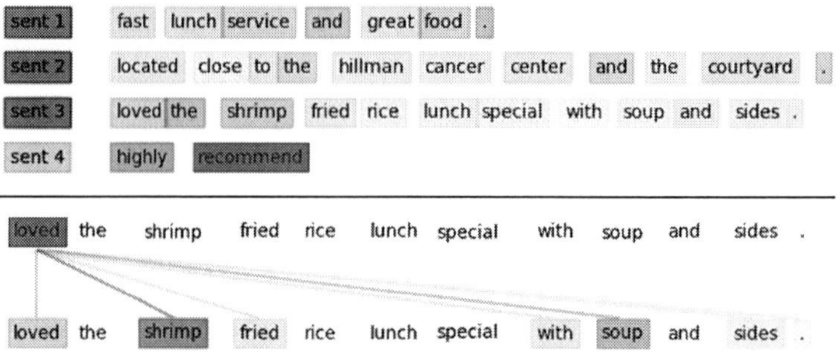

Figure 4: Attention weights assigned to a sample Yelp review by one attention head. The top portion shows the attention weights assigned to each word and sentence by the convolutional multihead target-attention. The bottom portion shows the attention weights assigned to the word "loved" in sentence 3 by the convolutional multihead self-attention.

HCANs and HANs utilize a hierarchical structure that first breaks a document down into its constituent sentences. Using this structure, the networks first locate the most critical information within each sentence and then establish the relationships between the critical information found from each sentence. Our results suggest that this approach works better for text classification than scanning the entire document in one single pass to look for key features.

On our tasks, we see that the HCAN achieves similar performance with the HAN but trains much faster. We attribute this to the fact that HCANs utilize a self-attention-based architecture instead of an RNN-based architecture to extract features. Self-attention utilizes a feed-forward structure, whereas an RNN must backpropagate onto itself over time. When computing gradients, this means that much more calculation is required for RNN-based architectures. For our HCAN, we utilized a self-attention mechanism with a width of 512 neurons and were able to perform faster than our HAN that used an RNN with only 50 GRUs.

Another important implication of self-attention is that it is easier to parallelize than RNNs. Self-attention utilizes a fixed number of feed-forward steps that remain the same regardless of the length of the input sequences. This makes it simple to split the model parameters associated with self-attention across multiple GPUs even when processing multiple documents of different lengths. On the other hand, the number of operations for an RNN is dependent on the length of the input sequence. This makes it challenging to efficiently split RNN parameters across multiple GPUs when dealing with a mini-batch of documents that vary

in length (Huang et al., 2013).

Utilizing an attention-based approach also increases the interpretability of the model. By examining the attention weights assigned to each word/sentence by the target attention mechanisms in each hierarchy of the HCAN, we can locate the words/sentences in a document that contribute most to its final label (Figure 4). Furthermore, we can also examine the attention weights assigned to each word/sentence in the self-attention mechanisms to establish how the HCAN is finding relationships between individual words/sentences when extracting important features (Figure 4).

Our results show that using two parallel self-attention mechanisms results in higher accuracy than using a single self-attention mechanism. Upon analyzing the attention weights assigned by the self-attention mechanisms, we found that using two parallel self-attentions captures more relationships involving modifier words than one single self-attention mechanism alone (Figure 5). Furthermore, we analyzed the documents that two parallel self-attentions classified correctly but one single self-attention did not. In sentiment analysis tasks, we found that many of these documents (1) begin positively but conclude negatively or vice versa, (2) contain a mix of positive and negative words, or (3) contain words that scale the meaning of another word or phrase (Supplementary A). This supports our hypothesis that two parallel self-attentions better distinguishes complex word relationships like scaling and negation.

To better understand how the HCAN functions in comparison with the HAN, we compared the attention weights assigned to each word/sentence by the target attention mechanisms in the two net-

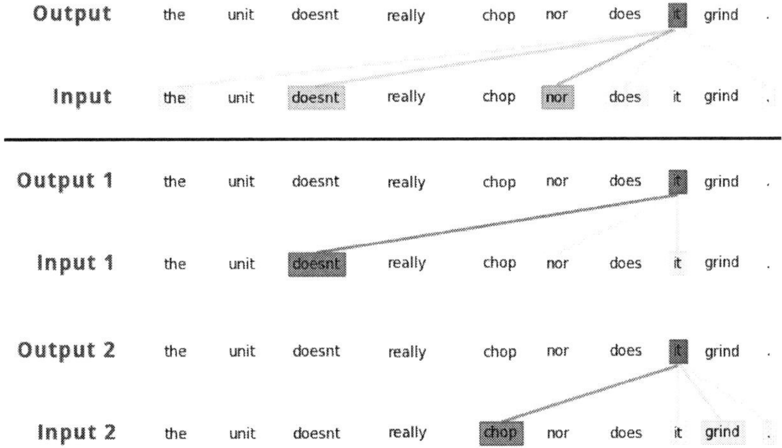

Figure 5: Self-attention weights assigned to a sample word 'it' by (top) HCAN with a single self-attention and (bottom) HCAN with two parallel self-attentions. With two self-attentions, the first self-attention captures the relationship between 'it' and 'doesnt' and the second self-attention captures the relationship between 'it' and 'chop'. This is a more nuanced negation relationship that isn't captured when using a single self-attention.

works. We found the HCAN weight assignments to be more spread out than those from the HAN (Supplementary B). Further analysis revealed that the self-attention mechanisms in the HCAN distribute the meaning of important keywords across many other words before the sequence is fed into the target attention mechanism, thus resulting in the wider distribution of attention weights.

6 Conclusion

In this work, we introduced a new self-attention-based text classification architecture, HCANs, and compared its performance with the current state-of-the-art, HANS, in four classification tasks: Yelp review sentiment, Amazon review sentiment, Amazon review product category, and Pubmed abstract topic. In all four tasks HCANs achieved slightly better performance than HANs while being more than twice as fast to train. Our results show that in time-critical NLP tasks, self-attention-based architectures may be able to replace RNN-based architectures to reduce training time without sacrificing accuracy. Moving forward, we plan to explore efficient implementations of data and model parallelism for self-attention-based architectures such as the HCAN. The code for our experiments is available online at `https://code.ornl.gov/v33/HCAN/`.

Acknowledgments

This work has been supported in part by the Joint Design of Advanced Computing Solutions for Cancer (JDACS4C) program established by the U.S. Department of Energy (DOE) and the National Cancer Institute (NCI) of the National Institutes of Health. This work was performed under the auspices of the U.S. Department of Energy by Argonne National Laboratory under Contract DE-AC02-06-CH11357, Lawrence Livermore National Laboratory under Contract DE-AC52-07NA27344, Los Alamos National Laboratory under Contract DE-AC5206NA25396, and Oak Ridge National Laboratory under Contract DE-AC05-00OR22725. This research was supported by the Exascale Computing Project (17-SC-20-SC), a collaborative effort of the U.S. Department of Energy Office of Science and the National Nuclear Security Administration. This research used resources of the Oak Ridge Leadership Computing Facility at the Oak Ridge National Laboratory, which is supported by the Office of Science of the U.S. Department of Energy under Contract No. DE-AC05-00OR22725.

References

Jimmy Lei Ba, Jamie Ryan Kiros, and Geoffrey E Hinton. 2016. Layer normalization. *arXiv preprint arXiv:1607.06450* .

Jianpeng Cheng, Li Dong, and Mirella Lapata. 2016. Long short-term memory-networks for machine reading. pages 551–561.

Kyunghyun Cho, Bart van Merrienboer, Caglar Gulcehre, Dzmitry Bahdanau, Fethi Bougares, Holger Schwenk, and Yoshua Bengio. 2014. Learning phrase representations using rnn encoder–decoder for statistical machine translation pages 1724–1734.

Junyoung Chung, Caglar Gulcehre, KyungHyun Cho, and Yoshua Bengio. 2014. Empirical evaluation of gated recurrent neural networks on sequence modeling. *arXiv preprint arXiv:1412.3555* .

Djork-Arn Clevert, Thomas Unterthiner, and Sepp Hochreiter. 2016. Fast and accurate deep network learning by exponential linear units (elus). *ICLR* .

Alexis Conneau, Holger Schwenk, Loc Barrault, and Yann Lecun. 2017. Very deep convolutional networks for text classification. In *ACL-EACL*. pages 1107–1116.

Cícero Nogueira Dos Santos and Maira Gatti. 2014. Deep convolutional neural networks for sentiment analysis of short texts. In *COLING*. pages 69–78.

Cicero Nogueira dos Santos, Bing Xiang, and Bowen Zhou. 2015. Classifying relations by ranking with convolutional neural networks pages 626–634.

Jonas Gehring, Michael Auli, David Grangier, Denis Yarats, and Yann N. Dauphin. 2017. Convolutional sequence to sequence learning. *ICML* pages 1243–1252.

Sebastian Gehrmann, Franck Dernoncourt, Yeran Li, Eric T Carlson, Joy T Wu, Jonathan Welt, John Foote Jr, Edward T Moseley, David W Grant, Patrick D Tyler, et al. 2017. Comparing rule-based and deep learning models for patient phenotyping. *arXiv preprint arXiv:1703.08705* .

Karl Moritz Hermann, Tomas Kocisky, Edward Grefenstette, Lasse Espeholt, Will Kay, Mustafa Suleyman, and Phil Blunsom. 2015. Teaching machines to read and comprehend. In *NIPS*. pages 1693–1701.

Zhiheng Huang, Geoffrey Zweig, Michael Levit, Benoit Dumoulin, Barlas Oguz, and Shawn Chang. 2013. Accelerating recurrent neural network training via two stage classes and parallelization. In *Proc IEEE Workshop Autom Speech Recognit Underst*. IEEE, pages 326–331.

Ozan Irsoy and Claire Cardie. 2014. Opinion mining with deep recurrent neural networks. In *EMNLP*. pages 720–728.

Yoon Kim. 2014. Convolutional neural networks for sentence classification. In *EMNLP*. pages 1746–1751.

Diederik P. Kingma and Jimmy Lei Ba. 2015. Adam: A method for stochastic optimization. *ICLR* .

Hoa T. Le, Christophe Cerisara, and Alexandre Denis. 2017. Do convolutional networks need to be deep for text classification? *CoRR* abs/1707.04108.

Zhouhan Lin, Minwei Feng, Cicero Nogueira dos Santos, Mo Yu, Bing Xiang, Bowen Zhou, and Yoshua Bengio. 2017. A structured self-attentive sentence embedding. In *ICLR*.

Pengfei Liu, Xipeng Qiu, and Xuanjing Huang. 2016. Recurrent neural network for text classification with multi-task learning. *IJCAI* pages 2873–2879.

Thang Luong, Hieu Pham, and Christopher D. Manning. 2015. Effective approaches to attention-based neural machine translation pages 1412–1421.

Julian McAuley and Jure Leskovec. 2013. Hidden factors and hidden topics: understanding rating dimensions with review text. In *ACM conference on Recommender systems*. ACM, pages 165–172.

Romain Paulus, Caiming Xiong, and Richard Socher. 2017. A deep reinforced model for abstractive summarization. *arXiv preprint arXiv:1705.04304* .

Hao Peng, Lili Mou, Ge Li, Yunchuan Chen, Yangyang Lu, and Zhi Jin. 2015. A comparative study on regularization strategies for embedding-based neural networks. In *EMNLP*. pages 2106–2111.

J Qiu, HJ Yoon, PA Fearn, et al. 2017. Deep learning for automated extraction of primary sites from cancer pathology reports. *IEEE J Biomed Health Inform* .

Fabrizio Sebastiani. 2005. Text categorization. In *Encyclopedia of Database Technologies and Applications*, IGI Global, pages 683–687.

Duyu Tang, Furu Wei, Nan Yang, Ming Zhou, Ting Liu, and Bing Qin. 2014. Learning sentiment-specific word embedding for twitter sentiment classification. In *ACL*. pages 1555–1565.

Ashish Vaswani, Noam Shazeer, Niki Parmar, Llion Jones, Jakob Uszkoreit, Aidan N Gomez, and ukasz Kaiser. 2017. Attention is all you need. *NIPS* .

Tao Wang, David J Wu, Adam Coates, and Andrew Y Ng. 2012. End-to-end text recognition with convolutional neural networks. In *ICPR*. IEEE, pages 3304–3308.

Kelvin Xu, Jimmy Ba, Ryan Kiros, Kyunghyun Cho, Aaron Courville, Ruslan Salakhudinov, Rich Zemel, and Yoshua Bengio. 2015. Show, attend and tell: Neural image caption generation with visual attention. In *ICML*. pages 2048–2057.

Zichao Yang, Diyi Yang, Chris Dyer, Xiaodong He, Alexander J Smola, and Eduard H Hovy. 2016. Hierarchical attention networks for document classification. In *HLT-NAACL*. pages 1480–1489.

Wenpeng Yin, Katharina Kann, Mo Yu, and Hinrich Schütze. 2017. Comparative study of cnn and rnn for natural language processing. *arXiv preprint arXiv:1702.01923* .

Tom Young, Devamanyu Hazarika, Soujanya Poria, and Erik Cambria. 2017. Recent trends in deep learning based natural language processing. *arXiv preprint arXiv:1708.02709* .

Daojian Zeng, Kang Liu, Siwei Lai, Guangyou Zhou, Jun Zhao, et al. 2014. Relation classification via convolutional deep neural network. In *COLING*. pages 2335–2344.

Xiang Zhang, Junbo Zhao, and Yann LeCun. 2015. Character-level convolutional networks for text classification. In *NIPS*. pages 649–657.

A Yelp Reviews Misclassified by Single Self-Attention

The following are examples of Yelp reviews that were misclassified when using a single self-attention mechanism but correctly classified when using two parallel self-attention mechanisms. Note in many of these reviews, one section of the review negates or scales the meaning in another section.

> i got this at a grocery store thinking it would be great since i only drink a little bit of wine or sake at a time . i ended up giving it away to goodwill after a few months because it doesnt really help the wine or sake at least not for weeks like im prone to need between glasses and it is annoying to use the plastic thingy trying to get it tight and worrying that youre going to break the bottle . i think a nice reusable cork kind of gadget would do just as good a job take up less drawer space and look prettier in the bottle .

> for those of you who criticized this book for lack of a plot i can only assume that you are much more suited to books in the mystery thriller genre . i loved it and found the characters very real and compelling . if you are a reader who likes books about relationships you are going to love it too .

> i hesitated buying this grill because there were so many negative reviews . im glad i decided to buy the grill . weve used it 5 times so far . to address some of the negative reviews . you can cook with the grill on both high and low with the cover closed . in the instructions you are actually directed to clean the grill for the first time with the burners on high and the cover closed . the stand is excellent . weve been using this at the beach . the stand and fold out tables save packing additional cargo in the car . as far as cleaning i dont know what people are expecting . its a bbq it gets dirty . the grates clean up real nice with brillo . the chrome area under the grill plates cleans up with a fantastic type cleaner .

> a feel good read . dean koontz does this type of book very very well . no horrid monsters except for the unscrupulous government people so dont expect nightmares from this one . it does have its suspense however .

> its fun in the begining . but the levels get harder and game play is not as fun . it got so hard it was not much fun to play . and has not much varity in it .

B Comparing Attention Weights from HAN and HCAN

The attention weights assigned by the target-attention for the HAN (Figure 6) are more focused on keywords than for the HCAN (Figure 7). This is because the self-attention in the HCAN redistributes the content of important keywords across other words before the sequence is sent into the target-attention (Figure 8).

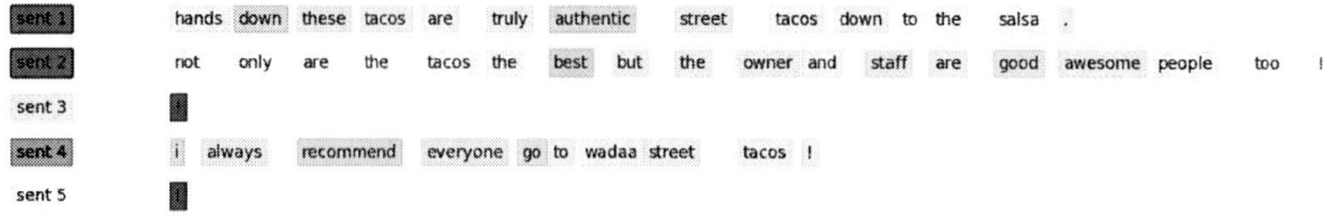

Figure 6: HAN target-attention weights assigned to a sample Yelp review. We see that the weights are primarily focused on sentiment keywords.

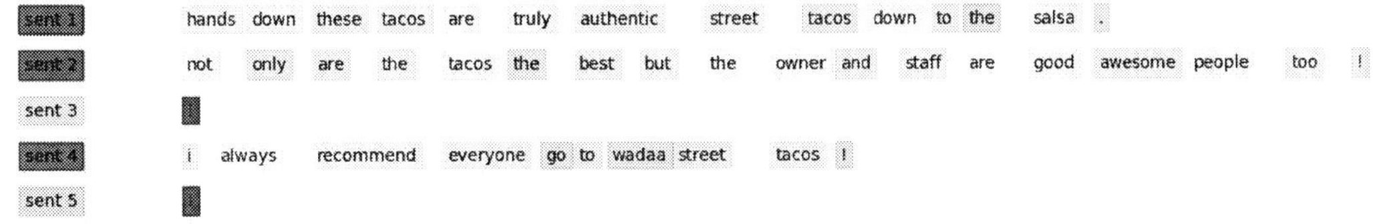

Figure 7: HCAN target-attention weights assigned to a sample Yelp review. We see that the weights are more spread out than in the HAN target-attention.

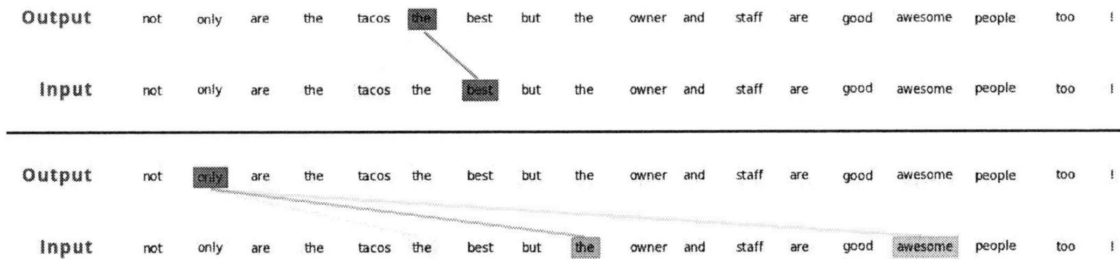

Figure 8: HCAN self-attention weights assigned to the words "the" and "only" in a sample Yelp review sentence. We see that meaning from sentiment keywords are redistributed among other words. In the two example shown above, we see that "best" is reassigned to "the" and "awesome" is reassigned to "only". Therefore, the HCAN target-attention weighs the words "the" and "only" higher because they contain content from sentiment keywords.

Extrofitting: Enriching Word Representation and its Vector Space with Semantic Lexicons

Hwiyeol Jo
AI Lab, LG Electronics
hwiyeolj@gmail.com

Stanley Jungkyu Choi
AI Lab, LG Electronics
stanley.choi@lge.com

Abstract

We propose post-processing method for enriching not only word representation but also its vector space using semantic lexicons, which we call *extrofitting*. The method consists of 3 steps as follows: (i) Expanding 1 or more dimension(s) on all the word vectors, filling with their representative value. (ii) Transferring semantic knowledge by averaging each representative values of synonyms and filling them in the expanded dimension(s). These two steps make representations of the synonyms close together. (iii) Projecting the vector space using Linear Discriminant Analysis, which eliminates the expanded dimension(s) with semantic knowledge. When experimenting with GloVe, we find that our method outperforms Faruqui's retrofitting on some of word similarity task. We also report further analysis on our method in respect to word vector dimensions, vocabulary size as well as other well-known pretrained word vectors (e.g., Word2Vec, Fasttext).

1 Introduction

As a method to represent natural language on computer, researchers have utilized distributed word representation. The distributed word representation is to represent a word as n-dimensional float vector, hypothesizing that some or all of the dimensions may capture semantic meaning of the word. The representation has worked well in various NLP tasks, substituting one-hot representation (Turian et al., 2010). Two major algorithms learning the distributed word representation are CBOW (Continuous Bag-of-Words) and skip-gram (Mikolov et al., 2013b). Both CBOW and skip-gram learn the representation using one hidden neural networks. The difference is that CBOW learns the representation of a center word from neighbor words whereas skip-gram gets the representation of neighbor words from a center word. Therefore, the algorithms have to depend on word order, because their objective function is to maximize the probability of occurrence of neighbor words given the center word. Then a problem occurs because the word representations do not have any information to distinguish synonyms and antonyms. For example, worthy and desirable should be mapped closely on the vector space as well as agree and disagree should be mapped apart, although they occur on a very similar pattern. Researchers have focused on the problem, and their main approaches are to use semantic lexicons (Faruqui et al., 2014; Mrkšić et al., 2016; Speer et al., 2017; Vulić et al., 2017; Camacho-Collados et al., 2015). One of the successful works is Faruqui's retrofitting[1], which can be summarized as pulling word vectors of synonyms close together by weighted averaging the word vectors on a fixed vector space (it will be explained in Section 2.1). The retrofitting greatly improves word similarity between synonyms, and the result not only corresponds with human intuition on words but also performs better on document classification tasks with comparison to original word embeddings (Kiela et al., 2015). From the idea of retrofitting, our method hypothesize that we can enrich not only word representation but also its vector space using semantic lexicons[2]. We call our method as *extrofitting*, which retrofits word vectors by expanding its dimensions.

---

[1] The retrofitting codes are available at
https://github.com/mfaruqui/retrofitting
[2] Our codes are available at
https://github.com/HwiyeolJo/Extrofitting

Proceedings of the 3rd Workshop on Representation Learning for NLP, pages 24–29
Melbourne, Australia, July 20, 2018. ©2018 Association for Computational Linguistics

2 Backgrounds

2.1 Retrofitting

Retrofitting (Faruqui et al., 2014) is a post-processing method to enrich word vectors using synonyms in semantic lexicons. The algorithm learns the word embedding matrix $Q = \{q_1, q_2, \ldots, q_n\}$ with the objective function $\Psi(Q)$:

$$\Psi(Q) = \sum_{i=1}^{n} [\alpha \|q_i - \hat{q}_i\|^2 + \sum_{(i,j)\in E} \beta_{ij} \|q_i - q_j\|^2] \tag{1}$$

where an original word vector is q_i, its synonym vector is q_j, and inferred word vector is $\hat{q}_i$. The hyperparameter α and β control the relative strengths of associations. The $\hat{q}_i$ can be derived by the following online update: $\hat{q}_i = \frac{\sum_{j:(i,j)\in E} \beta_{ij} q_j + \alpha_i q_i}{\sum_{j:(i,j)\in E} \beta_{ij} + \alpha_i}$

2.2 Linear Discriminant Analysis (LDA)

LDA (Welling, 2005) is one of the dimension reduction algorithms that project data into different vector space, while minimizing the loss of class information as much as possible. As a result, the algorithm finds linear vector spaces which minimize the distance of data in the same class as well as maximize the distance among the different class. The algorithm can be summarized as follows:

Calculating between-class scatter matrix S_B **and within-class scatter matrix** S_W**.**
When we denote data as x, classes as c, S_B and S_W can be formulated as follows:

$$S_B = \sum_{c} (\mu_i - \mu)(\mu_i - \mu)^T, \tag{2}$$

$$S_W = \sum_{c} \sum_{i \in c} (x_i - \mu_c)(x_i - \mu_c)^T, \tag{3}$$

where the overall average of x is μ, and the partial average in class i is denoted by μ_i.

Maximizing the objective function $J(w)$**.**
The objective function $J(w)$ that we should maximize can be defined as

$$J(w) = \frac{|U^T S_B U|}{|U^T S_W U|}, \tag{4}$$

and its solution can be reduced to find U that satisfies $S_W^{-1} S_B = U \Lambda U^T$. Therefore, U is derived by eigen-decomposition of $S_{W_i}^{-1} S_B$; choosing q eigen vectors which have the top-q eigen values, and composing transform matrix of U.

Transforming data onto new vector space
Using transform matrix U, we can get transformed data by $y = U^T x$

3 Enriching Representations of Word Vector and The Vector Space

3.1 Expanding Word Vector with Enrichment

We simply enrich the word vectors by expanding dimension(s) that add 1 or more dimension to original vectors, filling with its representative value r_i, which can be a mean value. We denote an original word vectors as $q_i = (e_1, e_2, \cdots, e_D)$ where D denotes the number of word vector dimension. Then, the representative value r_i can be formulated as $r_i = mean(e_1, e_2, \cdots, e_D)$. Intuitively, if we expand more additional dimensions, the word vectors will strengthen its own meaning. Likewise, the ratio of the number of expanded dimension to the number of original dimensions will affect the meaning of the word vectors.

3.2 Transferring Semantic Knowledge

To transfer semantic knowledge on the representative value r_i, we also take a simple approach of averaging all the representative values of each synonym pair, substituting each of its previous value. We get the synonym pairs from lexicons we introduced in Section 3. The transferred representative value $\bar{r}_i$ can be formulated as $\bar{r}_i = \sum_{s \in L} r_s / N$ where L refers to the lexicon consisting of synonym pairs s, and N is the number of synonyms. This manipulation makes the representation of the synonym pairs close to one another.

3.3 Enriching Vector Space

With the enriched vectors and the semantic knowledge, we perform Linear Discriminant Analysis for dimension reduction as well as clustering the synonyms from semantic knowledge. LDA finds new vector spaces to cluster and differentiate the labeled data, which are synonym pairs in this experiment. We can get the extrofitted word embedding matrix $\bar{w}$ as follows:

$$\bar{Q} = LDA(Q \oplus \bar{r}, l) \tag{5}$$

where Q is the word embedding matrix composed of word vectors q and l is the index of the synonym pair. We implement our method using Python2.7 with scikit-learn (Pedregosa et al., 2011).

4 Experiment Data

4.1 Pretrained Word Vectors

GloVe (Pennington et al., 2014) has lots of variations in respect to word dimension, number of to-

	MEN-3k	WS353	SL-999	RG-65	#Extrofitted	#Vocab.
`glove.6B.300d`	0.7486	0.5170	0.3705	0.7693	-	0.4M
+ PPDB	**0.7949**	0.5826	0.4387	0.8177	67,729	-
+ WordNet$_{syn}$	0.7884	0.5805	**0.4409**	0.7943	55,388	-
+ WordNet$_{all}$	0.7893	0.5714	0.4353	0.8010	55,388	-
+ FrameNet	0.7840	**0.5837**	0.4376	**0.8187**	7,592	-
`glove.42B.300d`	0.7435	0.5516	0.3738	0.8172	-	1.9M
+ PPDB	**0.8292**	0.6613	**0.4896**	0.8362	76,631	-
+ WordNet$_{syn}$	0.8230	0.6605	0.4884	**0.8634**	70,411	-
+ WordNet$_{all}$	0.8223	**0.6638**	0.4858	0.8561	70,411	-
+ FrameNet	0.8123	0.6448	0.4601	0.8556	7,809	-

Table 1: Spearman's correlation of extrofitted word vectors for word similarity tasks using semantic lexicon. Our method improves pretrained GloVe in different vocabulary size.

kens, and train sources. We used `glove.6B` trained on Wikipedia+Gigawords and `glove.42B.300d` trained on Common Crawl. The other pretrained GloVe do not fit in our experiment because they have different word dimension or are case-sensitive. We also use 300-dimensional **Word2Vec** (Mikolov et al., 2013a) with negative sampling trained on GoogleNews corpus. **Fasttext** (Bojanowski et al., 2016) is an extension of Word2Vec, which utilizes subword information to represent an original word. We used 300-dimensional pretrained Fasttext trained on Wikipedia (`wiki.en.vec`), using skip-gram.

4.2 Semantic Lexicons

We borrow the semantic lexicons from retrofitting (Faruqui et al., 2014). Faruqui et al. extracted the synonyms from **PPDB** (Ganitkevitch et al., 2013) by finding a word that more than two words in another language are corresponding with. Retrofitting also used **WordNet** (Miller, 1995) database which grouped words into set of synonyms (synsets). We used two versions of WordNet lexicon, one which consists of synonym only (WordNet$_{syn}$) and the other with additional hypernyms, hyponyms included (WordNet$_{all}$). Lastly, synonyms were extracted from **FrameNet** (Baker et al., 1998), which contains more than 200,000 manually annotated sentences linked to semantic frames. Faruqui et al. regarded words as synonyms if the words can be grouped with any of the frames.

4.3 Evaluation Data

We evaluate our methods on word similarity tasks using 4 different kinds of dataset. **MEN-3k** (Bruni et al., 2014) consists of 3000-word pairs rated from 0 to 50. **WordSim-353** (Finkelstein et al., 2001) consists of 353-word pairs rated from 0 to 10. **SimLex-999** (Hill et al., 2015) includes 999-word pairs rated from 0 to 10. **RG-65** (Rubenstein and Goodenough, 1965) has 65 words paired scored from 0 to 4. MEN-3k and WordSim-353 were split into train (or dev) set and test set, but we combined them together solely for evaluation purpose. The other datasets have lots of out-of-vocabulary, so we disregard them for future work.

5 Experiments on Word Similarity Task

The word similarity task is to calculate Spearman's correlation (Daniel, 1990) between two words as word vector format. We first apply extrofitting to GloVe from different data sources and present the result in Table 1. The result shows that although the number of the extrofitted word with FrameNet is less than the other lexicons, its performance is on par with other lexicons. We can also ensure that our method improves the performance of original pretrained word vectors.

Next, we perform extrofitting on GloVe in different word dimension and compare the performance with retrofitting. We use WordNet$_{all}$ lexicon on both retrofitting and extrofitting to compare the performances in the ideal environment for retrofitting. We present the results in Table 2. We can demonstrate that our method outperforms retrofitting on some of word similarity tasks, MEN-3k and WordSim-353. We believe that extrofitting on SimLex-999 and RG-65 is less powerful because all word pairs in the datasets are included on WordNet$_{all}$ lexicon. Since retrofitting forces the word similarity to be

	MEN-3k	**WS353**	**SL-999**	**RG-65**	Lexicon
`glove.6B.50d`	0.6574	0.4193	0.2646	0.5948	-
+ Retrofitting	0.6773	0.4121	**0.3761**	**0.7027**	WordNet$_{all}$
+ Extrofitting	**0.6876**	**0.4859**	0.2926	0.6743	WordNet$_{all}$
`glove.6B.100d`	0.6932	0.4488	0.2975	0.6762	-
+ Retrofitting	0.7052	0.4428	**0.4065**	**0.7863**	WordNet$_{all}$
+ Extrofitting	**0.7447**	**0.5337**	0.3733	0.7341	WordNet$_{all}$
`glove.6B.200d`	0.7244	0.4866	0.3403	0.7128	-
+ Retrofitting	0.7397	0.4799	**0.4415**	**0.8123**	WordNet$_{all}$
+ Extrofitting	**0.7689**	**0.5416**	0.4120	0.7389	WordNet$_{all}$
`glove.6B.300d`	0.7486	0.5130	0.3705	0.7693	-
+ Retrofitting	0.7681	0.5232	**0.4701**	**0.8499**	WordNet$_{all}$
+ Extrofitting	**0.7893**	**0.5714**	0.4353	0.8010	WordNet$_{all}$

Table 2: Comparison of Spearman's correlation of retrofitted or extrofitted word vectors for word similarity tasks. Our method, extrofitting, outperforms retrofitting on MEN-3k and WordSim-353.

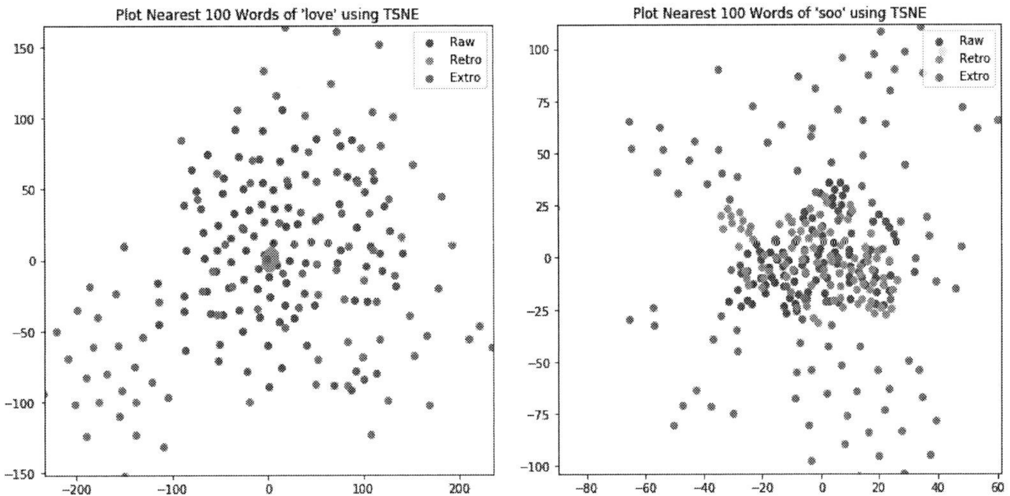

Figure 1: Plots of nearest top-100 words of cue words in different post-processing methods. We choose two cue words; one is included in semantic lexicons (`love`; left), and another is not (`soo`; right)

improved by weighted averaging their word vectors, it is prone to be overfitted on semantic lexicons. On the other hand, extrofitting also uses synonyms to improve word similarity but it works differently that extrofitting projects the synonyms both close together on a new vector space and far from the other words. Therefore, our method can make more generalized word representation than retrofitting. We plot top-100 nearest words using t-SNE (Maaten and Hinton, 2008), as shown in Figure 1. We can find that retrofitting strongly collects synonym words together whereas extrofitting weakly disperses the words, resulting loss in cosine similarity score. However, the result of ex-

trofitting can be interpreted as generalization that the word vectors strengthen its own meaning by being far away from each other, still keeping synonyms relatively close together (see Table 3). When we list up top-10 nearest words, extrofitting shows more favorable results than retrofitting. We can also observe that extrofitting even can be applied to words which are not included in semantic lexicons.

Lastly, we apply extrofitting to other well-known pretrained word vectors trained by different algorithms (see Subsection 4.1). The result is presented in Table 4. Extrofitting can be also applied to Word2Vec and Fasttext, enriching their word

Cue Word	Method	Top-10 Nearest Words(Cosine Similarity Score)
love	`glove.42B.300d`	loved(.7745), i(.7338), loves(.7311), know(.7286), loving(.7263), really(.7196), always(.7193), want(.7192), hope(.7127), think(.7110)
	+ Retrofitting	loved(.7857), know(.7826), like(.7781), want(.7736), i(.7707), feel(.7549), wish(.7549), think(.7491), enjoy(.7453), loving(.7451)
	+ Extrofitting	loved(.6008), adore(.5949), hate(.5949), luv(.5562), loving(.5391), loooove(.5321), looooove(.5233), loveeee(.5195), want(.5171), looove(.5107)
soo	`glove.42B.300d`	sooo(.8394), soooo(.7938), sooooo(.7715), soooooo(.7359), sooooooo(.6844), haha(.6574), hahah(.6320), damn(.6247), omg(.6244), hahaha(.6219)
	+ Retrofitting	sooo(.8394), soooo(.7938), sooooo(.7715), soooooo(.7359), haha(.6574), hahah(.6320), omg(.6244), hahaha(.6219), sooooooo(.6189)
	+ Extrofitting	sooo(.8329), soooo(.7896), sooooo(.7774), soooooo(.7560), sooooooo(.7256), soooooooo(.6867), sooooooooo(.6796), soooooooooo(.6517), tooo(.6493), sooooooooooo(.6423)

Table 3: List of top-10 nearest words of cue words in different post-processing methods. We show cosine similarity scores of two words included in semantic lexicon (`love`) or not (`soo`).

	MEN-3k	WS353	SL-999	RG-65	#Extrofitted	#Vocab.
`w2v-google-news`	0.7764	**0.6156**	0.4475	0.7558	-	3.0M
+ PPDB	**0.7883**	0.5935	**0.4799**	**0.7877**	63,825	-
+ WordNet$_{syn}$	0.7821	0.6004	0.4741	0.7844	64,248	-
+ WordNet$_{all}$	0.7782	0.6051	0.4733	0.7782	64,248	-
+ FrameNet	0.7784	0.6025	0.4651	0.7650	7,559	-
`wiki.en.vec`	0.7654	0.6301	0.3803	**0.8005**	-	2.5M
+ PPDB	**0.7737**	0.6363	0.4133	0.7723	69,237	-
+ WordNet$_{syn}$	0.7599	0.6326	**0.4135**	0.7633	70,542	-
+ WordNet$_{all}$	0.7569	**0.6421**	0.4093	0.7459	70,542	-
+ FrameNet	0.7594	0.6323	0.4051	0.7740	7,637	-

Table 4: Spearman's correlation of extrofitted word vectors for word similarity tasks on pretrained word vectors by Word2Vec and Fasttext. Extrofitting can be applied to other kinds of pretrained word vector.

representations except on WordSim-353 and RG-65, respectively. We find that our method can distort the well-established word embeddings. However, our results are noteworthy in that extrofitting can be applied to other kinds of pretrained word vectors for further enrichment.

6 Conclusion

We propose post-processing method for enriching not only word representation but also its vector space using semantic lexicons, which we call *extrofitting*. Our method takes a simple approach that (i) expanding word dimension (ii) transferring semantic knowledge on the word vectors (iii) projecting the vector space with enrichment. We show that our method outperforms another post-processing method, retrofitting, on some of word similarity task. Our method is robust in respect to the dimension of word vector and the size of vocabulary, only including an explainable hyperparameter; the number of dimension to be expanded. Further, our method does not depend on the order of synonym pairs. As a future work, we will do further research about our method to generalize and improve its performance; First, we can experiment on other word similarity datasets for generalization. Second, we can also utilize Autoencoder (Bengio et al., 2009) for non-linear projection with a constraint of preserving spatial information of each dimension of word vector.

Acknowledgments

Thanks for Jaeyoung Kim to discuss this idea. Also, greatly appreciate the reviewers for critical comments.

References

Collin F Baker, Charles J Fillmore, and John B Lowe. 1998. The berkeley framenet project. In *Proceedings of the 17th international conference on Computational linguistics-Volume 1*, pages 86–90. Association for Computational Linguistics.

Yoshua Bengio et al. 2009. Learning deep architectures for ai. *Foundations and trends® in Machine Learning*, 2(1):1–127.

Piotr Bojanowski, Edouard Grave, Armand Joulin, and Tomas Mikolov. 2016. Enriching word vectors with subword information. *arXiv preprint arXiv:1607.04606*.

Elia Bruni, N Tram, Marco Baroni, et al. 2014. Multimodal distributional semantics. *The Journal of Artificial Intelligence Research*, 49:1–47.

José Camacho-Collados, Mohammad Taher Pilehvar, and Roberto Navigli. 2015. Nasari: a novel approach to a semantically-aware representation of items. In *Proceedings of the 2015 Conference of the North American Chapter of the Association for Computational Linguistics: Human Language Technologies*, pages 567–577.

Wayne W Daniel. 1990. Spearman rank correlation coefficient. *Applied nonparametric statistics*, pages 358–365.

Manaal Faruqui, Jesse Dodge, Sujay K Jauhar, Chris Dyer, Eduard Hovy, and Noah A Smith. 2014. Retrofitting word vectors to semantic lexicons. *arXiv preprint arXiv:1411.4166*.

Lev Finkelstein, Evgeniy Gabrilovich, Yossi Matias, Ehud Rivlin, Zach Solan, Gadi Wolfman, and Eytan Ruppin. 2001. Placing search in context: The concept revisited. In *Proceedings of the 10th international conference on World Wide Web*, pages 406–414. ACM.

Juri Ganitkevitch, Benjamin Van Durme, and Chris Callison-Burch. 2013. Ppdb: The paraphrase database. In *Proceedings of the 2013 Conference of the North American Chapter of the Association for Computational Linguistics: Human Language Technologies*, pages 758–764.

Felix Hill, Roi Reichart, and Anna Korhonen. 2015. Simlex-999: Evaluating semantic models with (genuine) similarity estimation. *Computational Linguistics*, 41(4):665–695.

Douwe Kiela, Felix Hill, and Stephen Clark. 2015. Specializing word embeddings for similarity or relatedness. In *Proceedings of the 2015 Conference on Empirical Methods in Natural Language Processing*, pages 2044–2048.

Laurens van der Maaten and Geoffrey Hinton. 2008. Visualizing data using t-sne. *Journal of machine learning research*, 9(Nov):2579–2605.

Tomas Mikolov, Kai Chen, Greg Corrado, and Jeffrey Dean. 2013a. Efficient estimation of word representations in vector space. *arXiv preprint arXiv:1301.3781*.

Tomas Mikolov, Ilya Sutskever, Kai Chen, Greg S Corrado, and Jeff Dean. 2013b. Distributed representations of words and phrases and their compositionality. In *Advances in neural information processing systems*, pages 3111–3119.

George A Miller. 1995. Wordnet: a lexical database for english. *Communications of the ACM*, 38(11):39–41.

Nikola Mrkšić, Diarmuid O Séaghdha, Blaise Thomson, Milica Gašić, Lina Rojas-Barahona, Pei-Hao Su, David Vandyke, Tsung-Hsien Wen, and Steve Young. 2016. Counter-fitting word vectors to linguistic constraints. *arXiv preprint arXiv:1603.00892*.

F. Pedregosa, G. Varoquaux, A. Gramfort, V. Michel, B. Thirion, O. Grisel, M. Blondel, P. Prettenhofer, R. Weiss, V. Dubourg, J. Vanderplas, A. Passos, D. Cournapeau, M. Brucher, M. Perrot, and E. Duchesnay. 2011. Scikit-learn: Machine learning in Python. *Journal of Machine Learning Research*, 12:2825–2830.

Jeffrey Pennington, Richard Socher, and Christopher Manning. 2014. Glove: Global vectors for word representation. In *Proceedings of the 2014 conference on empirical methods in natural language processing (EMNLP)*, pages 1532–1543.

Herbert Rubenstein and John B Goodenough. 1965. Contextual correlates of synonymy. *Communications of the ACM*, 8(10):627–633.

Robert Speer, Joshua Chin, and Catherine Havasi. 2017. Conceptnet 5.5: An open multilingual graph of general knowledge. In *AAAI*, pages 4444–4451.

Joseph Turian, Lev Ratinov, and Yoshua Bengio. 2010. Word representations: a simple and general method for semi-supervised learning. In *Proceedings of the 48th annual meeting of the association for computational linguistics*, pages 384–394. Association for Computational Linguistics.

Ivan Vulić, Nikola Mrkšić, and Anna Korhonen. 2017. Cross-lingual induction and transfer of verb classes based on word vector space specialisation. *arXiv preprint arXiv:1707.06945*.

Max Welling. 2005. Fisher linear discriminant analysis. *Department of Computer Science, University of Toronto*, 3(1).

Chat Discrimination for Intelligent Conversational Agents with a Hybrid CNN-LMTGRU Network

Dennis Singh Moirangthem and Minho Lee
School of Electronics Engineering
Kyungpook National University
Daegu, South Korea
{mdennissingh,mholee}@gmail.com

Abstract

Recently, intelligent dialog systems and smart assistants have attracted the attention of many, and development of novel dialogue agents have become a research challenge. Intelligent agents that can handle both domain-specific task-oriented and open-domain chit-chat dialogs are one of the major requirements in the current systems. In order to address this issue and to realize such smart hybrid dialogue systems, we develop a model to discriminate user utterance between task-oriented and chit-chat conversations. We introduce a hybrid of convolutional neural network (CNN) and a lateral multiple timescale gated recurrent units (LMTGRU) that can represent multiple temporal scale dependencies for the discrimination task. With the help of the combined slow and fast units of the LMTGRU, our model effectively determines whether a user will have a chit-chat conversation or a task-specific conversation with the system. We also show that the LMTGRU structure helps the model to perform well on longer text inputs. We address the lack of dataset by constructing a dataset using Twitter and Maluuba Frames data. The results of the experiments demonstrate that the proposed hybrid network outperforms the conventional models on the chat discrimination task as well as performed comparable to the baselines on various benchmark datasets.

1 Introduction

Dialogue systems can be classified as domain-specific task-oriented and open-domain chit-chat dialog systems (Williams and Young, 2007; Wallace, 2009). The task-oriented dialog systems help users complete tasks in specific domains. The chit-chat dialog systems enable users to have an open-ended chat conversations with the system. While most of the functionalities offered by the two types of systems are complementary to each other, there have been very little efforts made to combine these two type of systems. Therefore, the potential of chat agents have been limited.

Recently, intelligent assistants have become popular with the integration of such systems in smartphones and home appliances. These intelligent assistants typically perform various tasks including weather forecast alerts, alarm settings, web search, and so on. Moreover, such assistants need to have the ability to perform chit-chat conversation with the users. This has led to the need for the development of novel and hybrid multi-domain task-oriented agents and open-domain chit-chat agents.

In order to develop such hybrid agents, we have to determine whether a user will have a chit-chat with the system or the user is looking for a task completion. For example, if a user says *"Hi, how are you doing?"*, then the user can be considered to have a chat with the system. Alternatively, if the user says *"I want a flight to Los Angeles,"* then the user is looking for a completion of a specific task. We address this task as a binary classification problem and call this task as *chat discrimination*.

Chat discrimination has not been sufficiently investigated in recent times. This is mainly because there are not enough studies to develop hybrids of task-oriented and chit-chat agents. Although task-oriented and chit-chat agents have long research histories, they do not require chat discrimination. We usually assume that the users of task-oriented agents will have task-oriented conversations with the systems and the users of chit-chat

Proceedings of the 3rd Workshop on Representation Learning for NLP, pages 30–40
Melbourne, Australia, July 20, 2018. ©2018 Association for Computational Linguistics

agents will always have non task-specific conversations with the systems. In a recent study, researchers in (Akasaki and Kaji, 2017) have tried chat detection using conventional classifiers with the help of a newly created dataset in Japanese language. But this dataset has not been released for further research or comparison.

In this work, we develop a hybrid network for chat discrimination by combining a convolutional neural network (CNN) and a gated recurrent unit (GRU). CNNs have been proven to be suitable for text classification problems (Kim, 2014; Johnson and Zhang, 2015a,b). Moreover, the temporal hierarchy concept with multiple timescale gated recurrent unit (MTGRU) (Kim et al., 2016) has also been proven to perform well in language modeling (Moirangthem and Lee, 2017; Moirangthem et al., 2017) and summarization (Kim et al., 2016) tasks. The MTGRU is known to handle long term dependency better with the help of the varying timescales to represent multiple compositionalities of language. The temporal hierarchy approach has also been shown to eliminate the need for complex structures and normalization techniques (Cooijmans et al., 2017; Krueger and Memisevic, 2016; Chung et al., 2017; Ha et al., 2017), and thereby increasing the computational efficiency of the model.

For our classification model, we develop a lateral multiple timescale structure. Our proposed lateral multiple timescale gated recurrent unit (LMTGRU) is significantly different from the conventional hierarchical MTGRU structure. The conventional MTGRU is most effective for handling long term dependencies in very long text inputs for applications such as summarization but performs comparable to vanilla GRU with shorter text inputs. Unlike the hierarchical architecture, the lateral connections in an LMTGRU will enable encoding of rich features that have different temporal dependencies from the input utterances in order to help classify the information correctly. LMTGRU follows a lateral (branch or root) architecture where the slow and fast units are directly connected to the inputs and the final output of the units are combined to form the final representation. This structure enables all the layers with different timescales to capture relevant features directly from the inputs unlike hierarchical multilayer structures. Since the data consist of utterances as input, and the input to the RNN is rep-

resented as higher order features from the CNN, LMTGRU proves to be more suitable for this task.

Our major contributions are as follows:

- We introduce a hybrid CNN-LMTGRU structure to build rich features from input texts to classify utterances correctly.

- The LMTGRU architecture enables our model to perform well on longer text sequences with the help of the slow layer as well as maintain comparable performance on shorter sequences.

- To address the lack of dataset, we create a dataset using Twitter data (Microsoft Research Social Media Conversation Corpus) (Sordoni et al., 2015) for chit-chat conversations and Maluuba Frames data (El Asri et al., 2017) for task-oriented conversations.

- In order to demonstrate that the proposed model performs well on other text classification tasks and to compare it to the existing baselines, we report the performance on various sentence classification benchmark datasets. The results of our experiments demonstrate that the proposed model performs well on the benchmark datasets as well.

2   Related Work

Although there have been enough studies for task-oriented and chit-chat agents independently, developing hybrid models of the two types of agents has not been explored enough. Therefore, few attempts have been made to develop a chat discrimination model.

Niculescu and Banchs (2015) tried to combine task-oriented agents and chit-chat agents, but the authors did not have a clear way to automatically determine when to switch back to the chit-chat agent. Lee et al. (2009) proposed to combine task-oriented and chit-chat agents with the help of an example-based dialogue manager, but it is difficult to integrate the current state-of-the-art deep learning model based classifiers as a component in such a framework.

Wang et al. (2014) and Sarikaya (2017) proposed to combine a multi-domain task-oriented agents and chit-chat agents using machine-learning-based frameworks. Robichaud et al. (2014); Sarikaya et al. (2016) approached domain classification as ranking between alternate "dialog experts". In a recent study, Akasaki and Kaji (2017) tried chat detection using conventional classifiers with the help of a newly created dataset in Japanese language. They used concatenated features from multiple feature extractors for the classification. An end-to-end model was not explored. Moreover, the dataset has not been released for further research or comparison.

Deep learning based models have achieved great success in many NLP tasks, including learning distributed word, sentence and document representation (Mikolov et al., 2013; Le and Mikolov, 2014), parsing (Socher et al., 2013), statistical machine translation (Cho et al., 2014), sentiment classification (Kim, 2014), etc. Learning distributed sentence representation through neural network models requires little external domain knowledge and can reach satisfactory results in related tasks like sentiment classification, text categorization etc.

In recent sentence representation learning works, neural network models are constructed upon either the input word sequences or the transformed syntactic parse tree. Among them, convolutional neural network (CNN) and recurrent neural network (RNN) are two popular ones. The capability of capturing local correlations along with extracting higher-level correlations through pooling empowers CNN to model sentences naturally from consecutive context windows. Kim (2014) proposed a CNN architecture with multiple filters and multiple channels for text classification.

RNNs are able to deal with variable-length input sequences and discover long-term dependencies. Various variants of RNNs have been proposed to better store and access memories. The most popular variants are long short-term memory (LSTM) (Hochreiter and Schmidhuber, 1997) and GRU (Cho et al., 2014). Recently proposed MTGRU (Kim et al., 2016), inspired by the concept of temporal hierarchy found in the human brain (Botvinick, 2007; Meunier et al., 2010), demonstrates the ability to capture multiple compositionalities similar to the findings of Ding et al. (2016). This better representation learning capability enhances the ability of the network to model longer sequences of text.

In this paper, we develop a hybrid of CNN and LMTGRU in a unified architecture for semantic sequence modeling. We apply CNN to text data and feed the features directly to the LMTGRU, and hence our architecture enables the network to learn multiple temporal scale dependencies from higher-order features. We hypothesize that the combination of slow and fast features will be beneficial for the chat discrimination task.

3 Proposed Model

We formulate chat discrimination as a binary classification problem. In this section, we explain the proposed hybrid classifier model shown in Figure 1.

3.1 The Convolutional Neural Network Layer

The CNN layer shown in Figure 1 is implemented using a single convolution and max-pooling layer and use a rectified linear unit (ReLU) as the non-linear activation function following Kim (2014). Let $\mathbf{x}_i \in \mathbf{R}^d$ be the word vector of dimension d corresponding to the i-th word in the input utterance. An utterance of length n, which are padded if necessary, can be represented as

$$\mathbf{x}_{1:n} = \mathbf{x}_1 \oplus \mathbf{x}_2 \oplus \ldots \oplus \mathbf{x}_n, \qquad (1)$$

where $\oplus$ is the concatenation operator. Let $\mathbf{x}_{i:i+j}$ be to the concatenation of words $\mathbf{x}_i, \mathbf{x}_{i+1}, \ldots, \mathbf{x}_{i+j}$. A convolution operation involves a *filter* $\mathbf{w} \in \mathbf{R}^{hd}$, which is applied to a window of h words to produce a new feature. For example, a feature c_i is generated from a window of words $\mathbf{x}_{i:i+h-1}$ by

$$c_i = f(\mathbf{w} \cdot \mathbf{x}_{i:i+h-1} + b). \qquad (2)$$

Here $b \in \mathbf{R}$ is a bias term and f is a non-linear function. This filter is applied to each possible window of words in the sentence $\{\mathbf{x}_{1:h}, \mathbf{x}_{2:h+1}, \ldots, \mathbf{x}_{n-h+1:n}\}$ to produce a feature map

$$\mathbf{c} = [c_1, c_2, \ldots, c_{n-h+1}], \qquad (3)$$

with $\mathbf{c} \in \mathbf{R}^{n-h+1}$. A max pooling operation (Collobert et al., 2011) over the feature map is applied, which takes the maximum value $\hat{c} = \max\{\mathbf{c}\}$ as the feature corresponding to this particular filter. The idea is to capture only the most important features.

The processes described above is for *one* feature being extracted from *one* filter. The proposed CNN model includes a number of filters with multiple window sizes to obtain various features. These features are then split into

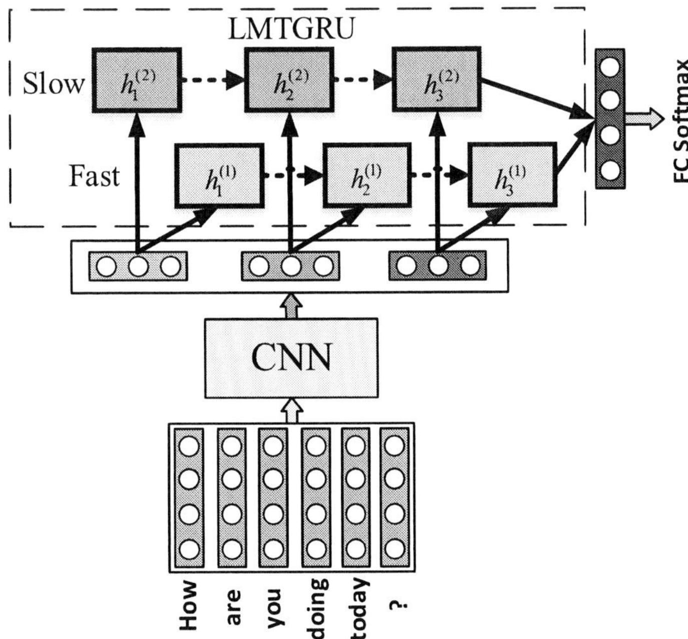

Figure 1: The proposed CNN-LMTGRU classifier. The input to the model is "How are you doing today?"

n/max_pool_size outputs and are passed on to the LMTGRU layer.

3.2 The Lateral MTGRU Layer

For this classification task, we implement a lateral multiple timescale architecture where half of the MTGRU units are fast and the remaining half are slow as shown in Figure 1. The fast and slow units can capture different temporal dependencies from the input sequence. The fast timescale layer can capture fast changing features (e.g. character or word) whereas slower timescales can represent phrase or sentence level features (Moirangthem et al., 2017). The proposed LMTGRU structure follows a lateral (branch or root) architecture where the slow and fast units are directly connected to the inputs. This lateral architecture is different from the conventional MTGRU with a hierarchical layer architecture, since the LMTGRU does not follow a multilayer structure. The LMTGRU structure is implemented using multiple single layer MTGRU networks whose timescales are different and the input to each layer comes directly from the input features. And the final output representation features of each layer are combined to form the penultimate representation of the input sequence that includes both fast and slow features.

The multiple timescales in an MTGRU network is implemented by applying a timescale variable at the end of a conventional GRU unit, essentially adding another gating unit that modulates the mixture of the past and current hidden states. In an MTGRU, each step takes as input $\mathbf{x}_t, \mathbf{h}_{t-1}$ and produces the hidden $\mathbf{h_t}$. The timescale τ added to the activation $\mathbf{h}_t$ of the MTGRU is shown in Eq. (4). τ is used to control the timescale of each GRU cell. Larger τ results in slower cell outputs but it makes the cell focus on the slow features and vice-versa. The timescale variable τ is scalar and one τ controls the slow cells and another τ controls the fast cells. We initialize the τ for each group of cells, e.g. larger τ for slow cells and smaller τ for fast cells. The τ is made as a trainable variable like any other weight of the network and is optimized during the training based on the final loss. An MTGRU cell is illustrated in Figure 2.

$$r_t = \sigma(W_{xr}x_t + W_{hr}h_{t-1})$$
$$z_t = \sigma(W_{xz}x_t + W_{hz}h_{t-1})$$
$$u_t = \tanh(W_{xu}x_t + W_{hu}(r_t \odot h_{t-1}))$$
$$\tilde{h}_t = z_t h_{t-1} + (1 - z_t)u_t$$
$$h_t = \tilde{h}_t \frac{1}{\tau} + (1 - \frac{1}{\tau})h_{t-1}$$

(4)

where $\sigma(\cdot)$ and $\tanh(\cdot)$ are the sigmoid and tangent hyperbolic activation functions, $\odot$ denotes

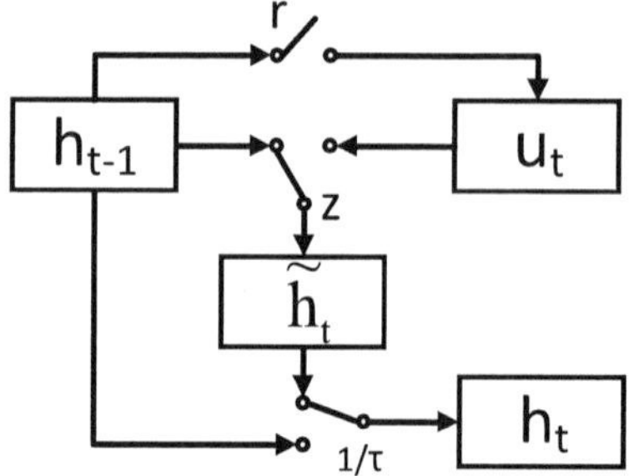

Figure 2: A Multiple Timescale Gated Recurrent Unit. The τ parameter is set for each layer and it controls the timescale of the layer.

the element-wise multiplication operator, and $\mathbf{r}_t$, $\mathbf{z}_t$ are referred to as *reset*, *update* gates respectively. $\mathbf{u}_t$ and $\tilde{\mathbf{h}}_t$ are the candidate activation and candidate hidden state of the MTGRU.

The proposed CNN-LMTGRU hybrid network consists of a CNN layer followed by a fast and a slow LMTGRU layer. The fast units as well as the slow units are directly connected to the CNN features. Finally the combined last hidden representation of the LMTGRU is passed to a fully connected softmax layer whose output is the probability distribution over the labels.

4 Chat Discrimination Dataset

Chat discrimination task requires a chat dataset like the one shown in Table 1. We address the lack of such a dataset by using the Microsoft Research Social Media Conversation Corpus[1] and Maluuba Frames[2] datasets. Microsoft Research Social Media Conversation Corpus is a collection of conversational snippets extracted from Twitter logs. The advantage of using this dataset is that it has been evaluated by crowd sourced annotators measuring quality of the response. These data are suitable for detecting open-domain non-task oriented chats. On the other hand, we use the Maluuba Frames dataset for the domain task-specific conversations. This corpus is for the travel agent domain where the users can inquire the agent and ask for booking of hotels and flights. The dialogs were recorded using 12 participants over a period of 20 days. We process the data to utilize only the user utterances in our chat discrimination dataset. Finally, we have 20,532 utterances with 10,266 in

[1]https://www.microsoft.com/en-us/download/details.aspx?id=52375

[2]https://datasets.maluuba.com/Frames

each class. We divide the data into 10% for validation, 10% for test, and the remaining for train.

5 Experiments and Results

We evaluate the performance of the proposed method and compare it to the conventional models using our chat discrimination dataset. In order to demonstrate that the proposed model performs well on other text classification datasets and to compare it to the existing baselines, we report the performance on various sentence classification benchmark datasets as well.

5.1 Experiment settings

We trained the proposed CNN-LMTGRU model in an end-to-end fashion, where we do not use any pre-trained word embedding. An embedding of size 300 was used for the model and was trained with the model. We used 128 filters of sizes $\{3, 4, 5\}$ for the CNN.

We used 300 units of MTGRU where half of the units are fast and the remaining are slow units to construct the LMTGRU structure. The τ for the fast units and the slow units were initialized to 1.0 and 1.25, respectively. We follow Moirangthem et al. (2017) to initialize the timescale parameter. In order to control the τ during training, we set the lower bound to 1.0 using clip by value. This is done as the fastest layer should have a τ of 1.0, however there is no upper bound for the slow layers. After training, the final τ values are 1.16 and 1.37 for the fast and the slow layers, respectively. The learning rate to update the τ, which is different from the global learning rate, is set to 0.00001 in order to avoid large changes in the timescale.

We used the RMSprop Optimizer (Tieleman and Hinton, 2012) to perform stochastic gradient descent with the decay set to 0.9 and the global learning rate to 0.001. For regularization we employ dropout of 0.5 on the final CNN output as well as in the LMTGRU layers to avoid overfitting. We utilized the validation performance for early stopping of the training for better generalization.

5.2 Baseline Models

The baseline models implemented for the comparison using our chat discrimination dataset are described as follows:

CNN We used the same parameters as before except the number of filters were increased to

Type	Example
Chit-Chat	Let's meet at the coffee place and talk about you.
	What is your hobby?
	I will visit my parents for the vacation.
	I like pop music.
	Do you like soccer?
	I don't know you, but you seem to be a serious person.
Task-oriented	Hello, I am looking to book a trip for 2 adults and 6 children.
	We are departing from Kochi for Denver.
	When would I be leaving for each of them?
	I would like to spend as much time in Denver as my budget will allow.
	Do these packages have different departure dates?
	Ok, I would like to purchase the trip with the 4-star hotel.

Table 1: Example utterances of the two kinds of conversations.

256. We followed (Kim, 2014) and used a fully connected softmax layer for the binary classification.

LSTM/GRU The same parameters were used as before except the number of hidden units is increased to 500. The LSTM/GRU takes every word vector in a sequence as input and the final representation is passed to a softmax layer for classification.

LMTGRU This LMTGRU model consists of a fast and a slow layer with 250 hidden units in each layer. The remaining settings are the same as the LSTM/GRU model.

CNN-LSTM/GRU This structure is almost identical to the proposed model, but instead of the LMTGRU, LSTM/GRU is used for comparison. The parameters remain the same.

5.3 Evaluation on Benchmark Datasets

Following Kim (2014), we test our model on various benchmarks. Summary statistics of the datasets are given below.

- **MR**: Movie reviews with one sentence per review. This binary classification task involves detecting positive/negative reviews (Pang and Lee, 2005). The average sequence length is 20 and the dataset size is $10,662$.

- **SST-1**: This is the Stanford Sentiment Treebank is an extension of MR with multiple labels (very positive, positive, neutral, negative, very negative) (Socher et al., 2013). The average sequence length is 18 and the dataset size is $11,855$.

- **SST-2**: This is similar to SST-1 but with binary labels. The average sequence length is 19 and the dataset size is $9,613$.

- **Subj**: Subjectivity dataset consists of sentences with binary labels (subjective or objective). The average sequence length is 23 and the dataset size is $10,000$ (Pang and Lee, 2004).

- **TREC**: The TREC task is a classification task to classify 6 types of question (questions about person, location, numeric information, etc.). The average sequence length is 10 and the dataset size is $5,952$ (Li and Roth, 2002).

- **CR**: Customer reviews of various products with positive/negative labels. The average sequence length is 19 and the dataset size is $3,775$ (Hu and Liu, 2004).

- **MPQA**: Opinion polarity detection is a subtask of the MPQA dataset with 2 classes. The average sequence length is 3 and the dataset size is $10,606$ (Wiebe et al., 2005).

For the evaluation on the benchmark datasets, we implemented a CNN-LMTGRU model that is identical to the one described in Section 5.1. The data for train, validation, and test for the benchmark datasets follow the previous works (Kim, 2014; Kalchbrenner et al., 2014).

5.4 Results

Table 2 illustrates the classification performance of the various models. The performance is given in accuracy and the results show that the proposed hybrid CNN-LMTGRU model outperforms

Model	Accuracy (%)
CNN	91.12
LSTM	89.67
GRU	90.56
LMTGRU	90.64
CNN-LSTM	92.31
CNN-GRU	93.01
Proposed CNN-LMTGRU	**94.69**

Table 2: Chat classification results on the test set.

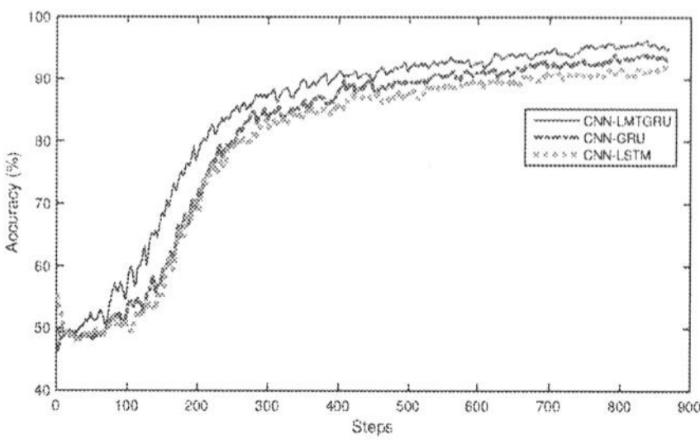

Figure 3: Classification accuracy curve on the validation set of the proposed method and the hybrid baseline models.

the baseline models. The performance curve of the hybrid models is shown in Figure 3, respectively.

In order to differentiate the performance of the proposed CNN-LMTGRU model and the CNN-GRU model, we divide the test data of the dialog classification dataset according to the length of the texts. Figure 4 shows the comparison of the performance accuracy on different lengths of test data. It can be seen that the LMTGRU structure enables the model to outperform GRU on longer text inputs and there is no significant performance degradation with the increase in input length. Whereas, the performance of GRU drops significantly with longer text inputs.

Table 3 shows the result of the comparison of our model with various other models using publicly available sentence classification datasets. These results illustrate that our proposed model either performed comparable to or outperformed existing models.

6 Discussion

When we look at the results illustrated in Table 2, the performance of the proposed CNN-LMTGRU increased significantly compared to CNN-GRU. As shown in Eq. (4), we know that if τ is close to 1, which is the case of a fast LMTGRU layer,

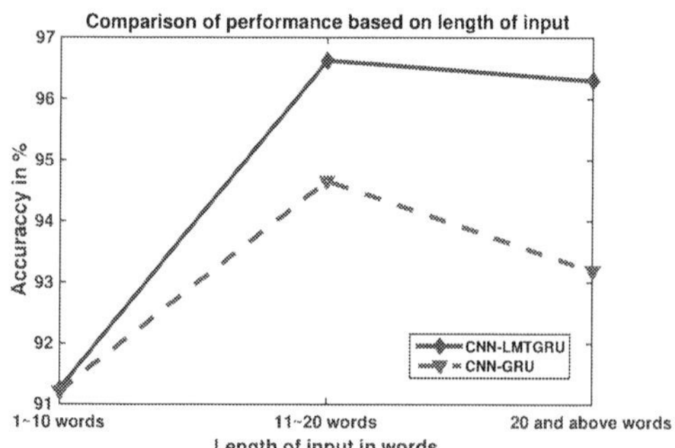

Figure 4: Classification performance comparison based on the length of input.

the model becomes a vanilla GRU. Therefore, a vanilla GRU is considered as a fast layer and hence, a CNN-GRU network can be considered as a network with only fast units. The difference in performance when we have all the RNN units as fast, i.e. CNN-GRU, and when we have a combination of slow and fast units, i.e. CNN-LMTGRU, show the effectiveness of the multiple timescale approach. The results in Figure 4 also show the significance of the features from slow and fast layers, where the fast features helps maintain the performance with shorter text inputs and the slow features enable the model to perform significantly better with longer text inputs. This confirms our hypotheses that the proposed LMTGRU with the help of both slow and fast units can help encode different dynamic features in order to help classify the sentences and utterances correctly. The results indicate that the LMTGRU architecture increases the capability of the model to learn multiple temporal dependencies better for the discrimination task. The results also demonstrate that our hybrid CNN-LMTGRU network performs significantly better than the existing hybrid models.

The results in Table 3 shows that our model performed fairly comparable to the baseline models. The enhanced performance of the proposed model in both SST-2 (average length of 19 words) and MPQA (average length of 3 words) over the baseline models also confirms our hypothesis that the rich features of the slow and fast layers help in the discrimination task even with diverse sequence lengths. However, for some of the datasets such as TREC, our end-to-end learning model cannot outperform the conventional models like SVM due to the limited size of the dataset.

The increased ability of the proposed model to

Model	MR	SST-1	SST-2	Subj	TREC	CR	MPQA
CNN-static (Kim, 2014)	81.0	45.5	86.8	93.0	92.8	84.7	89.6
CNN-non-static (Kim, 2014)	**81.5**	48.0	87.2	93.4	93.6	84.3	89.5
CNN-multichannel (Kim, 2014)	81.1	47.4	88.1	93.2	92.2	**85.0**	89.4
RAE (Socher et al., 2011)	77.7	43.2	82.4	–	–	–	86.4
MV-RNN (Socher et al., 2012)	79.0	44.4	82.9	–	–	–	–
RNTN (Socher et al., 2013)	–	45.7	85.4	–	–	–	–
DCNN (Kalchbrenner et al., 2014)	–	48.5	86.8	–	93.0	–	–
Paragraph-Vec (Le and Mikolov, 2014)	–	**48.7**	87.8	–	–	–	–
CCAE (Hermann and Blunsom, 2013)	77.8	–	–	–	–	–	87.2
Sent-Parser (Dong et al., 2015)	79.5	–	–	–	–	–	86.3
NBSVM (Wang and Manning, 2012)	79.4	–	–	93.2	–	81.8	86.3
MNB (Wang and Manning, 2012)	79.0	–	–	**93.6**	–	80.0	86.3
G-Dropout (Wang and Manning, 2013)	79.0	–	–	93.4	–	82.1	86.1
F-Dropout (Wang and Manning, 2013)	79.1	–	–	**93.6**	–	81.9	86.3
Tree-CRF (Nakagawa et al., 2010)	77.3	–	–	–	–	81.4	86.1
CRF-PR (Yang and Cardie, 2014)	–	–	–	–	–	82.7	–
SVM_S (Silva et al., 2011)	–	–	–	–	**95.0**	–	–
Proposed CNN-LMTGRU	80.9	48.4	**89.4**	93.4	93.8	84.8	**90.8**

Table 3: Results of our CNN-LMTGRU model against other methods on various sentence classification benchmark datasets.

discriminate between open-domain chit-chat conversations and domain-specific task-oriented utterances will definitely help in the development of hybrid intelligent dialog systems that can handle both types of conversation. Moreover, with the help of this kind of classifier, the chat agents can dynamically switch between utterances in order to conduct a more natural and intelligent conversation with the users.

7 Conclusion and Future Work

This paper addressed the issue of discriminating conversations for combining domain-specific task-oriented agents and open-domain chit-chat agents. We developed a hybrid model consisting of a CNN and an LMTRGU network to classify the conversations. The proposed LMTGRU was able to effectively determine the type of conversation that a user will have with a dialog system. Moreover, we addressed the lack of dataset by constructing a dataset with chit-chat conversations and a task-oriented conversation corpus. We also evaluated the performance of the proposed hybrid model on various benchmark sentence classification datasets in order to compare to several existing models. The results of our experiments illustrated that the proposed end-to-end learning hybrid network with multiple timescales not only performed signifi-

cantly better in case of longer texts inputs but also maintained good performance in case of shorter texts.

In the future, we plan to develop a more sophisticated dialog discrimination model to handle user utterances that are ambiguous in nature. It will be difficult for the standard classifiers to determine the actual type of conversation in such cases. One of the possible solution is to instruct the chat agent to follow up with clarification questions in case of ambiguity (Schlöder and Fernández, 2015). Another solution is to utilize contextual information by using previous dialogs from the system (Xu and Sarikaya, 2014). We plan to integrate features from the previous utterances for classification. This can be achieved by integrating the lateral architecture of an LMTGRU and the hierarchical organization of MTGRU along with the CNN features from the current and previous utterances to make the decision.

Although the studies on conversational agents have made significant progress in the recent years, it is still difficult for the systems to have a fluent conversation with the users (Higashinaka et al., 2015). We further plan to utilize the chat discrimination model to develop a hybrid system in order to improve such dialog agents. This will also allow us to evaluate the effectiveness of our model for this application.

Acknowledgments

This work was partly supported by the National Research Foundation of Korea (NRF) grant funded by the Korea government (MSIP) (No. NRF-2017M3C1B6071400)(40%), by the Institute for Information & communications Technology Promotion(IITP) grant funded by the Korea government(MSIT) (R7124-16-0004, Development of Intelligent Interaction Technology Based on Context Awareness and Human Intention Understanding)(30%), and by the Technology Innovation Program: Industrial Strategic Technology Development Program (10073162) funded By the Ministry of Trade, Industry & Energy(MOTIE, Korea)(30%).

References

Satoshi Akasaki and Nobuhiro Kaji. 2017. Chat detection in an intelligent assistant: Combining task-oriented and non-task-oriented spoken dialogue systems. *arXiv preprint arXiv:1705.00746* .

Matthew M Botvinick. 2007. Multilevel structure in behaviour and in the brain: a model of fuster's hierarchy. *Philosophical Transactions of the Royal Society B: Biological Sciences* 362(1485):1615–26.

Kyunghyun Cho, Bart van Merrienboer, Çaglar Gülçehre, Fethi Bougares, Holger Schwenk, and Yoshua Bengio. 2014. Learning phrase representations using RNN encoder-decoder for statistical machine translation. *CoRR* abs/1406.1078.

Junyoung Chung, Sungjin Ahn, and Yoshua Bengio. 2017. Hierarchical multiscale recurrent neural networks. In *Proceeding of the International Conference on Learning Representations*.

Ronan Collobert, Jason Weston, Léon Bottou, Michael Karlen, Koray Kavukcuoglu, and Pavel Kuksa. 2011. Natural language processing (almost) from scratch. *Journal of Machine Learning Research* 12(Aug):2493–2537.

Tim Cooijmans, Nicolas Ballas, César Laurent, Çağlar Gülçehre, and Aaron Courville. 2017. Recurrent batch normalization. In *Proceeding of the International Conference on Learning Representations*.

Nai Ding, Lucia Melloni, Hang Zhang, Xing Tian, and David Poeppel. 2016. Cortical tracking of hierarchical linguistic structures in connected speech. *Nature neuroscience* 19(1):158–164.

Li Dong, Furu Wei, Shujie Liu, Ming Zhou, and Ke Xu. 2015. A statistical parsing framework for sentiment classification. *Computational Linguistics* 41(2):293–336.

Layla El Asri, Hannes Schulz, Shikhar Sharma, Jeremie Zumer, Justin Harris, Emery Fine, Rahul Mehrotra, and Kaheer Suleman. 2017. Frames: A corpus for adding memory to goal-oriented dialogue systems. *arXiv preprint arXiv:1704.00057* .

David Ha, Andrew Dai, and Quoc V Le. 2017. Hypernetworks. In *Proceeding of the International Conference on Learning Representations*.

Karl Moritz Hermann and Phil Blunsom. 2013. The role of syntax in vector space models of compositional semantics. In *Proceedings of the 51st Annual Meeting of the Association for Computational Linguistics (Volume 1: Long Papers)*. volume 1, pages 894–904.

Ryuichiro Higashinaka, Kotaro Funakoshi, Masahiro Araki, Hiroshi Tsukahara, Yuka Kobayashi, and Masahiro Mizukami. 2015. Towards taxonomy of errors in chat-oriented dialogue systems. In *SIGDIAL Conference*. pages 87–95.

Sepp Hochreiter and Jürgen Schmidhuber. 1997. Long short-term memory. *Neural computation* 9(8):1735–1780.

Minqing Hu and Bing Liu. 2004. Mining and summarizing customer reviews. In *Proceedings of the tenth ACM SIGKDD international conference on Knowledge discovery and data mining*. ACM, pages 168–177.

Rie Johnson and Tong Zhang. 2015a. Effective use of word order for text categorization with convolutional neural networks pages 103–112.

Rie Johnson and Tong Zhang. 2015b. Semi-supervised convolutional neural networks for text categorization via region embedding. In *Advances in neural information processing systems*. pages 919–927.

Nal Kalchbrenner, Edward Grefenstette, and Phil Blunsom. 2014. A convolutional neural network for modelling sentences. In *Proceedings of the 52nd Annual Meeting of the Association for Computational Linguistics (Volume 1: Long Papers)*. volume 1, pages 655–665.

Minsoo Kim, Moirangthem Dennis Singh, and Minho Lee. 2016. Towards abstraction from extraction: Multiple timescale gated recurrent unit for summarization. In *1st Rep4NLP*. Association for Computational Linguistics, pages 70–77.

Yoon Kim. 2014. Convolutional neural networks for sentence classification. In *EMNLP*. Association for Computational Linguistics, pages 1746–1751.

David Krueger and Roland Memisevic. 2016. Regularizing rnns by stabilizing activations. In *Proceeding of the International Conference on Learning Representations*.

Quoc V Le and Tomas Mikolov. 2014. Distributed representations of sentences and documents. In *ICML*. volume 14, pages 1188–1196.

Cheongjae Lee, Sangkeun Jung, Seokhwan Kim, and Gary Geunbae Lee. 2009. Example-based dialog modeling for practical multi-domain dialog system. *Speech Communication* 51(5):466–484.

Xin Li and Dan Roth. 2002. Learning question classifiers. In *Proceedings of the 19th international conference on Computational linguistics-Volume 1*. Association for Computational Linguistics, pages 1–7.

D. Meunier, R. Lambiotte, A. Fornito, K. D. Ersche, and E. T. Bullmore. 2010. Hierarchical modularity in human brain functional networks. *ArXiv e-prints* .

Tomas Mikolov, Ilya Sutskever, Kai Chen, Greg S Corrado, and Jeff Dean. 2013. Distributed representations of words and phrases and their compositionality. In C. J. C. Burges, L. Bottou, M. Welling, Z. Ghahramani, and K. Q. Weinberger, editors, *Advances in Neural Information Processing Systems 26*, Curran Associates, Inc., pages 3111–3119.

Dennis Singh Moirangthem and Minho Lee. 2017. Temporal hierarchies in multilayer gated recurrent neural networks for language models. In *Neural Networks (IJCNN), 2017 International Joint Conference on*. IEEE, pages 2152–2157.

Dennis Singh Moirangthem, Jegyung Son, and Minho Lee. 2017. Representing compositionality based on multiple timescales gated recurrent neural networks with adaptive temporal hierarchy for character-level language models. In *Proceedings of the 2nd Workshop on Representation Learning for NLP*. Association for Computational Linguistics, pages 131–138.

Tetsuji Nakagawa, Kentaro Inui, and Sadao Kurohashi. 2010. Dependency tree-based sentiment classification using crfs with hidden variables. In *Human Language Technologies: The 2010 Annual Conference of the North American Chapter of the Association for Computational Linguistics*. Association for Computational Linguistics, pages 786–794.

Andreea I Niculescu and Rafael E Banchs. 2015. Strategies to cope with errors in human-machine spoken interactions: using chatbots as back-off mechanism for task-oriented dialogues. *Proceedings of ERRARE, Sinaia, Romania* .

Bo Pang and Lillian Lee. 2004. A sentimental education: Sentiment analysis using subjectivity summarization based on minimum cuts. In *Proceedings of the 42nd annual meeting on Association for Computational Linguistics*. Association for Computational Linguistics, page 271.

Bo Pang and Lillian Lee. 2005. Seeing stars: Exploiting class relationships for sentiment categorization with respect to rating scales. In *Proceedings of the 43rd annual meeting on association for computational linguistics*. Association for Computational Linguistics, pages 115–124.

Jean-Philippe Robichaud, Paul A Crook, Puyang Xu, Omar Zia Khan, and Ruhi Sarikaya. 2014. Hypotheses ranking for robust domain classification and tracking in dialogue systems. In *Fifteenth Annual Conference of the International Speech Communication Association*.

Ruhi Sarikaya. 2017. The technology behind personal digital assistants: An overview of the system architecture and key components. *IEEE Signal Processing Magazine* 34(1):67–81.

Ruhi Sarikaya, Paul A Crook, Alex Marin, Minwoo Jeong, Jean-Philippe Robichaud, Asli Celikyilmaz, Young-Bum Kim, Alexandre Rochette, Omar Zia Khan, Xiaohu Liu, et al. 2016. An overview of end-to-end language understanding and dialog management for personal digital assistants. In *Spoken Language Technology Workshop (SLT), 2016 IEEE*. IEEE, pages 391–397.

Julian J Schlöder and Raquel Fernández. 2015. Clarifying intentions in dialogue: A corpus study. In *IWCS*. pages 46–51.

Joao Silva, Luísa Coheur, Ana Cristina Mendes, and Andreas Wichert. 2011. From symbolic to subsymbolic information in question classification. *Artificial Intelligence Review* 35(2):137–154.

Richard Socher, Brody Huval, Christopher D Manning, and Andrew Y Ng. 2012. Semantic compositionality through recursive matrix-vector spaces. In *Proceedings of the 2012 joint conference on empirical methods in natural language processing and computational natural language learning*. Association for Computational Linguistics, pages 1201–1211.

Richard Socher, Jeffrey Pennington, Eric H Huang, Andrew Y Ng, and Christopher D Manning. 2011. Semi-supervised recursive autoencoders for predicting sentiment distributions. In *Proceedings of the conference on empirical methods in natural language processing*. Association for Computational Linguistics, pages 151–161.

Richard Socher, Alex Perelygin, Jean Wu, Jason Chuang, Christopher D Manning, Andrew Ng, and Christopher Potts. 2013. Recursive deep models for semantic compositionality over a sentiment treebank. In *Proceedings of the 2013 conference on empirical methods in natural language processing*. pages 1631–1642.

Alessandro Sordoni, Michel Galley, Michael Auli, Chris Brockett, Yangfeng Ji, Margaret Mitchell, Jian-Yun Nie, Jianfeng Gao, and Bill Dolan. 2015. A neural network approach to context-sensitive generation of conversational responses. In *NAACL–HLT*. Association for Computational Linguistics.

Tijmen Tieleman and Geoffrey Hinton. 2012. Lecture 6.5-rmsprop: Divide the gradient by a running average of its recent magnitude. *COURSERA: Neural networks for machine learning* 4(2):26–31.

Richard S Wallace. 2009. The anatomy of alice. *Parsing the Turing Test* pages 181–210.

Sida Wang and Christopher Manning. 2013. Fast dropout training. In *international conference on machine learning*. pages 118–126.

Sida Wang and Christopher D Manning. 2012. Baselines and bigrams: Simple, good sentiment and topic classification. In *Proceedings of the 50th Annual Meeting of the Association for Computational Linguistics: Short Papers-Volume 2*. Association for Computational Linguistics, pages 90–94.

Zhuoran Wang, Hongliang Chen, Guanchun Wang, Hao Tian, Hua Wu, and Haifeng Wang. 2014. Policy learning for domain selection in an extensible multi-domain spoken dialogue system. In *EMNLP*. Association for Computational Linguistics, pages 57–67.

Janyce Wiebe, Theresa Wilson, and Claire Cardie. 2005. Annotating expressions of opinions and emotions in language. *Language resources and evaluation* 39(2-3):165–210.

Jason D Williams and Steve Young. 2007. Partially observable markov decision processes for spoken dialog systems. *Computer Speech & Language* 21(2):393–422.

Puyang Xu and Ruhi Sarikaya. 2014. Contextual domain classification in spoken language understanding systems using recurrent neural network. In *Acoustics, Speech and Signal Processing (ICASSP), 2014 IEEE International Conference on*. IEEE, pages 136–140.

Bishan Yang and Claire Cardie. 2014. Context-aware learning for sentence-level sentiment analysis with posterior regularization. In *Proceedings of the 52nd Annual Meeting of the Association for Computational Linguistics (Volume 1: Long Papers)*. volume 1, pages 325–335.

Text Completion using a Context-Integrating Dependency Parser

Amr Rekaby Salama *
Department of Informatics
Universität Hamburg
Germany

Özge Alaçam *
Department of Informatics
Universität Hamburg
Germany

Wolfgang Menzel
Department of Informatics
Universität Hamburg
Germany

{salama,alacam,menzel}@informatik.uni-hamburg.de

Abstract

Incomplete linguistic input, i.e. due to a noisy environment, is one of the challenges that a successful communication system has to deal with. In this paper, we study text completion with a data set composed of sentences with gaps where a successful completion cannot be achieved through a uni-modal (language-based) approach. We present a solution based on a context-integrating dependency parser incorporating an additional non-linguistic modality. An incompleteness in one channel is compensated by information from another one and the parser learns the association between the two modalities from a multiple level knowledge representation. We examined several model variations by adjusting the degree of influence of different modalities in the decision making on possible filler words and their exact reference to a non-linguistic context element. Our model is able to fill the gap with 95.4% word and 95.2% exact reference accuracy hence the successful prediction can be achieved not only on the word level (such as *mug*) but also with respect to the correct identification of its context reference (such as *mug_2* among several mug instances).

1 Introduction

Text completion/prediction is a crucial element of communication systems, due to its role in increasing the fluency and the effectiveness of the communication in scenarios where the environment is noisy, or the communication partner suffers

from a motor, or cognitive impairment (Garay-Vitoria and Abascal, 2004). In this study, we tackle the problem of compensating the incompleteness of the verbal channel by additional information from visual modality. This capability for multi-modal integration can be a very specific yet crucial feature in resolving references and/or performing commands for i.e. a helper robot that aids people in their daily activities. To the authors' knowledge, there is no multi-modal data set for a text completion task that systematically addresses challenging linguistic structures (i.e. syntactic or referential ambiguities) for environments where helper robots, who have access to visual information, would be employed.

The completion is performed by predicting tenable fillers for the missing, unknown, or vague parts in the input sentences through varying techniques, using single or hybrid methods. The prediction process utilizes the available resources, usually linguistic information (morphological, syntactic, and semantic properties). It can also use additional information sources such as the linguistic, or visual context (Garay-Vitoria and Abascal, 2006). If only the linguistic level is available, a language model can be used to predict the probability of a syntactic category in a certain context (Asnani et al., 2015; Bickel et al., 2005). N-grams is a popular method for this task since they provide very robust predictions for local dependencies. Nevertheless, they loose their power for structures with long-range dependencies. Furthermore, if there are multiple instances of the same object class (c.f. Figure 1), a text completion based on N-gram could not differentiate between them to select the proper instance reference. As shown in several studies (Mirowski and Vlachos, 2015; Gubbins and Vlachos, 2013), a language model employing the syntactic dependencies of a sentence brings the relevant contexts

---

*These authors contributed equally to this work

Proceedings of the 3rd Workshop on Representation Learning for NLP, pages 41–49
Melbourne, Australia, July 20, 2018. ©2018 Association for Computational Linguistics

closer. Using the Microsoft Research Sentence Completion Challenge (Zweig and Burges, 2012), Gubbins and Vlachos (2013) have showed that incorporating syntactic information leads to grammatically better options for a semantic text completion task.

On the other hand, semantic clustering or classification (like in ontologies) can be used to derive predictions on the semantic level. However, when it comes to the description of daily activities, contextual information coming from another modality would be more beneficial, since linguistic distributions alone could hardly contribute enough clues to distinguish the action of *washing a pan* from *washing a mug*, which is a crucial difference for helper robots.

A popular trick in natural language processing consists in training a model on one task, and then apply it to an entirely different one. We adopt this method by training a multi-modal dependency parser using noise-free sentences combined with a description of their visual context. In the second step, we make use of the trained parser to predict the best fillers of the gaps (guided by the context modality).

The paper starts by introducing our multi-modal approach for the text completion task. In section 3, we present the experimental setup including the compiled dataset. The implementation is described in section 4. Experimental results are presented and discussed in section 5. Conclusions are drawn and future directions of research are pointed out at the end of the paper.

2   A Multi-Modal Approach for a Text Completion Task

Although closing the gaps in a sentence based only on a language model is a simple way to tackle the issue, in extremely ambiguous situations, gap reconstruction is almost impossible on a purely unimodal base. In this paper, we work on multi-modal data that consists of linguistic and context information. The linguistic part is provided by natural language sentences that refer to a particular visual scene. The context information is a meta-data description of that scene. Per input sentence, the context channel contains a set of context relations: $(argument, relation\_type, predicate)$ where $relation\_type$ is one of a predefined set of accepted relations, such as agent or theme while *Predicate* and *Argument* are tokens of the input

sentence. The complexity of the text completion task is controlled by creating challenging scenes along the following dimensions:

- Each scene is composed of different components (i.e., persons and objects).

- A scene might contain multiple instances of the same class (i.e., a blue mug (id: *mug_1*) and a green mug (id: *mug_2*).

- The different instances are taking part in various relations (more details are given in Section 2.2).

In a series of experiments, we assess the potential of a context-integrating dependency parser for correctly solving the text completion task. We not only try to determine whether we can fill the gap in the sentence with the correct word but also whether it is possible to correctly determine the exact reference to an entity in the context description given the contextual information, in particular if the linguistic input is noisy and a token of the input sentence is missing. At this stage of research, we work only on one gap per sentence.

2.1   Context-integrating Dependency Parser

Dependency parsing is an essential NLP task that determines the syntactic structure of the input sentence in form of a dependency tree. Each token of the input is represented as a tree node. The tree consists of the dependency relations between each word of the sentence and its *head* word (Nivre, 2004).

The standard input of a parser is a natural language sentence. To supply such a parser with additional information required for text completion in a multi-modal environment we have to make it sensitive to cues from the context.

In our previous research (Salama and Menzel, 2018, 2017), we have introduced a multi-modal dependency parser adopting the graph-based approach of Eisner (1996) and Mcdonald and Pereira (2006). Our model, called RBG-2, extends the RBG parser (Zhang et al., 2014) by enabling multi-channel input providing the parsing process with context information in addition to the natural language sentence. Integration is achieved by combining features from both input channels during the normal training procedure of the RBG parser.

2.2 The Data Set

In order to test how the model behaves for different linguistic structures, we used the nine different grammatical templates[1] given in Table 1 featuring active/passive voice, PP-attachments, relative clause (RC) attachments, and conjunctions. They are combined with several actions performed by different agents. The dependency structures are represented in the CONLL-X format. The data set consists of 429 individual sentences for 20 different visual scenes. We performed a 10-fold cross validation and introduced exactly one gap for either a noun, verb or adjective into each test sentence obtaining 1457 test sentences in total.

2.2.1 Linguistic Structures

In this section, we examplify the nine grammtical templates used in our data-set. The following examples belong to the scene in Figure 1:

- **T1. RC[2] Attachment Ambiguity-1**
  T1A. Active voice in RC. "It is a mug on a vitrine that the woman damages."
  Either the relative clause is low-attached (*the woman damages the vitrine*) or high-attached (*the woman damages the mug*).
  T1B. Passive voice in RC. "It is a mug on a vitrine that is damaged by the woman."

- **T2. RC Attachment Ambiguity-2**
  T2A. Active voice. "The woman damages the vitrine with a mug on it."
  T2B. Passive voice. "The vitrine with a mug on it is damaged by the woman."

- **T3. RC Attachment Ambiguity with a Genitive Object-3**
  T3A. Active voice in RC. "The woman removes the label of the medicine that lies on the shelf "
  T3B. Passive voice in RC. "The label of the medicine that lies on the shelf is removed by the woman."

- **T4. Scope Ambiguity**
  "There are a mug, a candle and books [that lie/lying] on the vitrine."

- **T5. Simple Imperative sentence**
  "bring me the mug [that lies/lying] on the vitrine [that the woman cleans]."

- **T6. Imperative sentence with modifiers**
  "bring me the blue mug [that lies/lying] on the vitrine [that the woman cleans]."

2.2.2 Context Representations

The visual information of a picture is represented in a knowledge base that contains the relationships between objects, characters and actions in the scene. This information has been manually annotated as triplets composed of argument, relation type and predicate. Currently, we consider six different context relations, namely *agent*, *theme*, *location*, *next-to*, *part-of/own*, as well as *property* assignments for color, material, shape etc. (e.g., *a blue mug* or *a ceramic vase*). Figure 1 exemplifies the context annotations of a visual scene with an additional concept map representation (bottom). In this scene, *the woman* is the *agent*, who performs the cleaning action, the *vitrine* is the *theme*, i.e. the entity undergoing a change of state, caused by the action. The entire data set and source code can be accessed from `https://github.com/rekaby/MD-TC.V1.0`

For the current study, the pictures, as the one given in Figure 1, serve illustrative purposes, because the computational model does only have access to the manually annotated representations. An automatic relation extraction is not within the scope of this study.

The different semantic roles are distributed in the data set as follows; Agent (%13.6), Theme (%13.6), Location (%33.1), Next to (%9.8), Property (%19.5), Own (%10.3). Table 2 presents a statistics for the amount of contextual information per scene.

3 Implementation

RBG-2 parser starts by creating a fully connected graph representing the input tokens as nodes. The parser decodes a minimum spanning tree out of the graph maximizing the aggregated scores of the arcs. The scores are calculated by combining the weights of linguistic features and context features between the pair of tokens as follows:

$$\overline{y} = \max_{y \in T(x,c)} \sum_{i=1}^{n} \omega_l.f(x_i, x_j, y) + \omega_c.\widehat{f}(c_i, c_j, y)$$

$$(1)$$

Where $\overline{y}$ is the best dependency tree, $T(x, c)$ is a set of all possible dependency trees for input sentence X and context c. The linguistic feature vector between node x_i and its dependency head x_j is

---

[1]inspired by the experimental setup of pyscholinguistic research

[2]Relative Clause

Types	Templates	Sentences	Gaps	Gap Types
T1A	PRO1$_{nom}$ VP1 NP1$_{acc}$ NP2$_{gen}$, WDT*$_{acc}$ PRO2$_{nom}$ VP2	41	130	NP(114), VP(16)
T1B	PRO1$_{nom}$ VP1 NP1$_{acc}$ NP2$_{gen}$, WDT*$_{acc}$ PRO2$_{nom}$ VP2	40	130	NP(115), VP(15)
T2A	PRO$_{nom}$ VP1 NP1$_{nom,pl.}$ NP1$_{nom,pl.}$, WDT $_{acc,pl.}$ VP2 PP1	50	177	NP(153), VP(24)
T2B	PRO$_{nom}$ VP1 NP1$_{nom,pl.}$ NP1$_{nom,pl.}$, WDT $_{acc,pl.}$ VP2 PP1	50	177	NP(153), VP(24)
T3A	NP$_{it-cleft}$ VP1 NP1$_{nom}$ NP2$_{dat}$, WDT $_{dat}$ PRO$_{3rd\text{-}sing.}$ ADV VP2	36	177	NP(139), VP(36), ADJ(2)
T3B	NP$_{it-cleft}$ VP1 NP1$_{nom}$ NP2$_{dat}$, WDT $_{dat}$ PRO$_{3rd\text{-}sing.}$ ADV VP2	29	145	NP(113), VP(30), ADJ(2)
T4	EX V$_{aux}$ NP1$_{nom}$ (CONJ NP2) WDT*$_{nom}$ VP1 Prep. NP3	58	156	NP(154), VP(0), ADJ(2)
T5	VP1 (Pro$_{dat}$ NP1 (WDT) VP2 Prep. NP2	63	141	NP(137), VP(1), ADJ(3)
T6	VP1 (Pro$_{dat}$ (Adj1) NP1 (WDT) VP2 Prep. (ADJ2) NP2	62	224	NP(135), VP(9), ADJ(80)
Total		429	1457	NP(1213), VP(155), ADJ(89)

Table 1: POS templates, the number of sentences and gaps for each sentence types, and the number of gaps for each POS category

Items	Mean
Relations (*Min.*=28, *Max.*=41)	34.8
Context entities (*Min.*=30, *Max.*=41)	35.6
Unique entities [5] (*Min.*=21, *Max.*=28)	25

Table 2: Complexity of the contextual information for the visual scenes in the data set

$f(x_i, x_j, y)$ with weights ω_l. The context feature vector is $\widehat{f}(c_i, c_j, y)$ with weights ω_c.

We build the context features using combinations of the predicates' and arguments' POS, lemma, and word. So far, we only use first-order features for both channels. That means, only information about immediately connected nodes in the graph (head-child relationships) is accounted for, but more complex, indirect connections (siblings, grantchilds, etc.) are ignored. We add the context features to the graph arc only if the pair of nodes (words) has a context relation in between. Using no higher-order features makes the learning process faster and simpler but introduces some limitations as discussed in the result section. Each record in the training data set consists of a complete input sentence, a set of context relations such as in Figure 1, and an exact context reference for each sentence token (if it exists in the context description).

In the testing (text completion) phase, the input sentence is incomplete (containing exactly one gap) while the context information is the same as in the training phase except the mapping between the input sentence and context references is missing as well. E.g. in the sentence *"The vitrine next to sofa is cleaned by the GAP"* accompanying the scene in Figure 1, we have multiple goals to determine

Algorithm 1 Text Completion Workflow using RBG-2

> $TR\text{-}L \leftarrow$ Training data (complete sentences).
> $TR\text{-}C \leftarrow$ Training data (context).
> $TE\text{-}L \leftarrow$ Testing data(sentences with gaps).
> $TE\text{-}C \leftarrow$ Testing data (context).
> $model \leftarrow$ train RBG-2(TR-L, TR-C)
> **for** each pair TE-L$_i$,TE-C$_i$ **do**
> $bestFillerScore \leftarrow -Inf.$
>   **for** each component TE-C$_{ij}$ $\in$ TE-C$_i$ **do**
>   **for** each POS$_t$ $\in$ POS tags **do**
>   TE-L$_i$ $\leftarrow$ SetGap(TE-C$_{ij}$,POS$_t$).
> $score \leftarrow$ parse(model,TE-L$_i$)
>   **if** $score > bestFillerScore$ **then**
> $bestFillerScore \leftarrow score.$
> $bestFiller \leftarrow$ TE-C$_{ij}$.
> $bestPOS \leftarrow$ POS$_t$.
>   TE-L$_i$ $\leftarrow$ fillGap(bestFiller,bestPOS).

- the filler word *(woman)*,
- the context filler reference *(woman_2)*,
- the context filler reference for all the other non-gap tokens in the input (if they exist). They are {*vitrine_2, sofa_1, clean_1*},
- the POS tag of the filler *(NN)*.

As shown in Algorithm 1, we train our data-driven RGB-2 parser on the multi-modal training set described above to learn the associations between the context knowledge representation and the the dependency structures. In the testing phase, we fill the gap by all the possible context components and parse the sentence in a multi-modal setup. We also iterate over different POS tags for the filler to compare the resulting dependency tree scores. The best filler (word, context-reference, and POS) means that this word/context-reference

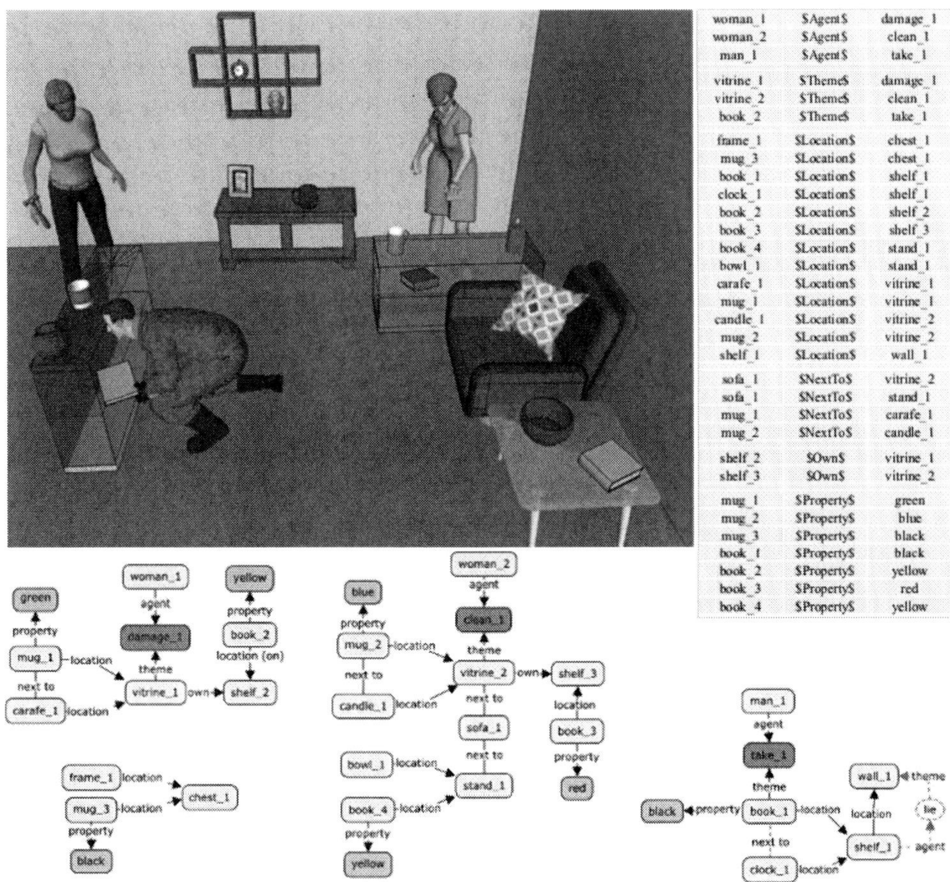

woman_1	$Agent$	damage_1
woman_2	$Agent$	clean_1
man_1	$Agent$	take_1
vitrine_1	$Theme$	damage_1
vitrine_2	$Theme$	clean_1
book_2	$Theme$	take_1
frame_1	$Location$	chest_1
mug_3	$Location$	chest_1
book_1	$Location$	shelf_1
clock_1	$Location$	shelf_1
book_2	$Location$	shelf_2
book_3	$Location$	shelf_3
book_4	$Location$	stand_1
bowl_1	$Location$	stand_1
carafe_1	$Location$	vitrine_1
mug_1	$Location$	vitrine_1
candle_1	$Location$	vitrine_2
mug_2	$Location$	vitrine_2
shelf_1	$Location$	wall_1
sofa_1	$NextTo$	vitrine_2
sofa_1	$NextTo$	stand_1
mug_1	$NextTo$	carafe_1
mug_2	$NextTo$	candle_1
shelf_2	Own	vitrine_1
shelf_3	Own	vitrine_2
mug_1	$Property$	green
mug_2	$Property$	blue
mug_3	$Property$	black
book_1	$Property$	black
book_2	$Property$	yellow
book_3	$Property$	red
book_4	$Property$	yellow

Figure 1: The corresponding image[4] for the sentences above and the semantic representations of the actions and relations in the image

is the best matching one that combines two perspectives: grammatical correctness and compatibility with the context information.

Although the ratio of contextual features to syntactic ones (first-order features) is 1:2.3, which is not high, trying all the possible context elements is rather expensive. For each sentence, we need to build $G * C * P * M$ dependency trees that have to be ranked to find the best one. Here, G is the number of gaps (1 in our experiments), C the number of context entities (35.6 in average), P the number of PoS tags (3) and $M = \prod_{i=1}^{N} M_i$, where M_i is the count of possible candidates references and N the number of sentence tokens with probable context references.

The search space could be reduced by avoiding irregular combinations of POS and filler words. In this stage of research, however, we do not prune it at all.

3.1 Context Data Preprocessing

In a preprocessing phase, we enrich the context information by inferring new relations from the original ones (colored red in Figure 1 and Figure 2). We have used two kinds of inferred relations:

Location to Agent/Theme: If we have a context relation such as $(X, Location, Y)$, this might appear in the linguistic modality in two different forms having either direct or indirect syntactic dependency. For example, *mug* and *vitrine* as in Figure 2A and 2B have a direct syntactic dependency and context relation respectively. In other sentence forms as in Figure 2C and 2D, there is no direct correspondence between the linguistic dependency and the context relation. Contextually, the two tokens are related through the *Location* relation, but syntactically they are daughters of the same action *lie* (no direct dependency). In this form, the *Location* relation is presented in the lin-

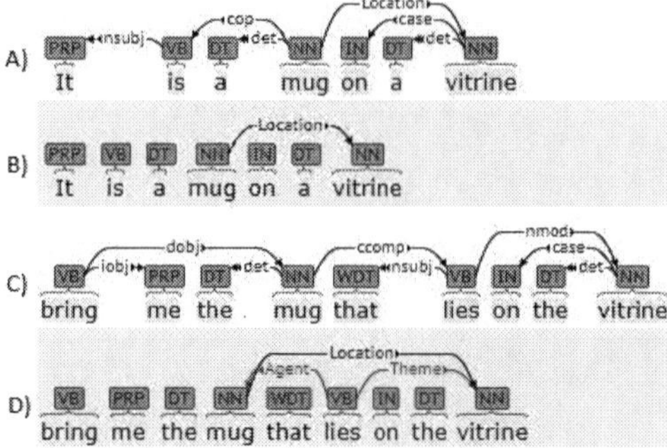

Figure 2: Location Inferred Agent/Theme Relations: A and C) dependency trees, B) original context information, D) original and inferred context relations

guistic modality using the verb to *lie*, which does not appear as a predicate in the context description.

To enrich the context repreresentation with information corresponding directly to the linguistic one, we define a set of verbs (LV) that have a location meaning (i.e., lie, stand, hang). From any location relation $(X, Location, Y)$, we infer another two relations $(X, Agent, LV_i)$ and $(X, Theme, LV_i)$, where $LV_i \in LV$ and LV_i is a token in the input sentence.

Location to Next_To relations: Given each pair of location relations $(X, Location, Z)$ and $(Y, Location, Z)$ we infer new relation $(X, Next - To, Y)$, where $X, Y, Z \in W$, W is the set of the input tokens. The inferred relations are added to the original list of the context input. In the rest of this paper, we use (IC) to refer to the Inferred Context relations and (OC) for the Original Context relations.

3.2 Model Variations

Varying syntactic/context's weight ratios (S2C): In the testing phase, we experiment with different ratios giving more influence (weight) to the context relations than to the linguistic ones. We assess different ratios (1to1,1to5, 1to10, and 1to25).

Original/Inferred relations' weight ratio (OC2IC): Similar to *S2C*, in the testing phase, we give more weight to the original relations than to the inferred ones by assigning the *OC2IC* ratio to 5to1.

4 Results

In order to show the effect of contextual information and to optimize the performance of the current model, we carried out several experiments with different parameters of the model by keeping the data set constant. We used 18 scenes (386 sentences in average) for training and kept the remaining 2 scenes (146 sentences on average) for test using a 10-fold cross-validation. In case the gap can be filled with more than one reference ($< 5\%$ of our dataset), we consider any possible one of them as correct. We used five evaluation metrics as listed below.

- POS-tag Accuracy
- Filler Word Accuracy
- Exact Filler Identification (*EFI*) Accuracy (i.e *mug_1* in contrast to *mug_2*)
- Non-gap Identification Accuracy, for all the other tokens in the input sentence.
- Complete Sentence Identification Accuracy
- Dependency Tree Accuracy (unlabeled attachment score, UAS)

Table 3 presents the results obtained from different variations of the model described in the previous section. We test a uni-modal parser (linguistic-only) only to show that the data set indeed is consisting of sentences, where reference resolution/text completion cannot be achieved on a purely uni-modal sense. For that purpose, the contribution of contextual information is turned off. Because of the uniform structure of the training dataset, the POS and dependency tree accuracies are very high 97.6% and 95.6% respectively. However, the model's prediction performance is drastically low for the gap words; 13.5% for the filler word and 7.8% for the exact filler identification.

As described in Section 3.2, the first model is based on having equal weights (S2C-1to1) for both syntactic (S) and contextual features (C) and the weights of original contextual (OC) features to the inferred features (IC) are kept equal as well (OC2IC-1to1). Giving equal weights leads to approx. 83% accuracy in both filler word and exact filler ID predictions, while increasing the influence of the context resulted in 95% accuracy[6].

---

[6]The other models with weights > 5 produced almost similar results.

Furthermore, giving more weight to the original relations over the inferred ones resulted in lower accuracy, therefore OCtoIC-1to1 variation is chosen as the standard for the analysis in this section. It is apparent from Table 3, a higher influence of the context is beneficial for a correct reference prediction. However, it should be noted that giving more weight to contextual features causes the model to be less sensitive about choosing a correct dependency tree. A closer look at the differences between the predictions of the S2C-1to5 and S2C-1to10 variations showed that 60 instances either in the dependency tree or in the filler ID were observed in the results. While S2C-1to5 builds 51 correct dependency trees and 43 correct references, S2C-1to10 chooses the correct dependency tree in only 12 instances, but even if the dependency tree is wrong, it fills the gap correctly in 48 out of 60 instances.

95 inaccurate EFI in 73 test sentences were observed. False predictions of the model variations can be categorized into several groups:

Inferred Relations. 60% of the inaccurate predictions occurred within this category. As explained in the Section 3.1, a phrase like *"an entity-1 that lies on an entity-2"* can be resolved due to an inferred relation. However, for sentences containing structures like *"an entity-1 that lie/stand/hang(s) next to an entity-2"* with a gap in a position of *entity-2*, the model prefers the most plausible filler that has a *location* relation (either original or inferred) with the *entity-1* instead of having a *next to* relation with it.

A Chain of Relations. This problem arises when for example there is a chain of location relations among the entities (7.4%), i.e. *(bird_1, Location, cage_1)*, and *(cage_1, Location, chest_1)* with a description *"It is a cage on a chest that the man cleans"* with a gap in a *chest* position. While the S2C-1to5 model correctly fills the gap, S2C-1to10 chooses *bird* for the gap position. Assigning more weight to the context information leads to similar scores for the various entities of the chain, which may cause some wrong filler predictions.

Less represented PP associations. Syntactically, all prepositions *(with, of, on and next to)* have the same PoS tag but semantically they differ. While preposition *of* is associated with the *own* relation, and preposition *next to* with *next-to*, there are two prepositions which are related to the *lo-*cation relation; *on/in* and *with*. The distribution of them is as follows; *with*: 21.3%, and *on/in/under*[7]: 78.7%. As shown in Figure 3, the most likely association between syntactic and contextual features (w.r.t. *location* relations) is *head to argument* and *dependent to predicate*. This association is flipped for the prepositional phrase like *"entity-2 with entity-1 on it"*. Regardless of giving more influence to the context in that case, the model makes the prediction more strongly biased to the canonical direction of prepositional phrases resulting a wrong text prediction.

A Verb in a Noun Position. This error occurs irrespective of the linguistic structure if more weight (1to10 or 1to25) is given to the context (6.3%). As an example, a gap in the *shelf* position in the sentence *"There are a cat, a flower and books on the shelf"* is filled with *chase*, caused by the *(cat_1, Theme, chase_1)* relation. In that case, a stronger contextual influence overrides the syntactic form of the PP-attachment, and favors a reference with the *theme* relation, which has a consistent syntactic representation; its argument always points to the predicate. The goal to find syntactically correct PP-attachment is overruled by the more powerful features of the context relations, and so *chase* is selected considering that *a cat* is the only entity with a *theme* relation among others.

Far-Attachments. Far-attachments of the relative clauses or prepositional phrases are not that frequent as short-attachments, yet they are grammatically correct and occur in a data set. The results indicate that giving more influence to contextual information (S2C-1to10 and 1to25) helps to correctly fill the gap, while a model with lower weight for the contextual information (S2C-1to1 and -1to5) tends to choose the wrong reference for the gap position. To illustrate, the sentence *"It is a blanket on a couch that is grasped by the woman"* refers to one instance of a blanket class, and the context contains two instances: *blanket_1* and *blanket_2*, where *blanket_2* is the theme of the *grasp* action. When the gap is in *the couch* position, S2C-1to5 chooses a dependency tree with a short attachment of the RC. It attaches the gap to the action *grasp* and thus fills it with *blanket_2*. This is consistent with the *theme* relation in the context, resulting a sentence *"It is a blanket_1 on*

---

[7]excluding the occurrences of *"on/in/under"* in the reflexive phrases as in *"with a mug on it"*

Model Variations	PoS	Filler Word	EFI	Non-Gap	Complete Sentence	DP-UAS
Uni-model (linguistic only)	97.58	13.50	7.75	62.05	2.21	95.60
S2C Weight (1to1) + OC2IC Weight (1to1)	98.34	83.53	83.11	97.35	83.60	95.60
S2C Weight (1to5) + OC2IC Weight (1to1)	98.89	95.36	95.22	99.24	94.67	95.11
S2C Weight (1to10) + OC2IC Weight (1to1)	98.48	95.57	95.50	99.07	94.81	94.80
S2C Weight (1to25) + OC2IC Weight (1to1)	98.13	95.57	95.50	99.36	94.81	94.51
S2C Weight (1to5) + OC2IC Weight (5to1)	98.82	92.39	92.32	98.85	91.76	95.05

Table 3: The results of the different model variations

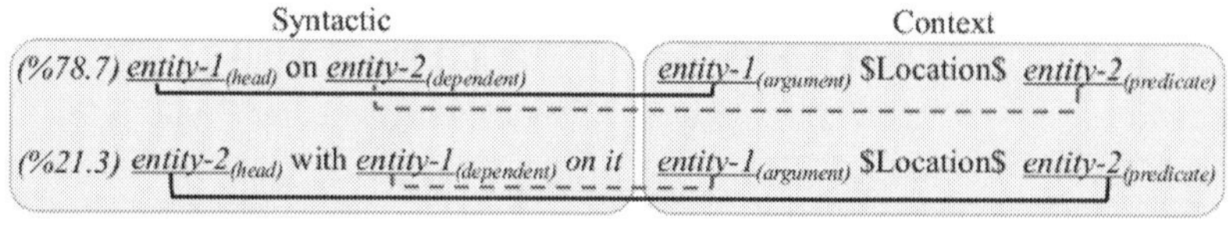

Syntactic   Context

(%78.7) *entity-1*$_{(head)}$ on *entity-2*$_{(dependent)}$ *entity-1*$_{(argument)}$ \$Location\$ *entity-2*$_{(predicate)}$

(%21.3) *entity-2*$_{(head)}$ with *entity-1*$_{(dependent)}$ *on it*   *entity-1*$_{(argument)}$ \$Location\$ *entity-2*$_{(predicate)}$

Figure 3: Syntactic/Context feature association for the prepositions *on* and *with*

a blanket_2 that is grasped by the woman"[8]. If the context had only one blanket, that instance of the blanket had to be assigned to a non-gap blanket position in the sentence, and then the model is forced to switch to another dependency tree with a lower score but a better alignment. On the other hand, a 1to10 model gives more influence to the context, resulting in a correct completion even if the dependency structure is wrong. This may indicate that in order to deal with more challenging contexts or less represented linguistic structures (like far-attachments) increasing the influence of the contextual information would be beneficial.

Contextually Challenging Cases. This category covers 10.5% of the errors. To illustrate, lets consider a context, which contains two different roles for the same agent *man_1* together with a sentence like *"The handle of the mug on the counter is hold by the man"*; namely an action *wash* with a *theme* relation to a *mug* and another action *hold* with a *theme* relation to a *handle*. Another relevant relation for this sentence is *(mug_1, Own, handle_1)*. If in such a case the gap is in the verb position, the model can choose the alternative actions associated with a *mug* instead of forcing a far-attachment which is also favored contextually.

5 Conclusion and Future Directions

In this paper, we present a data set for sentence completion consisting of problematic instances, which can not be effectively handled using linguistic features alone. We apply a context-integrating dependency parser to solve this problem. There are number of assumptions and constraints of the current model. First, allowed gaps are only nouns, verbs and adjectives. Pronouns are not used as a possible gap filler. Furthermore, each individual instance is allowed to occur in the sentence once[9], thus a context reference (i.e. *mug_1*) can not be assigned to more than one token of the input sentence. Morever, the set of context relations is restricted to the the six relations. Further studies will need to cover more variety to relax these limitations.

The results indicate that incorporating contextual information and giving a strong enough influence to them helps to solve a majority of the problems concerning different sentence structures with conjunctions, relative clauses or PP-attachments. There are still some challenging situations originating from high degrees of linguistic or contextual complexity, which need to be addressed in future work. Furthermore, we plan to address noisier linguistic input with multiple gaps in a sentence as well as mismatches between the sentence and its contextual information. We also target reference resolution at the earliest time possible by employing incremental processing.

Acknowledgments

This research was partially funded by the German Research Foundation - DFG Transregio SFB 169: Cross-Modal Learning, and German Academic Exchange Service (DAAD).

---

[8]Our assumption is not using same context reference twice

[9]This constraint is not based on linguistic phenomena, it is just the design decision for the current solution

References

Kavita Asnani, Douglas Vaz, Tanay PrabhuDesai, Surabhi Borgikar, Megha Bisht, Sharvari Bhosale, and Nikhil Balaji. 2015. Sentence completion using text prediction systems. In *Proceedings of the 3rd International Conference on Frontiers of Intelligent Computing: Theory and Applications (FICTA) 2014*. Springer, pages 397–404.

Steffen Bickel, Peter Haider, and Tobias Scheffer. 2005. Learning to complete sentences. In *European Conference on Machine Learning*. Springer, pages 497–504.

Jason M. Eisner. 1996. Three new probabilistic models for dependency parsing: An exploration. In *Proceedings of the 16th Conference on Computational Linguistics - Volume 1*. Association for Computational Linguistics, Stroudsburg, PA, USA, COLING '96, pages 340–345. https://doi.org/10.3115/992628.992688.

Nestor Garay-Vitoria and Julio Abascal. 2004. A comparison of prediction techniques to enhance the communication rate. In *ERCIM Workshop on User Interfaces for All*. Springer, pages 400–417.

Nestor Garay-Vitoria and Julio Abascal. 2006. Text prediction systems: a survey. *Universal Access in the Information Society* 4(3):188–203.

Joseph Gubbins and Andreas Vlachos. 2013. Dependency language models for sentence completion. In *Proceedings of the 2013 Conference on Empirical Methods in Natural Language Processing*. pages 1405–1410.

Ryan Mcdonald and Fernando Pereira. 2006. Online learning of approximate dependency parsing algorithms. In *In Proc. of EACL*. pages 81–88.

Piotr Mirowski and Andreas Vlachos. 2015. Dependency recurrent neural language models for sentence completion. *arXiv preprint arXiv:1507.01193* .

Joakim Nivre. 2004. Incrementality in deterministic dependency parsing. In *Proceedings of the Workshop on Incremental Parsing: Bringing Engineering and Cognition Together*. Association for Computational Linguistics, Stroudsburg, PA, USA, IncrementParsing '04, pages 50–57. http://dl.acm.org/citation.cfm?id=1613148.1613156.

Amr Rekaby Salama and Wolfgang Menzel. 2017. Multimodal graph-based dependency parsing of natural language. In *Proceedings of the International Conference on Advanced Intelligent Systems and Informatics 2016*. Springer International Publishing, pages 22–31.

Amr Rekaby Salama and Wolfgang Menzel. 2018. *Learning Context-Integration in a Dependency Parser for Natural Language*, Springer International Publishing, pages 545–569.

Yuan Zhang, Tao Lei, Regina Barzilay, Tommi Jaakkola, and Amir Globerson. 2014. Steps to excellence: Simple inference with refined scoring of dependency trees. In *Proceedings of the 52nd Annual Meeting of the Association for Computational Linguistics (Volume 1: Long Papers)*. Association for Computational Linguistics, Baltimore, Maryland, pages 197–207. http://www.aclweb.org/anthology/P14-1019.

Geoffrey Zweig and Chris JC Burges. 2012. A challenge set for advancing language modeling. In *Proceedings of the NAACL-HLT 2012 Workshop: Will We Ever Really Replace the N-gram Model? On the Future of Language Modeling for HLT*. Association for Computational Linguistics, pages 29–36.

Quantum-inspired Complex Word Embedding

Qiuchi Li[*]
University of Padova
Padova, Italy
`qiuchili@dei.unipd.it`

Sagar Uprety[*]
The Open University
Milton Keynes, UK
`sagar.uprety@open.ac.uk`

Benyou Wang
University of Padova
Padova, Italy
`wabyking@163.com`

Dawei Song
The Open University
Milton Keynes, UK
Beijing Institute of Technology
Beijing, China
`dawei.song@open.ac.uk`

Abstract

A challenging task for word embeddings is to capture the emergent meaning or polarity of a combination of individual words. For example, existing approaches in word embeddings will assign high probabilities to the words "Penguin" and "Fly" if they frequently co-occur, but it fails to capture the fact that they occur in an opposite sense - Penguins do not fly. We hypothesize that humans do not associate a single polarity or sentiment to each word. The word contributes to the overall polarity of a combination of words depending upon which other words it is combined with. This is analogous to the behavior of microscopic particles which exist in all possible states at the same time and interfere with each other to give rise to new states depending upon their relative phases. We make use of the Hilbert Space representation of such particles in Quantum Mechanics where we subscribe a relative phase to each word, which is a complex number, and investigate two such quantum inspired models to derive the meaning of a combination of words. The proposed models [1] achieve better performances than state-of-the-art non-quantum models on the binary sentence classification task.

1   Introduction

Word embeddings (Bengio et al., 2003; Mikolov et al., 2013; Pennington et al., 2014) are the

---

[*]Corresponding author

[1]https://github.com/complexembedding/
complex_word_embedding.git

current state of art techniques to form semantic representations of words based on their contexts. They have been successfully used in various downstream tasks such as text classification, text generation, etc. Building on word embeddings, various unsupervised (Kiros et al., 2015; Hill et al., 2016a) and supervised (Conneau et al., 2017) models for sentence embeddings have been proposed. The general idea behind word embeddings is to use word co-occurrence as the basis of semantic relationship between words. This naturally brings about the difficulty for word embedding approaches in capturing the emergent meaning of a combination of words, such as a phrase or a sentence. For example, the phrase "ivory tower" can hardly be modeled as a semantic combination of "ivory" and "tower". Or, the high frequency of occurrence of the words "Penguin" and "Fly" fails to suggest that they are negative correlated.

In the field of information retrieval (IR), various models based on the mathematical framework of Quantum Theory have been applied to capture and represent dependencies between words (Sordoni et al., 2013; Xie et al., 2015; Zhang et al., 2018), inspired by the pioneering work of Van Rijsbergen (2004). Sordoni et al. (2013) models a segment of text as a quantum mixed state, represented by a positive semi-definite matrix called density matrix in a Hilbert Space, whose non-diagonal entries entail word relations in a quantum manner(Quantum Interference). The resulting Quantum Language Model (QLM) outperforms various classical models on ad-hoc retrieval tasks. Xie et al. (2015) captures Unconditional Pure Dependence (UPD) (Hou et al., 2013) between words in a quantum way by demonstrating the equivalence relation between UPD and Quantum Entan-

Proceedings of the 3rd Workshop on Representation Learning for NLP, pages 50–57
Melbourne, Australia, July 20, 2018. ©2018 Association for Computational Linguistics

glement (QE) and providing a way to incorporate UPD information into QLM, leading to improved performance over the original QLM. Zhang et al. (2018) develops a well-performing question answering (QA) system by extracting various features and learning to compare the density matrices between a question and an answer.

The successful application of quantum-inspired models onto IR tasks (Wang et al., 2016) to some extent demonstrates the non-classical nature of word dependency relations. However, all these models simplify the space of interest to be space of real vectors $\mathbb{R}^n$, with the representation of a word or a text segment being a real-valued vector or matrix, largely due to the lack of proper textual features corresponding to the imaginary part. Since quantum phenomena cannot be faithfully expressed without complex numbers, these models are theoretically limited. In a recent work, Aerts et al. (2017) presents a theoretical quantum framework for modeling a collection of documents called QWeb, in which a concept is represented as a state in a Hilbert Space, and concept combination is represented as a superposition of the concept states. Under this framework, the complex phases of each concept have a natural correspondence to the extent of interference between concepts. However, the framework has not given rise to any applicable models onto IR or NLP tasks to the authors' knowledge.

Inspired by the potential of quantum-inspired models to represent word relations, we seek to build quantum models to represent words and word combinations, and explore the use of complex numbers in the modeling process. Our model is built on top of two hypothesis: I) A word is a linear combination of latent concepts with complex weights. II) A combination of words is viewed as a complex combination of word states, either a superposition state or a mixed state. The first hypothesis agrees with QWeb, but here we concretize a concept in QWeb to be a word. The second hypothesis is an extension of both QWeb and the work by Zhang et al. (2018), because QWeb restricts a combination of concepts to be a superposition state while the work by Zhang et al. (2018) assumes that a sentence is a complex mixture of word projectors.

This study sets foot in sentence-level analysis, and treats a sentence as a combination of words. We intend to model a word as a quantum state containing two parts: amplitudes and complex phases, and expect to capture the low-level word co-occurrence information by the amplitudes, while using the phases to represent the emergent meaning or polarity when a word is combined with other words. We investigate on two models to represent the combination of words, either as a superposition of word states or as a mixture of word projectors. The effectiveness of the two models are evaluated on 5 benchmarking binary sentence classification datasets, and the results show that the mixture model outperforms state-of-the-art word embedding approaches.

The motivation behind this paper stems from an analogy with Quantum Physics. Consider the phrase "Penguins fly". If we model it along the lines of the famous double slit experiment in Quantum Physics, the two slits corresponds to human interpretation of words "Penguins" and "Fly" (Verb sense of Fly). When only one slit is open at a time, the waves corresponding to the individual word will go through the slit and register onto the screen. The screen is made of a set of polarity detectors judging opinion or sentiment polarities.

In Figure 1.a the human mind sees the word 'Penguins' alone and detects it as a neutral word with a very high probability. This is analogous to the double slit experiment with one slit open. The same is the case for the word 'Fly' considered in isolation. By classical logic, when the two words are taken together as a phrase 'Penguins fly', the human mind should assign a high probability of it being neutral again. However, we know that it is a false statement (Figure 1.c).

Different from classical representation, this study hypothesizes that the combination of words can be viewed as a superposition or complex mixture of quantum entities which gives rise to a new state. In this way, the emerging meaning or polarity of a combination of words will manifest in the interference between words, and be captured inherently in the density matrix representation. For example, two or more words having a neutral sense individually may combine to give a negative sense, just like the case in the analogy given above.

2 Hilbert Space Representation of Words and Sentences

The section introduces the proposed quantum framework for representing words and sentences.

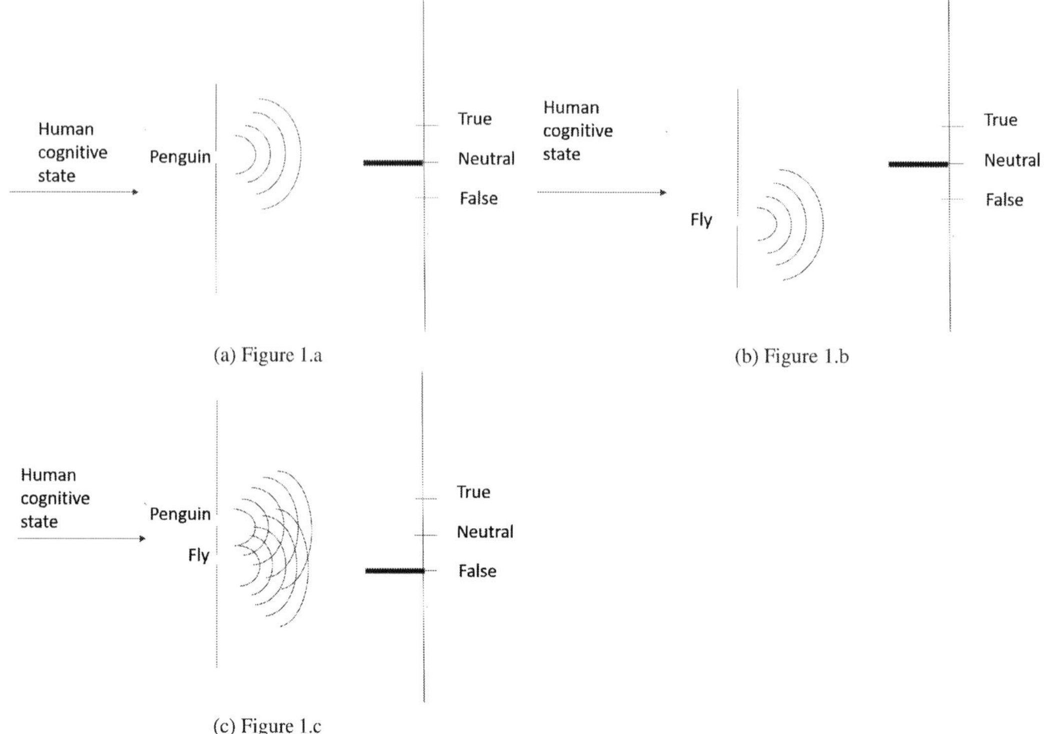

(a) Figure 1.a

(b) Figure 1.b

(c) Figure 1.c

Our research scope is currently limited to sentence and word level analysis. However, our proposed model is potentially capable of representing higher-level concepts such as paragraphs and documents, which we will investigate in the future. To be consistent with the quantum framework, we use Dirac notations, in which a unit vector $\vec{\mu}$ and its transpose $\vec{\mu}^T$ are denoted as ket $|u\rangle$ and bra $\langle u|$ respectively.

Suppose there are n independent latent concepts in the text collection, we then model words and sentences as quantum concepts defined on an n-dimensional Hilbert Space $\mathbb{H}^n$, where latent concepts form a set of pure orthonormal states of the space. Using Dirac notations, the concepts are denoted as $\{|C_i\rangle\}_{i=1}^n$. Intuitively, latent concepts correspond to the contexts in which words are used.

Each word t is modeled as a superposition state (Nielsen and Chuang, 2011) in the n-dimensional Hilbert Space $\mathbb{H}^n$. Equivalently, it can be viewed as a linear combination of $\{|C_i\rangle\}_{i=1}^n$ with complex weights, i.e. $|t\rangle = \sum_{k=1}^n e^{i\theta_k} w_k |C_k\rangle$, in which $\{w_i\}_{i=1}^n$ are real-valued amplitudes with $w_i > 0$ and $\sum_{i=1}^n w_i^2 = 1$, and $\theta_i \in [-\pi, \pi], i = 1, 2, ..., n$ are the corresponding complex phases. This representation can be seen as a generalization of previous word embedding approaches (Bengio et al., 2003; Mikolov et al., 2013; Pennington et al., 2014) in that it can be regarded as a complex embedding with unitary length of word vectors. A word has many different contexts associated with it. For example, 'Penguin' is associated with 'Bird', 'Antarctica', 'Snow', etc. When a quantum particle(e.g. electron) is said to be in a superposition state, it exists in a new state(e.g. position) of all of its possible outcomes(at all positions) at the same time. A particular outcome is observed upon measurement. Similarly a word exists in all of its contexts at the same time and depending upon its interaction with other words in a combination, a particular context is materialized. Note that because of reduced dimensionality, the contexts are latent concepts.

A sentence is a non-classical combination of words. Since each word is a superposition of latent concepts, a sentence s is also a non-classical combination of latent concepts $\{|C_i\rangle\}_{i=1}^n$. It is represented by a n by n density matrix ρ which is positive semi-definite with unitary trace: $\rho \geq 0$, $\text{Tr}(\rho) = 1$. The real diagonal values of ρ reflects the strength of concepts in the sentence, whereas the non-diagonal values encodes correlations between concepts in a quantum manner. The density matrix can be computed from the word states either directly or through a training strategy.

Our proposed approach is related to but largely differs from Sordoni et al. (2013) and Zhang et al. (2018). Sordoni et al. (2013) models queries and documents as density matrices and provides a training method for constructing density matrices from texts. Zhang et al. (2018) directly computes the density matrix of a sentence and put it into an end-to-end neural network for handling the Question Answering (QA) task. Both works view a segment of texts as a mixed state (Nielsen and Chuang, 2011) and use real-valued density matrix as a representation. Our study also directly computes the sentence representation from the word superposition states. However, different from both works, our study explores on treating a sentence as either a strictly mixed state or a superposition state. In either case, it can be represented as a complex density matrix with complex values for non-diagonal entries.

On top of the obtained sentence representation, different quantum operations can be applied to achieve a particular NLP target at hand. For sentence classification tasks, one can perform projective measurements onto the sentence representation to determine the sentiment polarity; for sentence text similarity task, the amplitude of the inner product between a sentence pair may provide evidence for judging to what extent they are similar to each other. Projective measurements and inner products are methods to compute probabilities in Quantum Theory (Nielsen and Chuang, 2011).

3 Complex Embedding Network for Text Classification

In this paper, we build a complex embedding network for text classification on the basis of Hilbert Space representation for words and sentences. The end-to-end network accepts a sentence sequence as input and computes its classification label in the procedure shown by Figure 2:

The input one-hot sequence is passed through an embedding layer with a complex valued lookup table, which maps each word into a complex vector representing its superposition state, resulting in a sequence of complex embedding vectors. Then the density matrix of the sentence is computed from the complex embedding vectors. Finally, a square projection matrix takes control of the measurement. For any sentence state ρ, the measurement probability is computed through Born's rule (Born, 1926):

$$p = Tr(P\rho) \qquad (1)$$

Where P is a projection matrix satisfying $P^2 = P, P = P^T$. The value of p determines the class of this sentence. The lookup table determining the complex embedding for each word is learned by feeding the network with a sufficient number of training data.

The crucial step of the process falls on how to compute the sentence density matrix from the sequence of complex word embeddings. As no previous research has attempted to build complex networks for text classification task, we investigate on two approaches for this step:

I) A sentence is viewed as a linear combination of all word vectors in the sentence, i.e. $|S\rangle = \frac{\sum_{l=1}^{m} \lambda_l |t_l\rangle}{\|\sum_{l=1}^{m} \lambda_l |t_l\rangle\|_2}$, with $\sum_{l=1}^{m} \lambda_l = 1$. Here λ_ls are real-valued weights indicating the relative degree of importance for each word in the sentence, and the state is divided by its 2-norm in order to guarantee it is a legal quantum state (i.e.,with unit length). The sentence is then a pure superposition state and the density matrix can be computed simply as $\rho = |S\rangle\langle S|$.

II) A sentence is viewed as a classical mixture of the word states in the sentence, i.e. $\rho = \sum_{l=1}^{m} \lambda_l |t_l\rangle\langle t_l|$, with $\sum_{l=1}^{m} \lambda_l = 1$. Here $|t_l\rangle\langle t_l|$ is the density matrix representing the superposition state of a word t_l. This equation guarantees the obtained ρ is a legal density matrix without any further normalization.

The constructed density matrix representing a sentence has real values for diagonal entries and non-zero complex values for non-diagonal entries. Intuitively, the diagonal entries tell us something about the distribution of latent concepts in the sentence, whereas the non-diagonal values entail information regarding the emergent meanings. Consider a very simple example where the complex phases represent positive, neutral or negative senses. Independently, both the words "Penguin" and "Fly" have neutral sense, $\theta_P = \theta_F = 0$. When they are combined together in a sentence, then sentence density matrix has a negative-phased complex value in the entry corresponding to them, i.e. $\theta_{PF} < 0$. Therefore, the combination of these two words will have a negative complex phase, implying the negative sense "Penguins cannot fly".

Figure 2: The process diagram of the proposed complex embedding network. $|V|$ is the vocabulary size, n is the embedding dimension, m is the maximum length of a sentence

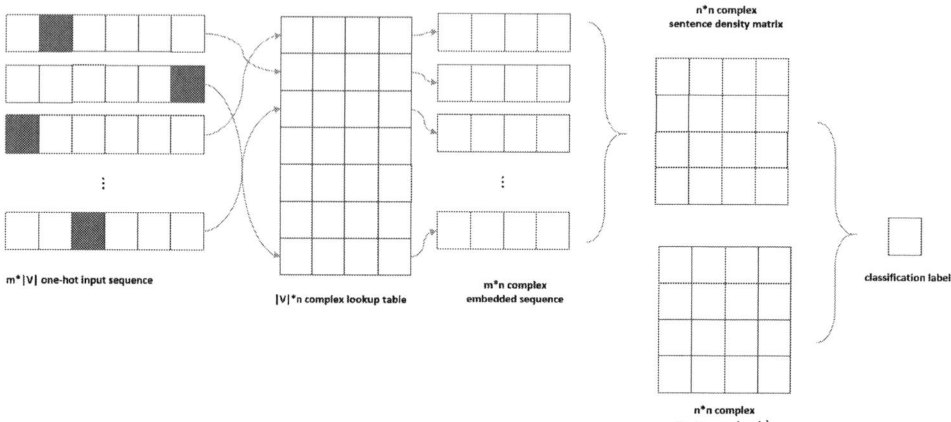

In practice, the connections between words are much more complicated, but we believe that by feeding the above-mentioned models with enough data, the constructed density matrix will be able to effectively capture and represent the emergent meanings of sentences.

The above-mentioned approaches lead to two different models, resulting in different embeddings learned from the same training data. Hence we name them as complex embedding superposition (CE-Sup) network and complex embedding mixture (CE-Mix) network respectively. For sake of simplicity, we assign equal importance of each word in the sentence representation in both models, i.e. $\lambda_l = \frac{1}{m}, l = 1, 2, ..., m$. In a relevant research, Zhang et al. (2018) learns the values of λ_ls in the training framework, while enforcing the word embeddings $|t_l\rangle$s to be fixed. By fixing λ_ls and learning $|t_l\rangle$s from the data, this paper is essentially aiming at obtaining better representation of each word from the training data, whereas Zhang et al.'s work directly takes existing word vectors trained from external corpus. It would be interesting to see what a co-training of $|t_l\rangle$s and λ_ls will bring about in future works.

4 Experimental Setup

The experiments are conducted on five benchmarking datasets for binary text classification: Customer Review dataset (CR) (Hu and Liu, 2014), Opinion polarity dataset (MPQA) (Wiebe et al., 2005), Sentence Subjectivity dataset (SUBJ) (Pang and Lee, 2005), Movie Review dataset (MR) (Pang and Lee, 2005), and Stanford Sentiment Treebank (SST) dataset [2]. The statistics for the datasets are shown in Table 1.

Table 1: Dataset Statistics

Dataset	#Count	Task	Classes
CR	4k	product reviews	pos/neg
MPQA	11k	opinion polarity	pos/neg
SUBJ	10k	subjectivity	subj/obj
MR	11k	movie reviews	pos/neg
SST	70k	movie reviews	pos/neg

In this paper, we compare the classification accuracy of our proposed Complex Embedding Superposition (CE-Sup) network and Complex Embedding Mixture (CE-Mix) network with three existing unsupervised representation training models, Unigram-TFIDF and fastText Bag-of-Words (BOW), as well as two existing supervised representation training models, namely CaptionRep BOW (Hill et al., 2016b) and DictRep BOW (Hill et al., 2016c). We directly take the performances of these systems on the 5 datasets from existing works. Since the performances for CaptionRep and DictRep are not available on SST, we use the performance of another model called Paragraph-Phrase (Bansal and Livescu, 2016). For a fair comparison, we also implement an end-to-end supervised real embedding network (Real-Embed),

---

[2]https://nlp.stanford.edu/sentiment/index.html

where each word is mapped to a real-valued vector in the embedding layer, based on which the sentence representation is obtained by averaging the embedding vectors for all words in the sentence, and a fully connected layer maps the sentence vector to the classification label. CE-mixture, CE-Superposition and Real-Embed are trained and tested in a completely identical process.

For the construction of training, validation and test data, they are readily available for SST dataset, and for the other four datasets we randomly split the whole data into 8:1:1 for training, validation and test data respectively. The embedding dimension is set to be 100. We use batch training with batch size being 32 for SST and 16 for the other datasets. We adopt Adam as the optimizer and use the default parameters for Adam in Keras [3].

The experiments are implemented in Keras and Tensorflow [4] under Python 3.6.4. The experiment is run on a desktop with NVidia Quadro M4000 and 16GB RAM.

5 Results and Discussion

In this study, we seek to answer the following two research questions:

RQ1. Do the proposed quantum-inspired complex embedding models outperform state-of-the art non-quantum approaches?

RQ2. Out of the two proposed model in this study, which one performs better?

Table 2 presents the classification accuracy values of all models experimented in this paper, where the bold values indicate the best-performing models for each dataset. It can be clearly seen from the table that CE-Mix is the best-performing model, because it occupies the highest accuracy value on 4 out of 5 benchmarking datasets, and on the remaining dataset it performs only slightly worse than the best-performed model.

In order to make the results more convincing, we also conduct two-tailed p-tests on the performances. The hypotheses are:

H0. There is no difference between two groups of performances on a particular dataset.

H1. There is a difference between two groups of performances on a particular dataset.

We use the threshold 0.05 to accept or reject the null hypothesis: when the obtained p-value $<$ 0.05, the null hypothesis is rejected; when p-value $>$0.05, the null hypothesis is accepted.

Regarding RQ1, it can be observed that CE-Sup and CE-Mix achieves consistently higher or comparable accuracy than non-quantum models under experiment. It illustrates the superiority of complex embedding network over traditional language model (Unigram-TFIDF) (p-value $<$ 0.05 on all datasets, rejecting the null hypothesis, and so forth), unsupervised embeddings trained from external corpus (word2vec, fastText) (p-value $<$ 0.05 on all datasets except MPQA), as well as supervised embedding methods (CaptionRep, DictRep and Paragram-Phrase) (p-value$<$ on all datasets except MPQA). The fair comparison with real embedding network (p-value $<$ 0.05 on all datasets) confirms the superiority of complex embedding over real embedding techniques.

Regarding RQ2, out of the two complex embedding models proposed in this study, CE-Mix performs consistently but insignificantly (p-value $>$ 0.05) better than CE-Sup in all datasets. Even though it is yet a fully convincing evidence, this result provides us with some intuition that it seems better to model a sentence as a classical mixture of word projectors rather than as a superposition state of latent concepts. For future work we will evaluate the performances of these two models on other datasets as well as other tasks to reach a more solid conclusion.

6 Conclusion and Future Work

This paper attempts to address the challenge of representing the combinatory meaning of words for word embedding. The successful applications of quantum-based models in IR tasks inspires us to construct Hilbert Space representation of words and sentences, and explore to build two quantum models for solving sentence classification task. The experimental result on five benchmarking datasets demonstrates their effectiveness.

This work contributes to the fields of both word embeddings and quantum-inspired IR. On the one hand, our work can be interpreted as an improved embedding approach, which tackles the challenge

---

[3] https://keras.io/
[4] https://www.tensorflow.org/

Table 2: Experimental Results in percentage(%). The best performed value for each dataset is in bold.

Model	CR	MPQA	MR	SST	SUBJ
Unigram-TFIDF	79.2	82.4	73.7	-	90.3
word2vec BOW	79.8	**88.3**	77.7	79.7	90.9
fastText BOW	78.9	87.4	76.5	78.8	91.6
CaptionRep BOW	69.3	70.8	61.9	-	77.4
DictRep BOW	78.7	87.2	76.7	-	90.7
Paragram-Phrase	-	-	-	79.7	-
Real-Embed	77.5	84.7	77.0	80.0	92.0
CE-Sup	80.0	85.7	78.4	82.6	92.6
CE-Mix	**81.1**	86.6	**79.8**	**83.3**	**92.8**

of capturing the emergent meaning of a combination of words. On the other hand, this can be viewed as a pioneering study on quantum-inspired language models with complex numbers, and also an trial effort to adopt the theoretical QWeb framework onto an application context.

For future work, it is necessary to conduct a more comprehensive evaluation of the proposed models, either by evaluating on more datasets or by evaluating the qualities of the trained complex embeddings. We are also looking forward to seek additional ways to model a sentence based on the word states, and the application of the models onto other NLP tasks.

ACKNOWLEDGEMENT

This work is supported by the Quantum Access and Retrieval Theory (QUARTZ) project, which has received funding from the European Union's Horizon 2020 research and innovation programme under the Marie Skodowska-Curie grant agreement No. 721321.

References

Diederik Aerts, Jonito Aerts Arguelles, Lester Beltran, Lyneth Beltran, Isaac Distrito, Massimiliano Sassoli de Bianchi, Sandro Sozzo, and Tomas Veloz. 2017. Towards a Quantum World Wide Web. *arXiv:1703.06642 [quant-ph]* ArXiv: 1703.06642. http://arxiv.org/abs/1703.06642.

John Wieting Mohit Bansal and Kevin Gimpel Karen Livescu. 2016. TOWARDS UNIVERSAL PARAPHRASTIC SENTENCE EMBEDDINGS page 19.

Yoshua Bengio, Réjean Ducharme, Pascal Vincent, and Christian Janvin. 2003. A neural probabilistic language model. *J. Mach. Learn. Res.* 3:1137–1155. http://dl.acm.org/citation.cfm?id=944919.944966.

Max Born. 1926. Zur Quantenmechanik der Sto\s svorgnge. *Zeitschrift fr Physik* 37(12):863–867. https://doi.org/10.1007/BF01397477.

Alexis Conneau, Douwe Kiela, Holger Schwenk, Loïc Barrault, and Antoine Bordes. 2017. Supervised learning of universal sentence representations from natural language inference data. In *Proceedings of the 2017 Conference on Empirical Methods in Natural Language Processing*. Association for Computational Linguistics, pages 670–680. http://aclweb.org/anthology/D17-1070.

Felix Hill, Kyunghyun Cho, and Anna Korhonen. 2016a. Learning distributed representations of sentences from unlabelled data. *CoRR* abs/1602.03483. http://arxiv.org/abs/1602.03483.

Felix Hill, Kyunghyun Cho, and Anna Korhonen. 2016b. Learning Distributed Representations of Sentences from Unlabelled Data. In *Proceedings of the 2016 Conference of the North American Chapter of the Association for Computational Linguistics: Human Language Technologies*. Association for Computational Linguistics, San Diego, California, pages 1367–1377. http://www.aclweb.org/anthology/N16-1162.

Felix Hill, KyungHyun Cho, Anna Korhonen, and Yoshua Bengio. 2016c. Learning to Understand Phrases by Embedding the Dictionary. *Transactions of the Association for Computational Linguistics* 4:17–30. https://tacl2013.cs.columbia.edu/ojs/index.php/tacl/article/view/711.

Yuexian Hou, Xiaozhao Zhao, Dawei Song, and Wenjie Li. 2013. Mining Pure High-order Word Associations via Information Geometry for Information Retrieval. *ACM Trans. Inf. Syst.* 31(3):12:1–12:32. https://doi.org/10.1145/2493175.2493177.

Minqing Hu and Bing Liu. 2014. Mining and Summarizing Customer Reviews page 10.

Ryan Kiros, Yukun Zhu, Ruslan Salakhutdinov, Richard S. Zemel, Antonio Torralba, Raquel Urtasun, and Sanja Fidler. 2015. Skip-thought vectors. In *Proceedings of the 28th International Conference on Neural Information Processing Systems - Volume 2*. MIT Press, Cambridge, MA, USA, NIPS'15, pages 3294–3302. http://dl.acm.org/citation.cfm?id=2969442.2969607.

Tomas Mikolov, Ilya Sutskever, Kai Chen, Greg Corrado, and Jeffrey Dean. 2013. Distributed representations of words and phrases and their compositionality. In *Proceedings of the 26th International Conference on Neural Information Processing Systems - Volume 2*. Curran Associates Inc., USA, NIPS'13, pages 3111–3119. http://dl.acm.org/citation.cfm?id=2999792.2999959.

Michael A. Nielsen and Isaac L. Chuang. 2011. *Quantum Computation and Quantum Information: 10th Anniversary Edition*. Cambridge University Press, New York, NY, USA, 10th edition.

Bo Pang and Lillian Lee. 2005. Seeing stars: exploiting class relationships for sentiment categorization with respect to rating scales. Association for Computational Linguistics, pages 115–124. https://doi.org/10.3115/1219840.1219855.

Jeffrey Pennington, Richard Socher, and Christopher D Manning. 2014. Glove: Global vectors for word representation. In *EMNLP*. volume 14, pages 1532–1543.

Alessandro Sordoni, Jian-Yun Nie, and Yoshua Bengio. 2013. Modeling Term Dependencies with Quantum Language Models for IR. In *Proceedings of the 36th International ACM SIGIR Conference on Research and Development in Information Retrieval*. ACM, New York, NY, USA, SIGIR '13, pages 653–662. https://doi.org/10.1145/2484028.2484098.

Cornelis Joost Van Rijsbergen. 2004. *The geometry of information retrieval*. Cambridge University Press.

Benyou Wang, Peng Zhang, Jingfei Li, Dawei Song, Yuexian Hou, and Zhenguo Shang. 2016. Exploration of quantum interference in document relevance judgement discrepancy. *Entropy* 18(4):144.

Janyce Wiebe, Theresa Wilson, and Claire Cardie. 2005. Annotating Expressions of Opinions and Emotions in Language. *Language Resources and Evaluation* 39(2-3):165–210. https://doi.org/10.1007/s10579-005-7880-9.

Mengjiao Xie, Yuexian Hou, Peng Zhang, Jingfei Li, Wenjie Li, and Dawei Song. 2015. Modeling Quantum Entanglements in Quantum Language Models. In *Proceedings of the 24th International Conference on Artificial Intelligence*. AAAI Press, Buenos Aires, Argentina, IJCAI'15, pages 1362–1368. http://dl.acm.org/citation.cfm?id=2832415.2832439.

Peng Zhang, Jiabin Niu, Zhan Su, Benyou Wang, Liqun Ma, and Dawei Song. 2018. End-to-End Quantum-like Language Models with Application to Question Answering .

Natural Language Inference with Definition Embedding Considering Context On the Fly

Kosuke Nishida,   Kyosuke Nishida,   Hisako Asano,   Junji Tomita

NTT Media Intelligence Laboratories, NTT Corporation

1-1 Hikarinooka Yokosuka, Kanagawa, Japan

`nishida.kosuke@lab.ntt.co.jp`

Abstract

Natural language inference (NLI) is one of the most important tasks in NLP. In this study, we propose a novel method using word dictionaries, which are pairs of a word and its definition, as external knowledge. Our neural definition embedding mechanism encodes input sentences with the definitions of each word of the sentences on the fly. It can encode definitions of words considering the context of the input sentences by using an attention mechanism. We evaluated our method using WordNet as a dictionary and confirmed that it performed better than baseline models when using the full or a subset of $100d$ GloVe as word embeddings.

1   Introduction

Recognition of the entailment relationship between two sentences is one of the most important tasks in the field of natural language processing. An understanding of entailment relationships among sentences is useful for performing tasks such as question answering, information retrieval, and summarization.

The task of recognizing the entailment relationship between two sentences is called recognizing textual entailment (RTE) or natural language inference (NLI). NLI has recently been getting more attention from researchers, owing to the release of large-scale corpora such as SNLI (Bowman et al., 2015) and MNLI (Williams et al., 2018).

These corpora consist of pairs of sentences, such as 'A soccer game with multiple males playing.' and 'Some men are playing a sport.', and ground-truth labels. Each label is a judgment of whether the latter sentence, which is the premise,

is inferred from the former one, which is the hypothesis. In this example, the label is 'entailment'.

In this study, we propose a novel method that uses word dictionaries as external knowledge. Word dictionaries are useful for domain adaptation, where we need to understand rare or novel words in which we do not have good embedding representations. For NLI, there is related work that does use dictionaries (Bahdanau et al., 2017). In it, a definition embedding method is proposed that obtains representations of out-of-vocabulary (OOV) words from dictionaries on the fly. In this method, however, the description of a word is converted into the same embedding anytime without considering the context of the input sentences.

On the other hand, we consider that word representation from dictionaries should reflect the context of the input sentences. In the dictionary, we can explain the meaning of a word from many aspects. However, the required information varies depending on the context of the input sentences. This problem also occurs for pre-trained word embeddings, which are usually fixed for all contexts in the previous studies.

The proposed method can obtain different representations of words according to the contexts of the input sentences. It introduces an attention mechanism that improves the encoded representations of each word in input sentences, by using the encoded word definitions of each word in the input sentences. Moreover, unlike Bahdanau's method, it obtains the representation of *all* words from dictionaries on the fly in order to improve the representations of non-OOV words.

2   Task Definition

We follow the task definition of SNLI (Bowman et al., 2015) and MNLI (Williams et al., 2018). We define a dictionary as follows.

58

Proceedings of the 3rd Workshop on Representation Learning for NLP, pages 58–63
Melbourne, Australia, July 20, 2018. ©2018 Association for Computational Linguistics

Def. 1 (Dictionary). A dictionary $\mathcal{D}$ has the following components.

Headword y is an arbitrary token. **Definition** D^y is represented as a token sequence that defines the headword y. This study assumes that each headword has only one definition. For a polysemic headword with multiple definitions, we use the concatenation of the definitions. **Vocabulary** V_D is the set of all headwords in the dictionary.

3 Related Work

Bahdanau et al. (2017) proposed a method that enables dictionary information to be used in NLP tasks, such as NLI, reading comprehension, and language modeling. Their method can obtain the embeddings of OOV words efficiently, because they obtain the definition embeddings for only OOV words instead of the random embeddings of the words. Our method is similar to theirs, but our purpose is different; we refine word embeddings considering the contexts of input sentences for all words.

The definition embedding is also useful for other tasks. Hill et al. (2016) used the definition embedding to understand the phrases. They presented two applications: reverse dictionaries and crossword question answering. They tackled these applications with phrase embeddings obtained from their definitions. Long et al. (2016) used the encoding of the word definition for the initialization of TransE (Bordes et al., 2013), which obtains the embedding of the relationship between two entities.

There is related work that uses other external resources for refining word representations. For NLI, Chen et al. (2017a) proposed a model that uses a knowledge graph to reflect word relationships (e.g., synonymy, hypernymy). Their method achieved state-of-the-art performance on SNLI; however, it cannot handle the definition description of each word.

Moreover, there are general frameworks to refine word embeddings by using external knowledge. Weissenborn et al. (2017) proposed a method that refines the word embedding by encoding the text transformation of ConceptNet (Speer and Havasi, 2012). McCann et al. (2017) proposed context vectors (CoVe), which uses a RNN encoder trained on machine translation datasets to introduce context information to the word embedding. Peters et al. (2018) proposed the Embeddings from Language Models (ELMo), which obtains contextualized word representations. They used the states of the middle layers in the deep language model. These methods are also effective at the NLI task.

4 Existing Methods

This section outlines the existing NLI models and describes the conventional model that uses a dictionary as external knowledge.

4.1 NLI model

In the architecture of a general NLI model (Bowman et al., 2015; Rocktäschel et al., 2016; Chen et al., 2017b), the input of the model is a pair of token sequences $\{X^s = (x_1^s, \cdots, x_{l_s}^s) : s \in \{\mathrm{P}, \mathrm{H}\}\}$, where l_s is the length of X^s. $s \in \{\mathrm{P}, \mathrm{H}\}$ means a premise or hypothesis.

We call the following two layers together the **Encoder**.

Encoder Word Embedding Layer (WEL) This layer takes X^s as input. Let $e(y) \in \mathbb{R}^{n_e}$ be the embedding of token y. It outputs a vector sequence $E^s = (e(x_1^s), \cdots, e(x_{l_s}^s)) \in \mathbb{R}^{n_e \times l_s}$.

Encoder Context Embedding Layer (CEL) This layer converts the vector sequence E^s into a contextualized vector sequence, $C^s = f(E^s) \in \mathbb{R}^{n_c \times l_s}$. The most common approach is to use an RNN as f.

The encoder outputs C^P and C^H for the premise and hypothesis sentences, respectively.

Decoder The input of the decoder is a pair of vector sequences $\{C^P, C^H\}$. The decoder outputs the score vector of the classification labels.

4.2 Definition Embedding Mechanism

We summarize the definition embedding mechanism (DEM) (Bahdanau et al., 2017) as it relates to NLI. They proposed dictionary embedding mechanisms with many variations, such as mean pooling or an RNN. We select one of their models with an RNN, because we also use an RNN for the definition embedding.

The DEM acts on each premise and hypothesis. Its input is a token sequence X^s and the encoder word embedding sequence E^s. The output is E'^s, and E'^s is passed to the encoder CEL instead of E^s. E'^s is obtained by adding E^s to the final state of the RNN encoding of the definition. The sizes of E^s and E'^s are each $n_e \times l_s$.

5 Proposed Method

We propose a novel DEM considering the contexts of the input sentences. Our contributions are threefold. First, we introduce an attention mechanism. Second, we implement the mechanism after the encoder. Third, we consider definition embeddings of words including non-OOV ones.

The input is a token sequence X^s together with the encoder word and context embedding sequence E^s and C^s, and the output is C'^s. C'^s is passed to the *decoder* instead of C^s, where the sizes of C^s and C'^s are each $n_c \times l_s$. The proposed mechanism has the following layers.

Definition Extracting Layer   Let V^s be the set of target tokens of the definition embedding which are in both the token sequence X^s and the vocabulary of the dictionary V_D. The definition D^y of token $y \in V^s$ is obtained from the dictionary $\mathcal{D}$. Let m_y be the length of D^y. This layer outputs a set of target tokens V^s and a set of definitions $\{D^y : y \in V^s\}$.

Definition WEL   This layer has the same parameters as the encoder WEL. For each element of D^y, it outputs a vector sequence $E^y = (e(d_1^y), \cdots, e(d_{m_y}^y)) \in \mathbb{R}^{n_c \times m_y}$.

Definition CEL   This layer has the same model as the encoder CEL. Parameters are not shared with the encoder CEL. It converts the vector sequence E^y into the output of this layer $C^y = f(E^y) \in \mathbb{R}^{n_c \times m_y}$.

Definition Attention Layer   This layer obtains a fixed-length vector representation of definition D^y with an attention mechanism. It takes the outputs of the previous layers E^y, C^y, C^s, and $C^{\bar{s}}$ as input, where $\bar{s} \in \{P, H\}$ indicates that either the premise or hypothesis is different from s.

For $C^y \in \mathbb{R}^{n_c \times m_y}, C^s \in \mathbb{R}^{n_c \times l_s}$, we define an attention matrix $A^{y,s} = \frac{1}{\sqrt{n_c}} C^{s\top} C^y$, and an attention vector $a^{y,s} = \left(\frac{1}{l_s} \sum_i A_{ij}^{y,s} \right)_{j=1,\cdots,m_y} \in \mathbb{R}^{m_y}$. The attention vector $a^{y,s}$ represents the extent that each token in definition D^y is related with the input sentence X^s. The attended definition vector to the input sentence X^s is

$$ h^{y,s} = \sum_i \text{softmax}_i(a^{y,s}) c_i^y \in \mathbb{R}^{n_c}, $$

where c_i^y is the i-th state of the definition context embedding C^y.

The last state of the definition context embedding is $c_{m_y}^y \in \mathbb{R}^{n_c}$. The output of this layer is a linear combination of the enhancements (Chen et al., 2017b) of the attended definition vectors,

$$ z^y = [c_{m_y}^y, h^{s,y,a}, h^{s,y,a} - c_{m_y}^y, h^{s,y,a} \odot c_{m_y}^y, \\ h^{\bar{s},y,a}, h^{\bar{s},y,a} - c_{m_y}^y, h^{\bar{s},y,a} \odot c_{m_y}^y]w, \tag{1} $$

where $w \in \mathbb{R}^7$ is a trainable parameter and $\odot$ is the element-wise product. n_c is the size of z^y.

Output Layer   The output of the proposed mechanism is expressed as

$$ c_i'^s = \begin{cases} c_i^s + z^{x_i^s} & (x_i^s \in V^s) \\ c_i^s & \text{otherwise} \end{cases}. \tag{2} $$

The decoder receives C'^s instead of C^s.

Algorithm 1 is the pseudo code of the definition embedding mechanism.

The above explanation only covers the case of NLI. However, the proposed method can be applied to any number of input sentences, because Equation (1) can take an arbitrary number of arguments. Therefore, it is applicable to other tasks that have text inputs, such as question answering and machine translation.

Algorithm 1 Definition Embedding

Input: $X^s, E^s, C^s, C^{\bar{s}}$
Output: C'^s
 1: $V^s, \{D^y : y \in V^s\} \leftarrow$ Def. Ext.(X^s)
 2: **for all** y in V^s **do**
 3:    $E^y \leftarrow$ Def. Word Emb.(D^y)
 4:    $C^y \leftarrow$ Def. Context Emb.(E^y)
 5:    $z^y \leftarrow$ Def. Att.$(E^y, C^y, C^s, C^{\bar{s}})$
 6: **end for**
 7: $C'^s \leftarrow$ Output$(E^s, C^s, V^s, \{z^y : y \in V^s\})$

---

6 Experiments

This section describes the results of the evaluation of the proposed method.

6.1 Experimental Setup

We chose ESIM (Chen et al., 2017b) and one of the methods in Bahdanau et al. (2017) (BDN) as the baseline models. ESIM is based on the model in Section 4.1. BDN and our method each add a DEM to ESIM. In BDN, the target tokens of the definition embedding are not contained in the pre-trained word embedding vocabulary, because

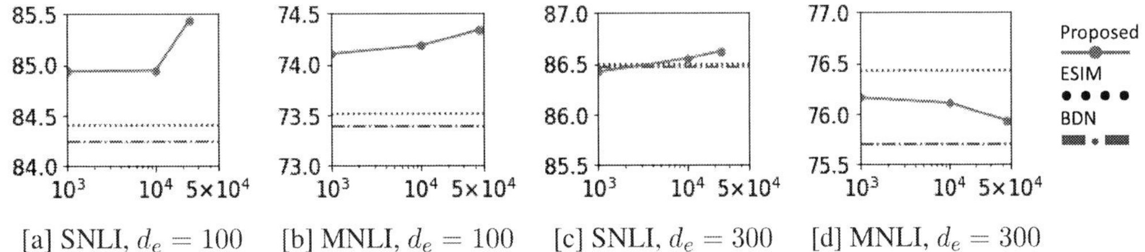

[a] SNLI, $d_e = 100$ [b] MNLI, $d_e = 100$ [c] SNLI, $d_e = 300$ [d] MNLI, $d_e = 300$

Figure 1: Classification accuracy of each model in the not-many-OOV setting. The vertical axis is accuracy, and the horizontal axis is the number of the vocabulary entries of the dictionary. The performance of ESIM and BDN was constant because their dictionary size is less than 1000.

BDN intends to supplement the embeddings of OOV words. However, in our method, the target tokens do not depend on a pre-trained word embedding vocabulary, because we intend to improve the representation of all the words by considering the context.

Our experiments were on the SNLI and MNLI benchmarks. For MNLI, we used a matched domain development dataset as our development data and a mismatched domain development dataset as our test data. The tokenizer was spaCy (Honnibal and Montani, 2018). The word embeddings were pre-trained $100d$ GloVe 6B vectors and $300d$ GloVe 840B vectors (Jeffrey Pennington and Manning, 2014). The embeddings were fixed during training, because we were interested in the difference in representation between pre-trained embeddings with and without dictionary information.

We used the vocabulary and definitions in WordNet (Miller, 1995) as dictionaries. For polysemic words with multiple definitions, we used the top-5 definitions connected in descending order of frequency of synsets, which are provided by WordNet. The number of headwords that appear in SNLI is 24103, and 45225 in MNLI.

The other settings are described in Appendix A.

6.2 Results

Does the proposed method refine the OOV word embedding? In order to investigate the effectiveness of our method against OOV words, we restricted the vocabulary of the $100d$ GloVe embedding to the most common 3000 words in each dataset and considered the other words as OOV (many-OOV setting). The word embeddings of the OOV words were randomly initialized according to a Gaussian distribution and fixed during training.

Table 1 shows the results. When there were many OOV words, our method improved test ac-

	SNLI	MNLI
ESIM	82.5	69.8
BDN	83.7	69.7
Proposed	**83.9**	**71.3**

Table 1: Test accuracy in the many-OOV setting

curacy by 1.4% in SNLI and 1.5% in MNLI. In contrast, BDN did not improve accuracy in MNLI.

Does the larger dictionary bring higher accuracy? We also evaluated our method with the whole $100d$ GloVe embedding (not-many-OOV setting). In this experiment, we used the whole vocabulary of WordNet or restricted the WordNet vocabulary to the 1000 and 10000 most common words in the each dataset.

Figures 1a and 1b show the results when using $100d$ GloVe. We confirmed that the larger dictionary raises accuracy. We think that the pre-trained GloVe embeddings for the frequent words were more appropriate than those for the rare words. This means that our method was effective for words that had relatively poor embeddings and occur sufficiently often in the training data.

We confirmed that the threefold originality of our method contributed to the improvement in the whole WordNet setting. The proposed method using the whole WordNet achieved the higher test accuracy on each dataset. The improvement from ESIM was 1.0% in SNLI and 0.8% in MNLI. Moreover, our method without the definition attention mechanism performed worse by 0.4% in SNLI and 0.5% in MNLI in comparison with the method with it. This implies that our definition embedding layer plays an important role in the definition embedding. In particular, the implementation of the attention mechanism after the encoder, which is essential to reflecting the context of input sentences, contributes to a refined representation.

BDN did not perform well. The number of

OOV words in SNLI (MNLI) is 415 (913); therefore, BDN could not sufficiently train the representations of the words with the sentences in the datasets.

Does the improvement depend on the quality of the word embedding? Figures 1c and 1d show the results when using $300d$ GloVe. In this setting, our method provided no significant improvement. It performed slightly better (worse) than ESIM in SNLI (MNLI). BDN, as well, did not perform better than ESIM. We think the $300d$ GloVe has sufficiently correct embeddings for most of the words in SNLI and MNLI, because it was created from a much larger corpora (340 billion tokens) than that of the 100d one (eight billion tokens).

To summarize the experimental results for the first and third research questions, the effectiveness of our method is dependent on the quality and coverage of word embeddings. That is, our method is effective for rare or novel words.

7 Conclusion

We proposed a novel definition embedding method. The method considers the contexts of the input sentences with an attention mechanism for the definition embeddings. It considers the definition embeddings of words including non-OOV words. Experimental results showed that it is effective for rare or novel words that do not have good pre-trained word embeddings.

References

Dzmitry Bahdanau, Tom Bosc, Stanislaw Jastrzebski, Edward Grefenstette, Pascal Vincent, and Yoshua Bengio. 2017. Learning to compute word embeddings on the fly. *arXiv preprint arXiv:1706.00286* .

Steven Bird, Ewan Klein, and Edward Loper. 2009. *Natural Language Processing with Python*. O'Reilly Media, Inc.

Antoine Bordes, Nicolas Usunier, Alberto Garcia-Duran, Jason Weston, and Oksana Yakhnenko. 2013. Translating embeddings for modeling multi-relational data. In *NIPS*. pages 2787–2795.

Samuel R. Bowman, Gabor Angeli, Christopher Potts, and Christopher D. Manning. 2015. A large annotated corpus for learning natural language inference. In *EMNLP*. pages 632–642. https://doi.org/10.18653/v1/D15-1075.

Qian Chen, Xiaodan Zhu, Zhen-Hua Ling, Diana Inkpen, and Si Wei. 2017a. Natural language inference with external knowledge. *arXiv preprint arXiv:1711.04289* .

Qian Chen, Xiaodan Zhu, Zhenhua Ling, Si Wei, Hui Jiang, and Diana Inkpen. 2017b. Enhanced LSTM for natural language inference. In *ACL*. pages 1657–1668. https://doi.org/10.18653/v1/P17-1152.

Xavier Glorot and Yoshua Bengio. 2010. Understanding the difficulty of training deep feedforward neural networks. In *AISTATS*. pages 249–256.

Felix Hill, Kyunghyun Cho, Anna Korhonen, and Yoshua Bengio. 2016. Learning to understand phrases by embedding the dictionary. *Transactions of ACL* 4:17–30.

Matthew Honnibal and Ines Montani. 2018. spaCy 2: Natural language understanding with bloom embeddings, convolutional neural networks and incremental parsing. *To appear* .

Richard Socher Jeffrey Pennington and Christopher D. Manning. 2014. GloVe: Global vectors for word representation. In *EMNLP*. pages 1532–1543. https://doi.org/10.3115/v1/D14-1162.

Tao Lei and Yu Zhang. 2017. Training RNNs as fast as CNNs. *arXiv preprint arXiv:1709.02755* .

Teng Long, Ryan Lowe, Jackie Chi Kit Cheung, and Doina Precup. 2016. Leveraging lexical resources for learning entity embeddings in multi-relational data. pages 112–117. https://doi.org/10.18653/v1/P16-2019.

Bryan McCann, James Bradbury, Caiming Xiong, and Richard Socher. 2017. Learned in translation: Contextualized word vectors. In *NIPS*.

George A. Miller. 1995. WordNet: A lexical database for english. *Commun. ACM* 38(11):39–41. https://doi.org/10.1145/219717.219748.

Adam Paszke, Sam Gross, Soumith Chintala, Gregory Chanan, Edward Yang, Zachary DeVito, Zeming Lin, Alban Desmaison, Luca Antiga, and Adam Lerer. 2017. Automatic differentiation in pytorch. In *NIPS Workshop Autodiff* .

Matthew E. Peters, Mark Neumann, Mohit Iyyer, Matt Gardner, Christopher Clark, Kenton Lee, and Luke Zettlemoyer. 2018. Deep contextualized word representations. In *NAACL*.

Tim Rocktäschel, Edward Grefenstette, Karl Moritz Hermann, Tomáš Kočiský, and Phil Blunsom. 2016. Reasoning about entailment with neural attention. In *ICLR*.

Robert Speer and Catherine Havasi. 2012. Representing general relational knowledge in conceptnet 5. In *LREC*. pages 3679–3686.

Dirk Weissenborn, Tomas Kocisky, and Chris Dyer.
2017. Dynamic integration of background knowledge in neural NLU systems. *arXiv preprint
arXiv:1706.02596* .

Adina Williams, Nikita Nangia, and Samuel R. Bowman. 2018. A broad-coverage challenge corpus
for sentence understanding through inference. In
NAACL.

Matthew D. Zeiler. 2012. ADADELTA: an adaptive learning rate method. *arXiv preprint
arXiv:1212.5701* .

A Details of the Implementation

The section describes our implementation so that
our experiments can be reproduced.

We implemented our method in PyTorch
(Paszke et al., 2017) and trained it on one Nvidia
GeForce GTX 1080 GPU. The RNNs in the encoder, decoder, and definition embedding mechanism were two-layer bi-directional simple recurrent units (SRUs) (Lei and Zhang, 2017). The size
of the output of the RNN was $n_c = 2n_e$. The activation function in the RNN was the tanh function.
Dropout with a keep ratio of 0.8 was applied to the
same layer as ESIM and the definition embedding
layer.

The parameters of the weights were initialized
using the Xavier normal initializer (Glorot and
Bengio, 2010), and the parameters of the biases
were initialized as zero vectors. Word embeddings
not contained in pre-trained GloVe were random-
ized according to a Gaussian distribution.

The mini-batch size was set to 16. The optimizer was Adadelta (Zeiler, 2012) with an initial
learning rate of 0.075 and ρ of 0.9. Early stopping
with a patience of 7 was used to avoid overfitting.

We removed words whose definition length
was one and stop words in the Natural Language
Toolkit (Bird et al., 2009) from the vocabulary of
the dictionary.

Comparison of Representations of Named Entities for Multi-label Document Classification with Convolutional Neural Networks

Lidia Pivovarova and **Roman Yangarber**
University of Helsinki, Finland
Department of Computer Science
`first.last@cs.helsinki.fi`

Abstract

We explore representations for multi-token names in the context of the Reuters topic and sector classification tasks (RCV1). We find that: the best way to treat names is to split them into tokens and use each token as a separate feature; NEs have more impact on sector classification than on topic classification; replacing all NEs with special entity-type tokens is not an effective strategy; representing tokens by different embeddings for proper names vs. common nouns does not improve results. We highlight the improvements over state-of-the-art results that our CNN models yield.

1 Introduction

This paper addresses large-scale multi-class text classification tasks: categorizing articles in the Reuters news corpus (RCV1) according to topic and to industry sectors. A topic is a broad news category, e.g., "Economics," "Sport," "Health." A sector defines a narrower business area, e.g., "Banking," "Telecommunications," "Insurance."

We use convolutional neural networks (CNNs), which take word embeddings as input. Typically word embeddings are built by treating a corpus as a sequence of tokens, where named entities (NEs) receive no special treatment. Yet NEs may be important features in some classification tasks: companies, e.g., are often linked to particular industry sectors, and certain industries are linked to locations. Thus company and location names may be important features for sector classification.

RCV1 is much smaller than corpora typically used to build word embeddings. Thus we utilize external resources—a corpus of approximately 10 million business news articles, collected using the PULS news monitoring system (Pivovarova et al., 2013). While nominally RCV1 contains *general* news, it is skewed toward business; many of the topic labels are business-related ("Markets", "Commodities", "Share Capital," etc.). Thus, we expect our business corpus to help in learning features for the Reuters classification tasks.

We compare several NE representation to find the most suitable name features for each task. We use the PULS NER system (Grishman et al., 2003; Huttunen et al., 2002a,b) to find NEs and their types—*company, location, person*, etc. We compare various representations of NEs, by building embeddings, and training CNNs to find the best representation. We also compare building embeddings on the RCV1 corpus vs. using much larger external corpora.

2 Data and Prior Work

RCV1 (Lewis et al., 2004) is a corpus of about 800K Reuters articles from 1996–1997 with manually assigned *sector* and *topic* labels. Both classifications are multi-label—each document may have zero or more labels. While all documents have topic labels, only 350K have sector labels.

While RCV1 appears frequently in published research, few authors tackle the full-scale classification problem. Typically they use subsets of the data: (Daniely et al., 2017; Duchi et al., 2011) use only the four most general topic labels; (Dredze et al., 2008) use 6 sector categories to explore binary classification, (Daniels and Metaxas, 2017) use a subset of 6K articles. Even when the entire dataset is used, the training-text split varies across papers, because the "original" split (Lewis et al., 2004) is impractical for most purposes: 23K instances for training, and 780K for testing.

Another problem that complicates comparison is the lack of consistency in evaluation metrics

Proceedings of the 3rd Workshop on Representation Learning for NLP, pages 64–68
Melbourne, Australia, July 20, 2018. ©2018 Association for Computational Linguistics

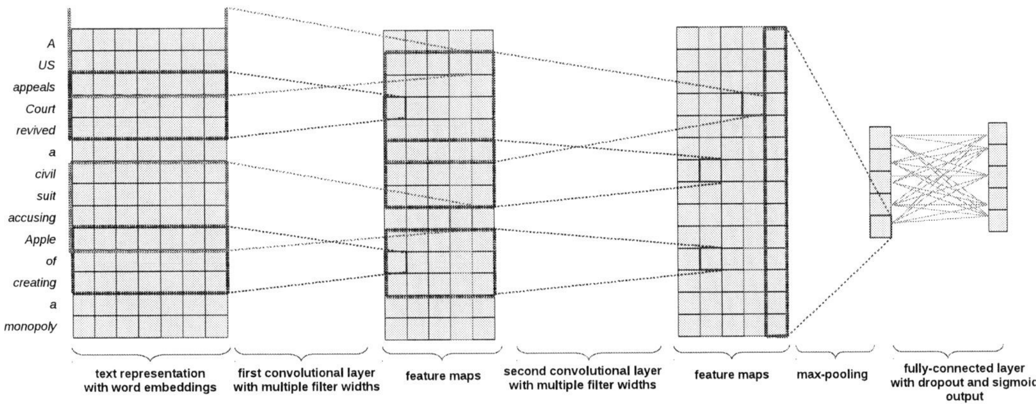

Figure 1: Architecture of the convolutional neural networks

used to evaluate classifier performance. The most common measures for multi-class classification are macro- and micro-averaged F-measure, which we use in this paper. However, others use other metrics. For example, (Liu et al., 2017) use precision and cumulative gain at top K—measures adopted from information retrieval. This is not comparable with other work, because these metrics are used not only to report results, but also to optimize the algorithms during training. The notion of the best classifier differs depending on which evaluation measure is used. Thus, although RCV1 is frequently used, we find few papers directly comparable to our research, in the sense that they use the *entire* RCV1 dataset and report micro- and macro-averaged F-measure.

To the best of our knowledge, our previous work (Du et al., 2015) was the only study of the utility of NEs for RCV1 classification. We demonstrated that using a combination of keyword-based and NE-based classifiers works better than either classifier alone. In that paper we applied a rule-based approach for NEs, and did not use NEs as features for machine learning.

3 Model

The architecture of our CNN is shown in Figure 1. The inputs are fed into the network as zero-padded text fragments of fixed size, with each word represented by a fixed-dimensional embedding vector. The inputs are fed into a layer of convolutional filters with multiple widths, optionally followed by deeper convolutional layers. The results of the last convolutional layer are max-pooled, producing a

vector with one scalar per filter. This is fed into a fully-connected layer with dropout regularization, with one sigmoid node in the output layer for each of the class labels. For each class label, a cross-entropy loss is computed. Losses are averaged across labels, and the gradient of the loss is back-propagated to update the weights. This is similar to the model (Kim, 2014) used for sentiment analysis. The key differences are that our model uses an arbitrary number of convolutions, and that we use sigmoid rather than softmax on output, since the labels are not mutually exclusive.

To train the model we used a random split: 80% of the data used for training, 10% development set, and 10% test set. The development set is used to determine when to stop training, and to tune a set of optimal thresholds $\{\theta_i\}$ for each label i—if the output probability p_i is higher than θ_i, the label is assigned to the instance, otherwise it is not. To find the optimal threshold, we optimize the F-measure for each label. The test set is used to obtain the final, reported performance scores.

Our focus is this paper is *data representation*, thus we defer the tuning of hyper-parameters for future work. All experiments use the same network structure: 3 convolution layers with filter sizes $\{3,7,11\}$, $\{3,7,11\}$, and $\{3,11\}$, with 512, 256 and 256 filters of each size, respectively. The runs differ only in the *input embeddings* they use.

4 Data Representation

We train the embeddings using GloVe (Pennington et al., 2014). As features we use lower-cased *lemmas* of all words. The rationale for this is that our corpora are relatively small, so the data are sparse and not sufficient to build embeddings from surface forms. We tune the embeddings while training the CNN, updating them at each iteration.

We explore several *name representations*, using our NER system:

- **type**: each entity is represented by a special token denoting its type—*C-company, C-person, C-location*, etc, and *C-name* if the type is not determined. The model learns one embedding for each of these tokens.
- **name**: each name gets its own embedding; multi-word names treated as *a single token*.
- **split-name**: multi-word names are split into tokens, and each token has its own embedding; the motivation is that some company names may contain informative parts—e.g., Air Baltic, Delta Airlines—which may indicate that these companies operate in the same field; these name parts may be more useful than the name as a whole.
- **split-name+common**: similar to the above, but tokens inside names and in common context are distinguished; the motivation is that some words may be used in names without any relation to the company's line of business—e.g., *Apple, Blackberry*—and their usage inside names should not be mixed with their usage as common nouns.

In the experiments, we build GloVe embeddings from two corpora: RCV1 only, and RCV1 plus our external corpus. For comparison, we also use 200-dimensional embeddings trained on a 6 billion general corpus (**glove-6B**), provided by the GloVe project.[0] This corresponds to our **split-name** representation mode.

To illustrate the effect of the different token representations, Table 1 shows ten words nearest to the sample lemmas: *apple* and *airline*. When **name** representation is used, the token *apple* is ambiguous, its nearest neighbors are both fruit words (*pear*) and computer words (*apple_computer*). In **type** representation, the "computer" meaning disappears, since all mentions of *Apple* as company are represented by the special token *C-company*. When using **glove-6B**, the fruit meaning is absent, and all neighbors are computer-related words. The token *airline* does not exhibit such ambiguity, and all representations produce similar nearest neighbors.

---

[0]https://nlp.stanford.edu/projects/glove/

apple		
name	**type**	**glove-6B**
pear	pear	iphone
unpasteurized	unpasteurized	microsoft
juice	juice	intel
apple_computer	fruit	macintosh
odwalla	salmonella	ipod
strawberry	peach	ibm
fruit	taint	ipad
macintosh	orange	software
meat	crate	google
pear_board	strawberry	itunes

airline		
name	**type**	**glove-6B**
carrier	carrier	airlines
flight	flight	airways
british_airways	passenger	lufthansa
american_airlines	aircraft	carrier
air_france	airport	flights
passenger	air	flight
lufthansa	pilot	pilots
air	route	qantas
united_airlines	plane	alitalia
aircraft	aviation	klm

split-name+common			
apple	*apple_NE*	*airline*	*airline_NE*
pear	computer_NE	airlines_NE	malaysian_NE
juice	macintosh_NE	airways_NE	scandinavian_NE
unpasteurized	amelio_NE	carrier	airlines_NE
odwalla_NE	operating-system	flight	system_NE
fruit	compaq_NE	air_NE	pilots_NE
anthrax	microsoft_NE	passenger	air_NE
salmonella	oracle_NE	lufthansa_NE	klm_NE
rotten	ibm_NE	pilot	passengers_NE
unpasteurised	software	aircraft	jet_NE
strawberry	jobs_NE	route	tajudin_NE

Table 1: Nearest neighbors for sample words using various word representations.

In the **split-name+common** representation mode, each lemma may produce two vectors, one for a common noun and one for a proper noun (inside a name). As the table shows, *apple* as a common noun has a clear "fruit" meaning; the one company appearing among the neighbors is a juice producer, *Odwalla*. The nearest neighbors for *apple_NE*, in name context, include IT companies. The tokens *airline* and *airline_NE* have no clear semantic distinction, with similar nearest neighbors. In such cases there is no clear advantage in using two embeddings rather than one.

We test all of the above name representations experimentally, to determine which is more useful in the document classification tasks.

5   Results and Discussion

Experimental results are presented in Tables 2 and 3. We compare our results with those found in related work, described in Section 2, focusing on micro- and macro-averaged F-measure—μ-F1 and M-F1, respectively. The experimental settings differ in the various papers, which makes precise comparison difficult. For example, several previous papers use the "standard split," (proposed in (Lewis et al., 2004)), which contains only 23K

Algorithm (prior)	M-F1	μ-F1
SVM (Lewis et al., 2004)	29.7	51.3
SVM (Zhuang et al., 2005)	30.1	52.0
Naive Bayes (Puurula, 2012)	—	70.5
Bloom Filters (Cisse et al., 2013)	47.8	*72.4*
SVM + NEs (Du et al., 2015)	*57.7*	63.8
RCV1 embeddings		
CNN type	32.2	58.4
CNN name	61.0	80.2
CNN split-name	**63.6**	**82.0**
CNN split-name+common	44.3	68.3
RCV1 + external corpus		
CNN type	47.7	72.6
CNN name	55.2	78.4
CNN split-name	60.7	80.3
CNN split-name+common	38.0	66.0
CNN split-name (*Glove-6B*)	55.7	78.4

Table 2: Sector classification results on RCV1.

Algorithm (prior)	M-F1	μ-F1
SVM (Lewis et al., 2004)	61.9	81.6
ANN (Nam et al., 2014)	*69.2*	85.3
CNN (Johnson and Zhang, 2015)	67.1	*85.7*
RCV1 embeddings		
CNN type	65.5	85.5
CNN name	66.7	**86.2**
CNN split-name	66.5	**86.2**
CNN split-name+common	66.6	**86.2**
RCV1 + external corpus		
CNN type	64.9	85.6
CNN name	66.4	**86.2**
CNN split-name	65.7	85.9
CNN split-name+common	65.6	85.8
CNN split-name (*Glove-6B*)	65.8	85.8

Table 3: Topic classification results on RCV1.

training instances, which is not sufficient for learning word embeddings.

Compared to the reported state-of-the-art results on Sector Classification (Table 2), our best model yields a 10% gain in μ-F1, (Cisse et al., 2013), and a 6% gain in M-F1 (Du et al., 2015). The best μ-F1 and M-F1 results are obtained by the same model.[1] On Topic Classification (Table 3), our μ-F1 results show a modest improvement of 0.5% in F-measure—or a 3.5% (averaged) error reduction—over state of the art (Johnson and Zhang, 2015).[2]

As seen in Table 2, the best data representation for Sector Classification, is **split-name**, where each token has the same embedding regardless whether it is used in a proper-name or a common-noun context. The worst performing name representation is **type**, where names are mapped to special "concepts" (*C-company, C-person* etc.), and each concept has its own embedding. This indicates the importance of the tokens inside the named entities for Sector Classification, and supports the notion that company names mentioned in text correlate with sector labels.

Results for Topic Classification are in Table 3. The best data representation is again **split-name**, though the difference between representations is less pronounced than in the case of Sector Classification, and using **type** does not lead to a significant drop in model performance. This suggests that proper names are less important for Topic

(event) classification, and supports the intuition that entity names (e.g., companies) are less correlated with the types of events in which the entities participate in business news. However, there may be correlations between industry sectors and topics/events: e.g., mining or petroleum companies rarely launch new products. This may explain why the **split-name** representation appears to be better for Topic Classification. One possible next step is to build CNNs that jointly model Topics and Sectors; we plan to explore this in future work.

Surprisingly, using external corpora did not improve the models' performance, as indicated by both Sector and Topic results (Tables 2 and 3, respectively). This may mean that the genre and the time period of the news corpus are more relevant for building embeddings than the size of the corpora. However, other factors may contribute as well, e.g., our hyper-parameter combination may not be optimal for these embeddings. Nevertheless, the results follow the same pattern: the best name representation is **split-name** and the difference between representations is more pronounced for Sector than for Topic classification.

In conclusion, our contribution is two-fold. On one classic large-scale classification task, *sectors*, our proposed CNNs yield substantial improvements over state-of-the-art; on *topics*—a modest improvement in μ-F-measure. Further, to the best of our knowledge, this is the first attempt at a systematic comparison of NE representation for text classification. More effective ways of representing NEs should be explored in future work, given their importance for the classification tasks, as demonstrated by the experiments we present in this paper.

---

[1]In prior work, state of the art was achieved by different models.

[2]Interestingly, the best result for M-F1 on Topics is still in prior work: i.e., these prior models perform better on *very infrequent* topics. This is to be explored in future work.

References

Moustapha M. Cisse, Nicolas Usunier, Thierry Arti, and Patrick Gallinari. 2013. Robust Bloom filters for large multilabel classification tasks. In *Advances in Neural Information Processing Systems*, pages 1851–1859.

Zachary Alan Daniels and Dimitris N Metaxas. 2017. Addressing imbalance in multi-label classification using structured hellinger forests. In *AAAI*, pages 1826–1832.

Amit Daniely, Nevena Lazic, Yoram Singer, and Kunal Talwar. 2017. Short and deep: Sketching and neural networks.

Mark Dredze, Koby Crammer, and Fernando Pereira. 2008. Confidence-weighted linear classification. In *Proceedings of the 25th International Conference on Machine Learning*, ICML '08, pages 264–271, New York, NY, USA. ACM.

Mian Du, Matthew Pierce, Lidia Pivovarova, and Roman Yangarber. 2015. Improving supervised classification using information extraction. In *International Conference on Applications of Natural Language to Information Systems*, pages 3–18. Springer.

John Duchi, Elad Hazan, and Yoram Singer. 2011. Adaptive subgradient methods for online learning and stochastic optimization. *J. Mach. Learn. Res.*, 12:2121–2159.

Ralph Grishman, Silja Huttunen, and Roman Yangarber. 2003. Information extraction for enhanced access to disease outbreak reports. *Journal of Biomedical Informatics*, **35**(4):236–246.

Silja Huttunen, Roman Yangarber, and Ralph Grishman. 2002a. Complexity of event structure in IE scenarios. In *Proceedings of the 19th International Conference on Computational Linguistics (COLING 2002)*, Taipei.

Silja Huttunen, Roman Yangarber, and Ralph Grishman. 2002b. Diversity of scenarios in information extraction. In *Proceedings of the Third International Conference on Language Resources and Evaluation (LREC 2002)*, Las Palmas de Gran Canaria, Spain.

Rie Johnson and Tong Zhang. 2015. Semi-supervised convolutional neural networks for text categorization via region embedding. In *Advances in neural information processing systems*, pages 919–927.

Yoon Kim. 2014. Convolutional neural networks for sentence classification. In *Proceedings of the Conference on Empirical Methods in Natural Language Processing (EMNLP)*.

David D. Lewis, Yiming Yang, Tony G. Rose, and Fan Li. 2004. RCV1: A new benchmark collection for text categorization research. *The Journal of Machine Learning Research*, 5:361–397.

Jingzhou Liu, Wei-Cheng Chang, Yuexin Wu, and Yiming Yang. 2017. Deep learning for extreme multi-label text classification. In *Proceedings of the 40th International ACM SIGIR Conference on Research and Development in Information Retrieval*, pages 115–124. ACM.

Jinseok Nam, Jungi Kim, Eneldo Loza Mencía, Iryna Gurevych, and Johannes Fürnkranz. 2014. Large-scale multi-label text classification—revisiting neural networks. In *Joint european conference on machine learning and knowledge discovery in databases*, pages 437–452. Springer.

Jeffrey Pennington, Richard Socher, and Christopher D. Manning. 2014. GloVe: Global vectors for word representation. In *Empirical Methods in Natural Language Processing (EMNLP)*, pages 1532–1543.

Lidia Pivovarova, Silja Huttunen, and Roman Yangarber. 2013. Event representation across genre. In *Proceedins of the 1st Workshop on Events: Definition, Detection, Coreference, and Representation*, NAACL HLT.

Antti Puurula. 2012. Scalable text classification with sparse generative modeling. In Patricia Anthony, Mitsuru Ishizuka, and Dickson Lukose, editors, *PRICAI 2012: Trends in Artificial Intelligence*, volume 7458 of *Lecture Notes in Computer Science*, pages 458–469. Springer Berlin Heidelberg.

Dong Zhuang, Benyu Zhang, Qiang Yang, Jun Yan, Zheng Chen, and Ying Chen. 2005. Efficient text classification by weighted proximal SVM. In *Fifth IEEE International Conference on Data Mining*.

Speeding up Context-based Sentence Representation Learning
with Non-autoregressive Convolutional Decoding

Shuai Tang[1], **Hailin Jin**[2], **Chen Fang**[2], **Zhaowen Wang**[2], **Virginia R. de Sa**[1]
[1] Department of Cognitive Science, UC San Diego
[2] Adobe Research
{shuaitang93,desa}@ucsd.edu, {hljin,cfang,zhawang}@adobe.com

Abstract

Context plays an important role in human language understanding, thus it may also be useful for machines learning vector representations of language. In this paper, we explore an asymmetric encoder-decoder structure for unsupervised context-based sentence representation learning. We carefully designed experiments to show that neither an autoregressive decoder nor an RNN decoder is required. After that, we designed a model which still keeps an RNN as the encoder, while using a non-autoregressive convolutional decoder. We further combine a suite of effective designs to significantly improve model efficiency while also achieving better performance. Our model is trained on two different large unlabelled corpora, and in both cases the transferability is evaluated on a set of downstream NLP tasks. We empirically show that our model is simple and fast while producing rich sentence representations that excel in downstream tasks.

1 Introduction

Learning distributed representations of sentences is an important and hard topic in both the deep learning and natural language processing communities, since it requires machines to encode a sentence with rich language content into a fixed-dimension vector filled with real numbers. Our goal is to build a distributed sentence encoder learnt in an unsupervised fashion by exploiting the structure and relationships in a large unlabelled corpus.

Numerous studies in human language processing have supported that rich semantics of a word or sentence can be inferred from its context (Harris, 1954; Firth, 1957). The idea of learning from the co-occurrence (Turney and Pantel, 2010) was recently successfully applied to vector representation learning for words in Mikolov et al. (2013) and Pennington et al. (2014).

A very recent successful application of the distributional hypothesis (Harris, 1954) at the sentence-level is the skip-thoughts model (Kiros et al., 2015). The skip-thoughts model learns to encode the current sentence and decode the surrounding two sentences instead of the input sentence itself, which achieves overall good performance on all tested downstream NLP tasks that cover various topics. The major issue is that the training takes too long since there are two RNN decoders to reconstruct the previous sentence and the next one independently. Intuitively, given the current sentence, inferring the previous sentence and inferring the next one should be different, which supports the usage of two independent decoders in the skip-thoughts model. However, Tang et al. (2017) proposed the skip-thought neighbour model, which only decodes the next sentence based on the current one, and has similar performance on downstream tasks compared to that of their implementation of the skip-thoughts model.

In the encoder-decoder models for learning sentence representations, only the encoder will be used to map sentences to vectors after training, which implies that the quality of the generated language is not our main concern. This leads to our two-step experiment to check the necessity of applying an autoregressive model as the decoder. In other words, since the decoder's performance on language modelling is not our main concern, it is preferred to reduce the complexity of the decoder to speed up the training process. In our experiments, the first step is to check whether "teacher-forcing" is required during training if we stick to using an autoregressive model as the decoder, and the second step is to check whether an autoregres-

Proceedings of the 3rd Workshop on Representation Learning for NLP, pages 69–78
Melbourne, Australia, July 20, 2018. ©2018 Association for Computational Linguistics

sive decoder is necessary to learn a good sentence encoder. Briefly, the experimental results show that an autoregressive decoder is indeed not essential in learning a good sentence encoder; thus the two findings of our experiments lead to our final model design.

Our proposed model has an asymmetric encoder-decoder structure, which keeps an RNN as the encoder and has a CNN as the decoder, and the model explores using only the subsequent context information as the supervision. The asymmetry in both model architecture and training pair reduces a large amount of the training time.

The contribution of our work is summarised as:

1. We design experiments to show that an autoregressive decoder or an RNN decoder is not necessary in the encoder-decoder type of models for learning sentence representations, and based on our results, we present two findings. **Finding I**: It is not necessary to input the correct words into an autoregressive decoder for learning sentence representations. **Finding II**: The model with an autoregressive decoder performs similarly to the model with a predict-all-words decoder.

2. The two findings above lead to our final model design, which keeps an RNN encoder while using a CNN decoder and learns to encode the current sentence and decode the subsequent contiguous words all at once.

3. With a suite of techniques, our model performs decently on the downstream tasks, and can be trained efficiently on a large unlabelled corpus.

The following sections will introduce the components in our "RNN-CNN" model, and discuss our experimental design.

2 RNN-CNN Model

Our model is highly asymmetric in terms of both the training pairs and the model structure. Specifically, our model has an RNN as the encoder, and a CNN as the decoder. During training, the encoder takes the i-th sentence S_i as the input, and then produces a fixed-dimension vector $\mathbf{z}_i$ as the sentence representation; the decoder is applied to reconstruct the paired target sequence T_i that contains the subsequent contiguous words. The distance between the generated sequence and the target one is measured by the cross-entropy loss at each position in T_i. An illustration is in Figure 1. (For simplicity, we omit the subscript i in this section.)

1. Encoder: The encoder is a bi-directional Gated Recurrent Unit (GRU, Chung et al. (2014))[1]. Suppose that an input sentence S contains M words, which are $\{w_s^1, w_s^2, ..., w_s^M\}$, and they are transformed by an embedding matrix $\mathbf{E} \in \mathbb{R}^{d_e \times |V|}$ to word vectors[2]. The bi-directional GRU takes one word vector at a time, and processes the input sentence in both the forward and backward directions; both sets of hidden states are concatenated to form the hidden state matrix $\mathbf{H} = [\mathbf{h}^1, \mathbf{h}^2, ..., \mathbf{h}^M] \in \mathbb{R}^{d_h \times M}$, where d_h is the dimension of the hidden states $\mathbf{h}^m = \left[\overleftarrow{\mathbf{h}^m}; \overrightarrow{\mathbf{h}^m}\right]$ ($\forall m \in \{1, 2, ..., M\}$).

2. Representation: We aim to provide a model with faster training speed and better transferability than existing algorithms; thus we choose to apply a parameter-free composition function, which is a concatenation of the outputs from a global mean pooling over time and a global max pooling over time, on the computed sequence of hidden states $\mathbf{H}$. The composition function is represented as

$$\mathbf{z} = \left[\frac{1}{M}\sum_{m=1}^{M}\mathbf{h}^m; \mathrm{MaxPool}(\mathbf{H})\right] \qquad (1)$$

where MaxPool is the max operation on each row of the matrix $\mathbf{H}$, which outputs a vector with dimension d_h. Thus the representation $\mathbf{z} \in \mathbb{R}^{2d_h}$.

3. Decoder: The decoder is a 3-layer CNN to reconstruct the paired target sequence T, which needs to expand $\mathbf{z}$, which can be considered as a sequence with only one element, to a sequence with T elements. Intuitively, the decoder could be a stack of deconvolution layers. For fast training speed, we optimised the architecture to make it possible to use fully-connected layers and convolution layers in the decoder, since generally, convolution layers run faster than deconvolution layers in modern deep learning frameworks.

Suppose that the target sequence T has N words, which are $\{w_t^1, w_t^2, ..., w_t^N\}$, the first layer of deconvolution will expand $\mathbf{z} \in \mathbb{R}^{2d_h \times 1}$, into a feature

---

[1]We experimented with both Long-short Term Memory (LSTM, Hochreiter and Schmidhuber (1997)) and GRU. Since LSTM didn't give us significant performance boost, and generally GRU runs faster than LSTM, in our experiments, we stick to using GRU in the encoder.

[2]V is the vocabulary, and $|V|$ is the number of unique words in the vocabulary. d_e is the dimension of each word vector.

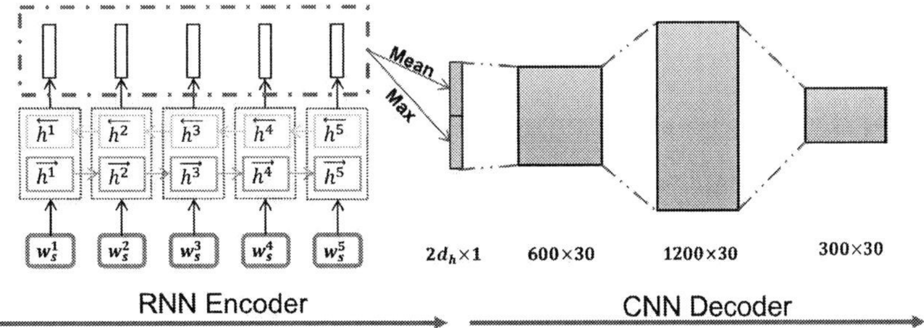

Figure 1: Our proposed model is composed of an RNN encoder, and a CNN decoder. During training, a batch of sentences are sent to the model, and the RNN encoder computes a vector representation for each of sentences; then the CNN decoder needs to reconstruct the paired target sequence, which contains 30 contiguous words right after the input sentence, given the vector representation. 300 is the dimension of word vectors. $2d_h$ is the dimension of the sentence representation which varies with the RNN encoder size. (Better view in colour.)

map with N elements. It can be easily implemented as a concatenation of outputs from N linear transformations in parallel. Then the second and third layer are 1D-convolution layers. The output feature map is $\mathbf{U} = [\mathbf{u}^1, \mathbf{u}^2, ..., \mathbf{u}^N] \in \mathbb{R}^{d_e \times N}$, where d_e is the dimension of the word vectors.

Note that our decoder is not an autoregressive model and has high training efficiency. We will discuss the reason for choosing this decoder which we call a predict-all-words CNN decoder.

4. Objective: The training objective is to maximise the likelihood of the target sequence being generated from the decoder. Since in our model, each word is predicted independently, a softmax layer is applied after the decoder to produce a probability distribution over words in V at each position, thus the probability of generating a word w_t^n in the target sequence is defined as:

$$P(w_t^n) = \frac{e^{\mathbf{E}(w_t^n)^\top \mathbf{u}^n}}{\sum_{w \in V} e^{\mathbf{E}(w)^\top \mathbf{u}^n}}, \quad (2)$$

where, $\mathbf{E}(w)$ is the vector representation of w in the embedding matrix $\mathbf{E}$, and $\mathbf{E}(w)^\top \mathbf{u}^n$ is the dot-product between the word vector and the feature vector produced by the decoder at position n . The training objective is to minimise the sum of the negative log-likelihood over all positions in the target sequence T:

$$\mathcal{L}(\boldsymbol{\phi}, \boldsymbol{\theta}) = -\log P(T|S; \boldsymbol{\phi}, \boldsymbol{\theta})$$
$$= -\sum_{n=1}^{N} \log P(w_t^n | w_s^1, w_s^2, ..., w_s^M; \boldsymbol{\phi}, \boldsymbol{\theta}), \quad (3)$$

where ϕ and θ contain the parameters in the encoder and the decoder, respectively. The training objective $\mathcal{L}(\phi, \theta)$ is summed over all sentences in the training corpus.

3 Architecture Design

We use an encoder-decoder model and use context for learning sentence representations in an unsupervised fashion. Since the decoder won't be used after training, and the quality of the generated sequences is not our main focus, it is important to study the design of the decoder. Generally, a fast training algorithm is preferred; thus proposing a new decoder with high training efficiency and also strong transferability is crucial for an encoder-decoder model.

3.1 CNN as the decoder

Our design of the decoder is basically a 3-layer ConvNet that predicts all words in the target sequence at once. In contrast, existing work, such as skip-thoughts (Kiros et al., 2015), and CNN-LSTM (Gan et al., 2017), use autoregressive RNNs as the decoders. As known, an autoregressive model is good at generating sequences with high quality, such as language and speech. However, an autoregressive decoder seems to be unnecessary in an encoder-decoder model for learning sentence representations, since it won't be used after training, and it takes up a large portion of the training time to compute the output and the gradient. Therefore, we conducted experiments to test the necessity of using an autoregressive decoder in learning sentence representations, and we had two findings.

Decoder	SICK-R	SICK-E	STS14	MSRP (Acc/F1)	SST	TREC
auto-regressive RNN as decoder						
Teacher-Forcing	0.8530	82.6	0.51/0.50	74.1 / 81.7	82.5	88.2
Always Sampling	0.8576	83.2	0.55/0.53	74.7 / 81.3	80.6	87.0
Uniform Sampling	0.8559	82.9	0.54/0.53	74.0 / 81.8	81.0	87.4
auto-regressive CNN as decoder						
Teacher-Forcing	0.8510	82.8	0.49/0.48	74.7 / 82.8	81.4	82.6
Always Sampling	0.8535	83.3	0.53/0.52	75.0 / 81.7	81.4	87.6
Uniform Sampling	0.8568	83.4	0.56/0.54	74.7 / 81.4	83.0	88.4
predict-all-words RNN as decoder						
RNN	0.8508	82.8	0.58/0.55	74.2 / 82.8	81.6	88.8
predict-all-words CNN as decoder						
CNN	0.8530	82.6	**0.58/0.56**	**75.6** / 82.9	82.8	89.2
CNN-MaxOnly	0.8465	82.6	0.50/0.47	73.3 / 81.5	79.1	82.2
Double-sized RNN Encoder						
CNN	**0.8631**	**83.9**	0.58/0.55	74.7 / **83.1**	**83.4**	**90.2**
CNN-MaxOnly	0.8485	83.2	0.47/0.44	72.9 / 80.8	82.2	86.6

Table 1: The models here all have a bi-directional GRU as the encoder (dimensionality 300 in each direction). The default way of producing the representation is a concatenation of outputs from a global *mean-pooling* and a global *max-pooling*, while "·-*MaxOnly*" refers to the model with only global max-pooling. Bold numbers are the best results among all presented models. We found that **1)** inputting correct words to an autoregressive decoder is not necessary; **2)** predict-all-words decoders work roughly the same as autoregressive decoders; **3)** mean+max pooling provides stronger transferability than the max-pooling alone does. The table supports our choice of the predict-all-words CNN decoder and the way of producing vector representations from the bi-directional RNN encoder.

Finding I: It is not necessary to input the correct words into an autoregressive decoder for learning sentence representations.

The experimental design was inspired by Bengio et al. (2015). The model we designed for the experiment has a bi-directional GRU as the encoder, and an autoregressive decoder, including both RNN and CNN. We started by analysing the effect of different sampling strategies of the input words on learning an auto-regressive decoder.

We compared three sampling strategies of input words in decoding the target sequence with an autoregressive decoder: (1) **Teacher-Forcing**: the decoder always gets the ground-truth words; (2) **Always Sampling**: at time step t, a word is sampled from the multinomial distribution predicted at time step $t-1$; (3) **Uniform Sampling**: a word is uniformly sampled from the dictionary V, then fed to the decoder at every time step.

The results are presented in Table 1 (top two subparts). As we can see, the three decoding settings do not differ significantly in terms of the performance on selected downstream tasks, with RNN or CNN as the decoder. The results show that, in terms of learning good sentence representations,

the autoregressive decoder doesn't require the correct ground-truth words as the inputs.

Finding II: The model with an autoregressive decoder performs similarly to the model with a predict-all-words decoder.

With **Finding I**, we conducted an experiment to test whether the model needs an autoregressive decoder at all. In this experiment, the goal is to compare the performance of the predict-all-words decoders and that of the autoregressive decoders separate from the RNN/CNN distinction, thus we designed a predict-all-words CNN decoder and RNN decoder. The predict-all-words CNN decoder is described in Section 2, which is a stack of three convolutional layers, and all words are predicted once at the output layer of the decoder. The predict-all-words RNN decoder is built based on our CNN decoder. To keep the number of parameters of the two predict-all-words decoder roughly the same, we replaced the last two convolutional layers with a bidirectional GRU.

The results are also presented in Table 1 (3rd and 4th subparts). The performance of the predict-all-words RNN decoder does not significantly differ from that of any one of the autoregressive RNN decoders, and the same situation can be also observed in CNN decoders.

These two findings indeed support our choice of using a predict-all-words CNN as the decoder, as it brings the model high training efficiency while maintaining strong transferability.

3.2 Mean+Max Pooling

Since the encoder is a bi-directional RNN in our model, we have multiple ways to select/compute on the generated hidden states to produce a sentence representation. Instead of using the last hidden state as the sentence representation as done in skip-thoughts (Kiros et al., 2015) and SDAE (Hill et al., 2016), we followed the idea proposed in Chen et al. (2016). They built a model for supervised training on the SNLI dataset (Bowman et al., 2015) that concatenates the outputs from a global mean pooling over time and a global max pooling over time to serve as the sentence representation, and showed a performance boost on the SNLI task. Conneau et al. (2017) found that the model with global max pooling function provides stronger transferability than the model with a global mean pooling function does.

In our proposed RNN-CNN model, we empirically show that the mean+max pooling provides stronger transferability than the max pooling alone does, and the results are presented in the last two sections of Table 1. The concatenation of a mean-pooling and a max pooling function is actually a parameter-free composition function, and the computation load is negligible compared to all the heavy matrix multiplications in the model. Also, the non-linearity of the max pooling function augments the mean pooling function for constructing a representation that captures a more complex composition of the syntactic information.

3.3 Tying Word Embeddings and Word Prediction Layer

We choose to share the parameters in the word embedding layer of the RNN encoder and the word prediction layer of the CNN decoder. Tying was shown in both Inan et al. (2016) and Press and Wolf (2017), and it generally helped to learn a better language model. In our model, tying also drastically reduces the number of parameters, which could potentially prevent overfitting.

Furthermore, we initialise the word embeddings with pretrained word vectors, such as word2vec (Mikolov et al., 2013) and GloVe (Pennington et al.,

2014), since it has been shown that these pretrained word vectors can serve as a good initialisation for deep learning models, and more likely lead to better results than a random initialisation.

3.4 Study of the Hyperparameters in Our Model Design

We studied hyperparameters in our model design based on three out of 10 downstream tasks, which are SICK-R, SICK-E (Marelli et al., 2014), and STS14 (Agirre et al., 2014). The first model we created, which is reported in Section 2, is a decent design, and the following variations didn't give us much performance change except improvements brought by increasing the dimensionality of the encoder. However, we think it is worth mentioning the effect of hyperparameters in our model design. We present the Table 1 in the supplementary material and we summarise it as follows:

1. Decoding the next sentence performed similarly to decoding the subsequent contiguous words.

2. Decoding the subsequent 30 words, which was adopted from the skip-thought training code[3], gave reasonably good performance. More words for decoding didn't give us a significant performance gain, and took longer to train.

3. Adding more layers into the decoder and enlarging the dimension of the convolutional layers indeed sightly improved the performance on the three downstream tasks, but as training efficiency is one of our main concerns, it wasn't worth sacrificing training efficiency for the minor performance gain.

4. Increasing the dimensionality of the RNN encoder improved the model performance, and the additional training time required was less than needed for increasing the complexity in the CNN decoder. We report results from both smallest and largest models in Table 2.

4 Experiment Settings

The vocabulary for unsupervised training contains the 20k most frequent words in BookCorpus. In order to generalise the model trained with a relatively small, fixed vocabulary to the much larger set of all possible English words, we followed the vocabulary expansion method proposed in Kiros et al. (2015), which learns a linear mapping from the pretrained word vectors to the learnt RNN word

---

[3]https://github.com/ryankiros/skip-thoughts/

Model	Hrs	SICK-R	SICK-E	STS14	MSRP	TREC	MR	CR	SUBJ	MPQA	SST
Measurement		r	Acc.	r/ρ	Acc./F1	Accuracy					
Unsupervised training with unordered sentences											
ParagraphVec	4	-	-	0.42/0.43	72.9/81.1	59.4	60.2	66.9	76.3	70.7	-
word2vec BOW	2	0.8030	78.7	0.65/**0.64**	72.5/81.4	83.6	77.7	**79.8**	90.9	**88.3**	79.7
fastText BOW	-	0.8000	77.9	0.63/0.62	72.4/81.2	81.8	76.5	78.9	**91.6**	87.4	78.8
SIF (GloVe+WR)	-	**0.8603**	**84.6**	**0.69**/ -	- / -	-	-	-	-	-	**82.2**
GloVe BOW	-	0.8000	78.6	0.54/0.56	72.1/80.9	83.6	**78.7**	78.5	**91.6**	87.6	79.8
SDAE	72	-	-	0.37/0.38	**73.7**/80.7	78.4	74.6	78.0	90.8	86.9	-
Unsupervised training with ordered sentences - BookCorpus											
FastSent	2	-	-	**0.63/0.64**	72.2/80.3	76.8	70.8	78.4	88.7	80.6	-
FastSent+AE	2	-	-	0.62/0.62	71.2/79.1	80.4	71.8	76.5	88.8	81.5	-
Skip-thoughts	336	0.8580	82.3	0.29/0.35	73.0/82.0	92.2	76.5	80.1	93.6	87.1	82.0
Skip-thought+LN	720	0.8580	79.5	0.44/0.45	-	88.4	79.4	**83.1**	93.7	89.3	82.9
combine CNN-LSTM	-	0.8618	-	-	**76.5/83.8**	**92.6**	77.8	82.1	93.6	**89.4**	-
small RNN-CNN†	20	0.8530	82.6	0.58/0.56	75.6/82.9	89.2	77.6	80.3	92.3	87.8	82.8
large RNN-CNN†	34	**0.8698**	**85.2**	0.59/0.57	75.1/83.2	92.2	**79.7**	81.9	**94.0**	88.7	**84.1**
Unsupervised training with ordered sentences - Amazon Book Review											
small RNN-CNN†	21	0.8476	82.7	**0.53/0.53**	73.8/81.5	84.8	83.3	83.0	94.7	88.2	87.8
large RNN-CNN†	33	**0.8616**	**84.3**	0.51/0.51	**75.7/82.8**	**90.8**	85.3	86.8	**95.3**	**89.0**	**88.3**
Unsupervised training with ordered sentences - Amazon Review											
BYTE m-LSTM	720	0.7920	-	-	75.0/**82.8**	-	**86.9**	**91.4**	94.6	88.5	-
Supervised training - Transfer learning											
DiscSent	8	-	-	-	75.0/ -	87.2	-	-	93.0	-	-
DisSent Books 8	-	0.8170	81.5	-	-/ -	87.2	**82.9**	81.4	**93.2**	90.0	80.2
CaptionRep BOW	24	-	-	0.46/0.42	-	72.2	61.9	69.3	77.4	70.8	-
DictRep BOW	24	-	-	0.67/**0.70**	68.4/76.8	81.0	76.7	78.7	90.7	87.2	-
InferSent(SNLI)	<24	**0.8850**	84.6	0.68/0.65	75.1/82.3	**88.7**	79.9	84.6	92.1	89.8	83.3
InferSent(AllNLI)	<24	0.8840	**86.3**	**0.70**/0.67	**76.2/83.1**	88.2	81.1	**86.3**	92.4	**90.2**	84.6

Table 2: **Related Work and Comparison.** As presented, our designed asymmetric RNN-CNN model has strong transferability, and is overall better than existing unsupervised models in terms of fast training speed and good performance on evaluation tasks. "†"s refer to our models, and "**small/large**" refers to the dimension of representation as 1200/4800. **Bold** numbers are the best ones among the models with same training and transferring setting, and underlined numbers are best results among all transfer learning models. The training time of each model was collected from the paper that proposed it.

vectors. Thus, the model benefits from the generalisation ability of the pretrained word embeddings.

The downstream tasks for evaluation include semantic relatedness (SICK, Marelli et al. (2014)), paraphrase detection (MSRP, Dolan et al. (2004)), question-type classification (TREC, Li and Roth (2002)), and five benchmark sentiment and subjective datasets, which include movie review sentiment (MR, Pang and Lee (2005), SST, Socher et al. (2013)), customer product reviews (CR, Hu and Liu (2004)), subjectivity/objectivity classification (SUBJ, Pang and Lee (2004)), opinion polarity (MPQA, Wiebe et al. (2005)), semantic textual similarity (STS14, Agirre et al. (2014)), and SNLI (Bowman et al., 2015). After unsupervised training, the encoder is fixed, and applied as a representation

extractor on the 10 tasks.

To compare the effect of different corpora, we also trained two models on Amazon Book Review dataset (without ratings) which is the largest subset of the Amazon Review dataset (McAuley et al., 2015) with 142 million sentences, about twice as large as BookCorpus.

Both training and evaluation of our models were conducted in PyTorch[4], and we used SentEval[5] provided by Conneau et al. (2017) to evaluate the transferability of our models. All the models were trained for the same number of iterations with the same batch size, and the performance was measured at the end of training for each of the models.

[4]http://pytorch.org/
[5]https://github.com/facebookresearch/SentEval

5   Related work and Comparison

Table 2 presents the results on 9 evaluation tasks of our proposed RNN-CNN models, and related work. The "**small RNN-CNN**" refers to the model with the dimension of representation as 1200, and the "**large RNN-CNN**" refers to that as 4800. The results of our "large RNN-CNN" model on SNLI is presented in Table 3.

Model	SNLI (Acc %)
Unsupervised Transfer Learning	
Skip-thoughts (Vendrov et al.)	81.5
large RNN-CNN *BookCorpus*	**81.7**
large RNN-CNN *Amazon*	81.5
Supervised Training	
ESIM (Chen et al.)	86.7
DIIN (Gong et al.)	**88.9**

Table 3: We implemented the same classifier as mentioned in Vendrov et al. (2015) on top of the features computed by our model. Our proposed RNN-CNN model gets similar result on SNLI as skip-thoughts, but with much less training time.

Our work was inspired by analysing the **skip-thoughts** model (Kiros et al., 2015). The skip-thoughts model successfully applied this form of learning from the context information into unsupervised representation learning for sentences, and then, Ba et al. (2016) augmented the LSTM with proposed layer-normalisation (**Skip-thought+LN**), which improved the skip-thoughts model generally on downstream tasks. In contrast, Hill et al. (2016) proposed the **FastSent** model which only learns source and target word embeddings and is an adaptation of **Skip-gram** (Mikolov et al., 2013) to sentence-level learning without word order information. Gan et al. (2017) applied a CNN as the encoder, but still applied LSTMs for decoding the adjacent sentences, which is called **CNN-LSTM**.

Our **RNN-CNN** model falls in the same category as it is an encoder-decoder model. Instead of decoding the surrounding two sentences as in skip-thoughts, FastSent and the compositional CNN-LSTM, our model only decodes the subsequent sequence with a fixed length. Compared with the hierarchical CNN-LSTM, our model showed that, with a proper model design, the context information from the subsequent words is sufficient for learning sentence representations. Particularly, our proposed **small RNN-CNN** model runs roughly three

times faster than our implemented skip-thoughts model[6] on the same GPU machine during training.

Proposed by Radford et al. (2017), **BYTE m-LSTM** model uses a multiplicative LSTM unit (Krause et al., 2016) to learn a language model. This model is simple, providing next-byte prediction, but achieves good results likely due to the extremely large training corpus (Amazon Review data, McAuley et al. (2015)) that is also highly related to many of the sentiment analysis downstream tasks (domain matching).

We experimented with the Amazon Book review dataset, the largest subset of the Amazon Review. This subset is significantly smaller than the full Amazon Review dataset but twice as large as Book-Corpus. Our RNN-CNN model trained on the Amazon Book review dataset resulted in performance improvement on all single-sentence classification tasks relative to that achieved with training under BookCorpus.

Unordered sentences are also useful for learning representations of sentences. **ParagraphVec** (Le and Mikolov, 2014) learns a fixed-dimension vector for each sentence by predicting the words within the given sentence. However, after training, the representation for a new sentence is hard to derive, since it requires optimising the sentence representation towards an objective. **SDAE** (Hill et al., 2016) learns the sentence representations with a denoising auto-encoder model. Our proposed RNN-CNN model trains faster than SDAE does, and also because we utilised the sentence-level continuity as a supervision which SDAE doesn't, our model largely performs better than SDAE.

Another transfer approach is to learn a supervised discriminative classifier by distinguishing whether the sentence pair or triple comes from the same context. Li and Hovy (2014) proposed a model that learns to classify whether the input sentence triplet contains three contiguous sentences. **DiscSent** (Jernite et al., 2017) and **DisSent** (Nie et al., 2017) both utilise the annotated explicit discourse relations, which is also good for learning sentence representations. It is a very promising research direction since the proposed models are generally computational efficient and have clear intuition, yet more investigations need to be done to augment the performance.

Supervised training for transfer learning is

---

[6]We reimplemented the skip-thoughts model in PyTorch, and it took roughly four days to train for only one epoch on BookCorpus.

also promising when a large amount of human-annotated data is accessible. Conneau et al. (2017) proposed the **InferSent** model, which applies a bi-directional LSTM as the sentence encoder with multiple fully-connected layers to classify whether the hypothesis sentence entails the premise sentence in SNLI (Bowman et al., 2015), and MultiNLI (Williams et al., 2017). The trained model demonstrates a very impressive transferability on downstream tasks, including both supervised and unsupervised. Our RNN-CNN model trained on Amazon Book Review data in an unsupervised way has better results on supervised tasks than **InferSent** but slightly inferior results on semantic relatedness tasks. We argue that labelling a large amount of training data is time-consuming and costly, while unsupervised learning provides great performance at a fraction of the cost. It could potentially be leveraged to initialise or more generally augment the costly human labelling, and make the overall system less costly and more efficient.

6 Discussion

In Hill et al. (2016), internal consistency is measured on five single sentence classification tasks (MR, CR, SUBJ, MPQA, TREC), MSRP and STS-14, and was found to be only above the "acceptable" threshold. They empirically showed that models that worked well on supervised evaluation tasks generally didn't perform well on unsupervised ones. This implies that we should consider supervised and unsupervised evaluations separately, since each group has higher internal consistency.

As presented in Table 2, the encoders that only sum over pretrained word vectors perform better overall than those with RNNs on unsupervised evaluation tasks, including STS14. In recent proposed log-bilinear models, such as **FastSent** (Hill et al., 2016) and **SiameseBOW** (Kenter et al., 2016), the sentence representation is composed by summing over all word representations, and the only tunable parameters in the models are word vectors. These resulting models perform very well on unsupervised tasks. By augmenting the pretrained word vectors with a weighted averaging process, and removing the top few principal components, which mainly encode frequently-used words, as proposed in Arora et al. (2017) and Mu et al. (2018), the performance on the unsupervised evaluation tasks gets even better. Prior work suggests that incorporating word-level information helps the model to perform better on cosine distance based semantic textual similarity tasks.

Our model predicts all words in the target sequence at once, without an autoregressive process, and ties the word embedding layer in the encoder with the prediction layer in the decoder, which explicitly uses the word vectors in the target sequence as the supervision in training. Thus, our model incorporates the word-level information by using word vectors as the targets, and it improves the model performance on STS14 compared to other RNN-based encoders.

Arora et al. (2017) conducted an experiment to show that the word order information is crucial in getting better results on supervised tasks. In our model, the encoder is still an RNN, which explicitly utilises the word order information. We believe that the combination of encoding a sentence with its word order information and decoding all words in a sentence independently inherently leverages the benefits from both log-linear models and RNN-based models.

7 Conclusion

Inspired by learning to exploit the contextual information present in adjacent sentences, we proposed an asymmetric encoder-decoder model with a suite of techniques for improving context-based unsupervised sentence representation learning. Since we believe that a simple model will be faster in training and easier to analyse, we opt to use simple techniques in our proposed model, including 1) an RNN as the encoder, and a predict-all-words CNN as the decoder, 2) learning by inferring subsequent contiguous words, 3) mean+max pooling, and 4) tying word vectors with word prediction. With thorough discussion and extensive evaluation, we justify our decision making for each component in our RNN-CNN model. In terms of the performance and the efficiency of training, we justify that our model is a fast and simple algorithm for learning generic sentence representations from unlabelled corpora. Further research will focus on how to maximise the utility of the context information, and how to design simple architectures to best make use of it.

References

Eneko Agirre, Carmen Banea, Claire Cardie, Daniel M. Cer, Mona T. Diab, Aitor Gonzalez-Agirre, Weiwei Guo, Rada Mihalcea, German Rigau, and Janyce Wiebe. 2014. Semeval-2014 task 10: Multilingual semantic textual similarity. In *SemEval@COLING*.

Sanjeev Arora, Yingyu Liang, and Tengyu Ma. 2017. A simple but tough-to-beat baseline for sentence embeddings. In *ICLR*.

Jimmy Ba, Ryan Kiros, and Geoffrey E. Hinton. 2016. Layer normalization. *CoRR*, abs/1607.06450.

Samy Bengio, Oriol Vinyals, Navdeep Jaitly, and Noam Shazeer. 2015. Scheduled sampling for sequence prediction with recurrent neural networks. In *NIPS*.

Samuel R. Bowman, Gabor Angeli, Christopher Potts, and Christopher D. Manning. 2015. A large annotated corpus for learning natural language inference. In *EMNLP*.

Qian Chen, Xiaodan Zhu, Zhenhua Ling, Si Wei, and Hui Jiang. 2016. Enhancing and combining sequential and tree lstm for natural language inference. *arXiv preprint arXiv:1609.06038*.

Junyoung Chung, Caglar Gulcehre, KyungHyun Cho, and Yoshua Bengio. 2014. Empirical evaluation of gated recurrent neural networks on sequence modeling. *arXiv preprint arXiv:1412.3555*.

Alexis Conneau, Douwe Kiela, Holger Schwenk, Loïc Barrault, and Antoine Bordes. 2017. Supervised learning of universal sentence representations from natural language inference data. In *EMNLP*.

William B. Dolan, Chris Quirk, and Chris Brockett. 2004. Unsupervised construction of large paraphrase corpora: Exploiting massively parallel news sources. In *COLING*.

J. R. Firth. 1957. A synopsis of linguistic theory.

Zhe Gan, Yunchen Pu, Ricardo Henao, Chunyuan Li, Xiaodong He, and Lawrence Carin. 2017. Learning generic sentence representations using convolutional neural networks. In *EMNLP*.

Yichen Gong, Heng Luo, and Jian Zhang. 2017. Natural language inference over interaction space. *CoRR*, abs/1709.04348.

Zellig S Harris. 1954. Distributional structure. *Word*, 10(2-3):146–162.

Felix Hill, Kyunghyun Cho, and Anna Korhonen. 2016. Learning distributed representations of sentences from unlabelled data. In *HLT-NAACL*.

Sepp Hochreiter and Juergen Schmidhuber. 1997. Long short-term memory. *Neural Computation*, 9:1735–1780.

Minqing Hu and Bing Liu. 2004. Mining and summarizing customer reviews. In *KDD*.

Hakan Inan, Khashayar Khosravi, and Richard Socher. 2016. Tying word vectors and word classifiers: A loss framework for language modeling. *CoRR*, abs/1611.01462.

Yacine Jernite, Samuel R. Bowman, and David Sontag. 2017. Discourse-based objectives for fast unsupervised sentence representation learning. *CoRR*, abs/1705.00557.

Tom Kenter, Alexey Borisov, and Maarten de Rijke. 2016. Siamese cbow: Optimizing word embeddings for sentence representations. In *ACL*.

Jamie Ryan Kiros, Yukun Zhu, Ruslan Salakhutdinov, Richard S. Zemel, Raquel Urtasun, Antonio Torralba, and Sanja Fidler. 2015. Skip-thought vectors. In *NIPS*.

Ben Krause, Liang Lu, Iain Murray, and Steve Renals. 2016. Multiplicative lstm for sequence modelling. *CoRR*, abs/1609.07959.

Quoc V. Le and Tomas Mikolov. 2014. Distributed representations of sentences and documents. In *ICML*.

Jiwei Li and Eduard H. Hovy. 2014. A model of coherence based on distributed sentence representation. In *EMNLP*.

Xin Li and Dan Roth. 2002. Learning question classifiers. In *COLING*.

Marco Marelli, Stefano Menini, Marco Baroni, Luisa Bentivogli, Raffaella Bernardi, and Roberto Zamparelli. 2014. A sick cure for the evaluation of compositional distributional semantic models. In *LREC*.

Julian J. McAuley, Christopher Targett, Qinfeng Shi, and Anton van den Hengel. 2015. Image-based recommendations on styles and substitutes. In *SIGIR*.

Tomas Mikolov, Ilya Sutskever, Kai Chen, Gregory S. Corrado, and Jeffrey Dean. 2013. Distributed representations of words and phrases and their compositionality. In *NIPS*.

Jiaqi Mu, Suma Bhat, and Pramod Viswanath. 2018. All-but-the-top: Simple and effective postprocessing for word representations. In *ICLR*.

Allen Nie, Erin D. Bennett, and Noah D. Goodman. 2017. Dissent: Sentence representation learning from explicit discourse relations. *CoRR*, abs/1710.04334.

Bo Pang and Lillian Lee. 2004. A sentimental education: Sentiment analysis using subjectivity summarization based on minimum cuts. In *ACL*.

Bo Pang and Lillian Lee. 2005. Seeing stars: Exploiting class relationships for sentiment categorization with respect to rating scales. In *ACL*.

Jeffrey Pennington, Richard Socher, and Christopher D. Manning. 2014. Glove: Global vectors for word representation. In *EMNLP*.

Ofir Press and Lior Wolf. 2017. Using the output embedding to improve language models. In *EACL*.

Alec Radford, Rafal Józefowicz, and Ilya Sutskever. 2017. Learning to generate reviews and discovering sentiment. *CoRR*, abs/1704.01444.

Richard Socher, Alex Perelygin, Jean Wu, Jason Chuang, Christopher D. Manning, Andrew Ng, and Christopher Potts. 2013. Recursive deep models for semantic compositionality over a sentiment treebank. In *EMNLP*.

Shuai Tang, Hailin Jin, Chen Fang, Zhaowen Wang, and Virginia R. de Sa. 2017. Rethinking skip-thought: A neighborhood based approach. In *RepL4NLP, ACL Workshop*.

Peter D. Turney and Patrick Pantel. 2010. From frequency to meaning: Vector space models of semantics. *J. Artif. Intell. Res.*, 37:141–188.

Ivan Vendrov, Jamie Ryan Kiros, Sanja Fidler, and Raquel Urtasun. 2015. Order-embeddings of images and language. *CoRR*, abs/1511.06361.

Janyce Wiebe, Theresa Wilson, and Claire Cardie. 2005. Annotating expressions of opinions and emotions in language. *Language Resources and Evaluation*, 39:165–210.

Adina Williams, Nikita Nangia, and Samuel R. Bowman. 2017. A broad-coverage challenge corpus for sentence understanding through inference. *CoRR*, abs/1704.05426.

Connecting Supervised and Unsupervised Sentence Embeddings

Gil Levi
Tel Aviv University
gil.levi100@gmail.com

Abstract

Representing sentences as numerical vectors while capturing their semantic context is an important and useful intermediate step in natural language processing. Representations that are both general and discriminative can serve as a tool for tackling various NLP tasks.

While common sentence representation methods are unsupervised in nature, recently, an approach for learning universal sentence representation in a supervised setting was presented in (Conneau et al., 2017). We argue that although promising results were obtained, an improvement can be reached by adding various unsupervised constraints that are motivated by auto-encoders and by language models. We show that by adding such constraints, superior sentence embeddings can be achieved. We compare our method with the original implementation and show improvements in several tasks.

1 Introduction

Word embeddings are considered one of the key building blocks in natural language processing and are widely used for various applications (Mikolov et al., 2013; Pennington et al., 2014). While word representations has been successfully used, representing the more complicated and nuanced nature of the next element in the hierarchy - a full sentence - is still considered a challenge. Once trained, universal sentence representations can be used as an out-of-the-box tool for solving various NLP and computer vision problems. Even though their importance is unquestionable, it seems that current results are still far from satisfactory.

More concretely, given a set of sentences $\{s_i\}_{i=1}^n$, sentence embedding methods are designed to map them to some feature space $\mathcal{F}$ along with a distance metric $\mathcal{M}$ such that given two sentences s_i and s_j that have similar semantic meaning, their distance $\mathcal{M}(s_i, s_j)$ would be small. The challenge is learning a mapping $\mathbf{T} : \{s_i\}_{i=1}^n \to \mathcal{F}$ that manages to capture the semantics of each s_i. While sentence embedding are not always used in similarity probing, we find this formulation useful as the similarity assumption is implicitly made when training classifiers on top of the embeddings in downstream tasks.

Sentences embedding methods were mostly trained in an unsupervised setting. In (Le and Mikolov, 2014) the ParagraphVector model was proposed which is trained to predict words in the document. SkipThought (Kiros et al., 2015) vectors rely on the continuity of text to train an encoder-decoder model that tries to reconstruct the surrounding sentences of a given passage. In Sequential Denoising Autoencoders (SDAE) (Hill et al., 2016) high-dimensional input data is corrupted according to some noise function, and the model is trained to recover the original data from the corrupted version. FastSent (Hill et al., 2016) learns to predicts a Bag-Of-Word (BOW) representation of adjacent sentences given a BOW representation of some sentence. In (Klein et al., 2015) a Hybrid Gaussian Laplacian density function is fitted to the sentence to derive Fisher Vectors.

While previous methods train sentence embeddings in an unsupervised manner, a recent work (Conneau et al., 2017) argued that better representations can be achieved via supervised training on a general sentence inference dataset (Bowman et al., 2015). To this end, the authors use the Stanford Natural Language Inference (SNLI) dataset (Bowman et al., 2015) to train different

Proceedings of the 3rd Workshop on Representation Learning for NLP, pages 79–83
Melbourne, Australia, July 20, 2018. ©2018 Association for Computational Linguistics

Method	MR	CR	SUBJ	MPQA	SST	TREC	MRPC	SICK-R	SICK-E	STS14
FastSent	70.8	78.4	88.7	80.6	-	76.8	72.2/80.3	-	-	.63/.64
SkipThought	76.5	80.1	**93.6**	87.1	82.0	**92.2**	73.0/82.0	0.858	82.3	.29/.35
BiLSTM	79.9	84.6	92.1	89.8	83.3	88.7	75.1/82.3	0.885	86.3	**.68/.65**
AE Reg	79.0	84.4	91.8	90.0	82.4	88.8	75.0/82.4	**0.888**	86.8	.66/.65
LM Reg	79.1	**85.3**	92.2	**90.2**	83.6	87.6	75.7/**82.8**	**0.888**	86.3	.66/.65
Combined	**80.04**	84.56	91.96	90.19	**84.07**	87.8	74.84/82.34	0.888	86.44	.67/.65
Bi-AE Reg	**79.9**	84.1	92.1	**90.2**	83.8	89	**75.9**/82.6	**0.888**	**87.7**	.66/.65
Bi-LM Reg	79.1	84.6	91.2	90.0	82.6	89.4	74.4/81.8	**0.888**	86.4	.66/.64

Table 1: **Sentence embedding results.** BiLSTM refers to the original BiLSTM followed by Max-Pooling implementation of (Conneau et al., 2017) which is the baseline for our work. AE Reg and LM Reg refers to the Auto-Encoder and Language-Model regularization terms described in 2.1 and Combined refers to optimizing with both terms. Bi-AE Reg and Bi-LM Reg refers to the bi-directional Auto-Encoder and bi-directional Language-Model regularization terms described in 2.2. As evident from the results, adding simple unsupervised regularization terms improves the results of the model on almost all the evaluated tasks.

sentence embedding methods and compare them on various benchmarks. The SNLI dataset is composed of 570K pairs of sentences with a label depicting the relationship between them, which can be either 'neutral', 'contradiction' or 'entailment'. The authors show that by leveraging the dataset, state-of-the-art representations can be obtained which are universal and general enough for solving various NLP tasks.

A different, unsupervised, task in NLP is estimating the probability of word sequences. A family of algorithms for this task titled *word language models* seek to model the problem as estimating the probability of a word, given the previous words in the text. In (Bengio et al., 2003) neural networks were employed and (Mikolov et al., 2010) was among the first methods to use recurrent neural networks (RNN) for modeling the problem, where the probability of the a word is estimated based on the previous words fed to the RNN. A variant of RNN - Long Short Term Memory (LSTM) networks (Hochreiter and Schmidhuber, 1997) - were used in (Sundermeyer et al., 2012). Following that, (Zaremba et al., 2014) proposed a dropout augmented LSTM.

We note that there exists a connection between those two problems and try to model it more explicitly. Recently, the incorporation of the hidden states of neural language models in downstream supervised-learning models have been shown to improve the results of the latter (e.g. ElMo - Peters et al. (2018), CoVe - McCann et al. (2017) Peters et al. (2017), Salant and Berant (2017)) – in this work we jointly train the unsupervised

and supervised tasks. To this end, we incorporate unsupervised regularization terms motivated by language modeling and auto-encoders in the training framework proposed by (Conneau et al., 2017). We test our proposed model on a set of NLP tasks and show improved results over the baseline framework of (Conneau et al., 2017).

2 Method

Our approach builds upon the previous work of (Conneau et al., 2017). Specifically, we use their BiLSTM model with max pooling. More concretely, given a sequence of T words, $\{w_t\}_{t=1,...,T}$ with given word embedding (Mikolov et al., 2013; Pennington et al., 2014) $\{v_t\}_{t=1,...,T}$,a bidirectional LSTM computes a set of T vectors $\{h_t\}_{t=1,...,T}$ where each h_t is the concatenation of a forward LSTM and a backward LSTM that read the sentences in two opposite directions. We denote $\{\overrightarrow{h_t}\}$ and $\{\overleftarrow{h_t}\}$ as the hidden states of the left and right LSTM's respectively, where $t = 1, \ldots, T$. The final sentence representation is obtained by taking the maximal value of each dimension of the $\{h_t\}$ hidden units (i.e.: max pooling). The original model of (Conneau et al., 2017) was trained on the SNLI dataset in a supervised fashion - given pairs of sentences s_1 and s_2, denote their representation by $\bar{s}_1$ and $\bar{s}_2$. During training, the concatenation of $\bar{s}_1$, $\bar{s}_2$, $|\bar{s}_1 - \bar{s}_2|$ and $\bar{s}_1 * \bar{s}_2$ is fed to a three layer fully connected network followed by a softmax classifier.

2.1 Regularization terms

We note that by training on SNLI, the model might overfit and would not be general enough to provide universal sentence embedding. We devise several regularization criteria that incentivize the hidden states to maintain more information about the input sequence.

Specifically, denote the dimension of the word embedding by d and the dimension of the hidden state by l. We add a linear transformation layer $L_{l \times d} : H \rightarrow W$ on top of the BiLSTM to transform the hidden states back to the dimension of word embeddings and denote its output by $\{w'_t\}_{t=1,\dots,T}$. Recall that in the training process, we minimize the log-likelihood loss of the fully connected network predictions which we denote by y_i where y_{gt} is the prediction score given to the correct ground truth class. Now, the total loss criteria with our regularization term can be written as

$$\mathcal{L} = -log \left(\frac{e^{y_{gt}}}{\sum_j e^{y_j}} \right) + \lambda \sum_{t=1}^{T} \|w'_t - w_t\|^2 \quad (1)$$

or as

$$\mathcal{L} = -log \left(\frac{e^{y_{gt}}}{\sum_j e^{y_j}} \right) + \lambda \sum_{t=1}^{T-1} \|w'_t - w_{t+1}\|^2$$
$$(2)$$

where the first term in both (1) and (2) is the original classification loss. We call the second regularization term in (1) an *auto-encoder regularization* term and in (2) a *language model regularization* term. Intuitively, since each w'_t is obtained by a linear transformation of h_t, it enforces the hidden state h_t to maintain enough information on each w_t such it can be reconstructed back from h_t or such that the following word w_{t+1} can be predicted from h_t. This aids in obtaining a more general sentence representation and mitigates the risk of overfitting to the SNLI training set. The constant λ in (1) and (2) is a hyper-parameter that controls the amount of regularization and was set to 1 in our experiments.

We have also experimented with combining the two terms, giving equal weight to each of them in optimizing the model.

2.2 Bi-directional Regularization terms

Similarly to regularization terms described in 2.1, we devise variants of (1) and (2) which take into account the bi-directional architecture of the model. Here, we add two linear transformation layers: $\overrightarrow{L}_{\frac{l}{2} \times d} : \overrightarrow{H} \rightarrow W$ and $\overleftarrow{L}_{\frac{l}{2} \times d} : \overleftarrow{H} \rightarrow W$ on top of the forward LSTM and backward LSTM, respectively, and denote their output as $\{\overrightarrow{w}'_t\}$ and $\{\overleftarrow{w}'_t\}$, respectively, where $t = 1, \dots, T$.

Now, equations (1) and (2) are re-written as:

$$\mathcal{L} = -log \left(\frac{e^{y_{gt}}}{\sum_j e^{y_j}} \right) + \lambda_1 \sum_{t=1}^{T} \|\overrightarrow{w}'_t - w_t\|^2 \quad (3)$$
$$+ \lambda_2 \sum_{t=1}^{T} \|\overleftarrow{w}'_t - w_t\|^2$$

and

$$\mathcal{L} = -log \left(\frac{e^{y_{gt}}}{\sum_j e^{y_j}} \right) + \lambda_1 \sum_{t=1}^{T-1} \|\overrightarrow{w}'_t - w_{t+1}\|^2$$
$$(4)$$
$$+ \lambda_2 \sum_{t=2}^{T} \|\overleftarrow{w}'_t - w_{t-1}\|^2$$

We call the second regularization term in (3) a *bi-directional auto-encoder regularization* and in (4) a *bi-directional language model regularization* term. Again, λ_1 and λ_2 are hyper-parameters controlling the amount of regularization and were set to 0.5 in our experiments.

3 Experiments

Following (Conneau et al., 2017) we have tested our approach on a wide array of classification tasks, including sentiment analysis (MR – Pang and Lee (2005), SST – Socher et al. (2013)), question-type (TREC – Li and Roth (2002)), product reviews (CR – Hu and Liu (2004)), subjectivity/objectivity (SUBJ – Pang and Lee (2005)) and opinion polarity (MPQA – Wiebe et al. (2005)). We also tested our approach on semantic textual similarity (STS 14 – Agirre et al. (2014)), paraphrase detection (MRPC – Dolan et al. (2004)), entailment and semantic relatedness tasks (SICK-R and SICK-E – Marelli et al. (2014)), though those tasks are more close in nature to the task of the SNLI dataset which the model was trained on. In our experiments we have set λ from eq. (1) and eq. (2) to be 1 and λ_1, λ_2 from eq. (3) and eq. (4) to be 0.5. All other hyper-parameters and implementation details were left unchanged to provide a fair comparison to the baseline method of (Conneau et al., 2017).

Our results are summarized in table 1. We compared out method against the baseline BiLSTM implementation of (Conneau et al., 2017) and included FastSent (Hill et al., 2016) and SkipThought vectors (Kiros et al., 2015) as a reference.

As evident from table 1 in almost all the tasks evaluated, adding the proposed regularization terms improves performance. This serve to show that in a supervised learning setting, additional information on the input sequence can be leveraged and injected to the model by adding simple unsupervised loss criteria.

4 Conclusions

In our work, we have sought to connect unsupervised and supervised learning in the context of sentence embeddings. Leveraging supervision given by some general task aided in obtaining state-of-the-art sentence representations (Conneau et al., 2017). However, every supervised learning tasks is prone to overfit. In this context, overfitting to the learning task will result in a model which generalizes less well to new tasks.

We alleviate this problem by incorporating unsupervised regularization criteria in the model's loss function which are motivated by auto-encoders and language models. We note that the added regularization terms do come at the price of increasing the model size by ld parameters (where d and l are the dimensions of the word embedding and the LSTM hidden state, respectively) due to the added linear transformation (see 2.1). However, as evident from our results, this does not hinder the model performance, even though we did not increase the amount of training data. Moreover, since those term are unsupervised in nature, it is possible to pre-train the model on unlabeled data and then finetune it on the SNLI dataset.

In conclusion, our experiments show that adding the proposed regularization terms results in a more general model and superior sentence embeddings. This validates our assumption that while the a supervised signal is general enough for learning sentence embeddings, it can be further improved by incorporated a second unsupervised signal.

5 Acknowledgments

We would like to thank Shimi Salant and Ofir Press for their helpful comments.

References

Eneko Agirre, Carmen Banea, Claire Cardie, Daniel Cer, Mona Diab, Aitor Gonzalez-Agirre, Weiwei Guo, Rada Mihalcea, German Rigau, and Janyce Wiebe. 2014. Semeval-2014 task 10: Multilingual semantic textual similarity. In *Proceedings of the 8th international workshop on semantic evaluation (SemEval 2014)*. pages 81–91.

Yoshua Bengio, Réjean Ducharme, Pascal Vincent, and Christian Jauvin. 2003. A neural probabilistic language model. *Journal of machine learning research* 3(Feb):1137–1155.

Samuel R Bowman, Gabor Angeli, Christopher Potts, and Christopher D Manning. 2015. A large annotated corpus for learning natural language inference. *arXiv preprint arXiv:1508.05326* .

Alexis Conneau, Douwe Kiela, Holger Schwenk, Loïc Barrault, and Antoine Bordes. 2017. Supervised learning of universal sentence representations from natural language inference data. In *Proceedings of the 2017 Conference on Empirical Methods in Natural Language Processing*. pages 670–680.

Bill Dolan, Chris Quirk, and Chris Brockett. 2004. Unsupervised construction of large paraphrase corpora: Exploiting massively parallel news sources. In *Proceedings of the 20th international conference on Computational Linguistics*. Association for Computational Linguistics, page 350.

Felix Hill, Kyunghyun Cho, and Anna Korhonen. 2016. Learning distributed representations of sentences from unlabelled data. In *Proceedings of NAACL-HLT*. pages 1367–1377.

Sepp Hochreiter and Jürgen Schmidhuber. 1997. Long short-term memory. *Neural computation* 9(8):1735–1780.

Minqing Hu and Bing Liu. 2004. Mining and summarizing customer reviews. In *Proceedings of the tenth ACM SIGKDD international conference on Knowledge discovery and data mining*. ACM, pages 168–177.

Ryan Kiros, Yukun Zhu, Ruslan R Salakhutdinov, Richard Zemel, Raquel Urtasun, Antonio Torralba, and Sanja Fidler. 2015. Skip-thought vectors. In *Advances in neural information processing systems*. pages 3294–3302.

Benjamin Klein, Guy Lev, Gil Sadeh, and Lior Wolf. 2015. Associating neural word embeddings with deep image representations using fisher vectors. In *Proceedings of the IEEE Conference on Computer Vision and Pattern Recognition*. pages 4437–4446.

Quoc Le and Tomas Mikolov. 2014. Distributed representations of sentences and documents. In *International Conference on Machine Learning*. pages 1188–1196.

Xin Li and Dan Roth. 2002. Learning question classifiers. In *Proceedings of the 19th international conference on Computational linguistics-Volume 1*. Association for Computational Linguistics, pages 1–7.

Marco Marelli, Stefano Menini, Marco Baroni, Luisa Bentivogli, Raffaella Bernardi, Roberto Zamparelli, et al. 2014. A sick cure for the evaluation of compositional distributional semantic models. In *LREC*. pages 216–223.

Bryan McCann, James Bradbury, Caiming Xiong, and Richard Socher. 2017. Learned in translation: Contextualized word vectors. In *Advances in Neural Information Processing Systems*. pages 6297–6308.

Tomas Mikolov, Martin Karafiát, Lukas Burget, Jan Cernocký, and Sanjeev Khudanpur. 2010. Recurrent neural network based language model. In *Interspeech*. volume 2, page 3.

Tomas Mikolov, Ilya Sutskever, Kai Chen, Greg S Corrado, and Jeff Dean. 2013. Distributed representations of words and phrases and their compositionality. In *Advances in neural information processing systems*. pages 3111–3119.

Bo Pang and Lillian Lee. 2005. Seeing stars: Exploiting class relationships for sentiment categorization with respect to rating scales. In *Proceedings of the 43rd annual meeting on association for computational linguistics*. Association for Computational Linguistics, pages 115–124.

Jeffrey Pennington, Richard Socher, and Christopher Manning. 2014. Glove: Global vectors for word representation. In *Proceedings of the 2014 conference on empirical methods in natural language processing (EMNLP)*. pages 1532–1543.

Matthew Peters, Waleed Ammar, Chandra Bhagavatula, and Russell Power. 2017. Semi-supervised sequence tagging with bidirectional language models. In *Proceedings of the 55th Annual Meeting of the Association for Computational Linguistics (Volume 1: Long Papers)*. volume 1, pages 1756–1765.

Matthew E Peters, Mark Neumann, Mohit Iyyer, Matt Gardner, Christopher Clark, Kenton Lee, and Luke Zettlemoyer. 2018. Deep contextualized word representations. *arXiv preprint arXiv:1802.05365* .

Shimi Salant and Jonathan Berant. 2017. Contextualized word representations for reading comprehension. *arXiv preprint arXiv:1712.03609* .

Richard Socher, Alex Perelygin, Jean Wu, Jason Chuang, Christopher D Manning, Andrew Ng, and Christopher Potts. 2013. Recursive deep models for semantic compositionality over a sentiment treebank. In *Proceedings of the 2013 conference on empirical methods in natural language processing*. pages 1631–1642.

Martin Sundermeyer, Ralf Schlüter, and Hermann Ney. 2012. Lstm neural networks for language modeling. In *Thirteenth Annual Conference of the International Speech Communication Association*.

Janyce Wiebe, Theresa Wilson, and Claire Cardie. 2005. Annotating expressions of opinions and emotions in language. *Language resources and evaluation* 39(2-3):165–210.

Wojciech Zaremba, Ilya Sutskever, and Oriol Vinyals. 2014. Recurrent neural network regularization. *arXiv preprint arXiv:1409.2329* .

A Hybrid Learning Scheme for Chinese Word Embedding

Wenfan Chen[1] and **Weiguo Sheng**[2,*]

[1] School of Computer Science and Technology, Zhejiang University of Technology, Hangzhou, P.R.China
[2] Department of Computer Science, Hangzhou Normal University, Hangzhou, P.R.China

Abstract

To improve word embedding, subword information has been widely employed in state-of-the-art methods. These methods can be classified to either compositional or predictive models. In this paper, we propose a hybrid learning scheme, which integrates compositional and predictive model for word embedding. Such a scheme can take advantage of both models, thus effectively learning word embedding. The proposed scheme has been applied to learn word representation on Chinese. Our results show that the proposed scheme can significantly improve the performance of word embedding in terms of analogical reasoning and is robust to the size of training data.

1 Introduction

Word embedding, also known as distributed word representation, represents a word as a real-valued low-dimensional vector and encodes its semantic meaning into the vector. It is a fundamental task of natural language processing (NLP), such as language modeling (Bengio et al., 2003; Mnih and Hinton, 2009), machine translation (Bahdanau et al., 2014; Sutskever et al., 2014), caption generation (Xu et al., 2015; Devlin et al., 2015) and question answering (Hermann et al., 2015).

Most previous word embedding methods suffer from high computational complexity and have difficulty to be applied to large-scale corpora. Recently, Continuous Bag-Of-Words (CBOW) and Skip-Gram (SG) models (Mikolov et al., 2013a), which can alleviate the above issue, have received much attention. However, these models take a word as a basic unit but ignore rich subword information, which could significantly limit their performance. To improve the performance of word embedding, subword information, such as

morphemes and character n-grams, has been employed (Luong et al., 2013; Qiu et al., 2014; Cao and Rei, 2016; Sun et al., 2016a; Wieting et al., 2016; Bojanowski et al., 2017). While these methods are effective, they are originally developed for alphabetic writing systems and can't be applied directly to other writing systems, like Chinese.

In Chinese, each word typically consists of less characters than in English[1], while each character can have a complicated structure of its meaning. Typically, a Chinese character can be decomposed into components (部), where each component has its own meaning. The internal semantic meaning of a Chinese word emerges from such a structure. For example, the Chinese word "海水 (seawater)" is composed by "海 (sea)" and "水 (water)". The semantic component of "海 (sea)" is "氵", which is the transformation of "水 (water)" and indicates it is related to "水 (water)". Therefore, the word "海水 (seawater)" has the meaning of "water from the sea".

Based on the linguistic feature of Chinese, recent methods have used subword information to improve Chinese word embedding. For example, Chen et al. (2015) proposed a character-enhanced word embedding (CWE) model, which departed from CBOW of representing context words with both character embeddings and word embeddings. Shi et al. (2015) proposed a radical embedding method, which used the CBOW framework but replacing word embeddings with radical embeddings. Yin et al. (2016) and Xu et al. (2016) extended the CWE model in different ways: the former presented a multi-granularity embedding (MGE) model, additionally using the embeddings associated with radicals detected in the target word; the latter proposed a similarity-based character-enhanced word embedding (SCWE) model, considering the similarity between a word and its

---

* Corresponding author. E-mail: w.sheng@ieee.org

[1] https://en.wikipedia.org/wiki/Written_Chinese

Proceedings of the 3rd Workshop on Representation Learning for NLP, pages 84–90
Melbourne, Australia, July 20, 2018. ©2018 Association for Computational Linguistics

component characters. Yu et al. (2017) introduced a joint learning word embedding (JWE) model, which jointly learned embeddings for words, characters and components, and predicted the target word, respectively. Cao et al. (2018), on the other hand, represented Chinese words as sequences of strokes[2] and learned word embedding with stroke n-grams information.

The above methods can be divided into two types: compositional and predictive model. The compositional model composes rich information into one vector to predict the target word. In this type of model, information works in a cooperative manner for word embedding. By contrast, the predictive model decouples various information to predict the target word. The information in this type of model works competitively for word embedding. Both models can effectively learn word embedding and give good estimation for rare and unseen words. By combining richer information, the compositional model can more accurately represent the target word. However, information is usually composed in a sophisticated way. The predictive model, on the other hand, is simple and can directly capture the interaction between words and their internal information. This type of model, however, typically ignores the interrelationship between various information.

To take advantage of both models, in this paper, we propose a hybrid learning scheme for word embedding. The proposed scheme learns word embedding in a competitive and cooperative manner. Specifically, in our scheme, the decoupled representations are used to capture the semantic meaning of target word respectively while making their composition semantically consistent with the target word. The performance of proposed scheme has been evaluated on Chinese in terms of word similarity and analogy tasks. The results show that our proposed scheme can effectively learn word representation and is robust to the size of training data.

2 Proposed Scheme

In this section, we present the details of our proposed hybrid learning scheme for word embedding. We denote the proposed scheme as **Co-Opetition Word Embedding (COWE)**. It consists of predictive and compositional parts, which will be described in subsection 2.1 and subsection 2.2,

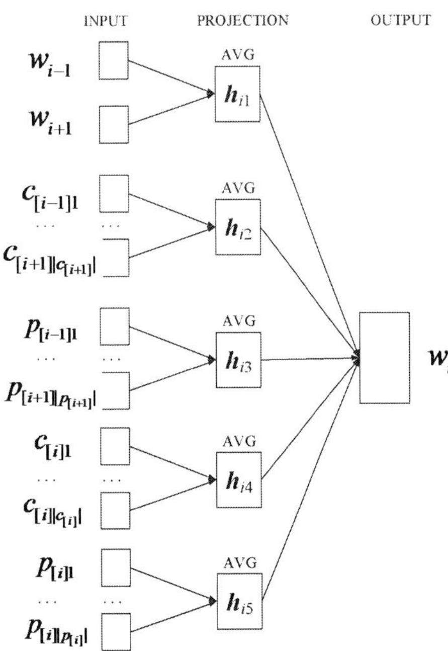

Figure 1: Illustration of the predictive part of COWE.

respectively. This is followed by describing the objective function.

The meaning of notation used in this section is as follows. We denote the training corpus as $\mathcal{D}$, word vocabulary as $\mathcal{W}$, character vocabulary as $\mathcal{C}$, components vocabulary as $\mathcal{P}$. Each word $w \in \mathcal{W}$, character $c \in \mathcal{C}$ and component $p \in \mathcal{P}$ are associated with vectors $w \in \mathbb{R}^d$, $c \in \mathbb{R}^d$, $p \in \mathbb{R}^d$, respectively, where d is the vector dimension. The characters and components in word w_i are denoted as $c_{[i]}$ and $p_{[i]}$, where $|c_{[i]}|$ and $|p_{[i]}|$ denote the number of characters and components in w_i, respectively.

2.1 Predictive Part

In the predictive part, the compositions of context words, characters and components as well as compositions of characters and components in target word are used to predict the target word, as illustrated in Figure 1. These separate predictions by various compositions can be considered as competitions for the semantic meaning of target word. In order to maintain similar length between different compositions, COWE uses an average operation as the composition operation.

---

[2] https://en.wikipedia.org/wiki/Stroke_(CJKV_character)

The goal of this part is to maximize the sum of log likelihoods of all predictive conditional probabilities:

$$\mathcal{L}_p(w_i) = \sum_{k=1}^{5} \log p(w_i|h_{ik}),\qquad(1)$$

where h_{i1}, h_{i2}, h_{i3}, h_{i4} and h_{i5} correspond to the above mentioned five compositions, respectively. Here, h_{i1} is defined as:

$$h_{i1} = \frac{1}{2N}\sum_{-N\leq j\leq N, j\neq 0} w_{i+j}.\qquad(2)$$

where N is the context window size. h_{i2}, h_{i3}, h_{i4} and h_{i5} are defined in a similar way. The conditional probability is defined using a softmax function as:

$$p(w_i|h_{ik}) = \frac{\exp(w_i \cdot h_{ik})}{\sum_{w_{i'}\in W}\exp(w_{i'} \cdot h_{ik})},\ \ k = 1,2,3,4,5.\ (3)$$

This objective function is similar to the one used in JWE (Yu et al., 2017). The main difference is that we further decouple components in the context words and target word, and leverage characters in the target word in addition.

2.2 Compositional Part

In the compositional part, all compositions mentioned above work in a cooperative manner, where their composition is used to predict the target word. We consider the composition as *semantic consistency point* of various representations, and the prediction loss as *consistency loss*, as shown in Figure 2.

The goal of this part is to maximize the following objective function:

$$\mathcal{L}_c(w_i) = \log p(w_i|a_i),\qquad(4)$$

where a_i is the semantic consistency point, and is defined as:

$$a_i = \frac{1}{5}\sum_{k=1}^{5} h_{ik}.\qquad(5)$$

Similar to the predictive part, the conditional probability is defined using the softmax function (see Equation (3)).

2.3 Objective Function

As COWE consists of predictive and compositional parts, its objective function is therefore consisted of the sum of all prediction losses and the consistency loss:

$$\mathcal{L}(\mathcal{D}) = \sum_{w_i\in\mathcal{D}} \mathcal{L}_p(w_i) + \mathcal{L}_c(w_i).\qquad(6)$$

To solve the above optimization problem, we employ the negative sampling technique (Mikolov et al., 2013b). Note that only the consistency loss

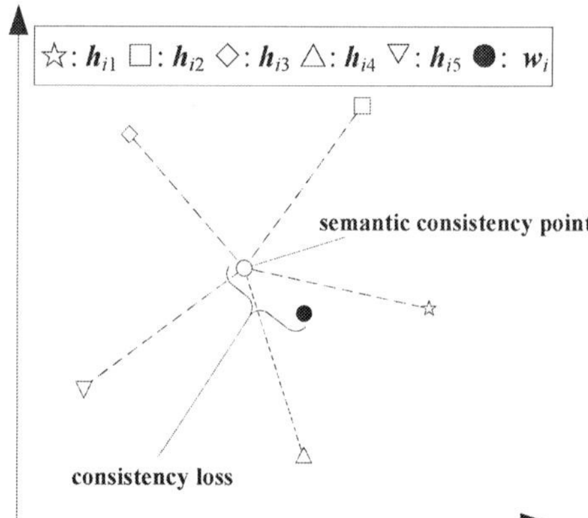

Figure 2: Illustration of the semantic consistency point and the consistency loss.

between semantic consistency point and target word is considered. In preliminary experiments, we also tried the consistency losses between semantic consistency point and sampled negative words, but observed reduced performance.

As a result, the final objective function can be written as:

$$\mathcal{L}(\mathcal{D}) = \sum_{w_i\in\mathcal{D}}\sum_{k=1}^{5}\log\sigma(w_i \cdot h_{ik}) +$$
$$\lambda\mathbb{E}_{\tilde{w}\sim P_{\tilde{W}}}[\sum_{k=1}^{5}\log\sigma(\tilde{w}\cdot h_{ik})] + \log\sigma(w_i \cdot a_i),\qquad(7)$$

where σ is a sigmoid function: $\sigma(x) = 1/(1 + \exp(-x))$, λ is the number of negative words, $\tilde{w}$ is the sampled negative word and $P_{\tilde{W}}$ is the distribution of negative words.

3 Experiments

In this section, we evaluate COWE on Chinese in terms of word similarity computation and analogical reasoning.

3.1 Experimental Settings

We use Chinese Wikipedia dump dated on March 1, 2018[3] for embedding learning, which contains 310K Chinese Wikipedia articles. The data is preprocessed as follows. Firstly, construct training corpus from the Wikipedia dump with `WikiCorpus` in the `gensim` toolkit[4]. Secondly, convert traditional Chinese characters to simplified Chinese characters with the `opencc` toolkit[5]. Thirdly, remove all non-Chinese characters and Chinese words whose frequencies are less than 10

---

[3] https://dumps.wikimedia.org/zhwiki/20180301/
[4] https://radimrehurek.com/gensim/corpora/wikicorpus.html
[5] https://github.com/BYVoid/OpenCC

in the corpus. Finally, perform Chinese word segmentation with THULAC[6] (Sun et al., 2016b). In addition, we perform POS tagging on the training corpus using THULAC and identify all entity names for CWE (Chen et al., 2015), as it does not use the character information for non-compositional words. We use the subword files provided by Yu et al. (2017). As a result, we obtain a 1 GB training corpus with 165,507,601 words, 368,408 unique words, 20,885 unique characters and 13,232 unique components.

We compare COWE with CBOW (Mikolov et al., 2013a)[7], CWE (Chen et al., 2015)[8] and JWE (Yu et al., 2017)[9]. To further evaluate the effect of consistency loss and components, we create two variants of COWE, denoted as COWE-c2 and COWE-p. The former is indeed the JWE model with an additional consistency loss, while the latter is COWE without using component information. The same parameter settings are used for all models. Specifically, the vector dimension is set to 200, the training iteration is set to 100, both the size of context window and number of negative samples are set to 5, the initial learning rate is set to 0.025, and the subsampling threshold is set to 10^{-4}.

3.2 Word Similarity

This task is to evaluate the effectiveness of word embedding in capturing semantic similarity of word pairs. Following Yu et al. (2017), we adopt wordsim-240 and wordsim-296 datasets (Jin and Wu, 2012). Both datasets contain manually-annotated similarity scores for word pairs. In wordsim-240, words in 234 pairs appear in the training corpus, and in wordsim-296, words in 286 pairs appear in the training corpus. Unseen words are removed. The performance of word embedding is evaluated by ranking the pairs according to their cosine similarity and measuring the Spearman correlation ρ with human ratings. The results are shown in Table 1.

The results, on the wordsim-240 dataset, show that CWE performs better than CBOW, but outperformed by all other models. This could indicate the benefits of using rich information. COWE-c2 is not so good as JWE, COWE-p and COWE perform even worse. This suggests that the introduc-

Model	wordsim-240	wordsim-296
CBOW	0.4861	0.5658
CWE	0.5151	0.5684
JWE	**0.5496**	**0.6355**
COWE-c2	0.5473	0.5899
COWE-p	0.5180	0.5844
COWE	0.5412	0.5674

Table 1: Results on word similarity evaluation.

tion of consistency loss, to some extent, may limit the performance of word representation. This may be due to the fact that our average semantic consistency point considers the contributions of various representations equally. With the evolution of history, however, meanings of some Chinese characters or components have degraded, making them less expressive. We plan to investigate the composition operation further in future work.

3.3 Word Analogy

This task is to evaluate the effectiveness of word embedding in capturing semantic relations between pairs of words. The goal is to answer the analogy questions of the form "a is to a* as b is to b*", where b* is hidden, and must be reasoned out from the vocabulary. We use the Chinese word analogy dataset provided by Chen et al. (2015). It consists of 1,124 analogy questions, categorized into 3 types: 1) capitals of countries (677 groups), 2) capitals of provinces/states (175 groups), and 3) family relationships (272 groups). The analogy questions are answered using 3CosAdd (Mikolov et al., 2013a) as well as 3CosMul (Levy and Goldberg, 2014)[10]. We abbreviate the two methods as "Add" and "Mul", respectively. The evaluation metric for this task is the percentage of questions for which the argmax result is the correct answer b*. The results are shown in Table 2[11].

It can be found that CBOW performs better than CWE and JWE on the Capital and Family tasks. This is due to that using internal information improperly could be harmful in cases where words are non-compositional or irrelevant words sharing similar internal structures. For example, the words "儿子 (son)" and "妻子 (wife)" share the same character "子", which means "son" in the former but makes no sense in the latter. We observe that COWE-c2 achieves the best results

---

[6] http://thulac.thunlp.org/
[7] https://code.google.com/archive/p/word2vec/
[8] https://github.com/Leonard-Xu/CWE
[9] https://github.com/HKUST-KnowComp/JWE

[10] https://bitbucket.org/omerlevy/hyperwords
[11] The results do not agree with that reported in (Yu et al., 2017). We suggest that these discrepancies stem from differences in training corpus and parameter settings.

Model	Capital Add/Mul	State Add/Mul	Family Add/Mul
CBOW	87.00/85.82	93.14/92.00	76.84/73.90
CWE	86.71/85.08	91.43/90.29	75.74/70.96
JWE	86.12/83.90	**94.29/94.29**	70.96/69.49
COWE-c2	83.16/83.31	90.29/86.29	**77.94/74.63**
COWE-p	**87.74**/85.82	92.57/**94.29**	73.16/69.85
COWE	85.82/**86.12**	94.29/93.71	76.10/74.26

Table 2: Results on word analogy evaluation.

on the Family task and outperforms JWE by large margins. This shows the effectiveness of consistency loss in helping with learning from various information. COWE-p and COWE perform best on the other tasks, respectively. The fact suggests that different information could help in different ways.

3.4 Performance on Low-Resource Corpora

To evaluate the performance of different models on low-resource corpora, we conduct the same experiments on 5%, 10% and 20% randomly selected Wikipedia articles, respectively. As less training data introducing more noises, this makes it more difficult for models to learn good word representations. The results are shown in Table 3.

The results indicate the superiority of our models on low-resource corpora. We observe that as the size of dataset decreases, the performance of baselines drops rapidly, while the performance decrement of COWE and its variants is much smaller. This shows the robustness of our proposed models. COWE-p is generally more robust than COWE-c2, however, COWE-c2 performs more robustly on the Family task. Taking both characters and components into account, COWE achieves the most robust results.

We also observe that on the Capital task, the performance of CWE and JWE drops more quick than CBOW, which agrees with the previous findings. However, with the consistency loss, COWE-c2 always performs better than JWE, and usually outperforms CBOW. We believe that the consistency loss, in cases where some embeddings are useless, would encourage weak embeddings to close to strong embeddings, letting weak embeddings acquire some helpful features, and prevent strong embeddings from overfitting. On the State and Family tasks, where the character and component embeddings could be useful, all of our models still outperform the baselines by large margins. This should be due to the fact that the consistency

Model	Capital Add/Mul	State Add/Mul	Family Add/Mul
CBOW	57.46/52.14	28.00/23.43	34.19/29.04
CWE	51.99/47.12	36.00/31.43	16.18/13.60
JWE	44.76/40.77	49.14/44.57	31.99/27.57
COWE-c2	61.74/58.64	67.43/65.14	**44.49**/35.29
COWE-p	**79.17**/77.40	80.00/81.71	37.87/37.50
COWE	78.14/**79.03**	**81.71**/82.86	41.91/**41.18**

(a) 5% Wikipedia articles

Model	Capital Add/Mul	State Add/Mul	Family Add/Mul
CBOW	73.12/69.42	54.29/50.29	48.90/43.38
CWE	66.03/64.40	54.29/53.14	39.71/37.13
JWE	63.81/63.22	62.86/58.29	40.07/36.40
COWE-c2	70.16/67.50	77.71/73.14	59.19/56.62
COWE-p	77.70/**78.58**	79.43/**80.00**	54.78/52.21
COWE	**78.43**/78.58	**80.00**/77.71	**60.29/56.99**

(b) 10% Wikipedia articles

Model	Capital Add/Mul	State Add/Mul	Family Add/Mul
CBOW	70.75/68.39	69.71/64.57	59.19/54.78
CWE	67.80/65.58	66.29/63.43	50.00/44.49
JWE	70.46/69.28	81.71/78.86	48.90/48.16
COWE-c2	74.89/72.97	**90.29/87.43**	**59.93/56.25**
COWE-p	81.83/81.83	89.71/86.86	58.46/54.78
COWE	**84.79/83.60**	87.43/86.86	58.46/55.51

(c) 20% Wikipedia articles

Table 3: Results on word analogy evaluation, trained on 5%/10%20% Wikipedia articles.

loss prevents various learned embeddings from contradicting each other, thus making all of them close to the true target word embedding.

3.5 Case Study

To gain a better understanding of the quality of learned word embedding, we take the word "癌症 (cancer)" as an example and show its nearest neighbors in Table 4, where cosine similarity is used as the distance metric.

All words yielded by different models are disease-related. Specifically, words yielded by CWE contain the character "癌 (cancer)", including some weird words, like "国家癌症 (national cancer)" and "抑癌 (anti-cancer)"[12]. This implies that CWE has overused the internal information. For

---

[12] Translation by Google Translate.

CWE	JWE	COWE
肾癌	肺癌	肺癌
(renal cr)	(lung cr)	(lung cr)
癌病	肝癌	并发症
(cr)	(liver cr)	(complication)
肺癌	癌	癌
(lung cr)	(cr)	(cr)
胰腺癌	胃癌	白血病
(pancreatic cr)	(gastric cr)	(leukemia)
国家癌症	白血病	乳腺癌
(national cr)	(leukemia)	(breast cr)
抑癌	肺结核	胃癌
(anti-cr)	(tuberculosis)	(gastric cr)
肝癌	胰腺癌	肝癌
(liver cr)	(pancreatic cr)	(liver cr)
脑癌	肺炎	肺结核
(brain cr)	(pneumonia)	(tuberculosis)
胰脏腺癌	心脏病	大肠癌
(pancreatic cr)	(heart disease)	(colorectal cr)
癌	并发症	肺炎
(cr)	(complication)	(pneumonia)

Table 4: Nearest neighbors of "癌症 (cancer)". "cr" is abbreviation for "cancer".

JWE and COWE, which directly capture the interaction between the words and their internal information, they yield disease-related words that do not contain the component "疒", such as "肺结核 (pneumonia)". This indicates that they make full use of external and internal information, and avoid the above issue. Compared to JWE, COWE yields more words that are semantically relevant to the target word.

4 Conclusion

This paper proposes a scheme, which combines predictive and compositional models to jointly learn various word representations in a competitive and cooperative manner. The predictive part of the proposed scheme is based on various external and internal information, which is used to capture corresponding representation. In the compositional part, the semantic consistency point and the consistency loss are introduced. They connect separate learned representations and prevent them from contradicting each other. The experimental results show that the proposed scheme outperforms baseline models on word analogy tasks and achieves competitive results on word similarity tasks. The results also show that our model is robust to the size of training data. Therefore, our proposed scheme is suitable to be applied on low-resource corpora, for example task-specific corpora, where data is often very scarce.

Acknowledgements

This work was supported by the National Natural Science Foundation of China (Grant Nos. 61573316). We also thank Yuehua Wan and Xiaoxu Wu for their help and very valuable feedback.

References

Dzmitry Bahdanau, Kyunghyun Cho, and Yoshua Bengio. 2014. Neural Machine Translation by Jointly Learning to Align and Translate. *arXiv preprint arXiv:1409.0473*:1–15, September.

Yoshua Bengio, Réjean Ducharme, Pascal Vincent, and Christian Janvin. 2003. A Neural Probabilistic Language Model. *The Journal of Machine Learning Research*, 3:1137–1155.

Piotr Bojanowski, Edouard Grave, Armand Joulin, and Tomas Mikolov. 2017. Enriching Word Vectors with Subword Information. *Transactions of the Association for Computational Linguistics*, 5(1):135–146. http://aclweb.org/anthology/Q17-1010

Kris Cao and Marek Rei. 2016. A Joint Model for Word Embedding and Word Morphology. In *Proceedings of the 1st Workshop on Representation Learning for NLP*, pages 18–26. Association for Computational Linguistics. https://doi.org/10.18653/v1/W16-1603

Shaosheng Cao, Wei Lu, Jun Zhou, and Xiaolong Li. 2018. cw2vec: Learning Chinese Word Embeddings with Stroke n-gram Information. In *Proceedings of the 32th AAAI Conference on Artificial Intelligence*, pages 1–8.

Xinxiong Chen, Lei Xu, Zhiyuan Liu, Maosong Sun, and Huanbo Luan. 2015. Joint learning of character and word embeddings. In *Proceedings of the 24th International Conference on Artificial Intelligence*, pages 1236–1242.

Jacob Devlin, Hao Cheng, Hao Fang, Saurabh Gupta, Li Deng, Xiaodong He, Geoffrey Zweig, and Margaret Mitchell. 2015. Language Models for Image Captioning: The Quirks and What Works. In *Proceedings of the 53rd Annual Meeting of the Association for Computational Linguistics and the 7th International Joint Conference on Natural Language Processing (Volume 2: Short Papers)*, pages 100–105, A Neural Probabilistic Language Model. Association for Computational Linguistics. https://doi.org/10.3115/v1/P15-2017

Karl Moritz Hermann, Tomáš Kočiský, Edward Grefenstette, Lasse Espeholt, Will Kay, Mustafa Suleyman, and Phil Blunsom. 2015. Teaching Machines to Read and Comprehend. In *Proceedings of the 28th International Conference on Neural Information Processing Systems*, pages 1693–1701. June.

Peng Jin and Yunfang Wu. 2012. SemEval-2012 Task 4: Evaluating Chinese Word Similarity. In **SEM 2012: The First Joint Conference on Lexical and Computational Semantics -- Volume 1: Proceedings of the main conference and the shared task, and Volume 2: Proceedings of the Sixth International Workshop on Semantic Evaluation (SemEval 2012)*, pages 374–377. Association for Computational Linguistics. http://www.aclweb.org/anthology/S12-1049

Omer Levy and Yoav Goldberg. 2014. Linguistic Regularities in Sparse and Explicit Word Representations. In *Proceedings of the Eighteenth Conference on Computational Natural Language Learning*, pages 171–180. Association for Computational Linguistics. https://doi.org/10.3115/v1/W14-1618

Minh-Thang Luong, Richard Socher, and Christopher D. Manning. 2013. Better Word Representations with Recursive Neural Networks for Morphology. In *Proceedings of the Seventeenth Conference on Computational Natural Language Learning*, pages 104–113. http://www.aclweb.org/anthology/W13-3512

Tomas Mikolov, Kai Chen, Greg Corrado, and Jeffrey Dean. 2013a. Efficient Estimation of Word Representations in Vector Space. *arXiv preprint arXiv:1301.3781*:1–12, January.

Tomas Mikolov, Ilya Sutskever, Kai Chen, Greg Corrado, and Jeffrey Dean. 2013b. Distributed Representations of Words and Phrases and their Compositionality. *Advances in neural information processing systems*:3111–3119, October.

Andriy Mnih and Geoffrey E. Hinton. 2009. A Scalable Hierarchical Distributed Language Model. In *Advances in neural information processing systems*, pages 1081–1088.

Siyu Qiu, Qing Cui, Jiang Bian, Bin Gao, and Tie-Yan Liu. 2014. Co-learning of Word Representations and Morpheme Representations. In *Proceedings of COLING 2014, the 25th International Conference on Computational Linguistics: Technical Papers*, pages 141–150. Dublin City University and Association for Computational Linguistics. https://www.aclweb.org/anthology/C14-1015

Xinlei Shi, Junjie Zhai, Xudong Yang, Zehua Xie, and Chao Liu. 2015. Radical Embedding: Delving Deeper to Chinese Radicals. In *Proceedings of the 53rd Annual Meeting of the Association for Computational Linguistics and the 7th International Joint Conference on Natural Language Processing (Volume 2: Short Papers)*, pages 594–598. Association for Computational Linguistics. https://doi.org/10.3115/v1/P15-2098

Fei Sun, Jiafeng Guo, Yanyan Lan, Jun Xu, and Xueqi Cheng. 2016a. Inside Out: Two Jointly Predictive Models for Word Representations and Phrase Representations. In *Proceedings of the Thirtieth AAAI Conference on Artificial Intelligence*, pages 2821–2827.

Maosong Sun, Xinxiong Chen, Kaixu Zhang, Zhipeng Guo, Zhiyuan Liu. 2016b. THULAC: An Efficient Lexical Analyzer for Chinese.

Ilya Sutskever, Oriol Vinyals, and Quoc V. Le. 2014. Sequence to Sequence Learning with Neural Networks. In *Proceedings of the 27th International Conference on Neural Information Processing Systems*, pages 3104–3112. September.

John Wieting, Mohit Bansal, Kevin Gimpel, and Karen Livescu. 2016. Charagram: Embedding Words and Sentences via Character n-grams. In *Proceedings of the 2016 Conference on Empirical Methods in Natural Language Processing*, pages 1504–1515. Association for Computational Linguistics. https://doi.org/10.18653/v1/D16-1157

Jian Xu, Jiawei Liu, Liangang Zhang, Zhengyu Li, and Huanhuan Chen. 2016. Improve Chinese Word Embeddings by Exploiting Internal Structure. In *Proceedings of the 2016 Conference of the North American Chapter of the Association for Computational Linguistics: Human Language Technologies*, pages 1041–1050. Association for Computational Linguistics. https://doi.org/10.18653/v1/N16-1119

Kelvin Xu, Jimmy Ba, Ryan Kiros, Kyunghyun Cho, Aaron Courville, Ruslan Salakhutdinov, Richard Zemel, and Yoshua Bengio. 2015. Show, Attend and Tell: Neural Image Caption Generation with Visual Attention. In *International Conference on Machine Learning*, pages 2048–2057.

Rongchao Yin, Quan Wang, Peng Li, Rui Li, and Bin Wang. 2016. Multi-Granularity Chinese Word Embedding. In *Proceedings of the 2016 Conference on Empirical Methods in Natural Language Processing*, pages 981–986. Association for Computational Linguistics. https://doi.org/10.18653/v1/D16-1100

Jinxing Yu, Xun Jian, Hao Xin, and Yangqiu Song. 2017. Joint Embeddings of Chinese Words, Characters, and Fine-grained Subcharacter Components. In *Proceedings of the 2017 Conference on Empirical Methods in Natural Language Processing*, pages 286–291. Association for Computational Linguistics. https://doi.org/10.18653/v1/D17-1027

Unsupervised Random Walk Sentence Embeddings:
A Strong but Simple Baseline

Kawin Ethayarajh

Department of Computer Science, University of Toronto
`kawin@cs.toronto.edu`

Abstract

Using a random walk model of text generation, Arora et al. (2017) proposed a strong baseline for computing sentence embeddings: take a weighted average of word embeddings and modify with SVD. This simple method even outperforms far more complex approaches such as LSTMs on textual similarity tasks. In this paper, we first show that word vector length has a confounding effect on the probability of a sentence being generated in Arora et al.'s model. We propose a random walk model that is robust to this confound, where the probability of word generation is inversely related to the angular distance between the word and sentence embeddings. Our approach beats Arora et al.'s by up to 44.4% on textual similarity tasks and is competitive with state-of-the-art methods. Unlike Arora et al.'s method, ours requires no hyperparameter tuning, which means it can be used when there is no labelled data.

1 Introduction

Distributed representations of words, better known as word embeddings, have become fixtures of current methods in natural language processing. Word embeddings can be generated in a number of ways (Bengio et al., 2003; Collobert and Weston, 2008; Pennington et al., 2014; Mikolov et al., 2013) by capturing the semantics of a word using the contexts it appears in. Recent work has tried to extend that intuition to sequences of words, using methods ranging from a weighted average of word embeddings to convolutional, recursive, and recurrent neural networks (Le and Mikolov, 2014; Kiros et al., 2015; Luong et al., 2013; Tai et al., 2015). Still, Wieting et al. (2016b) found that

these sophisticated architectures are often outperformed, particularly in transfer learning settings, by sentence embeddings generated as a simple average of tuned word embeddings.

Arora et al. (2017) provided a more powerful approach: compute the sentence embeddings as weighted averages of word embeddings, then subtract from each one the vector projection on their first principal component. The weighting scheme, *smoothed inverse frequency* (SIF), is derived from a random walk model where words in a sentence s are produced by the random walk of a latent discourse vector c_s. A word unrelated to c_s can be produced by chance or if it is part of frequent discourse such as stopwords. This approach evens outperforms more complex models such as LSTMs on textual similarity tasks. Arora et al. argued that the simplicity and effectiveness of their method make it a tough-to-beat baseline for sentence embeddings. Though they call their approach unsupervised, others have noted that it is actually 'weakly supervised', since it requires hyperparameter tuning (Cer et al., 2017).

In this paper, we first propose a class of worst-case scenarios for Arora et al.'s (2017) random walk model. Specifically, given some sentence g that is dominated by words with zero similarity, and some sentence h that is dominated by identical words, we show that their approach can return two discourse vectors c_g and c_h such that $p(g|c_g) \approx p(h|c_h)$, provided that the word vectors for g have a sufficiently greater length than those for h. In other words, word vector length has a confounding effect on the probability of a sentence being generated, and this effect can be strong enough to yield completely unintuitive results. This problem is not endemic to these scenarios, though they are the most illustrative of it; because of the underlying log-linear word production model, Arora et al.'s model is fundamentally

Proceedings of the 3rd Workshop on Representation Learning for NLP, pages 91–100
Melbourne, Australia, July 20, 2018. ©2018 Association for Computational Linguistics

sensitive to word vector length.

Our contributions in this paper are three-fold. First, we propose a random walk model that is robust to distortion by vector length, where the probability of a word vector being generated by a discourse vector is inversely related to the angular distance between them. Second, we derive a weighting scheme from this model and compute a MAP estimate for the sentence embedding as follows: normalize the word vectors, take a weighted average of them, and then subtract from each weighted average vector the projection on their first m principal components. We call the weighting scheme derived from our random walk model *unsupervised smoothed inverse frequency* (uSIF). It is similar to SIF (Arora et al., 2017) in practice, but requires no hyperparameter tuning at all – it is completely unsupervised, allowing it to be used when there is no labelled data. Lastly, we show that our approach outperforms Arora et al.'s by up to 44.4% on textual similarity tasks, and is even competitive with state-of-the-art methods. Given the simplicity, effectiveness, and unsupervised nature of our method, we suggest it be used as a baseline for computing sentence embeddings.

2   Related Work

Word Embeddings   Word embeddings are distributed representations of words, typically in a low-dimensional continuous space. These word vectors can capture semantic and lexical properties of words, even allowing some relationships to be captured algebraically (e.g., $v_{\text{Berlin}} - v_{\text{Germany}} + v_{\text{France}} \approx v_{\text{Paris}}$) (Mikolov et al., 2013). Word embeddings are generally obtained in two ways: (a) from internal representations of words in shallow neural networks (Bengio et al., 2003; Mikolov et al., 2013; Collobert and Weston, 2008); (b) from low rank approximations of co-occurrence matrices (Pennington et al., 2014).

Word Sequence Embeddings   Embeddings for sequences of words (e.g., sentences) are created by composing word embeddings. This can be done simply, by doing coordinate-wise multiplication (Mitchell and Lapata, 2008) or taking an unweighted average (Mikolov et al., 2013) of the word vectors. More sophisticated architectures can also be used: for instance, recursive neural networks (Socher et al., 2011, 2013), LSTMs (Tai et al., 2015), and convolutional neural networks (Kalchbrenner et al., 2014) can be defined and

trained on parse and dependency trees.

Other approaches are based on the presence of a latent vector for the entire sequence. Paragraph vectors (Le and Mikolov, 2014) are latent representations that influence the distribution of words. Skip-thought vectors (Kiros et al., 2015) are hidden representations of a neural network that encodes a sentence by trying to reconstruct its surrounding sentences. Conneau et al. (2017) leverage transfer learning by using the hidden representation of a sentence in an LSTM trained for another task, such as textual entailment. The inspiration for Arora et al. (2017) is Wieting et al. (2016b), who use word averaging after updating word embeddings by tuning them on paraphrase pairs. A later work by Wieting et al. (2017a) tried trigram-averaging and LSTM-averaging in addition to word-averaging. In that approach, vectors were tuned on the ParaNMT-50M dataset, created by using neural machine translation to translate 51M Czech-English sentence pairs into English-English pairs. This yielded state-of-the-art results on textual similarity tasks, beating the previous baseline by a wide margin.

3   Approach

3.1   The Log-Linear Random Walk Model

In Arora et al.'s original model (2016), words are generated dynamically by the random walk of a time-variant discourse vector $c_t \in \mathbb{R}^d$, representing "what is being talked about". Words are represented as $v_w \in \mathbb{R}^d$. The probability of a word w being generated at time t is given by a log-linear production model (Mnih and Hinton, 2007):

$$p(w|c_t) \propto \exp\left(\langle c_t, v_w \rangle\right) \qquad (1)$$

Assuming that the discourse vector c_t does not change much over the course of the sentence, Arora et al. replace the sequence of discourse vectors $\{c_t\}$ across all time steps with a single discourse vector c_s. The MAP estimate of c_s is then the unweighted average of word vectors (ignoring any scalar multiplication).

Arora et al.'s improved random walk model (2017) allows words to also be generated: (a) by chance, with probability $\alpha \cdot p(w)$, where α is some scalar and $p(w)$ is the frequency; (b) if the word is correlated with the common discourse vector, which represents frequent discourse such as stopwords. We use c_0 to denote the common discourse vector, to be consistent with the literature. Among other things, these changes help explain words that appear frequently despite being poorly correlated with the discourse vectors — words like *the*, for example. The probability of a word w being generated by a discourse vector c_s is then given as:

$$p(w|c_s) = \alpha \cdot p(w) + (1 - \alpha) \cdot \frac{\exp\left(\langle \widetilde{c}_s, v_w \rangle\right)}{Z_{\widetilde{c}_s}},$$

$$\text{where } \widetilde{c}_s \triangleq \beta \cdot c_0 + (1 - \beta) \cdot c_s, c_0 \perp c_s$$

$$Z_{\widetilde{c}_s} \triangleq \sum_{w' \in \mathcal{V}} \exp\left(\langle \widetilde{c}_s, v_{w'} \rangle\right)$$

where α, β are scalar hyperparameters, $\mathcal{V}$ is the vocabulary, $\widetilde{c}_s$ is a linear combination of the discourse and common discourse vectors parameterized by β, and $Z_{\widetilde{c}_s}$ is the partition function.

The sentence embedding for a sentence is defined as the MAP estimate of the discourse vector c_s that generated the sentence. To compute this tractably, Arora et al. (2017) assume that word vectors v_w are roughly uniformly dispersed in the latent space. This implies that the partition function $Z_{\widetilde{c}_s}$ is roughly the same for all $\widetilde{c}_s$, allowing it to be replaced with a constant Z. Assuming a uniform prior over $\widetilde{c}_s$, the maximum likelihood estimator for $\widetilde{c}_s$ on the unit sphere (ignoring normalization) is then approximately proportional to:

$$\frac{1}{|s|} \sum_{w \in s} \frac{a}{a + p(w)} \cdot v_w, \text{where } a \triangleq \frac{1 - \alpha}{\alpha \cdot Z}$$

Since Z cannot be evaluated, and α is not known, a is a hyperparameter that needs tuning. This weighting scheme is called *smoothed inverse frequency* (SIF) and places a lower weight on more frequent words. The first principal component of all $\{\widetilde{c}_s\}$ in the corpus is used as the estimate for the common discourse vector c_0. The final discourse vector c_s is then produced by subtracting the projection of the weighted average on the common component (*common component removal*):

$$c_s \triangleq \widetilde{c}_s - \text{proj}_{c_0} \widetilde{c}_s$$

Arora et al. call their approach unsupervised, but others (Cer et al., 2017) have correctly noted that it is weakly supervised, since the hyperparameter a needs to be tuned on a validation set.

3.2 The Confounding Effect of Vector Length

We now propose worst-case scenarios where word vector length clearly distorts $p(s|c_s)$ due to the underlying log-linear word production model. Note that we discuss these scenarios because they are illustrative, not because they circumscribe the universe of all scenarios in which word vector length has a confounding effect.

Consider a sentence g comprising two rare words x and y, where x and y have zero similarity. Also consider some sentence h, where the only word z appears twice. g might not occur naturally, but its weighted average $\widetilde{c}_g$ would be similar to that of some longer sentence where x, y are the only non-stopwords (i.e., those with non-negligible weight). For simplicity, further assume that common component removal has negligible effect:

$$\langle v_x, v_y \rangle = 0$$

$$c_g = \widetilde{c}_g = \frac{1}{2} \left(\frac{a}{a + p(x)} \cdot v_x + \frac{a}{a + p(y)} \cdot v_y \right)$$

$$c_h = \widetilde{c}_h = \frac{a}{a + p(z)} \cdot v_z$$

$$(2)$$

Words x, y, z are so infrequent that the probability of them being produced by chance or by the common discourse vector is negligible; the likelihood of them being produced is therefore proportional to the inner product of the discourse and word vectors. Given that the words $x, y \in g$ have zero similarity, and given that the only word $z \in h$ is identical to its discourse vector, we would expect:

$$p(h|c_h) \gg p(g|c_g) \tag{3}$$

However, (3) does not always hold. Suppose that the word embeddings lie in $\mathbb{R}^2$. Then any scalar k can be used to create a valid set of assignments for word embeddings v_x, v_y, v_z that satisfy (2):

$$v_x = \begin{bmatrix} 2k \\ 0 \end{bmatrix}, v_y = \begin{bmatrix} 0 \\ 2k \end{bmatrix}, v_z = \begin{bmatrix} k \\ k \end{bmatrix} \tag{4}$$

Assuming the words x, y, z have roughly the same frequency, they should have the same SIF-weight. Then the weighted averages, and by extension the discourse vectors (2), are the same:

$$c_g = c_h = \frac{a}{a + p(x)} \begin{bmatrix} k \\ k \end{bmatrix}$$

$$\Rightarrow \langle c_g, x \rangle = \langle c_g, y \rangle = \langle c_h, z \rangle = \frac{a}{a + p(x)} \cdot 2k^2$$

$$\Rightarrow p(g|c_g) = p(h|c_h)$$

Thus it is possible for g to be generated by discourse vector c_g with roughly the same probability as h by c_h, contradicting (3). How is this possible, given that the words in g have zero similarity with each other while those in h are identical to each other? The answer can be found in the word vector lengths. Because $||v_x||_2 = \sqrt{2}||v_z||_2$, and $p(w|c_s)$ depends on the inner product of the word and discourse vectors (1), words with longer word vectors are more likely to be produced. In fact, if v_x and v_y were multiplied by some scalar greater than 1, then $p(h|c_h)$ would be less than $p(g|c_g)$.

Generalizing Worst-Case Scenarios By manipulating the word vector length, we can also come up with a more general class of assignments that can contradict (3):

$$v_x = \begin{bmatrix} \beta k_1 \sigma \\ \beta k_2 (1-\sigma) \end{bmatrix} v_y = \begin{bmatrix} \beta k_1 (1-\sigma) \\ \beta k_2 \sigma \end{bmatrix} v_z = \begin{bmatrix} k_1 \\ k_2 \end{bmatrix} \tag{5}$$

where $\sigma \in [0,1], \beta \in \mathbb{R}, \beta \geq 2$. For convenience, we replace $\frac{a}{a+p(x)}$ with C below:

$$c_g = C \begin{bmatrix} \frac{1}{2}\beta k_1 \\ \frac{1}{2}\beta k_2 \end{bmatrix}, c_h = C \begin{bmatrix} k_1 \\ k_2 \end{bmatrix}$$

For simplicity, we assume that the words x, y, z across the two sentences are so infrequent that the probability of them being generated by chance is zero. Then the conditional probabilities of the sentences being generated are:

$$p(g|c_g) \propto \exp\left(\langle c_g, v_x \rangle + \langle c_g, v_y \rangle\right)$$
$$= \exp\left(\frac{1}{2}\beta^2 C \left(k_1{}^2 + k_2{}^2\right)\right)$$
$$p(h|c_h) \propto \exp\left(\langle c_h, v_z \rangle + \langle c_h, v_z \rangle\right) \tag{6}$$
$$= \exp\left(2C \left(k_1{}^2 + k_2{}^2\right)\right)$$
$$\therefore \beta \geq 2 \Rightarrow p(g|c_g) \geq p(h|c_h)$$

In this general formulation, not all scenarios are worst-case. This describes a spectrum of scenarios ranging from acceptable (e.g., $v_x = v_y = v_z$ when $\beta = 2, \sigma = 0.5$) to completely counter-intuitive (see (4)). Though these assignments only apply for word vectors in $\mathbb{R}^2$, they can easily be extended to higher-dimensional spaces.

The confound of vector length persists for longer, naturally occurring sentences. Ultimately, the underlying log-linear word production model (1) means that words with longer word vectors are more likely to be generated. Because this confound is due to model design, rather than the MLE, removing it requires redesigning the model. The exact degree of the confound varies across sentences, but in theory, it is unbounded.

3.3 An Angular Distance–Based Random Walk Model

To address the confounding effect of word vector length, we propose a random walk model where the probability of observing a word w at time t is inversely related to the angular distance between the time-variant discourse vector $c_t \in \mathbb{R}^d$ and the word vector $v_w \in \mathbb{R}^d$:

$$p(w|c_t) \propto 1 - \frac{\arccos\left(\cos\left(v_w, c_t\right)\right)}{\pi},$$
$$\text{where } \cos\left(v_w, c_t\right) \triangleq \frac{v_w \cdot c_t}{||v_w||_2 \cdot ||c_t||_2} \tag{7}$$

where $\arccos\left(\cos\left(v_w, c_t\right)\right)$ is the angular distance. For the intuition behind the use of this distance metric, note that the angular distance between two vectors is equal to the geodesic distance between them on the unit sphere. Thus the angular distance can also be interpreted as the length of the shortest path between the L_2 normalized word vector and the L_2 normalized discourse vector on the unit sphere. Since the angular distance lies in $[0, \pi]$, we divide it by π to bound it in $[0, 1]$. Our choice of angular distance – as opposed to, say, the exponentiated cosine similarity – is critical to avoiding hyperparameter tuning.

Assuming that the discourse vector c_t does not change much over the course of the sentence, the sequence of discourse vectors $\{c_t\}$ across all time steps can be replaced with a single discourse vector c_s for the sentence s. To model sentences more realistically, we allow words to be generated in two additional ways, as proposed in Arora et al. (2017): (a) by chance, with probability $\alpha \cdot p(w)$, where α is some scalar and $p(w)$ is the frequency; (b) if the word is correlated with one of m common discourse vectors $\{c'_m\}$, which represent various types of frequent discourse, such as stopwords. The probability of a word w being generated by discourse vector c_s is then:

$$p(w|c_s) = \alpha \cdot p(w) + (1-\alpha) \cdot \frac{d\left(\widetilde{c}_s, v_w\right)}{Z_{\widetilde{c}_s}},$$
$$\text{where } \widetilde{c}_s \triangleq (1-\beta) c_s + \beta \sum_{i=1}^{m} \lambda_i\, c'_i, \;\; c_s \perp c'_i \tag{8}$$
$$d\left(\widetilde{c}_s, v_w\right) \triangleq 1 - \frac{\arccos\left(\cos\left(v_w, c_t\right)\right)}{\pi},$$
$$Z_{\widetilde{c}_s} \triangleq \sum_{w' \in \mathcal{V}} d\left(\widetilde{c}_s, v_{w'}\right)$$

where $\alpha, \beta, \{\lambda_i\}$ are scalar hyperparameters, $\mathcal{V}$ is the vocabulary, $\widetilde{c}_s$ is a linear combination of the discourse and common discourse vectors parameterized by β and $\{\lambda_i\}$, and $Z_{\widetilde{c}_s}$ is the partition function. Instead of searching for the optimal hyperparameter values over some large space, as Arora et al. (2017) did, we make some simple assumptions to directly compute them.

We define the sentence embedding for some sentence s to be the MAP estimate of the discourse vector c_s that generates s. Assuming a uniform prior over possible c_s, the MAP estimate is also the MLE estimate for c_s. The log-likelihood of a sentence s is:

$$\log p(s|c_s) = \sum_{w \in s} \log p(w|c_s)$$

To maximize $\log p(s|c_s)$, we can approximate $\log p(w|c_s)$ using a first-degree Taylor polynomial:

$$f_w(\widetilde{c}_s) \triangleq \log p(w|\widetilde{c}_s)$$

$$\nabla f_w(\widetilde{c}_s) = \left[\frac{1-\alpha}{\pi \cdot Z_{\widetilde{c}_s} \cdot \exp\left(f_w(\widetilde{c}_s)\right)} \right] \frac{\frac{\partial}{\partial \widetilde{c}_s} \cos\left(v_w, \widetilde{c}_s\right)}{\sqrt{1 - \cos^2\left(v_w, \widetilde{c}_s\right)}},$$

$$\frac{\partial}{\partial \widetilde{c}_s} \cos = \frac{v_w}{\|v_w\|_2 \cdot \|\widetilde{c}_s\|_2} - \cos\left(v_w, \widetilde{c}_s\right) \frac{\widetilde{c}_s}{\|\widetilde{c}_s\|_2^2}$$

Where $a \triangleq (1-\alpha)/(\alpha Z_{\widetilde{c}_s})$, C is a constant, and v_w' is a vector orthogonal to v_w with length $\|v_w\|^{-1}$:

$$f_w(\widetilde{c}_s) \approx f_w(v_w') + \nabla f_w(v_w')^\top \left(\widetilde{c}_s - v_w'\right)$$

$$= C + \frac{a}{\pi \cdot \left(p(w) + \frac{1}{2} \cdot a\right)} \cdot v_w \left(\widetilde{c}_s - v_w'\right)$$

$$= C + \frac{1}{\pi} \left(\frac{a}{p(w) + \frac{1}{2} \cdot a} \langle \widetilde{c}_s, v_w \rangle \right)$$

The MLE for $\widetilde{c}_s$ on the unit sphere (ignoring normalization) is then approximately proportional to:

$$\frac{1}{|s|} \sum_{w \in s} \frac{a}{p(w) + \frac{1}{2}a} \cdot v_w \qquad (9)$$

The MLE of $\widetilde{c}_s$ is approximately a weighted average of word vectors, where more frequent words are down-weighted. In fact, it very closely resembles the SIF weighting scheme (Arora et al., 2017)! However, there are two key differences. For one, as we show later in this subsection, we have derived this weighting scheme from a model that is robust to the confounding effect of word vector length. Secondly, in SIF, a is a hyperparameter that needs to be tuned on a validation set. We now show that in our approach, we can calculate a directly as a function of the vocabulary $\mathcal{V}$ and the number of words in the sentence, $|s|$.

Normalization Before weighting the word vectors, we normalize them along each dimension: we construct a matrix $[v_{w_1}...w_{w_{|s|}}]$ and take the L_2 norm of each row, which corresponds to a single dimension in $\mathbb{R}^d$. We then multiply this d-dimensional vector element-wise with every vector in the sentence. This helps reduce the difference in variance across the dimensions.

Partition Function To calculate $Z_{\widetilde{c}_s}$, we borrow the key assumption from Arora et al. (2017) that the word vectors v_w are roughly uniformly dispersed in the latent space. Then the expected geodesic distance between a latent discourse vector and a word vector on the unit sphere is $\pi/2$, so $\mathbb{E}_{w' \in \mathcal{V}}[d(\widetilde{c}_s, v_{w'})] = \frac{1}{2}$. Then:

$$Z_{\widetilde{c}_s} = \sum_{w' \in \mathcal{V}} d(\widetilde{c}_s, v_{w'})$$
$$= |\mathcal{V}| \, \mathbb{E}_{w' \in \mathcal{V}}[d(\widetilde{c}_s, v_{w'})] = \frac{1}{2}|\mathcal{V}| \qquad (10)$$

Odds of Random Production α is the probability that a word w will be produced by chance instead of by the discourse or common discourse vectors. To estimate α, we first consider the probability that a random word w will be produced by a discourse vector c_s at least once over n steps of a random walk:

$$p(w|c_s^1, ..., c_s^n) = 1 - \prod_{t=1}^{n} \left[1 - \frac{d(c_s^t, v_w)}{Z_{c_s}} \right]$$

$$\mathbb{E}_{w \sim \mathcal{V}}[p(w|c_s^1, ..., c_s^n)] = 1 - \left(1 - \frac{1}{|\mathcal{V}|}\right)^n$$

The number of steps taken during the random walk is itself a random variable, so we let $n = \mathbb{E}_{s \in S}|s|$. We assume that if the frequency is greater than this expectation, then the word is always produced by chance; less than this expectation, and it is always produced by the discourse or common discourse vectors. α is the proportion of the vocabulary with $p(w)$ above this threshold:

$$\alpha = \frac{\sum_{w \in \mathcal{V}} \mathbb{1}\left[p(w) > \mathbb{E}_{w \sim \mathcal{V}}[p(w|c_s^1, ..., c_s^n)]\right]}{|\mathcal{V}|}$$
$$(11)$$

Since we can directly calculate $Z_{\widetilde{c}_s}$ and α, we can also directly calculate $a = (1-\alpha)/(\alpha Z_{\widetilde{c}_s})$.

Common Discourse Vectors We estimate the m common discourse vectors as the first m singular vectors from the singular value decomposition of the weighted average vectors. $\{\lambda_i\}$ are the weights on the common discourse vectors. In reality, these are unique to the word for which $p(w|c_s)$ is being evaluated. However, we let λ_i be:

$$\lambda_i = \frac{\sigma_i^2}{\sum_j^m \sigma_j^2}$$

where σ_i is the singular value for c_i'. λ_i can be interpreted as the proportion of variance explained by $\{c_1', ..., c_m'\}$ that is explained by c_i'. If removing the common discourse vectors is a form of denoising (Arora et al., 2017), increasing m, in theory, should improve results. Because the variance explained by a singular vector falls with every additional vector that is included, the choice of m is thus a trade-off between variance explained and computational cost. When $m = 1$, this is equivalent to the removal in Arora et al. (2017). We fix m at 5, since we find empirically that singular vectors beyond that do not explain much more variance. To get c_s, we subtract from $\widetilde{c}_s$ the weighted projection on each singular vector:

$$c_s \triangleq \widetilde{c}_s - \sum_{i=1}^{m} \lambda_i \operatorname{proj}_{c_i'} \widetilde{c}_s$$

We call this *piecewise common component removal*. Because our weighting scheme requires no hyperparameter tuning, it is completely unsupervised. For this reason, we call it *unsupervised smoothed inverse frequency* (uSIF). The full algorithm is given in Algorithm 1.

Note that while it is certainly *possible* to tune the hyperparameters in our model to achieve optimal results, it is not necessary to do so, which allows our method to be used when there is no labelled data. By contrast, in Arora et al.'s model (2017), hyperparameter tuning is a necessity.

Confound of Vector Length To understand why this model is not prone to the confound of word vector length, we reconsider the class of assignments for v_x, v_y, v_z in (5) and the resulting values for $\widetilde{c}_g$ and $\widetilde{c}_h$. Recall that in our example, sentence g comprises words x, y and sentence h comprises two instances of the word z. Under our new weighting scheme, C in (5) is replaced with $C' = \frac{a}{p(x) + \frac{1}{2}a}$. Note that we use $p(x)$ in C' because of the simplifying assumption that $p(x) = p(y) = p(z)$. Assuming again that $p(x) \approx 0$ and that piecewise common component removal has negligible effect,

---

Algorithm 1 uSIF Sentence Embedding

Input: vocabulary $\mathcal{V}$, word vectors $\{v_w : w \in \mathcal{V}\}$, frequencies $\{p(w) : w \in \mathcal{V}\}$, sentences $\mathcal{S}$
Output: sentence embeddings $\{c_s : s \in \mathcal{S}\}$

1: **procedure** EMBED
2:      $m \leftarrow 5$
3:      $n \leftarrow \mathbb{E}_{s \in \mathcal{S}} |s|$
4:      **for all** $s \in \mathcal{S}$ **do**
5:          $\alpha \leftarrow \dfrac{\sum_{w \in \mathcal{V}} \mathbb{1}\left[p(w) > 1 - \left(1 - \frac{1}{|\mathcal{V}|}\right)^n\right]}{|\mathcal{V}|}$
6:          $Z \leftarrow |\mathcal{V}|/2$
7:          $a \leftarrow (1 - \alpha)/(\alpha \cdot Z)$
8:          $\widetilde{c}_s \leftarrow \frac{1}{|s|} \sum_{w \in s} \frac{a}{p(w) + \frac{1}{2}a} v_w$
9:      **end for**
10:     $\mathcal{A} \leftarrow \left(\widetilde{c}_{s_1} \dots \widetilde{c}_{s_n}\right)$
11:     **for all** i in 1...m **do**
12:         $c_i' \leftarrow i^{\text{th}}$ singular vector of $\mathcal{A}$
13:         $\sigma_i \leftarrow i^{\text{th}}$ singular value of $\mathcal{A}$
14:     **end for**
15:     **for all** i in 1...m **do**
16:         $\lambda_i \leftarrow \frac{\sigma_i^2}{\sum_j^m \sigma_j^2}$
17:     **end for**
18:     **for all** $s \in \mathcal{S}$ **do**
19:         $c_s \leftarrow \widetilde{c}_s - \sum_{i=1}^{m} \lambda_i \operatorname{proj}_{c_i'} \widetilde{c}_s$
20:     **end for**
21: **end procedure**

---

we can see how $p(g|c_g)$ and $p(h|c_h)$ change in our random walk model:

$$p(g|c_g) \propto \prod_{w \in \{x, y\}} \left(1 - \frac{\arccos\left(\cos\left(c_g, v_w\right)\right)}{\pi}\right)$$

$$p(h|c_h) \propto \left(1 - \frac{\arccos\left(\cos\left(c_h, v_z\right)\right)}{\pi}\right)^2 = 1$$

Because $p(g|c_g)$ is ultimately based on the cosine similarities between the discourse vector and word vectors, it is a function of the parameter $\sigma \in [0, 1]$ that controls the degree of similarity between v_x and v_y. For example, for the worst-case assignments (4), $p(g|c_g) \propto 9/16$. Conversely, when $v_x = v_y = v_z$, we get $p(g|c_g) = p(h|c_h) \propto 1$. Recall that in Arora et al.'s model (2017), $\beta \geq 2$ was sufficient to ensure the counter-intuitive result of $p(g|c_g) \geq p(h|c_h)$ (6), where β was a scalar that controlled the word vector length. In contrast, in our random walk model, the effect of β – and thus the confound of vector length – is entirely absent; only the similarity between the word vectors is influential.

4 Results and Discussion

4.1 Textual Similarity Tasks

We test our approach on the SemEval semantic textual similarity (STS) tasks (2012-2015) (Agirre et al., 2012, 2013, 2014, 2015), the SemEval 2014 Relatedness task (SICK'14) (Marelli et al., 2014), and the STS Benchmark dataset (Cer et al., 2017). In these tasks, the goal is to determine the semantic similarity between a given pair of sentences; the evaluation criterion is the Pearson correlation coefficient between the predicted and actual similarity scores. To predict the similarity score, we simply encode each sentence and take the cosine similarity of their vectors. The individual scores for STS tasks are in Table 4 in the Appendix and the average scores are in Table 1. The STS benchmark scores are in Table 2. We compare our results with those from several methods, which are categorized by Cer et al. (2017) as 'unsupervised', 'weakly supervised', or 'supervised'.

4.2 Experimental Settings

For a fair comparison with Arora et al. (2017), we use the unigram probability distribution used by them, based on the enwiki dataset (Wikipedia, 3B words). Our preprocessing of the sentences is limited to tokenization. We try our method with three types of word vectors: GloVe vectors (Pennington et al., 2014), PARAGRAM-SL999 (PSL) vectors (Wieting et al., 2015), tuned on the SimLex999 dataset, and ParaNMT-50 vectors (Wieting and Gimpel, 2017a), tuned on 51M English-English sentence pairs translated from English-Czech sentence pairs. The value of n in (11) is $\mathbb{E}_{s \in S}|s| \approx 11$ and was estimated using sentences from all corpora. The value of a in (9) is then 1.2×10^{-3}. Our results are denoted as **X+UP**, where $\mathbf{X} \in \{$ 'GloVe', 'PSL', 'ParaNMT' $\}$, **U** denotes uSIF-weighting, and **P** denotes piecewise common component removal.

4.3 Results

Our model outperforms Arora et al.'s by up to 44.4% on individual tasks (see GloVe+UP vs. GloVe+WR for the STS'12 MSRpar task in Table 4) and by up to 15.5% on yearly averages (see GloVe+UP vs. GloVe+WR for STS'12 in Table 1). Our approach proves most useful in cases where Arora et al. (2017) underperform others, such as for STS'12, where our models – GloVe+UP and PSL+UP – outperform their equivalents in Arora

Model	STS'12	STS'13	STS'14	STS'15	SICK14
Wieting et al. (2016b) - unsupervised					
PP	58.7	55.8	70.9	75.8	71.6
PP-XXL	61.5	58.9	73.1	77.0	72.7
tfidf-GloVe	58.7	52.1	63.8	60.6	69.4
skip-thought	30.8	24.8	31.4	31.0	49.8
Arora et al. (2017) - weakly supervised					
GloVe+WR	56.2	56.6	68.5	71.7	72.2
PSL+WR	59.5	61.8	73.5	76.3	72.9
Wieting et al.(2017b) - weakly supervised					
LSTM AVG	64.8	63.1	75.8	76.7	71.3
AVG	61.6	59.4	75.8	77.9	72.4
GRAN	62.5	63.4	75.9	77.7	72.9
Conneau et al. (2017) - unsupervised (transfer learning)					
InferSent (AllSNLI)	58.6	51.5	67.8	68.3	-
InferSent (SNLI)	57.1	50.4	66.2	65.2	-
Wieting et al. (2017a) - unsupervised					
ParaNMT Word Avg.	66.2	61.8	76.2	79.3	-
ParaNMT BiLSTM Avg.	67.4	60.3	76.4	79.7	-
ParaNMT Trigram-Word	67.8	62.7	77.4	**80.3**	-
Our Approach - unsupervised					
GloVe+UP	64.9	63.6	74.4	76.1	73.0
PSL+UP	65.8	65.2	75.9	77.6	72.3
ParaNMT+UP	**68.3**	**66.1**	**78.4**	79.0	**73.5**

Table 1: Average results (Pearson's $r \times 100$) on textual similarity tasks. The highest score in each column is in bold. "Glove+UP" is the application of uSIF-weighting (U) and piecewise common component removal (P) to GloVe word vectors; "PSL+UP" to PSL word vectors; "ParaNMT+UP", to ParaNMT word vectors.

et al.'s results by 15.5% and 10.6% respectively. On average, our approach outperforms Arora et al.'s by around 7.6%, but the improvement is highly variable. This may be because the hyperparameter values we derived may be closer to the optima for some corpora more than others or because our other improvements – normalization and piecewise common component removal – are more effective for certain datasets.

Our best model, ParaNMT+UP, is also competitive with the state-of-the-art model, ParaNMT Trigram-Word, an average of trigram and word embeddings tuned on the ParaNMT-dataset. ParaNMT+UP outperforms ParaNMT Trigram-Word on STS'12, STS'13, and STS'14; it is narrowly outperformed on STS'15 and the STS benchmark. ParaNMT Trigram-Word's inclusion of trigram embeddings gives it an edge over our model for out-of-vocabulary words (Wieting and Gimpel, 2017a). It should be noted that ParaNMT+UP outperforms both ParaNMT Word Avg. and ParaNMT BiLSTM Avg., implying that our model composes words better than both simple averaging and BiLSTMs. Similarly, our model PSL+UP outperforms PP-XXL (Wieting et al., 2016b), despite the latter using the same word vectors and a learned projection instead.

Ablation Study On average, our weighting scheme alone is responsible for a roughly 4.4%

Unsupervised	
Doc2Vec DBOW (Le and Mikolov, 2014)	64.9
GloVe+UP	71.5
Charagram (Wieting et al., 2016a)	71.6
Paragram-Phrase (Wieting et al., 2016b)	73.2
PSL+UP	74.8
Sent2vec (Pagliardini et al., 2017)	75.5
InferSent (bi-LSTM trained on SNLI) (Conneau et al., 2017)	75.8
ParaNMT Word Avg. (Wieting and Gimpel, 2017a)	79.2
ParaNMT BiLSTM Avg. (Wieting and Gimpel, 2017a)	79.2
ParaNMT+UP	79.5
ParaNMT Trigram-Word Addition (Wieting and Gimpel, 2017a)	**79.9**
Weakly Supervised	
GloVe+WR (Arora et al., 2017)	72.0
GRAN (Wieting and Gimpel, 2017b)	76.4
Supervised	
Constituency Tree-LSTM (Tai et al., 2015)	71.9
CNN (HCTI) (Shao, 2017)	78.4

Table 2: Results (Pearson's $r \times 100$) on the STS Benchmark dataset. The highest score is in bold. The scores of our approaches are underlined.

Model	SST	SICK-R	SICK-E
ParaNMT-based (Wieting and Gimpel, 2017a)			
ParaNMT Word Avg. (300d)	80.0	83.6	80.6
ParaNMT Trigram Avg. (300d)	73.6	79.3	78.0
ParaNMT LSTM Avg. (300d)	80.6	83.9	81.9
LSTM (600d)	80.0	85.2	82.6
LSTM (900d)	81.6	86.0	83.0
BiLSTM (600d)	79.1	85.4	84.3
BiLSTM (900d)	81.3	85.8	84.4
Trigram-Word (600d, concatenation)	79.7	84.6	82.0
Trigram-Word-LSTM (900d, concatenation)	82.0	85.4	83.8
BILSTM AVG (4096)	82.8	85.9	83.8
ParaNMT+WR[†] (Arora et al., 2017)	80.5	83.9	80.9
ParaNMT+UP[†] (ours)	80.7	83.8	81.1
Other Approaches			
BiLSTM-Max (on AllNLI) (Conneau et al., 2017)	84.6	**88.4**	**86.3**
skip-thought (Kiros et al., 2015)	82.0	85.8	82.3
BYTE mLSTM (Radford et al., 2017)	**91.8**	79.2	-

Table 3: Results on the SST, SICK-R, and SICK-E tasks. The best score for each task is bolded. † indicates our implementation.

improvement over Arora et al. The piecewise common component removal alone is responsible for a roughly 5.1% improvement, and the normalization alone is responsible for a roughly 6.7% improvement. This suggests that the benefits of our individual contributions have much overlap. The choice of tuned word vectors (e.g., ParaNMT over GloVe) can also improve results by up to 11.2%.

4.4 Supervised Tasks

We also test our approach on three supervised tasks: the SICK similarity task (SICK-R), the SICK entailment task (SICK-E), and the Stanford Sentiment Treebank (SST) binary classification task (Socher et al., 2013). To a large extent, performance on these tasks depends on the architecture that is trained with the sentence embeddings. We take the embeddings that perform best on the textual similarity tasks, ParaNMT+UP, and follow the setup in Wieting et al. (2016b). As seen in Table 3, both SIF-weighting with common component removal (Arora et al., 2017) and uSIF-weighting with piecewise common component removal (ours) perform slightly better than simple word averaging, but not as well as more sophisticated models. Past work has found that tuning the word embeddings in addition to the parameters of the model yields much better performance (Wieting et al., 2016b), as does increasing the size of the hidden layer in the classifier (Arora et al., 2017). The results here, however, suggest that regardless of such changes, our approach would not be any more effective than Arora et al.'s on these tasks. Still, our approach retains the advantage of being a completely unsupervised method that can be used when there is no labelled data.

5 Future Work

There are several possibilities for future work. For one, the values we derived for $Z_{\tilde{c}_s}, \alpha, a$ and $\{\lambda_i\}$ are not necessarily optimal. While they are based on reasonable assumptions, there are likely sentence-specific and task-specific values that yield better results. Hyperparameter search is one way of finding these values, but that would require supervision. It may be possible, however, to theoretically derive more optimal values.

6 Conclusion

We first showed that word vector length has a confounding effect on the log-linear random walk model of generating text (Arora et al., 2017), the basis of a strong baseline method for sentence embeddings. We then proposed an angular distance–based random walk model where the probability of a sentence being generated is robust to distortion from word vector length. From this model, we derived a simple approach for creating sentence embeddings: normalize the word vectors, compute a weighted average, and then modify it using SVD. Unlike in Arora et al., our approach does not require hyperparameter tuning – it is completely unsupervised and can therefore be used when there is no labelled data. Our approach outperforms Arora et al.'s by up to 44.4% on textual similarity tasks and is even competitive with state-of-the-art methods. Because our simple approach is tough-to-beat, robust, and unsupervised, it is an ideal baseline for computing sentence embeddings.

Acknowledgments

We thank the Natural Sciences and Engineering Research Council of Canada (NSERC) for financial support. We thank John Wieting for providing pre-trained ParaNMT word embeddings and Graeme Hirst for his many insightful suggestions.

References

Eneko Agirre, Carmen Banea, Claire Cardie, Daniel M Cer, Mona T Diab, Aitor Gonzalez-Agirre, Weiwei Guo, Inigo Lopez-Gazpio, Montse Maritxalar, Rada Mihalcea, et al. 2015. Semeval-2015 task 2: Semantic textual similarity, English, Spanish and pilot on interpretability. In *Proceedings SemEval@ NAACL-HLT*, pages 252–263.

Eneko Agirre, Carmen Banea, Claire Cardie, Daniel M Cer, Mona T Diab, Aitor Gonzalez-Agirre, Weiwei Guo, Rada Mihalcea, German Rigau, and Janyce Wiebe. 2014. Semeval-2014 task 10: Multilingual semantic textual similarity. In *Proceedings SemEval@ COLING*, pages 81–91.

Eneko Agirre, Daniel Cer, Mona Diab, Aitor Gonzalez-Agirre, and Weiwei Guo. 2013. Sem 2013 shared task: Semantic textual similarity, including a pilot on typed-similarity. In *SEM 2013: The Second Joint Conference on Lexical and Computational Semantics*. Association for Computational Linguistics.

Eneko Agirre, Mona Diab, Daniel Cer, and Aitor Gonzalez-Agirre. 2012. Semeval-2012 task 6: A pilot on semantic textual similarity. In *Proceedings of the First Joint Conference on Lexical and Computational Semantics-Volume 1: Proceedings of the main conference and the shared task, and Volume 2: Proceedings of the Sixth International Workshop on Semantic Evaluation*, pages 385–393. Association for Computational Linguistics.

Sanjeev Arora, Yuanzhi Li, Yingyu Liang, Tengyu Ma, and Andrej Risteski. 2016. A latent variable model approach to PMI-based word embeddings. *Transactions of the Association for Computational Linguistics*, 4:385–399.

Sanjeev Arora, Yingyu Liang, and Tengyu Ma. 2017. A simple but tough-to-beat baseline for sentence embeddings. In *International Conference on Learning Representations*.

Yoshua Bengio, Réjean Ducharme, Pascal Vincent, and Christian Jauvin. 2003. A neural probabilistic language model. *Journal of Machine Learning Research*, 3(Feb):1137–1155.

Daniel Cer, Mona Diab, Eneko Agirre, Inigo Lopez-Gazpio, and Lucia Specia. 2017. Semeval-2017 task 1: Semantic textual similarity-multilingual and cross-lingual focused evaluation. *arXiv preprint arXiv:1708.00055*.

Ronan Collobert and Jason Weston. 2008. A unified architecture for natural language processing: Deep neural networks with multitask learning. In *Proceedings of the 25th International Conference on Machine Learning*, pages 160–167. ACM.

Alexis Conneau, Douwe Kiela, Holger Schwenk, Loic Barrault, and Antoine Bordes. 2017. Supervised learning of universal sentence representations from natural language inference data. *arXiv preprint arXiv:1705.02364*.

Nal Kalchbrenner, Edward Grefenstette, and Phil Blunsom. 2014. A convolutional neural network for modelling sentences. In *Proceedings of the 52nd Annual Meeting of the Association for Computational Linguistics*, pages 655–665.

Ryan Kiros, Yukun Zhu, Ruslan R Salakhutdinov, Richard Zemel, Raquel Urtasun, Antonio Torralba, and Sanja Fidler. 2015. Skip-thought vectors. In *Advances in Neural Information Processing Systems*, pages 3294–3302.

Quoc Le and Tomas Mikolov. 2014. Distributed representations of sentences and documents. In *Proceedings of the 31st International Conference on Machine Learning (ICML-14)*, pages 1188–1196.

Thang Luong, Richard Socher, and Christopher D Manning. 2013. Better word representations with recursive neural networks for morphology. In *SIGNLL Conference on Computational Natural Language Learning (CoNLL)*, pages 104–113.

Marco Marelli, Luisa Bentivogli, Marco Baroni, Raffaella Bernardi, Stefano Menini, and Roberto Zamparelli. 2014. Semeval-2014 task 1: Evaluation of compositional distributional semantic models on full sentences through semantic relatedness and textual entailment. In *Proceedings SemEval@ COLING*, pages 1–8.

Tomas Mikolov, Ilya Sutskever, Kai Chen, Greg S Corrado, and Jeff Dean. 2013. Distributed representations of words and phrases and their compositionality. In *Advances in Neural Information Processing Systems*, pages 3111–3119.

Jeff Mitchell and Mirella Lapata. 2008. Vector-based models of semantic composition. In *Proceedings of the 46th Annual Meeting of the Association for Computational Linguistics*, pages 236–244.

Andriy Mnih and Geoffrey Hinton. 2007. Three new graphical models for statistical language modelling. In *Proceedings of the 24th International Conference on Machine Learning*, pages 641–648. ACM.

Matteo Pagliardini, Prakhar Gupta, and Martin Jaggi. 2017. Unsupervised learning of sentence embeddings using compositional n-gram features. *arXiv preprint arXiv:1703.02507*.

Jeffrey Pennington, Richard Socher, and Christopher Manning. 2014. Glove: Global vectors for word representation. In *Proceedings of the 2014 Conference on Empirical Methods in Natural Language Processing (EMNLP)*, pages 1532–1543.

Alec Radford, Rafal Jozefowicz, and Ilya Sutskever. 2017. Learning to generate reviews and discovering sentiment. *arXiv preprint arXiv:1704.01444.*

Yang Shao. 2017. Hcti at semeval-2017 task 1: Use convolutional neural network to evaluate semantic textual similarity. In *Proceedings of the 11th International Workshop on Semantic Evaluation (SemEval-2017)*, pages 130–133.

Richard Socher, Eric H Huang, Jeffrey Pennin, Christopher D Manning, and Andrew Y Ng. 2011. Dynamic pooling and unfolding recursive autoencoders for paraphrase detection. In *Advances in Neural Information Processing Systems*, pages 801–809.

Richard Socher, Alex Perelygin, Jean Wu, Jason Chuang, Christopher D Manning, Andrew Ng, and Christopher Potts. 2013. Recursive deep models for semantic compositionality over a sentiment treebank. In *Proceedings of the 2013 Conference on Empirical Methods in Natural Language Processing*, pages 1631–1642.

Kai Sheng Tai, Richard Socher, and Christopher D Manning. 2015. Improved semantic representations from tree-structured long short-term memory networks. *Proceedings of the 53rd Annual Meeting of the Association for Computational Linguistics.*

John Wieting, Mohit Bansal, Kevin Gimpel, and Karen Livescu. 2016a. Charagram: Embedding words and sentences via character n-grams. *arXiv preprint arXiv:1607.02789.*

John Wieting, Mohit Bansal, Kevin Gimpel, and Karen Livescu. 2016b. Towards universal paraphrastic sentence embeddings. In *International Conference on Learning Representations.*

John Wieting, Mohit Bansal, Kevin Gimpel, Karen Livescu, and Dan Roth. 2015. From paraphrase database to compositional paraphrase model and back. *Transactions of the Association for Computational Linguistics*, 3:345–358.

John Wieting and Kevin Gimpel. 2017a. Pushing the limits of paraphrastic sentence embeddings with millions of machine translations. *arXiv preprint arXiv:1711.05732.*

John Wieting and Kevin Gimpel. 2017b. Revisiting recurrent networks for paraphrastic sentence embeddings. *arXiv preprint arXiv:1705.00364.*

Evaluating Word Embeddings
in Multi-label Classification
Using Fine-grained Name Typing

Yadollah Yaghoobzadeh[1]   Katharina Kann[2]   Hinrich Schütze[3]

[1]Mirosoft Research, Montreal, Canada
[2]Center for Data Science, New York University, USA
[3]CIS, LMU Munich, Germany
yayaghoo@microsoft.com

Abstract

Embedding models typically associate each word with a single real-valued vector, representing its different properties. Evaluation methods, therefore, need to analyze the accuracy and completeness of these properties in embeddings. This requires fine-grained analysis of embedding subspaces. Multi-label classification is an appropriate way to do so. We propose a new evaluation method for word embeddings based on multi-label classification given a word embedding. The task we use is fine-grained name typing: given a large corpus, find all types that a name can refer to based on the name embedding. Given the scale of entities in knowledge bases, we can build datasets for this task that are complementary to the current embedding evaluation datasets in: they are very large, contain fine-grained classes, and allow the direct evaluation of embeddings without confounding factors like sentence context.

1   Introduction

Distributed representation of words, aka word embedding, is an important element of many natural language processing applications. The quality of word embeddings is assessed using different methods. Baroni et al. (2014) evaluate word embeddings on different intrinsic tests: similarity, analogy, synonym detection, categorization and selectional preference. Different concept categorization datasets are introduced. These datasets are small ($<$500) (Baroni et al., 2014; Rubinstein et al., 2015) and therefore measure the goodness of embeddings by the quality of their clustering. Usually cosine is used as the similarity metric between embeddings, ignoring subspace similarities.

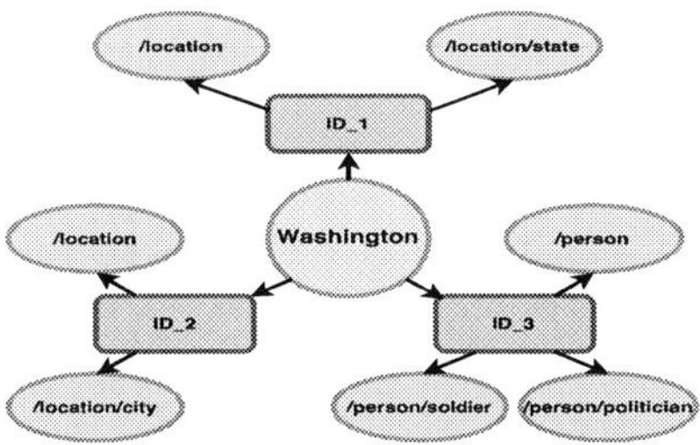

Figure 1: Types (ellipses; green) of the entities (rectangles; red), to which the name "Washington" can refer. Ideally, the embedding for "Washington" should represent all these types.

Extrinsic evaluations are also used, cf. Li and Jurafsky (2015). In these tasks, embeddings are used in context/sentence representations with composition involved.

In this paper, we propose a new evaluation method. In contrast to the prior work on *intrinsic evaluation*, our method is supervised, large-scale, fine-grained, automatically built, and evaluates embeddings in a classification setting where different subspaces of embeddings need to be analyzed. In contrast to the prior work on *extrinsic evaluation*, we evaluate embeddings in isolation, without confounding factors like sentence contexts or composition functions.

Our evaluation is based on an entity-oriented task in information extraction (IE). Different areas of IE try to predict relevant data about entities from text, either locally (i.e., at the context-level), or globally (i.e., at the corpus-level). For example, local (Zeng et al., 2014) and global (Riedel et al., 2013) in relation extraction, or local (Ling and Weld, 2012) and global (Yaghoobzadeh and Schütze, 2015) in entity typing. In most global tasks, each entity is indexed with an identifier (ID) that usually comes from knowledge bases such as

Proceedings of the 3rd Workshop on Representation Learning for NLP, pages 101–106
Melbourne, Australia, July 20, 2018. ©2018 Association for Computational Linguistics

Freebase. Exceptions are tasks in lexicon generation or population like entity set expansion (ESE) (Thelen and Riloff, 2002), which are global but without entity IDs. ESE usually starts from a few seed entities per set and completes the set using pattern-based methods.

Here, we address the task of *fine-grained name typing (FNT)*, a global prediction task, operating on the surface names of entities. FNT and ESE share applications in name lexicon population. FNT is different from ESE because we assume to have sufficient training instances for each type to train supervised models.

The challenging goal of FNT is to find the types of all entities a name can refer to. For example, "Washington" might refer to several entities which in turn may belong to multiple types, see Figure 1. In this example, "Washington" refers to "Washington DC (city)", "Washington (state)", or "George Washington (president)". Also, each entity can belong to several types, e.g., "George Washington" is a POLITICIAN, a PERSON and a SOLDIER, or "Washington (state)" is a STATE and a LOCATION.

Learning global representations for entities is very effective for global prediction tasks in IE (cf., Yaghoobzadeh and Schütze (2015)). For our task, FNT, we also learn a global representation for each name. By doing so, we see this task as a challenging evaluation for embedding models. We intend to use FNT to answer the following questions: (i) How well can embeddings represent distinctive information, i.e., different types or senses? (ii) Which properties are important for an embedding model to do well on this task?

We build a novel large-scale dataset of (name, types) from Freebase with millions of examples. The size of the dataset enables supervised approaches to work, an important requirement to be able to look at different subspaces of embeddings (Yaghoobzadeh and Schütze, 2016). Also, in FNT names are—in contrast to concept categorization datasets—multi-labeled, which requires to look at multiple subspaces of embeddings.

In summary, our contributions are (i) introducing a new evaluation method for word embeddings (ii) publishing a new dataset that is a good resource for evaluating word embeddings and is complementary to prior work: it is very large, contains more different classes than previous word categorization datasets, and allows the direct evaluation of embeddings without confounding factors like sentence context[1].

2   Related Work

Embedding evaluation. Baroni et al. (2014) evaluate embeddings on different intrinsic tests: similarity, analogy, synonym detection, categorization and selectional preference. Schnabel et al. (2015) introduce tasks with more fine-grained datasets. The concept categorization datasets used for embedding evaluation are mostly small (<500) (Baroni et al., 2014) and therefore measure the goodness of embeddings by the quality of their clustering. In contrast, we test embeddings in a classification setting and different subspaces of embeddings are analyzed. Extrinsic evaluations are also used (Li and Jurafsky, 2015; Köhn, 2015; Lai et al., 2015). In most tasks, embeddings are used in context/sentence representations with composition involved. In this work, we evaluate embeddings in isolation, on their ability to represent multiple senses.

Related tasks and datasets. Our proposed task is fine-grained name typing (FNT). A related task is entity set expansion (ESE): given a set of a few seed entities of a particular class, find other entities (Thelen and Riloff, 2002; Gupta and Manning, 2014). We can formulate FNT as ESE, however, there is a difference in the training data assumption. For our task, we assume to have enough instances for each type available, and, therefore, to be able to use a supervised learning approach. In contrast, for ESE, mostly only 3-5 seeds are given as training seeds for a set, which makes an evaluation like ours impossible.

Named entity recognition (NER) consists of recognizing and classifying mentions of entities locally in a particular context (Finkel et al., 2005). Recently, there has been increased interest in fine-grained typing of mentions (Ling and Weld, 2012; Yogatama et al., 2015; Ren et al., 2016; Shimaoka et al., 2016). One way of solving our task is to collect every mention of a name, use NER to predict the context-dependent types of mentions, and then take all predictions as the global types of the name. However, our focus in this paper is on how embedding models perform and propose this task as a good evaluation method. We leave the comparison to an NER-based approach for future work.

Corpus-level fine-grained entity typing is the

---

[1] Our dataset is available at: `https://github.com/ yyaghoobzadeh/name_typing`

task of predicting all types of *entities* based on their mentions in a corpus (Yaghoobzadeh and Schütze, 2015; Yaghoobzadeh and Schütze, 2017; Yaghoobzadeh et al., 2018). This is similar to our task, FNT, but in FNT the goals is to find the corpus-level types of *names*. Corpus-level entity typing has also been used for embedding evaluation (Yaghoobzadeh and Schütze, 2016). However, they need an annotated corpus with entities. For FNT, however, pretrained word embeddings are sufficient for the evaluation.

Finally, there exists some previous work on FNT, e.g., Chesney et al. (2017). In contrast to us, they do not explicitly focus on the evaluation of embedding models, such that their dataset only contains a limited number of types. In contrast, we use 50 different types, making our dataset suitable for the type of evaluation intended.

3 Multi-label Classification of Word Embeddings

Word embeddings are global representations of word properties learned from the context distribution of words. Words are usually ambiguous and belong to multiple classes, e.g., multiple part-of-speech tags or multiple meanings. A good word embedding should represent all information about the word, including its multiple classes. Our evaluation methodology is based on this hypothesis and tries to test this through multi-label classification of word embeddings. Here, we focus on the semantic property of nouns and entity names. We try to find all categories or types of a noun given its embedding.

Multi-label classification of embedding has multiple advantages over current evaluation methods: (i) large datasets can be created without much human annotation; (ii) more fine-grained analysis of the results is possible through analyzing classification performance; (iii) it allows the direct evaluation of embeddings without confounding factors like sentence context.

4 Fine-grained Name Typing

We assume to have the following: a set of names N, a set of types T and a membership function $m : N \times T \mapsto \{0, 1\}$ such that $m(n, t) = 1$ iff name n has type t; and a large corpus C. In this problem setting, we address the task of *fine-grained name typing (FNT)*: we want to infer from the corpus for each pair of name n and type t whether $m(n, t) =$

1 holds.

For example, for the name "Hamilton", we should find all of the following: LOCATION, OR-GANIZATION, PERSON, CITY, SPORTS_TEAM and SOLDIER, since "Hamilton" can describe entities belonging to those types. Another example is "Falcon" which is used for ANIMAL, AIRPLANE, SOFTWARE, ART. FNT sheds light on to which level these fine-grained types can be inferred from a corpus using embeddings.

4.1 Embedding-based Model

We aim to find $P(t|n)$, i.e., the probability of name n having type t. Given sufficient training instances for each type t, we can formulate the problem as a multi-label classification task. As input, we use a representation for n, learned from the corpus C. Distributional representations have shown to capture various types of information about a word, especially their categories or types (Yaghoobzadeh and Schütze, 2015).

After learning an embedding for n, we train two kinds of binary classifiers for each type t to to estimate $P(t|n)$: (i) linear: logistic regression (LR) with stochastic gradient decent; and (ii) non-linear: multi-layer perceptron (MLP) with one hidden layer and ReLU as the non-linearity. We use the Scikit-learn (Pedregosa et al., 2011) toolkit for training our classifiers.

5 Dataset

Using Freebase (Bollacker et al., 2008), we first retrieve the set of all entities E_n for each name n.[2] Then, we consider the types of all $e \in E_n$ the types of n. See Figure 1 for an example: all of the shown types belong to the name "Washington".

Since some of the about 1,500 Freebase types have very few instances, we map them first to the FIGER (Ling and Weld, 2012) type-set, which contains 113 types. We then further restrict our set to the top 50 most frequent types. See Table 5 for the list of types.

In order to be able to evaluate each embedding on its own, we divide our dataset into single-word (891,241 names) and multi-word (8,907,715 names). In this work, the multi-word set is not used. We then set a frequency threshold of 100 in our lowercased Wikipedia corpus [3] and select

---

[2]What we call "names" here are either *names* or *aliases* in the Freebase terminology.

[3]Our Wikipedia dump is from 2014.

/art, /art/film, /astral_body, /biology, /broadcast_network, /broadcast_program, /building, /building/restaurant, /chemistry, /computer/programming_language, /disease, /event, /food, /game, /geography/island, /geography/mountain, /god, /internet/website, /living_thing, /location, /location/body_of_water, /location/cemetery, /location/city, /location/county, /medicine/drug, /medicine/medical_treatment, /medicine/symptom, /music, /organization, /organization/airline, /organization/company, /organization/educational_institution, /organization/sports_team, /people/ethnicity, /person, /person/actor, /person/artist, /person/athlete, /person/author, /person/director, /person/engineer, /person/musician, /play, /product, /product/airplane, /product/instrument, /product/ship, /software, /title, /written_work

Table 1: List of the 50 types in our FNT dataset.

	#names	avg #types per name
train	50,000	3.78
dev	20,000	3.77
test	30,000	3.77

Table 2: Some statistics (number of names; average number of types per name) for our name typing dataset.

randomly 100,000 of our dataset names that pass this threshold. We then divide the names into train (50%), dev (20%) and test (30%). Some statistics of the single-word FNT dataset are shown in Table 2.

6 Experiments

6.1 FNT for Embedding Evaluation

Embedding models. We choose four different embedding models for our comparisons: (i) Skip-Gram (henceforth SKIP) (skipgram bag-of-words model) (Mikolov et al., 2013), (ii) CBOW (continuous bag-of-words model) (Mikolov et al., 2013), (iii) Structured SkipGram (henceforth SSKIP) (Ling et al., 2015), (iv) CWindow (henceforth CWIN) (continuous window model) (Ling et al., 2015), and SSKIP and CWIN are order-aware, i.e, they take the order of the context tokens into account, while SKIP and CBOW are bag-of-words models.

Results and analysis. We report the results for all embedding models using LR and MLP in Table 3. We use the following evaluation measures, which are used in entity typing (Yaghoobzadeh and Schütze, 2015): (i) ACC (accuracy): percentage of test examples where all predictions are correct, (ii) Micro-F1: the global F1 computed over all the predictions.

Models in lines 1-5 in Table 3 are trained on

	LR		MLP	
	ACC	Micro-F1	ACC	Micro-F1
1 CBOW	19.2	47.8	24.9	**54.6**
2 SKIP	22.6	49.3	**25.2**	53.5
3 CWIN	22.6	49.8	25.1	54.2
4 SSKIP	**23.4**	**50.5**	**25.2**	53.6

Table 3: Accuracy and micro-F1 results on FNT for different embedding models using two classifiers (LR and MLP). Best result in each column is bold.

the Wikipedia corpus. We set the min frequency in corpus to 100. Window size = 3; negative sampling with $n = 10$. Based on the results of LR, order-aware architectures are better than their bag-of-words counterparts, i.e., SSKIP > SKIP and CWIN > CBOW. Overall, SSKIP is the best using LR classification. In MLP results, however, CBOW works best on micro-F1 measure and SSKIP and SKIP are bests on accuracy. There is no significant difference between CBOW and CWIN, or SSKIP and SKIP, respectively. Overall, the nonlinear classifier (MLP) with one hidden layer outperforms the linear classifier (LR) substantially, emphasizing that the encoded information about different types is easier to extract with stronger models.

Analysis on the number of name types. As a separate analysis, we measure how the classification performance depends on the N number of types of a name. To do so, we group test names based on their number of types. We keep the groups that have more than 100 members. Then, we plot the F1 results of CBOW and CWIN models trained using MLP classifier in Figure 2.

As it is shown, both models get their best results on names with $N = 2$. We suppose that the bad performance of $N = 1$ is related to the fact that one-type names have missing types in our dataset due to the incompleteness of Freebase. The worse F1 of $N >= 3$ compared to $N = 2$ is expected since bigger N means that the models need to predict more types from the name embeddings. From $N = 4$, somewhat surprisingly the F1 increases as N increases. This is perhaps related to the frequency of names in the corpus, and its relation to the number of names types: as N increases, the frequency of words increases and the embedding has a better quality. However, this is only a hypothesis and more investigation is required. The other observation is in the trend of CBOW and CWIN results. CBOW is worse for $N <= 2$, but

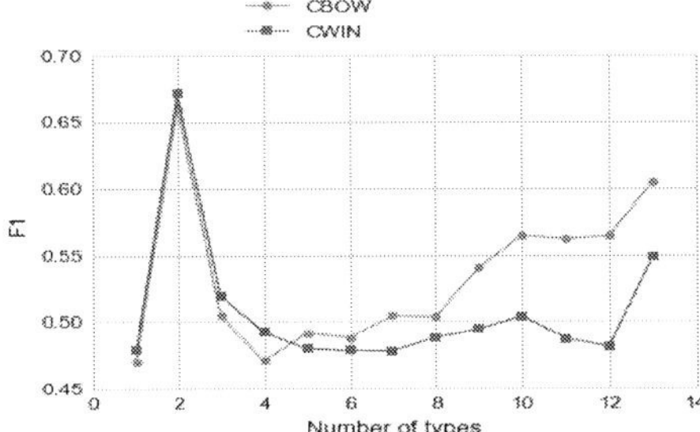

Figure 2: Micro-F1 for names with different number of types.

it works clearly better for $N > 2$. This shows that the embedding models behave differently for different number of classes they belong to. This could also be related to the frequency of words. Analysis of the reasons would be interesting. We leave it for the future work.

7 Conclusion

We proposed multi-label classification of word embeddings using the task of fine-grained typing of entity names. The dataset we built is a resource that is complementary to prior work in embedding evaluation: it is very large, its examples are multi-labeled with very fine-grained classes, and it allows the direct evaluation of embeddings without the need for context. We analyzed the performance of different embedding models on this dataset, showing differences in their performance as well as some of their limits in representing types accurately and completely.

More analysis and evaluation is necessary though, but we believe by using this kind of dataset, we are able to do much more than what we could do before with the small manually built word similarity and categorization benchmarks.

References

Marco Baroni, Georgiana Dinu, and Germán Kruszewski. 2014. Don't count, predict! A systematic comparison of context-counting vs. context-predicting semantic vectors. In *Proceedings of the 52nd Annual Meeting of the Association for Computational Linguistics, ACL 2014*, pages 238–247.

Kurt D. Bollacker, Colin Evans, Praveen Paritosh, Tim Sturge, and Jamie Taylor. 2008. Freebase: a collaboratively created graph database for structuring human knowledge. In *Proceedings of the ACM SIGMOD International Conference on Management of Data, SIGMOD 2008, Vancouver, BC, Canada, June 10-12, 2008*, pages 1247–1250.

Sophie Chesney, Guillaume Jacquet, Ralf Steinberger, and Jakub Piskorski. 2017. Multi-word entity classification in a highly multilingual environment. In *MWE*.

Jenny Rose Finkel, Trond Grenager, and Christopher Manning. 2005. Incorporating non-local information into information extraction systems by gibbs sampling. In *Proceedings of the 43rd Annual Meeting of the Association for Computational Linguistics (ACL'05)*, pages 363–370, Ann Arbor, Michigan. Association for Computational Linguistics.

Sonal Gupta and Christopher D. Manning. 2014. Improved pattern learning for bootstrapped entity extraction. In *Proceedings of the Eighteenth Conference on Computational Natural Language Learning, CoNLL 2014, Baltimore, Maryland, USA, June 26-27, 2014*, pages 98–108.

Arne Köhn. 2015. What?s in an embedding? analyzing word embeddings through multilingual evaluation. In *Proceedings of the 2015 Conference on Empirical Methods in Natural Language Processing*, pages 2067–2073, Lisbon, Portugal.

Siwei Lai, Kang Liu, Liheng Xu, and Jun Zhao. 2015. How to generate a good word embedding? *CoRR*, abs/1507.05523.

Jiwei Li and Dan Jurafsky. 2015. Do multi-sense embeddings improve natural language understanding? In *Proceedings of the 2015 Conference on Empirical Methods in Natural Language Processing*, pages 1722–1732, Lisbon, Portugal.

Wang Ling, Chris Dyer, Alan W. Black, and Isabel Trancoso. 2015. Two/too simple adaptations of word2vec for syntax problems. In *NAACL HLT 2015, The 2015 Conference of the North American Chapter of the Association for Computational Linguistics: Human Language Technologies, Denver, Colorado, USA, May 31 - June 5, 2015*, pages 1299–1304.

Xiao Ling and Daniel S. Weld. 2012. Fine-grained entity recognition. In *Proceedings of the Twenty-Sixth AAAI Conference on Artificial Intelligence*, Toronto, Ontario, Canada.

Tomas Mikolov, Kai Chen, Greg Corrado, and Jeffrey Dean. 2013. Efficient estimation of word representations in vector space. *CoRR*, abs/1301.3781.

Fabian Pedregosa, Gaël Varoquaux, Alexandre Gramfort, Vincent Michel, Bertrand Thirion, Olivier Grisel, Mathieu Blondel, Peter Prettenhofer, Ron Weiss, Vincent Dubourg, Jake VanderPlas, Alexandre Passos, David Cournapeau, Matthieu Brucher, Matthieu Perrot, and Edouard Duchesnay. 2011. Scikit-learn: Machine learning in python. *Journal of Machine Learning Research*, 12:2825–2830.

Xiang Ren, Wenqi He, Meng Qu, Lifu Huang, Heng Ji, and Jiawei Han. 2016. Afet: Automatic fine-grained entity typing by hierarchical partial-label embedding. In *Proceedings of the 2016 Conference on Empirical Methods in Natural Language Processing*, pages 1369–1378, Austin, Texas. Association for Computational Linguistics.

Sebastian Riedel, Limin Yao, Andrew McCallum, and Benjamin M. Marlin. 2013. Relation extraction with matrix factorization and universal schemas. In *Proceedings of the 2013 Conference of the North American Chapter of the Association for Computational Linguistics: Human Language Technologies*, pages 74–84, Atlanta, Georgia. Association for Computational Linguistics.

Dana Rubinstein, Effi Levi, Roy Schwartz, and Ari Rappoport. 2015. How well do distributional models capture different types of semantic knowledge? In *Proceedings of the 53rd Annual Meeting of the Association for Computational Linguistics and the 7th International Joint Conference on Natural Language Processing of the Asian Federation of Natural Language Processing, ACL 2015, July 26-31, 2015, Beijing, China, Volume 2: Short Papers*, pages 726–730.

Tobias Schnabel, Igor Labutov, David Mimno, and Thorsten Joachims. 2015. Evaluation methods for unsupervised word embeddings. In *Proceedings of the 2015 Conference on Empirical Methods in Natural Language Processing*, pages 298–307, Lisbon, Portugal.

Sonse Shimaoka, Pontus Stenetorp, Kentaro Inui, and Sebastian Riedel. 2016. An attentive neural architecture for fine-grained entity type classification. In *Proceedings of the 5th Workshop on Automated Knowledge Base Construction*, pages 69–74, San Diego, CA. Association for Computational Linguistics.

Michael Thelen and Ellen Riloff. 2002. A bootstrapping method for learning semantic lexicons using extraction pattern contexts. In *Proceedings of the 2002 Conference on Empirical Methods in Natural Language Processing*, pages 214–221. Association for Computational Linguistics.

Yadollah Yaghoobzadeh, Heike Adel, and Hinrich Schuetze. 2018. Corpus-level fine-grained entity typing. *Journal of Artificial Intelligence Research*, 61:835–862.

Yadollah Yaghoobzadeh and Hinrich Schütze. 2015. Corpus-level fine-grained entity typing using contextual information. In *Proceedings of the 2015 Conference on Empirical Methods in Natural Language Processing*, pages 715–725, Lisbon, Portugal.

Yadollah Yaghoobzadeh and Hinrich Schütze. 2016. Intrinsic subspace evaluation of word embedding representations. In *Proceedings of the 54th Annual Meeting of the Association for Computational Linguistics (Volume 1: Long Papers)*, pages 236–246, Berlin, Germany. Association for Computational Linguistics.

Yadollah Yaghoobzadeh and Hinrich Schütze. 2017. Multi-level representations for fine-grained typing of knowledge base entities. In *Proceedings of the 15th Conference of the European Chapter of the Association for Computational Linguistics: Volume 1, Long Papers*, pages 578–589. Association for Computational Linguistics.

Dani Yogatama, Daniel Gillick, and Nevena Lazic. 2015. Embedding methods for fine grained entity type classification. In *Proceedings of the 53rd Annual Meeting of the Association for Computational Linguistics and the 7th International Joint Conference on Natural Language Processing (Volume 2: Short Papers)*, pages 291–296, Beijing, China. Association for Computational Linguistics.

Daojian Zeng, Kang Liu, Siwei Lai, Guangyou Zhou, and Jun Zhao. 2014. Relation classification via convolutional deep neural network. In *COLING 2014, 25th International Conference on Computational Linguistics, Proceedings of the Conference: Technical Papers, August 23-29, 2014, Dublin, Ireland*, pages 2335–2344.

A Dense Vector Representation for Open-Domain Relation Tuples

Ade Romadhony[1], Alfan Farizki Wicaksono[2], Ayu Purwarianti[3] and Dwi Hendratmo Widyantoro[4]

[1,3,4]School of Electrical Engineering and Informatics, Bandung Institute of Technology
[1]{*ade_romadhony*}@*students.itb.ac.id*
[3,4]{*ayu,dwi*}@*stei.itb.ac.id*
[2]Faculty of Computer Science, University of Indonesia
[2]{*alfan*}@*cs.ui.ac.id*

Abstract

Open Information Extraction (Open IE), which has been extensively studied as a new paradigm on unrestricted information extraction, produces relation tuples (results) which serve as intermediate structures in several natural language processing tasks, such as question answering system. In this paper, we investigate ways to learn the vector representation of Open IE relation tuples using various approaches, ranging from simple vector composition to more advanced methods, such as recursive autoencoder (RAE). The quality of vector representation was evaluated by conducting experiments on the relation tuple similarity task. While the experiment result shows that simple linear combination (i.e., averaging the vectors of the words participating in the tuple) outperforms any other methods, including RAE, RAE itself has its own advantage in dealing with a case, in which the similarity criterion is characterized by each element in the tuple, where the simple linear combination unable to identify.

1 Introduction

Open information extraction (Open IE) is an extraction paradigm that applies no restriction on information type. This paradigm was first introduced by Banko et al. (2007), as a solution for alleviating the difficulty on conventional extraction paradigm, which commonly requires predefined information types. However, defining information type on diverse and large scale environment is certainly a daunting and expensive task. By applying Open IE paradigm, the extraction goal is to gather all possible relations while also retaining the low complexity of the process underlying the extraction.

An Open IE system extracts relation tuples from text, in the form of $(e_i, r_{i,j}, e_j)$, where both e_i and e_j denote a pair of entities and $r_{i,j}$ denotes the relation between them. There are several Open IE systems: TextRunner (Banko et al., 2007), ReVerb (Etzioni et al., 2011), Ollie (Schmitz et al., 2012), NELL (Carlson et al., 2010), Exemplar (Mesquita et al., 2013), ClauseIE (Del Corro and Gemulla, 2013), Stanford Open IE (Angeli et al., 2015), and MinIE (Gashteovski et al., 2017). Each of them has different characteristics according to the following criteria: (1) extraction degree (binary or n-ary), (2) extraction features (part-of-speech, phrase type, named-entity class, and dependency type), (3) extraction method, and (4) output granularity. However, all of them still maintain one main characteristic of Open IE system which aims at extracting open-domain relation tuples.

It has been widely known that the results of Open IE extraction can be applied to several task or system, such as question answering and knowledge based system. Stanovsky et al. (2015) conducted a study on employing Open IE results as an intermediate structure for other applications. The study revealed that Open IE structure is more effective on particular semantic applications, as compared to other structures, such as dependency tree and semantic role labeling (SRL). Stanford CoreNLP, which is an established natural language processing tool, also includes Open IE as an output type of their processing tools.

Although Open IE relation tuples have been widely used as input in some downstream applications (Mausam, 2016), most approaches that involve the relation tuples similarity generally require a two-step process. For example, in identifying other tuples which are similar to a particular relation tuple, Yates and Etzioni (2009) treated the relation similarity as a string similarity problem combined with relation tuple similarity that employs extracted shared property based on re-

Proceedings of the 3rd Workshop on Representation Learning for NLP, pages 107–112
Melbourne, Australia, July 20, 2018. ©2018 Association for Computational Linguistics

Sentence	Relation Tuple
MPAA sues six BitTorrent sites linking to TV shows.	SUBJ:MPAA:ORG; Trigger: sues; DOBJ: sites, POBJ-OF:BitTorrent:ORG
Microsoft co-founder Bill Gates spoke at a conference on Monday	SUBJ:Bill Gates:PER; Trigger: spoke; POBJ-ON:Monday:DATE

Table 1: Example of an Open IE System Input and Output

lation arguments. Another study on extracting large event schemas based on Open IE relation tuples processes the whole relation and then checks the arguments relatedness (Balasubramanian et al., 2013). To the best of our knowledge, there is no previous study on learning vector representation of Open IE relation tuple.

By representing a relation tuple in its original string form and processing the semantic information of its relation and arguments separately, it causes lack of semantic meaning. Studies on word representation as vector showed that it boosts the system performance on particular tasks related with semantic such as word similarity and word relatedness (Niraula et al., 2015). Representing a relation tuple as a single vector representation attempts to solve the weakness of string-based representation.

We investigate several methods to represent a relation tuple as a dense vector. There are different methods to solve this compositional semantic problem, including simple linear combination and recursive autoencoder (RAE) method. To compare the methods, we perform an evaluation on relation tuple similarity task. The dataset we use is Open Event Extraction (ASTRE) dataset (Nguyen et al., 2016). In addition to investigating the vector representation methods, the use of vector combination is also examined by incorporating word corpus-based vector and knowledge-based vector. This combination of different sources was introduced to achieve better performance on word similarity and word relatedness (Niraula et al., 2015) (Goikoetxea et al., 2016).

2   Related Work

Several Open IE systems have different ways on presenting relation tuples. ReVerb (Fader et al., 2011), Ollie (Carlson et al., 2010), and Stanford Open IE (Angeli et al., 2015) do not provide entity type of the arguments, since they only require that an argument should be a noun phrase, rather than a Named Entity. On the other hand, Exemplar restricts that an argument must be a Named Entity

with People/Organization/Location/Miscellanous class. Other Open IE systems such as PATTY (Nakashole et al., 2012) puts entity type information based on external knowledge base. Existing Open IE systems also differ in term of attaching argument type, whether the argument is subject or object. Exemplar and Stanford Open IE attach the subject and object information, while the other Open IE systems do not provide the information. Table 1 shows example of an Open IE system (Exemplar) input and output.

The differences on relation tuple structures affect different approaches on performing similarity task. However, no previous studies on relation tuple similarity has used vector representation. An early study on resolving the relation tuple synonym, Resolver, is based on string matching algorithm and relation property similarity (Yates and Etzioni, 2009). Other studies such as PATTY uses the argument type information to group similar relation tuples (Nakashole et al., 2012), and Rel-Grams uses the whole strings in a relation tuple as the feature of PMI-based similarity method (Balasubramanian et al., 2013).

Meanwhile, latest studies on word similarity show significance performance when word vector representation is used (Niraula et al., 2015). Representing a word as a vector enables us to perform vector operation on words, and infer several relationships between words. An Open IE relation tuple has similar characteristic to a clause or a sentence. Based on their similar characteristic, we adapt the methods on compositional semantic problem that has been applied to sentence: simple linear combination and RAE method, to represent a relation tuple as a dense vector.

3   Method

3.1   Dense Vector Composition

As we stated earlier, an Open IE relation tuple structure consists of a relation (trigger) and two or more arguments. Several Open IE systems including Exemplar and Stanford Open IE distinguish the arguments into subject and object. We use the trigger, subject and object information to build the vector, and use word vector as the basis for vector composition. In this study, we use Exemplar as the Open IE system that produces the relation tuples[1]. In contrast with several Open IE systems that pro-

---

[1] https://github.com/U-Alberta/exemplar

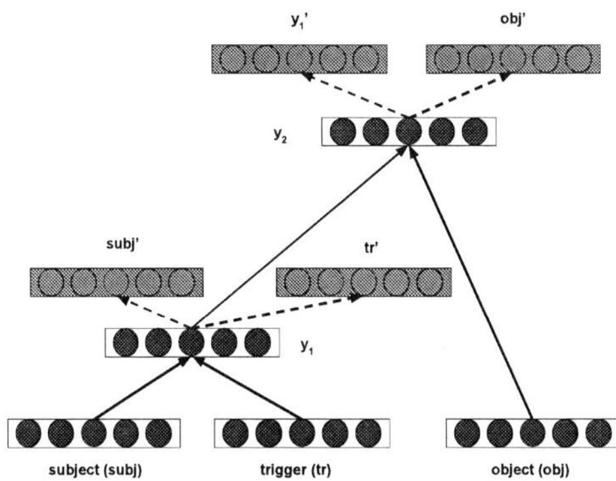

Figure 1: Relation Tuple Vector Composition

vide whole clause as relation argument, Exemplar only outputs the clause head as relation argument.

Simple Linear Composition A relation tuple consists of several words, therefore building a single vector representation of a relation tuple utilizes vector combination method. The most common vector combination method are addition/sum and averaging (Foltz et al., 1998). There are several studies on word vector operation to capture a phrase meaning, including Mitchell and Lapata (2008) work. They performed several vector operations such as averaging, while addition operation was not implemented because it treats the words as a bag of words, ignoring the syntax (Mitchell and Lapata, 2008).

In this study, we perform sum/addition and averaging operation on word vectors. We also employ the sum operation since Exemplar relation tuples do not contain complete phrase or clause, only the head words. Therefore, we think bag of words model operation could be applied.

Recursive Autoencoder / RAE

We adapt the RAE method from Socher et al. (2011) work, which goal was to learn vector representation for multi-word phrases. According to relation tuple structure, we define a tree structure as shown in Figure 1, under assumption that it is a static structure, because there is no dependency type information on a relation tuple. On learning the structure, first we build a composition vector from subject and trigger vector, followed by building a composition from subject-trigger and object vector. In each step, we learn an autoencoder model, which maps a concatenated vector of $2 * n$ dimensions to a vector of n dimensions. For each element: subject, trigger, and object, we

perform averaging operation to obtain single vector. We perform the linear word vector combination because it works well when the semantic of the words is sum of its parts, and no words modify the meaning of another word (Socher et al., 2012).

Given an input relation tuple, the autoencoder return a vector representation (y_2):

$$y_2 = f(W_1[y_1; V_{obj}] + b_1) \qquad (1)$$

The final output (y_2) is obtained from a vector that is the result of subject and trigger vector composition (y_1) and object vector. The subject and trigger composition (y_1) is defined as follows :

$$y_1 = f(W_1[V_{subj}; V_{tr}] + b_1) \qquad (2)$$

The W_1 weight was used in dense vector construction from subject and trigger vector, and from subject-trigger (y_1) and object vector. The construction process will result a vector with reduced dimension, from n + n (2n) to n dimension. According to Socher et al. (2011), we need to perform re-reconstruction after each dense vector construction:

$$[V_{subj}'; V_{tr}'] = f(W_2.y_1 + b_2) \qquad (3)$$

$$[y_1'; V_{obj}'] = f(W_2.y_2 + b_2) \qquad (4)$$

The W_2 weight was used in the re-reconstruction process after y_1 or y_2 was constructed, in which it expands the constructed vector dimension. The re-reconstruction process aim is to ensure that y_1 and y_2 represent the vector composition well.

The weight and bias parameters $\theta = (W_1, b_1, W_2, b_2)$ were estimated from data through gradient descent optimization with loss function based on the sum of all errors in dense vector construction and re-reconstruction process:

$$L = E_{rec}([V_{subj}; V_{tr}], [V_{subj}'; V_{tr}']) + \\ E_{rec}([y_1; V_{obj}], [y_1'; V_{obj}']) \qquad (5)$$

We define the reconstruction error as a MSE function:

$$Erec = \frac{1}{2}||u - v||^2 \qquad (6)$$

that measures the difference between input vector u and re-reconstructed vector v.

3.2 Word Vector Source

Besides using the word vectors obtained from corpus, we also examine another word vector source. Based on Goikoetxea et al. (2016) work, the use of word vectors combination performs better in several tasks on word similarity and word relatedness.

Relation Tuple
(MPAA, sue site, BitTorrent)
(He, sue, Acacia Mortgage Corp. 2001)
(Motion Picture Association of America, launch separate lawsuit, crackdown Internet sites)
(MPAA, commence legal action, BitTorrent)
(MPAA, target Usenet related site, Usenet)

Table 2: Example of Gold Relation Tuples

Therefore, we use concatenated corpus-based vector and WordNet-based vector as one of our experiment settings[2], to test whether this combination can capture better semantic relatedness.

3.3 Similarity Function

To measure relation tuple vector similarity, we use euclidean distance:

$$sim_{r_1,r_2} = \alpha(sim_{r_1,r_2}) + (1-\alpha)(sim_{tr_{(r1)},tr_{(r2)}}) \tag{7}$$

Our experiment default setting for similarity calculation is based on euclidean distance of relation tuple vector pair. However, we observe that a relation trigger may has stronger influence on relation tuple semantic rather than the relation tuple arguments (subject and object). We then examine other similarity function, i.e. combination of relation tuple vector similarity and relation trigger similarity. Formula 7 shows the similarity combination between the relation tuple vector similarity denotes by sim_{r_1,r_2} and the relation trigger similarity denotes by $sim_{tr_{r1},tr_{r2}}$. We use α 0.5 in our experiment.

4 Experiments

4.1 The Dataset

We use an English Open Event Extraction Dataset/ASTRE (Nguyen et al., 2016) in the experiment. The dataset is built for event schema induction task, and the development and test dataset were annotated with event type information on word that was denoted as event trigger. The event type annotation was performed based on the TAC KBP event annotation guidelines. We use small english wikipedia corpus[3] that was merged with relevant dataset to build the word vectors as the basis for learning the Open IE relation tuple vector, and use test dataset for generating the gold similarity label.

<hr>

[2]http://ixa2.si.ehu.eus/ukb/
[3]https://sites.google.com/site/rmyeid/projects/polyglot

4.2 Relation Tuple Similarity Task

In order to evaluate the relation tuple vector representation methods, we perform relation tuple similarity task. In contrast with other established tasks such as paraphrasing and sentence similarity, there is no standard evaluation dataset on relation tuple similarity. Hence, we adapt the available information on ASTRE event dataset to build our evaluation dataset.

We borrow the idea from information retrieval evaluation on performing the evaluation through relation tuple similarity task. Given a relation tuple, we evaluate how many other relation tuples with the same event type are having high similarity value. The similarity between two relation tuples was measured based on euclidean distance between both vectors. We conclude a better vector representation method has higher performance on getting more similar/relevant (i.e having the same event type) relation tuples, which is denoted by n-top similar tuples ranked by their similarity value.

Table 2 shows a list of relation tuples with *Sue* event type label. For each of relation tuple on the list, we compute their similarity value with all other relation tuples on the dataset. A perfect result is obtained when the top-n highest similarity values come from the relation tuples having the same event type. For instance, when performing the similarity computation on *(MPAA, sue site, BitTorrent)*, the expected result is having the other four relation tuples to have highest similarity value.

4.3 Results

For each relation tuples in gold label dataset, we take the top 10 most similar relation tuples (retrieved tuples), and then compare it to other gold relation tuples with the same event type (relevant tuples). Table 3 shows the F1 of relation tuple similarity evaluation. Overal result shows that averaging method with trigger similarity combination (avg-trigger) outperforms other settings. Although the simple linear method has better performance than the RAE method on majority event types, the RAE has better performance on *Sue* event type.

Based on our observation, the RAE has advantage on a case where the relation tuple characteristics depend heavily on syntax structure and element order. The RAE method preserves each element (subject, trigger, and object) characteristic, which can be observed on the retrieved similar tu-

| Composition Method | Event Type | | | | | | | | | | | | | | Avg |
and Similarity Setting	1	2	3	4	5	6	7	8	9	10	11	12	13	14	
sum	**0.17**	0.08	0.10	0.08	0.13	0.00	0.09	0.00	0.09	0.00	0.34	0.21	0.14	0.05	0.11
sum-trigger	0.11	**0.38**	0.17	0.20	0.30	0.00	0.21	0.06	**0.18**	0.00	**0.57**	**0.38**	0.23	0.21	0.22
avg	0.11	0.04	0.06	0.10	0.13	0.00	0.13	0.06	**0.18**	0.00	0.20	0.31	0.26	0.12	0.12
avg-trigger	0.11	0.35	**0.19**	**0.21**	**0.32**	0.00	**0.24**	0.14	**0.18**	0.00	**0.57**	**0.38**	0.31	**0.30**	**0.24**
RAE	0.00	0.00	0.02	0.04	0.07	0.00	0.02	0.06	0.00	0.00	0.03	0.12	0.34	0.00	0.05
RAE-trigger	0.11	0.23	0.12	0.15	0.26	0.00	0.17	0.11	0.00	0.00	**0.57**	0.30	**0.37**	0.11	0.18
RAECAT	0.00	0.04	0.04	0.04	0.04	0.00	0.03	0.06	0.00	0.00	0.09	0.15	0.31	0.02	0.06
RAECAT-trigger	0.11	0.27	0.18	0.20	0.30	0.00	0.20	**0.17**	0.09	**0.09**	**0.57**	0.27	0.31	0.25	0.22

Table 3: F1 similarity evaluation on each event type. (1) acquit, (2) appeal, (3) arrest-jail, (4) attack, (5) charge-indict, (6) convict, (7) die, (8) execute, (9) fine, (10) injure, (11) release-parole, (12) sentence, (13) sue, (14) trial-hearing.

Avg Method	RAE Method
(Denpasar court, sentence remain member, life Bali)	(court, sentence fine, US plea **years** secrets)
(he, serve, **years** sentence)	(canoeist, miss, **years**)
(life, sentence, Cyprus killing)	(she, face, **years**)
(years imprisonment, request, prosecutors)	(he, serve, **years** sentence)
(Texas judge, hand three-year prison sentence, US **three-year** prison)	(Glenn Simpkins, have, **weeks**)
(years, minimum penalty, **years** imprisonment)	(two sides, meet, **weeks**)
(court, sentence, Schwartz addition **days**)	(children, range, **years**)
(charges, carry minimum penalty, **years** imprisonment)	(charges, carry minimum penalty, **years** imprisonment)
(Tom DeLay, sentence, **years**)	(years, minimum penalty, **years** imprisonment)
(court, sentence fine, US plea **years** secrets)	(Tom DeLay, sentence, **years**)

Table 4: Top 10 most similar relation tuples to *(Jefferson, face maximum sentence, years)*

ples. For instance, we compare the top 10 most similar relation tuples to *(Jefferson, face maximum sentence, years)* retrieved from averaging and RAE method. As shown in Table 4, we found that all retrieved relation tuples from RAE method contains objects that are similar to the word *years*, such as: *years* and *weeks*. Meanwhile, a number of retrieved relation tuples from averaging method do not contain objects that are similar to *years*.

As for the word vector combination, the use of WordNet word vector shows effect on identifying more relevant words. The performance comparison between RAE and RAECAT and between RAE-trigger and RAECAT-trigger show that word vector combination has better performance on most event types.

5   Conclusion

We present an investigation of several methods on representing Open IE relation tuples as dense vectors based on word vector. The result on relation tuple similarity task shows that simple linear combination has better performance on most cases than RAE method. However, the RAE method has better performance on identifying similar relation tuples in a case where word or element order is important. In future, we plan to explore other

methods on learning dense vector model for open-domain relation tuple.

In future, we plan to explore other methods on learning dense vector model for open-domain relation tuple and also explore any other downstream application for evaluation. There are several more advanced methods on learning dense vector that may give better semantic representation than the ones we explored in this paper. The evaluation task on downstream applications also may give better reflection on the effectiveness of vector representation, rather than the similarity task that put more attention on the vector composition quality.

References

Gabor Angeli, Melvin Jose Johnson Premkumar, and Christopher D Manning. 2015. Leveraging linguistic structure for open domain information extraction. In *Proceedings of the 53rd Annual Meeting of the Association for Computational Linguistics and the 7th International Joint Conference on Natural Language Processing (Volume 1: Long Papers)*, volume 1, pages 344–354.

Niranjan Balasubramanian, Stephen Soderland, Oren Etzioni Mausam, and Oren Etzioni. 2013. Generating coherent event schemas at scale. In *EMNLP*, pages 1721–1731.

Michele Banko, Michael J Cafarella, Stephen Soderland, Matthew Broadhead, and Oren Etzioni. 2007. Open information extraction from the web. In *IJCAI*, volume 7, pages 2670–2676.

Andrew Carlson, Justin Betteridge, Bryan Kisiel, Burr Settles, Estevam R Hruschka Jr, and Tom M Mitchell. 2010. Toward an architecture for never-ending language learning. In *AAAI*, volume 5, page 3. Atlanta.

Luciano Del Corro and Rainer Gemulla. 2013. Clausie: clause-based open information extraction. In *Proceedings of the 22nd international conference on World Wide Web*, pages 355–366. ACM.

Oren Etzioni, Anthony Fader, Janara Christensen, Stephen Soderland, and Mausam Mausam. 2011. Open information extraction: The second generation. In *IJCAI*, volume 11, pages 3–10.

Anthony Fader, Stephen Soderland, and Oren Etzioni. 2011. Identifying relations for open information extraction. In *Proceedings of the conference on empirical methods in natural language processing*, pages 1535–1545. Association for Computational Linguistics.

Peter W Foltz, Walter Kintsch, and Thomas K Landauer. 1998. The measurement of textual coherence with latent semantic analysis. *Discourse processes*, 25(2-3):285–307.

Kiril Gashteovski, Rainer Gemulla, and Luciano Del Corro. 2017. Minie: Minimizing facts in open information extraction. In *Proceedings of the 2017 Conference on Empirical Methods in Natural Language Processing*, pages 2620–2630.

Josu Goikoetxea, Eneko Agirre, and Aitor Soroa. 2016. Single or multiple? combining word representations independently learned from text and wordnet. In *AAAI*, pages 2608–2614.

Mausam Mausam. 2016. Open information extraction systems and downstream applications. In *Proceedings of the Twenty-Fifth International Joint Conference on Artificial Intelligence*, pages 4074–4077. AAAI Press.

Filipe Mesquita, Jordan Schmidek, and Denilson Barbosa. 2013. Effectiveness and efficiency of open relation extraction. *New York Times*, 500:150.

Jeff Mitchell and Mirella Lapata. 2008. Vector-based models of semantic composition. *proceedings of ACL-08: HLT*, pages 236–244.

Ndapandula Nakashole, Gerhard Weikum, and Fabian Suchanek. 2012. Discovering and exploring relations on the web. *Proceedings of the VLDB Endowment*, 5(12):1982–1985.

Kiem-Hieu Nguyen, Xavier Tannier, Olivier Ferret, and Romaric Besançon. 2016. A dataset for open event extraction in english. In *LREC*.

Nobal B Niraula, Dipesh Gautam, Rajendra Banjade, Nabin Maharjan, and Vasile Rus. 2015. Combining word representations for measuring word relatedness and similarity. In *FLAIRS Conference*, pages 199–204.

Michael Schmitz, Robert Bart, Stephen Soderland, Oren Etzioni, et al. 2012. Open language learning for information extraction. In *Proceedings of the 2012 Joint Conference on Empirical Methods in Natural Language Processing and Computational Natural Language Learning*, pages 523–534. Association for Computational Linguistics.

Richard Socher, Brody Huval, Christopher D Manning, and Andrew Y Ng. 2012. Semantic compositionality through recursive matrix-vector spaces. In *Proceedings of the 2012 joint conference on empirical methods in natural language processing and computational natural language learning*, pages 1201–1211. Association for Computational Linguistics.

Richard Socher, Jeffrey Pennington, Eric H Huang, Andrew Y Ng, and Christopher D Manning. 2011. Semi-supervised recursive autoencoders for predicting sentiment distributions. In *Proceedings of the conference on empirical methods in natural language processing*, pages 151–161. Association for Computational Linguistics.

Gabriel Stanovsky, Ido Dagan, et al. 2015. Open ie as an intermediate structure for semantic tasks. In *Proceedings of the 53rd Annual Meeting of the Association for Computational Linguistics and the 7th International Joint Conference on Natural Language Processing (Volume 2: Short Papers)*, volume 2, pages 303–308.

Alexander Pieter Yates and Oren Etzioni. 2009. Unsupervised methods for determining object and relation synonyms on the web. *Journal of Artificial Intelligence Research*.

Exploiting Common Characters in Chinese and Japanese to Learn Cross-lingual Word Embeddings via Matrix Factorization

Jilei Wang *†
Tsinghua University, China
wangjileiruc@gmail.com

Shiying Luo †
Northeastern University, China
neulsy@hotmail.com

Weiyan Shi
University of California, Berkeley, USA
wyshi@berkeley.edu

Tao Dai
Tsinghua University, China
dait14@mails.tsinghua.edu.cn

Shu-Tao Xia *
Tsinghua University, China
xiast@sz.tsinghua.edu.cn

Abstract

Learning vector space representation of words (i.e., word embeddings) has recently attracted wide research interests, and has been extended to cross-lingual scenario. Currently most cross-lingual word embedding learning models are based on sentence alignment, which inevitably introduces much noise. In this paper, we show in Chinese and Japanese, the acquisition of semantic relation among words can benefit from the large number of common characters shared by both languages; inspired by this unique feature, we design a method named CJC targeting to generate cross-lingual context of words. We combine CJC with GloVe based on matrix factorization, and then propose an integrated model named CJ-Glo. Taking two sentence-aligned models and CJ-BOC (also exploits common characters but is based on CBOW) as baseline algorithms, we compare them with CJ-Glo on a series of NLP tasks including cross-lingual synonym, word analogy and sentence alignment. The result indicates CJ-Glo achieves the best performance among these methods, and is more stable in cross-lingual tasks; moreover, compared with CJ-BOC, CJ-Glo is less sensitive to the alteration of parameters.

1 Introduction

Word representation is critical to various NLP tasks, and the traditional one-hot representation, despite its simplicity, suffers from at least two aspects: the vector dimensionality increases with vocabulary size, leading to "curse of dimensionality"; more importantly, it fails to capture the semantic relation among words.

Due to the defects of one-hot representation, the majority of research interests now have switched to distributed word representation (also known as "word embedding"), which represents word as a real-valued vector. Represented as vectors, the semantics of words are better reflected, as the relatedness of words can be quantified using vector arithmetic.

To efficiently train word embeddings, a range of models have been proposed, most of them targeting to train monolingual word embedding. Though word embedding is often discussed under monolingual scenario, cross-lingual embedding can serve as a useful tool in several NLP tasks including machine translation (Wu et al., 2016), word sense disambiguation (Chen et al., 2014), and so on. This is because cross-lingual word embeddings map words from two languages into one vector space, thereby making it possible to measure the semantic relation among words from different languages. However, compared with the bulk of works studying monolingual word embedding, cross-lingual word embedding is still at its initial stage, with no learning model being widely accepted.

In this paper, we present a method named CJC (Chinese-Japanese Common Character)

---

* Corresponding authors.
† Contributed equally to the paper.

113

Proceedings of the 3rd Workshop on Representation Learning for NLP, pages 113–121
Melbourne, Australia, July 20, 2018. ©2018 Association for Computational Linguistics

aiming to extract cross-lingual context of words from sentence aligned Chinese-Japanese corpus. Given the large amount of common characters shared by both languages and the rich semantic connections thereof, we exploit them to acquire potential word level alignment. The acquired cross-lingual contexts can be flexibly integrated with various models; in this paper, CJC is mainly integrated with a matrix factorization model called Glove (Pennington et al., 2014), and the integrated model is thus called CJ-Glo.

To evaluate the performance of CJ-Glo, we take 2 sentence aligned models respectively based on CBOW(Mikolov et al., 2013a) and GloVe, and CJ-BOC model (based on Common Character + CBOW) (Wang et al., 2016) as contrast, and compare the trained word embeddings of these methods using three typical NLP tasks, including cross-lingual synonym, word analogy and sentence alignment. According to the experiment results, the acquired word embeddings by using CJ-Glo have better quality than those of the other models; moreover, CJ-Glo performs more stably than its competitors, and is less sensitive to parameter alteration.

2 Related work

Word embedding was initiated by Hinton (1986), which essentially encodes word using a real-valued vector. With word embeddings, the intrinsic relatedness among words can be explicitly measured as the distances or angles between word pairs. This favorable feature of word embedding soon led to its popularity in industry and academia in past decades. Specifically, word embedding has found its applications in machine translation (Wu et al., 2016; Lample et al., 2017), word sense disambiguation (Chen et al., 2014; Guo et al., 2014), information retrieval (Vulić and Moens, 2015) and so on.

To efficiently acquire high-quality word embeddings, vast research efforts have therefore emerged. A representative framework to learn word embeddings is Neural Network Language Model (NNLM) proposed by Bengio et al. (2003), which adopts back-propagation when training word embeddings and parameters for the model. Another typical approach is matrix factorization, whose basic idea is to approximate original matrices with low-rank matrices by leveraging statistic information. For example, GloVe (Pennington et al., 2014) explicitly factorizes the co-occurrence matrix, training only non-zero elements instead of an entire spare matrix.

Traditionally, word embedding was studied under monolingual setting, and then naturally extended to bilingual scenario. Compared with monolingual word embeddings, bilingual word embedding reveals the internal relation among words of different languages; and such capability makes bilingual word embeddings a powerful tool to assist machine translation, or even serves as a substitute for word mapping matrix and dictionary in previous machine translation methods. A range of works have been proposed to learn bilingual word embeddings, such as (Mikolov et al., 2013b), which attempts to map separately trained word embeddings into one vector space, and acquire bilingual word embeddings. BilBOWA is a model proposed in (Gouws et al., 2015), whose most notable merit is the whole training process does not require word alignment or dictionary. word alignment or dictionary. (Shi et al., 2015) is another work that utilizes matrix factorization in word embeddings learning. Ruder et al. (2017) provides a detailed survey, which enumerates the input format and basic principles of various bilingual word embedding learning methods.

When it comes to non-alphabet-based language like Chinese and Japanese, an essential difference from alphabet-based languages is that each character in a word contains abundant information, and makes sense itself. In addition to this, an underlying correlation between Chinese and Japanese is the large portion of shared characters in both languages; with the help of these characters, Chu et al. (2014) extracted texts from Wikipedia web pages of Chinese and Japanese version, based on which they then constructed a Chinese-Japanese parallel corpus. A natural conjecture about the common characters is the semantic similarity or even equivalence among them. In light of this, we proposed CJ-BOC model in our previous work (Wang et al., 2016) to learn Chinese-Japanese bilingual word embeddings, which outperforms sentence-alignment approaches in terms of embedding quality. To our knowledge, our previous work is the first attempt to learn Chinese-Japanese word embeddings using common Chinese characters.

3 Chinese-Japanese Common Character

Historically, Chinese character has spread to a group of countries in East Asia as a major carrier of Chinese culture, thereby influencing the writing systems in these countries. Traditional Chinese, Simplified Chinese and Japanese Kanji are now being used, all developing from Traditional Chinese; and given the same root of them, these three writing systems actually share a large portion of common characters: for a certain character in one of them, we can find its counterparts in the other two, with minor variation or even of the same shape. Chu et al. (2012) proposed a Chinese character table comparing traditional Chinese, simplified Chinese and Japanese. As summarized in Table 1, the glyphs of such common characters can be 1) the same in all these three writing systems; 2) consistent in two of them; 3) different in all these three.

And with regard to their semantics, simplified and traditional Chinese are only two written forms of the same language, and therefore common characters within them are semantically equivalent. For Japanese Kanji, most characters are semantically equivalent or relevant to their counterparts in Chinese.

We in our previous work (Wang et al., 2016) quantified such semantic relatedness from the view of information theory using mutual information (MI) and conditional mutual information (CMI). By repeating the experiments in this paper, we acquired the results in Table 2. All these 5 characters have multiple meanings in both Chinese and Japanese, and their respective meanings differ to some extent in both languages. Normally CMI should be larger than MI, which indicates that in a translation-sentence pair, if 2 words from each sentence share a common character, they are likely to form a translation word pair. The results of shown in Table 2 are no exception, providing theoretical root for our model which will be proposed in section 4.

4 Model

4.1 Context of Word and CJC Method

Before delving into the learning models, we should first clarify the concept of context. In natural language processing, a widely adopted semantic representation model is Bag-of-Words (Zhang et al., 2010). The fundamental assumption of this model is: within a given sentence or paragraph, the target word is prone to have the most intimate semantic relation with its closest context words. Formally define a sentence S with l words as an ordered sequence: $S = \langle w_0, w_1, ..., w_l \rangle$, and context function $Ctx(\cdot)$ is often formulated as:

$$Ctx(w_i, S) = \{w_k | i - K \leq k \leq i + K\}. \quad (1)$$

In cross-lingual scenario, besides two monolingual corpora of both languages, a parallel corpus is often required in most models, which is aligned in either word-level (Guo et al., 2016) or sentence-level. Some recent works attempted to learn embeddings without using parallel corpus, such as (Artetxe et al., 2017).

Now try to consider bilingual context of a given target word in aligned parallel corpus. Let $\langle S_{zh}, S_{ja} \rangle$ be a sentence pair, then define:

$$\begin{aligned} Ctx(w_{zh,i}) &= Ctx(w_{zh,i}, S_{zh}) \\ &\cup Ctx(w_{zh,i}, S_{ja}). \end{aligned} \quad (2)$$

As formulated above, the context of a target word is the union of its contexts in both sentences. Therefore in word-aligned parallel corpus, let $\langle w_{zh,i}, w_{ja,j} \rangle$ be a pair of aligned words, and the cross-lingual context $Ctx_w(w_{zh,i}, S_{ja})$ is equal to $Ctx_w(w_{ja,j}, S_{ja})$, since contexts in both languages are taken into account in this definition. In sentence-aligned parallel corpus, the cross-lingual context $Ctx_s(w_{zh,i}, S_{ja})$ is defined as the set of all the words in the respective sentence.

In real applications, sentence alignment data are usually easier to acquire. For example, Chu et al. (2014) proposed an approach to align Chinese-Japanese cross-lingual wiki corpus, using the common characters between both languages.

According to the analysis in Section 3, given an aligned Chinese-Japanese sentence pair, word alignment can be performed upon word pairs that share common characters. Based on

Type	Example of Characters with Unicode				Percentage
	SC	TC	KJ	Meaning	
1 - AAA	人 (U+4EBA)	人 (U+4EBA)	人 (U+4EBA)	People	56.55
2 - AAB	窗 (U+7A97)	窗 (U+7A97)	窓 (U+7A93)	Window	4.63
3 - ABA	国 (U+56FD)	國 (U+570B)	国 (U+56FD)	Country	3.45
4 - ABB	习 (U+4E60)	習 (U+7FD2)	習 (U+7FD2)	Study	29.17
5 - ABC	图 (U+56FE)	圖 (U+5716)	図 (U+56F3)	Picture	6.19

Table 1: Corresponding examples and percentages(%) of common characters in Simplified Chinese (SC), Traditional Chinese (TC), and Japanese Kanji (KJ).

Table 2: Estimated MI and CMI of 5 Common Characters.

	MI	CMI
天	0.3369	30.3057
地	0.5804	87.4515
人	0.8942	151.0069
中	0.7337	138.9676
学	0.4173	119.8921

this conclusion, using common characters, we can now give a definition for context similar to context in sentence-align corpus.

Define a character matching function $CC(\cdot)$ that generates a set of word in which each word has at least one common character with target word $w_{zh,i}$:

$$CC(w_{zh,i}, S_{ja}) = \quad \{w_{ja}|w_{ja} \in S_{ja}, \\ c \in w_{zh,i}, c \in w_{ja}\}. \quad (3)$$

Thus parallel context $Ctx_c(w_{zh,i}, S_{ja})$ can be acquired via common character matching:

$$Ctx_c(w_{zh,i}, S_{ja}) = \quad \{w|w \in Ctx(w_{ja}, S_{ja}), \\ w_{ja} \in CC(w_{zh,i}, S_{ja})\}. \quad (4)$$

Hence, when multiple words in the corresponding sentence have common characters with the target word, all of them will be included in $Ctx_c(w_{zh,i}, S_{ja})$. However, such case rarely occurs during our experiments.

For example, "天气/不错/一起/去/散步/吧" and "天気/が/良い/から/散歩/しま/しょう" are a parallel sentence-pair, meaning "The weather is nice, let's take a walk". There are two corresponding word pairs detected by common characters: "天气-天気 (Weather)" and "散步-散歩 (Take a walk)". Two words in a pair share their respective context during training.

We name this method as CJC (Chinese-Japanese Common Character) which uses $CC(\cdot)$ to determine context. Different from our previous work (Wang et al., 2016) which exploited common characters to facilitate only CBOW, this CJC method is more of a generalized scheme that can be integrated with various models including CBOW, Skip-Gram, GloVe etc.

4.2 CBOW-like Models

CBOW was a model proposed by Mikolov et al. in (Mikolov et al., 2013a), whose optimization goal is maximizing a probabilistic language model. In cross-lingual especially Chinese-Japanese scenario, the objective function for training $w_{zh,i}$ is:

$$L(S_{zh}) = \quad \frac{1}{N} \sum_{i=1}^{N} \Big\{ P_{zh,i,zh} \\ + \quad \lambda \cdot P_{zh,i,ja,c} \\ + \quad \mu \cdot P_{zh,i,ja,s} \Big\}, \quad (5)$$

where $P_{zh,i,zh}$, $P_{zh,i,ja,c}$, $and P_{zh,i,ja,s}$ are softmax function of the target word $w_{zh,i}$ to its corresponding monolingual context, sentence aligned cross-lingual context, and CJC context. Both λ and μ here are parameters of the model. If $\lambda = 0$, this is a trial sentence aligned CBOW model, otherwise it is a CJC+CBOW model; the CJ-BOC model in our previous work (Wang et al., 2016) used similar approach, and would be used as a baseline in our experiments.

4.3 GloVe-like Models

4.3.1 GloVe

GloVe model was originally proposed by Pennington et al. (2014). As the name implies, GloVe utilizes the global information of the corpus for vector training. GloVe and CBOW, as commonly adopted learning models, however differ a lot in terms of mathematical models, as they are respectively based on matrix factorization and neural network. The process of GloVe is as follows:

First, construct a word-word cooccurence matrix $M = (m_{ij})_{n \times n}$, where n is the size of the corpus, and m_{ij} represents the number of occurrence of w_j in the context of w_i in all the sentences S.

The learning problem of GloVe can then be transformed into the optimization of function $F(\cdot)$, such that for any word embeddings x_i, x_j and probe word embedding $\tilde{x}_k$, the objective function is defined below:

$$L = \sum_{i,j=1}^{n} f(m_{ij})(x_i^T \tilde{x}_j + b_i + \tilde{b}_j - \log m_{ij})^2, \quad (6)$$

$$f(m) = \begin{cases} (\frac{m}{m_{max}})^\alpha & \text{if } m < m_{max} \\ 1 & \text{otherwise.} \end{cases} \quad (7)$$

In this function, both b_i and b_j are bias, and f is a weighing function aiming to mitigate the impact of dataset size on training results. In GloVe, m_{max} is set to 100 and α to $\frac{3}{4}$.

4.3.2 Cross-lingual GloVe and CJ-Glo

To fit GloVe in cross-lingual scenario, one should first expand the word-word co-occurrence matrix. Suppose two languages respectively contain n and t words, the new matrix would have a size of If w_i and w_j belong to the same language, m_{ij} can be computed using exactly the same way as in GloVe; otherwise, suppose (S_{zh}, S_{ja}) is a pair of parallel sentences, $w_i \in S_{zh}$, $w_j \in S_{ja}$, and we have:

$$m_{ij} = \sum_{(S_{zh}, S_{ja})} (\lambda \cdot C_{ij,c} + \mu \cdot C_{ij,s}), \quad (8)$$

$$\begin{aligned} C_{ij,c} &= Cnt(w_j, Ctx_c(w_i, S_{ja})), \\ C_{ij,s} &= Cnt(w_j, Ctx_s(w_i, S_{ja})), \end{aligned} \quad (9)$$

$Cnt(\cdot)$ counts the frequency of w_j in certain context of w_i, either sentence aligned context or CJC context.

Once the cross-lingual word-word co-occurence matrix is obtained, the following optimization unfolds similarly with the monolingual GloVe model, using the objective function (6) and weighting function (7) to train.

Similar to Cross-lingual CBOW model, if the CJC learning rate $\lambda = 0$ in equation

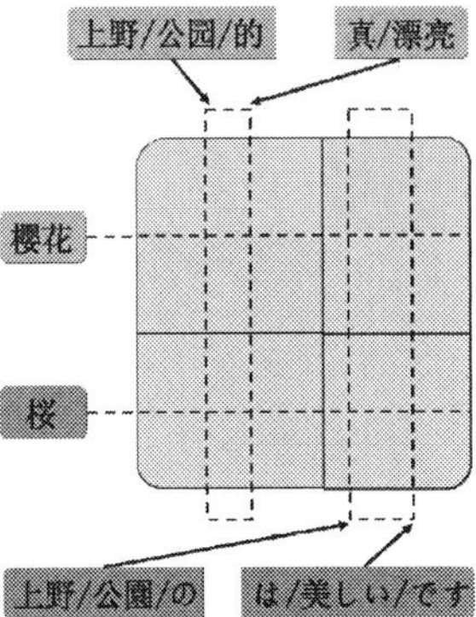

Figure 1: An example of CJ-Glo model, where the window size is 7 and the common character is "櫻 (桜)".

(8), this is a sentence aligned cross-lingual GloVe model. Otherwise, it is a CJC-enhanced model, and is thus called CJ-Glo.

Figure 1 demonstrates the operational principle of CJ-Glo: the square in this figure is a cross-lingual word co-occurrence matrix, in which the green square is a Chinese monolingual co-occurrence sub-matrix, and the orange square is for Japanese. The blue sections are cross-lingual sub-matrices and elements in them are calculated using equation (8). When two parallel sentences each contain a word sharing common characters, each word would be taken as a co-occurrence in the context of the other. Every point crossed by dotted lines and dotted rectangles represents an element to increment when processing the sentence pair.

5 Experiments and Analysis

5.1 Evaluation Methods

To evaluate the quality of cross-lingual word embeddings obtained from various models, we conducted three groups of experiments: 1) the straightforward cross-lingual synonym comparison; 2) cross-lingual word analogy; 3) sentence alignment.

Cross-lingual synonym comparison.

In monolingual scenario, the word embeddings of a pair of synonyms should have a high cosine similarity. This property is also applicable in cross-lingual word embeddings, i.e., the cosine similarity between a word embedding and its translated counterpart should also be high. In real applications, the correspondence between words in source language and words in target language can be one-to-one, one-to-many, or vice versa. To effectively eliminate ambiguity, we picked 200 one-to-one corresponding word pairs $\langle w_{zh}, w_{ja} \rangle$ at random, then for each word pair, calculated the cosine similarity between w_{zh} and w_{ja}, denoted as d, and computed the rank of d among the cosine similarities from w_{zh} to every Japanese word in corpus V_{ja}. Use the rank to calculate its relative rate among all words:

$$rate = (1 - \frac{rank - 1}{total\_word\_num}) \times 100\%. \quad (10)$$

Conducted the same operation for w_{ja} and all words in corpus V_{zh}. Calculate the average rate for all the 200 word pairs, and acquire the average rate of $w_{zh} \rightarrow w_{ja}$ and $w_{ja} \rightarrow w_{zh}$ respectively. Ambiguity is eliminated in all these word pairs, so a large rate is therefore favored.

Cross-lingual word analogy.

Word analogy is probably the most widely adopted task to evaluate the performance of word embeddings, because it depicts the connection between trained vector space and word semantics. Both CBOW(Mikolov et al., 2013a) and GloVe(Pennington et al., 2014) used a dataset with 19,544 queries for evaluation.

Given several related words from different languages, cross-lingual analogical reasoning works as follows: y=v(はは)-v(ちち)+v(男孩), we hope that the relatedness between Japanese words "はは (mother)" and "ちち (father)" could help us find the Chinese word "女孩 (girl)" and Japanese "女の子 (girl)" through Chinese word "男孩 (boy)".

More formally, the cross-lingual analogy task was undertaken as follows:
1. Input a quadruple of word embeddings $\langle w_1 : w_2 :: w_3 : w_4 \rangle$, where each word could be either Chinese or Japanese;
2. Compute the target vector $u = w_2 - w_1 + w_3$, acquire the corresponding rank and rate as in cross-lingual synonym comparison for $u \rightarrow w_4$;
3. Based on the ratio of Chinese word count to Japanese word count in the quadruple $\langle w_1 : w_2 :: w_3 : w_4 \rangle$, the word analogy task is divided into 5 subtasks, whose ratio are $(0 : 4)$, $(1 : 3)$, $(2 : 2)$, $(3 : 1)$ and $(4 : 0)$, and their respective

query amount is 420, 1680, 2520, 1680, and 420 in our experiment;
4. Calculate the average rate on every subtask.

Also, the average rate here is expected to be as large as possible.

Sentence alignment.

The above experiments respectively evaluated the direct similarity and cross-lingual feature of word embeddings. And now we consider a more complicated task: sentence alignment. In the dataset from (Chu et al., 2014), other than training data, a manual test dataset was also attached, which are 198 sentence pairs. Using this dataset, we conduct this experiment as follows:
1. For a Chinese sentence $S_{zh,i}$, calculate its average vector $U_{zh,i}$ and all U_{ja} of all sentences S_{ja}, and compute the cosine similarity.
2. Sort all the cosine similarities in step 2, and acquire the rank of the average vector $U_{ja,i}$ of $S_{ja,i}$ (the parallel sentence of $S_{zh,i}$).
3. Transform rank into rate using formula 10, where total number is 198.
4. Compute the average rate $S_{zh} \rightarrow S_{ja}$;
5. Follow the same steps above to generate $S_{ja} \rightarrow S_{zh}$.

Compared with the previous experiments, which evaluate only the relation between individual word embeddings, sentence alignment is a comprehensive task using word embedding, and is a critical indicator for the overall quality of the trained word embeddings.

5.2 Dataset and Training Details

As mentioned previously, (Chu et al., 2014) generated a parallel corpus including Chinese-Japanese sentence pairs from Wikipedia; train.ja and train.zh in this dataset were used throughout our empirical study, both containing 126,811 lines of text. Concretely, every single line in these two files is a complete sentence, which is parallel to its counterpart in the other file. As the preprocessing for datasets, both files were segmented using MeCab[1] and Jieba[2] for Japanese and Chinese, respectively. During the preprocessing, we assured the segmentation on Chinese and

---

[1] http://taku910.github.io/mecab, accessed date: December 20, 2017.
[2] https://github.com/fxsjy/jieba, commit number: cb0de2973b2fafaa67a0245a14206d8be70db515.

Table 3: Parameters of CJC and sentence learning rates in each models.

Model	λ	μ
SenBow	0	0.2
CJ-BOC	0.4	0.2
SenGlo	0	0.2
CJ-Glo	0.4	0.2

Table 4: Cross-lingual synonym comparison results on 200 one-to-one word pairs, the average rates(%) of each models.

Model	$w_{zh} \to w_{ja}$	$w_{ja} \to w_{zh}$
SenBow	83.97	83.76
CJ-BOC	96.75	97.61
SenGlo	91.17	90.05
CJ-Glo	**97.97**	**98.80**

Japanese were approximately grained, by tuning parameters.

Four models in total are put into comparison in our experiment:

1. *SenBow* model is the bilingual CBOW model applying sentence-aligned method;

2. *CJ-BOC* model from (Wang et al., 2016), considered as a CJC+CBOW model;

3. *SenGlo* model applies sentence-aligned method to GloVe model;

4. *CJ-Glo* model is our CJC method enhanced GloVe model.

The parameters of CJC learning rate λ and sentence learning rate μ are showed in Table 3. Both SenGlo and CJ-Glo have a m_{max} of 100, and an α of $\frac{3}{4}$. The thread count is 16 in the implementations of all these four models, the output vector dimensionality is 100, and the training process is iterated 15 times. We set the parameters to the above values, since these models achieved the optimal performances under such settings in our evaluation. All models are implemented using C language, and the code can be found on GitHub[3].

---

[3]https://github.com/jileiwang/CJC, commit number: a10592d200bc15f7b53d81a8f895e7de9ef8676d.

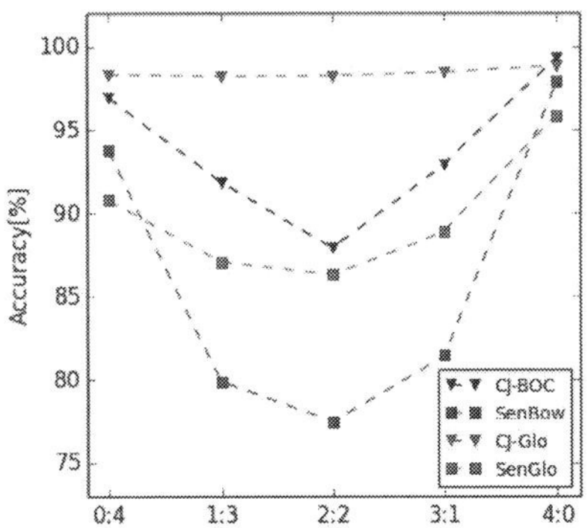

Figure 2: Cross-lingual word analogy experiment result. X-axis is the number ratio of Chinese words and Japanese words in the analogy query ($w_1 : w_2 :: w_3 : w_4$).

5.3 Results

The result of cross-lingual synonym comparison is shown in Table 4, from which we can see the integration of Common Character leads to obvious performance improvement for both CBOW-like and GloVe-like models, compared with sentence-aligned models, and CJ-Glo achieve the best result.

Figure 2 summarizes the results of the cross-lingual word analogy task, whose X-axis represents the ratio of Chinese word count to Japanese word count. In the figure, the leftmost point represents the result of pure Japanese word analogy, and the rightmost is the pure Chinese word analogy. We can see that all 4 models achieve fair performances in pure Chinese/Japanese word analogy. However, when it comes to the cross-lingual word analogy, CJ- models outperform Sen- models, and GloVe-like models generally beat CBOW-like ones. Another noticeable fact is that CJ-Glo performs approximately good under all 5 ratios, showing basically no difference between cross-lingual and monolingual word analogy.

We display the sentence alignment results in Table 5. Similarly, we still find CJ- models outperform Sen-, and GloVe-like models beat CBOW-like ones. Again, CJ-Glo has the best performance.

According to the above experiments, we can see compared with typical sentence-aligned methods, Common Character enhanced mod-

Table 5: Sentence alignment results on 198 parallel sentence pairs, the average rates(%) of each models.

Model	$S_{zh} \to S_{ja}$	$S_{ja} \to S_{zh}$
SenBow	79.14	74.63
CJ-BOC	86.39	83.14
SenGlo	90.33	84.90
CJ-Glo	**91.57**	**86.00**

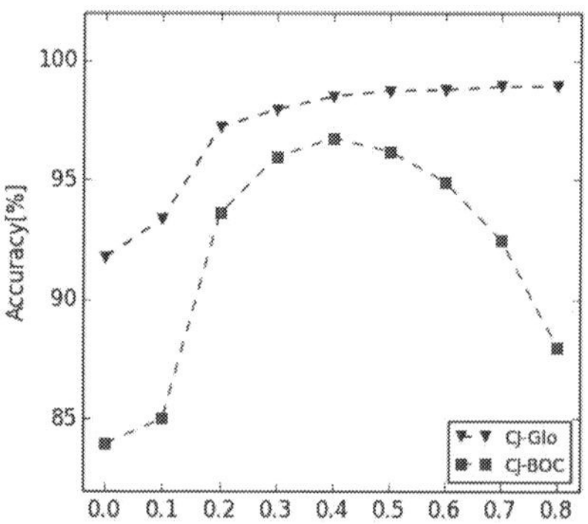

Figure 3: Accuracy of CJ-BOC and CJ-Glo Models on cross-lingual synonym $w_{zh} \to w_{ja}$ with different CC learning rate.

els are superior in learning Chinese-Japanese cross-lingual word embeddings, as it achieves obvious performance boost in various tasks. Moreover, CJ-Glo performs better than CJ-BOC, and is non-sensitive in cross-lingual tasks.

5.4 Model Analysis: CJC Learning Rate

CJC learning rate here refers to the multiplying factor of CJC context $Ctx_c(\cdot)$, which is λ in CJ-BOC and CJ-Glo. It worths discussion that how would CJC learning rate affects the performance of our proposed models. To explore this issue, we conduct a simple experiment: fixing the other parameters as set in section 5.2, we only change CJC learning rate, and apply the acquired word embeddings to synonym $w_{zh} \to w_{ja}$ tasks. The results are displayed in Figure 3 , in which we can find as λ increases in CJ-BOC, the accuracy declines after an increase, showing a obvious local optimal. While in CJ-Glo, the accuracy keeps improving with the increase of λ. Note that both parameters should be less than 1, because otherwise the impact of cross-lingual context would dominate the learning process, obviously resulting in overfit. CJ-Glo is more stable during the change of CJC learning rate, this interesting difference between both models is related to the their underlying learning mechanisms.

6 Conclusion and Future Work

In this paper, we quantified the semantic connection among common characters shared by Chinese and Japanese, and utilized it as the theoretical root to propose our cross-lingual context extracting method CJC. CJC makes use of common characters of both languages to assist the acquisition of parallel contexts. The effectiveness of CJC enhanced matrix factorization model CJ-Glo was verified via a series of tasks including cross-lingual synonym, word analogy and sentence alignment. As the experiment result shows, models like CBOW and GloVe achieved notable performance gain after integrated with CJC. Furthermore, CJ-Glo performed the best among all evaluated state-of-the-art methods, and showed its stability on cross-lingual tasks and non-sensitiveness of training parameter changing.

Below are several directions we may work on in the future: 1) The idea of training character and word embeddings jointly (Chen et al., 2015) is applicable to Chinese-Japanese word embedding training. Meanwhile, we can also align common characters and train cross-lingual character embeddings to further improve the quality of trained word embeddings. 2) A recent work (Lai et al., 2016) indicates that the performances of a model may vary given different tasks. Therefore, we shall study the performance fluctuation of CJ-Glo with more tasks including machine translation.

Acknowledgments

This work is supported by the National Natural Science Foundation of China under grant Nos. 61771273, 61371078.

The authors would like to thank Xinyu Zhou, Minghao Li, Yanning Li, and Qi Tang for the insightful discussions and suggestions that helped us improve the manuscript.

References

Mikel Artetxe, Gorka Labaka, and Eneko Agirre. 2017. Learning bilingual word embeddings with (almost) no bilingual data. In *Proceedings of the 55th Annual Meeting of the Association for Computational Linguistics (Volume 1: Long Papers)*, volume 1, pages 451–462.

Yoshua Bengio, Réjean Ducharme, Pascal Vincent, and Christian Jauvin. 2003. A neural probabilistic language model. *Journal of machine learning research*, 3(Feb):1137–1155.

Xinxiong Chen, Zhiyuan Liu, and Maosong Sun. 2014. A unified model for word sense representation and disambiguation. In *Proceedings of the 2014 conference on empirical methods in natural language processing (EMNLP)*, pages 1025–1035.

Xinxiong Chen, Lei Xu, Zhiyuan Liu, Maosong Sun, and Huan-Bo Luan. 2015. Joint learning of character and word embeddings. In *Proceedings of the 24th International Joint Conference On Artificial Intelligence (IJCAI)*, pages 1236–1242.

Chenhui Chu, Toshiaki Nakazawa, and Sadao Kurohashi. 2012. Chinese characters mapping table of japanese, traditional chinese and simplified chinese. In *Proceedings of the 8th Conference on International Language Resources and Evaluation Conference (LREC)*, pages 2149–2152. Citeseer.

Chenhui Chu, Toshiaki Nakazawa, and Sadao Kurohashi. 2014. Constructing a chinese japanese parallel corpus from wikipedia. In *Proceedings of the 9th Conference on International Language Resources and Evaluation Conference (LREC)*, pages 642–647.

Stephan Gouws, Yoshua Bengio, and Greg Corrado. 2015. Bilbowa: Fast bilingual distributed representations without word alignments. In *Proceedings of the 32nd International Conference on Machine Learning (ICML)*, pages 748–756.

Jiang Guo, Wanxiang Che, Haifeng Wang, and Ting Liu. 2014. Learning sense-specific word embeddings by exploiting bilingual resources. In *Proceedings of the 25th International Conference on Computational Linguistics: Technical Papers (COLING)*, pages 497–507.

Jiang Guo, Wanxiang Che, David Yarowsky, Haifeng Wang, and Ting Liu. 2016. A representation learning framework for multi-source transfer parsing. In *AAAI*, pages 2734–2740.

Geoffrey E Hinton. 1986. Learning distributed representations of concepts. In *Proceedings of the eighth annual conference of the cognitive science society*, volume 1, page 12. Amherst, MA.

Siwei Lai, Kang Liu, Shizhu He, and Jun Zhao. 2016. How to generate a good word embedding. *IEEE Intelligent Systems*, 31(6):5–14.

Guillaume Lample, Ludovic Denoyer, and Marc'Aurelio Ranzato. 2017. Unsupervised machine translation using monolingual corpora only. *arXiv preprint arXiv:1711.00043*.

Tomas Mikolov, Kai Chen, Greg Corrado, and Jeffrey Dean. 2013a. Efficient estimation of word representations in vector space. *arXiv preprint arXiv:1301.3781*.

Tomas Mikolov, Quoc V Le, and Ilya Sutskever. 2013b. Exploiting similarities among languages for machine translation. *arXiv preprint arXiv:1309.4168*.

Jeffrey Pennington, Richard Socher, and Christopher Manning. 2014. Glove: Global vectors for word representation. In *Proceedings of the 2014 conference on empirical methods in natural language processing (EMNLP)*, pages 1532–1543.

Sebastian Ruder, Ivan Vulić, and Anders Søgaard. 2017. A survey of cross-lingual word embedding models. *arXiv preprint arXiv:1706.04902*.

Tianze Shi, Zhiyuan Liu, Yang Liu, and Maosong Sun. 2015. Learning cross-lingual word embeddings via matrix co-factorization. In *Proceedings of the 53rd Annual Meeting of the Association for Computational Linguistics and the 7th International Joint Conference on Natural Language Processing (Volume 2: Short Papers)*, volume 2, pages 567–572.

Ivan Vulić and Marie-Francine Moens. 2015. Monolingual and cross-lingual information retrieval models based on (bilingual) word embeddings. In *Proceedings of the 38th International ACM SIGIR Conference on Research and Development in Information Retrieval*, pages 363–372. ACM.

Jilei Wang, Shiying Luo, Yanning Li, and Shu-Tao Xia. 2016. Learning chinese-japanese bilingual word embedding by using common characters. In *International Conference on Knowledge Science, Engineering and Management*, pages 82–93. Springer.

Yonghui Wu, Mike Schuster, Zhifeng Chen, Quoc V Le, Mohammad Norouzi, Wolfgang Macherey, Maxim Krikun, Yuan Cao, Qin Gao, Klaus Macherey, et al. 2016. Google's neural machine translation system: Bridging the gap between human and machine translation. *arXiv preprint arXiv:1609.08144*.

Yin Zhang, Rong Jin, and Zhi-Hua Zhou. 2010. Understanding bag-of-words model: a statistical framework. *International Journal of Machine Learning and Cybernetics*, 1(1-4):43–52.

WordNet Embeddings

Chakaveh Saedi, António Branco, João António Rodrigues, João Ricardo Silva
University of Lisbon
NLX-Natural Language and Speech Group, Department of Informatics
Faculdade de Ciências
Campo Grande, 1749-016 Lisboa, Portugal
{chakaveh.saedi, antonio.branco, joao.rodrigues, jsilva}@di.fc.ul.pt

Abstract

Semantic networks and semantic spaces have been two prominent approaches to represent lexical semantics. While a unified account of the lexical meaning relies on one being able to convert between these representations, in both directions, the conversion direction from semantic networks into semantic spaces started to attract more attention recently. In this paper we present a methodology for this conversion and assess it with a case study. When it is applied over WordNet, the performance of the resulting embeddings in a mainstream semantic similarity task is very good, substantially superior to the performance of word embeddings based on very large collections of texts like word2vec.

1 Introduction

The study of lexical semantics has been at the core of the research on language science and technology as the meaning of linguistic forms results from the meaning of their lexical units and from the way these are combined (Pelletier, 2016). How to represent lexical semantics has thus been a central topic of inquiry. Three broad families of approaches have emerged in this respect, namely those advocating that lexical semantics is represented as a semantic network (Quillan, 1966), a feature-based model (Minsky, 1975; Bobrow and Norman, 1975), or a semantic space (Harris, 1954; Osgood et al., 1957).

In terms of data structures, under a semantic network approach, the meaning of a lexical unit is represented as a node in a graph whose edges between nodes encode different types of semantic relations holding among the units (e.g. hyper-nymy, meronymy, etc.). In a feature-based model, the semantics of a lexicon is represented by a hash table where a key is the lexical unit of interest and the respective value is a set of other units denoting typical characteristics of the denotation of the unit in the key (e.g. role, usage or shape, etc.). Under a semantic space perspective, in turn, the meaning of a lexical unit is represented by a vector in a high-dimensional space, where each component is based on some frequency level of co-occurrence with the other units in contexts of language usage.

The motivation for these three families of lexical representation is to be found in their different suitability and success in explaining a wide range of empirical phenomena, in terms of how these are manifest in ordinary language usage and how they are elicited in laboratory experimentation. These phenomena are related to the acquisition, storage and retrieval of lexical knowledge (e.g. the spread activation effect (Meyer and Schvaneveldt, 1971), the fan effect (Anderson, 1974), among many others) and to how this knowledge interacts with other cognitive faculties or tasks, including categorization (Estes, 1994), reasoning (Rips, 1975), problem solving (Holyoak and Koh, 1987), learning (Ross, 1984), etc.

In the scope of the formal and computational modeling of lexical semantics, these approaches have inspired a number of initiatives to build repositories of lexical knowledge. Popular examples of such repositories are, for semantic networks, WordNet (Fellbaum, 1998), for feature-based models, Small World of Words (De Deyne et al., 2013), and for the semantic space, word2vec (Mikolov et al., 2013a), among many others. Interestingly, to achieve the highest quality, repositories of different types typically resort to different empirical sources of data. For instance, WordNet is constructed on the basis of systematic lexical intuitions handled by human experts; the informa-

Proceedings of the 3rd Workshop on Representation Learning for NLP, pages 122–131
Melbourne, Australia, July 20, 2018. ©2018 Association for Computational Linguistics

tion encoded in Small World of Words is evoked from laypersons; and word2vec is built on the basis of the co-occurrence frequency of lexical units in a collection of documents.

Even when motivated in the first place by psycholinguistic research goals, these repositories of lexical knowledge have been extraordinarily important for language technology. They have been instrumental for major advances in language processing tasks and applications such as word sense disambiguation, part-of-speech tagging, named entity recognition, sentiment analysis (e.g. (Li and Jurafsky, 2015)), parsing (e.g. (Socher et al., 2013)), textual entailment (e.g. (Baroni et al., 2012)), discourse analysis (e.g. (Ji and Eisenstein, 2014)), among many others.[1]

The proliferation of different types of representation for the same object of research is common in science, and searching for a unified rendering of a given research domain has been a major goal in many disciplines. To a large extent, such search focuses on finding ways of converting from one type of representation into another. Once this is made possible, it brings not only the theoretical satisfaction of getting a better unified insight into the research object, but also important instrumental rewards of reapplying results, resources and tools that had been obtained under one representation to the other representations, thus opening the potential for further research advances.

This is the case also in what concerns the research on lexical semantics. Establishing whether and how any given lexical representation can be converted into another representation is important for a more unified account of it. On the language science side, this will likely enhance the plausibility of our empirical modeling about how the mindbrain handles lexical meaning. On the language technology side, in turn, this will permit to reuse resources and find new ways to combine different sources of lexical information for better application results.

In the present paper, we seek to contribute towards a unified account of lexical semantics. We report on the methodology we used to convert from a semantic network based representation of lexical meaning into a semantic space based one, and on the successful evaluation results obtained when applying that methodology. We resorted to

Princeton WordNet version 3 as a repository of the lexical semantics of the English language, represented as a semantic graph, and converted a subgraph of it with half of its concepts into wnet2vec, a collection of vectors in a high-dimension space. These WordNet embeddings were evaluated under the same conditions that semantic space based repositories like word2vec are, namely under the processing task of determining the semantic similarity between pairs of lexical units. The evaluation results obtained for wnet2vec are around 15% superior to the results obtained for word2vec with the same mainstream evaluation data set SimLex-999 (Hill et al., 2016).

2 Distributional vectors from ontological graphs

For a given word w, its distributional representation $\vec{w}$ (aka word embedding) is a high dimension vector whose elements $\vec{w}_i$ record real valued scores expressing the strength of the semantic affinity of w with other words in the vocabulary. The usual source of these scores, and ultimately the empirical base of word embeddings, has been the frequency of co-occurrence between words taken from large collections of text.

The goal here instead is to use semantic networks as the empirical source of word embeddings. This will permit that the lexical knowledge that is encoded in a semantic graph be re-encoded as an embeddings matrix compiling the distributional vectors of the words in the vocabulary.

To determine the strength of semantic affinity of two words from their representation in a semantic graph, we follow this intuition: the larger the number of paths and the shorter the paths connecting any two nodes the stronger is their affinity.

To make this intuition operative we resort to the following procedure, to be refined later on. First, the semantic graph G is represented as an adjacency matrix M such that iff two nodes of G with words w_i and w_j are related by an edge representing a direct semantic relation between them, the element M_{ij} is set to 1 (to 0 otherwise).

Second, to enrich M with scores that represent the strength of semantic affinity of nodes not directly connected with each other by an edge, the following cumulative iteration is resorted to

$$M_G^{(n)} = I + \alpha M + \alpha^2 M^2 + \ldots + \alpha^n M^n \quad (1)$$

where I is the identity matrix; the n-th power of

---

[1] For the vast number of applications of WordNet, see http://lit.csci.unt.edu/~wordnet

the transition matrix, M^n, is the matrix where each M_{ij} counts the number of paths of lenght n between nodes i and j; and $\alpha < 1$ is a decay factor determining how longer paths are dominated by shorter ones.

Third, this iterative procedure is pursued until it converges into matrix M_G, which is analytically obtained by an inverse matrix operation given by[2]

$$M_G = \sum_{e=0}^{\infty} (\alpha M)^e = (I - \alpha M)^{-1} \qquad (2)$$

3 WordNet embeddings

In order to assess this procedure, we use it to convert a mainstream ontological graph into an embeddings matrix. We use Princeton WordNet (Fellbaum, 1998) as our working semantic network. This is a lexical ontology for English with over 120k concepts that are related by over 25 types of semantic relations and comprise over 155k words (lemmas), from the categories Noun (with 117k words), Verb, Adjective and Adverb.

The quality of the resulting semantic space (based on a semantic network) is assessed by resorting to the mainstream procedure to evaluate semantic spaces: (i) it is used to solve the task of determining the semantic similarity between words in a mainstream test data set used in the literature; (ii) its performance is compared to the performance of a mainstream semantic space (based on a text collection), namely word2vec (Mikolov et al., 2013b), which serves as our baseline.

The base data set was obtained by extracting a sub-graph from WordNet that supports a 60k word distributional matrix. All parts of speech in Word-Net were considered.

The nodes in WordNet are related by different types of semantic relations (e.g. hypernymy, meronymy, etc.). Relations of different types were taken into account with identical weight for the sake of the conversion of the graph into a matrix.

Upon applying the conversion procedure by resolving equation (2),[3] its outcome M_G was subject to the Positive Point-wise Mutual Information transformation (PMI+) seeking to reduce the eventual bias introduced by the conversion towards words with more senses.

Model	Similarity
wnet2vec	0.50
word2vec	0.44

Table 1: Performance in semantic similarity task over SimLex-999 given by Spearman's coefficient (higher score is better).

For the sound application of the conversion, each line in M_G was normalized, using L2-norm, so that it corresponds to a vector whose scores sum to 1, corresponding to a transition matrix.

Finally, we used Principal Component Analysis (PCA) (Wold et al., 1987) to transform the matrix, reducing the size of the vectors and setting to 850 the dimension of the encoded semantic space.

To assess the quality of the resulting semantic space, we resorted to the test data set SimLex-999 (Hill et al., 2016), containing a list of 999 pairs of words. Each pair is associated with a score, on a 0-10 scale, that indicates the strength of the semantic similarity between the words in that pair. For each pair, with the resulting embedding matrix, the cosine between the vectors of the words in that pair is calculated and mapped into the 0-10 scale. The outcome is compared to the gold standard scores in SimLex-999 resorting to Spearman's rank correlation coefficient.[4] The respective scores are displayed in Table 1.

4 Discussion

These results indicate a clear advantage of around 15% of the WordNet embeddings, scoring 0.50, over the word2vec embeddings, scoring 0.44. This indicates that the proposed conversion procedure is very effective.

WordNet embeddings is a semantic space empirically based on an internal language resource: on a systematic elicitation and recording of the semantic relations between words, thus being closely aligned with the lexical knowledge in the minds of speakers. Word2vec, in turn, is a semantic space empirically based on an external language resource: on records of contingent language usage, namely some texts that were produced by a population of language users and happened to be

---

[2] This is equation (7.63) in (Newman, 2010) where it is presented as a regular equivalence measure termed Katz similarity.

[3] We used `linalg.inv` from the `numpy` package for the inverse matrix calculation.

[4] We used the `evaluate_word_pairs` function from `Gensim` package (Řehůřek and Sojka, 2010) to determine the performance of both semantic spaces, the wnet2vec and the word2vec embeddings.

collected together. Hence, while words related by some semantic relation are likely to be linked in WordNet, they may happen to rarely or never occur in relevant context windows, as practical constraints on the production and usage of language may not favor that. This may help to explain the advantage of wnet2vec over word2vec.[5]

The conversion procedure is composed by a number of steps where each may receive a range of configurations. This opens a large experimental space of which the experiment in Section 3 instantiates one set of coordinates. In the remainder of the present section we justify the eventual empirical settings used and discuss the lessons learned by exploring this experimental space. The conversion procedure will be revisited in a backwards fashion, from its final to its initial steps, with the experiments being performed over the 60k subset identified in Subsection 4.3.

4.1 Matrix manipulation

Vector dimension: There have been studies indicating the positive effect of the reduction of the dimensionality of the semantic space (e.g. (Underhill et al., 2007; Grünauer and Vincze, 2015)). We experimented with a range of final vector dimensions, namely sizes 100, 300, 850, 1000 and 3000, also over evaluation data sets other than just SimLex-999.[6] Results obtained consistently indicated that size 850 leads to better performance.[7]

Dimensionality reduction: We compared two different techniques for dimensionality reduction, PCA (Wold et al., 1987) and a neural network approach. For the neural solution, the encoder-decoder architecture with a Sigmoid activation function was employed. The model was trained using a Nadam optimizer with binary cross entropy as loss metric. Experimentation consistently indicated that PCA is substantially more successful.

Normalization and bias: We contrasted the performance of the WordNet embeddings obtained with and without normalization of the distribu-

tional vectors. Results consistently indicated the advantage of doing normalization, even if for a small margin, with a delta of around 0.08.

Ablation tests were done also with respect to PMI+, which indicated a clear advantage of applying it.

4.2 Graph manipulation

Decay factor: The best results were achieved with $\alpha = 0.75$, after experimenting with values in the range 0.65 to 0.85.

Picking semantic relations: Concepts in WordNet are connected via semantic relations of different types. The relations of Hypernymy/Hyponymy, Synonymy and Antonymy play an essential role in structuring a semantic network, as without them the network could not exist. We undertook experiments where all semantic relations or only these kernel relations were taken into account for the conversion procedure, with results indicating a clear advantage for using all relations.

Weighting semantic relations: In the definition of a semantic network, some types of relations appear as necessary (e.g. Hypernymy), while other appears as more secondary (e.g. Meronymy). It might thus happen that the conversion of a semantic network into a semantic space might be optimized if different weights were assigned to different relations accordingly. We ran an experiment where different weights were assigned to different relations, namely hypernymy, hyponymy, antonymy and synonymy got 1, meronymy and holonymy 0.8 and other relations 0.5; and another experiment where all types of semantic relation were assigned the same weight. Better results were obtained with the latter.

4.3 Base data sets

Subgraphs: The conversion procedure relies on equation (2), whose complexity is dominated by the calculation of the inverse matrix, which is of exponential order. For the Princeton WordNet graph, with over 120k concepts, given the size of the adjacency matrix M^1 is over 120k $\times$ 120k, its calculation and the overall conversion of the ontological graph into the final embeddings matrix faces substantial challenges in terms of the memory footprint. To cope with this issue, we resorted to initial subgraphs of manageable size.[8]

---

[5]Naturally, the comparative advantage between a semantic space based on a semantic network and another based on a collection of texts depends also on the sizes of the network and of the collection. The training corpus of word2vec-GoogleNews-vectors we used is one of the largest, with an impressive amount of 100 billion tokens, and a vocabulary of 3 million types, which differently from the vocabulary units in WordNet, are wordforms, not lemmas (Mikolov et al., 2013a).

[6]More on evaluation data sets in Section 4.4

[7]The vector size in word2vec embeddings is 300.

[8]To invert a 60k matrix, numpy used all memory available in a machine with 32 CPUs/2.50GHz and 430Gb RAM.

We reduced the size of M^1 by eliminating more sparse rows (rows with more zero elements), corresponding to eliminating words in concepts with lower number of outgoing edges in Word-Net. Rows were ordered by decreasing sparsity, with rows with identical level of sparsity (identical number of zero elements) randomly ordered among themselves. The first 25k, 30k, 45k and 60k rows were extracted and used in the conversion process. To maximize overlap wth test set SimLex-999, its words in WordNet were retained. The performance scores of the resulting models are displayed in Table 2.

Random subgraphs	25k	30k	45k	60k
Semantic similarity	0.45	0.47	0.49	0.50

Table 2: Performance of wnet2vec in similarity task over SimLex-999 (Spearman's coefficient).

The larger the size of the WordNet subgraph the better is the performance of the resulting embeddings. As they contain more concepts, which on average are closer to each other, larger subgraphs tend to be denser and generate less sparse adjacency matrices. This supports semantic spaces with distributional vectors with more discriminative information on the semantic affinity of a word with respect to others.

The progression of scores in Table 2, for subgraphs with matrices in the range 25k-60k, supports the conjecture that when enough computational means are available and the full 155k word WordNet be used, the performance of the resulting embeddings may still improve by a substantial margin over the result now observed for the 60k matrix, with less than half of the words.

Additionally, we experimented with two specific subgraphs that were **not** randomly extracted from WordNet, namely: the subgraph supporting the matrix with the 13k most frequent words of English;[9] and the subgraph supporting the matrix with the 13k words used in (De Deyne et al., 2016),[10] which have been selected to act as cue words in psycholinguistic experiments for eliciting associated words from subjects. The performance results of the resulting models are dis-

played in Table 3.

Specific subgraphs	13k most frequent	13k cue words
Similarity	0.47	0.50

Table 3: Performance of wnet2vec in similarity task over SimLex-999 given by Spearman's coefficient. First row indicates the sizes of the matrices supported by specific subgraphs.

These matrices have less than $1/4$ of the size of the 60k matrix, and yet they show a better than expected approximation to its performance, taking into account the progression registered in Table 2. These results indicate that larger size is not the only factor improving the performance of Word-Net embeddings. Very interestingly, they seem to indicate that words more commonly used may support semantic spaces that are more accurate to discriminate semantic similarity.

Frequency of occurence in texts plays no direct role in the conversion of semantic networks into semantic spaces by equation (2). Hence this effect likely results from the fact captured by one of the Zipf word distributions, that on average more frequent words are more ambiguous than less frequent ones: On average more frequent words express more concepts — that is, they occur in more WordNet synsets — and thus enter in more outgoing edges in the semantic network, and this should support less sparse vectors in the semantic space.

This explanation is empirically supported by the fact that the word ambiguity rates are 2.7 and 2.8, in the sugraphs with 13k cue words and with 13k most frequent words, respectively, while there is a lower word ambiguity rate of around 1.5 for the random graph with 60k words.[11]

Parts of Speech: Princeton WordNet covers nouns, adjectives, verbs and adverbs. Nouns (117k) are the largest portion of all words (155k) in the graph and, among the different POS, they support the most dense subgraph of semantic relations. We run experiments with words from all POS categories, and where only Nouns where considered. While results obtained with Nouns only (0.44) are not that distant from the results obtained with all POS (0.50), the latter setting consistently showed better performance.

---

[9]To reach 13k, we used the 10k most common English words, as determined by n-gram frequency analysis of the Google's Trillion Word Corpus, from (Kaufman, 2017), supplemented with non repeating words from Wiktionary frequency lists (Wiktionary, 2017).

[10]Available from https://smallworldofwords.org/en

[11]This is obtained by counting n lemmas for a word that enters WordNet under n POS categories. Word ambiguity rate of the whole WordNet is 1.3.

4.4 Testing data and metrics

To assess the robustness of the results obtained, experiments were undertaken with: (i) yet another evaluation metric, namely Pearson's correlation coefficient; (ii) further evaluation data sets for semantic similarity, namely RG1965 (Rubenstein and Goodenough, 1965) and Wordsim-353-Similarity (Agirre et al., 2009); (iii) and testing over another task, namely semantic relatedness, with the evaluation data sets Wordsim-353-Relatedness (Agirre et al., 2009), MEN (Bruni et al., 2012) and MTurk-771 (Halawi et al., 2012). In these experiments we used our best settings, with a random 60k subgraph, and our second best settings, with the best model with a specific 13k subgraph, cf. Subsection 4.3.

Additional metric: The evaluation scores obtained over SimLex-999 with the Pearson's coefficient are basically aligned with the scores already obtained with Spearman's coefficient, confirming the superiority of the WordNet embeddings.

Additional data sets: Even with a number of test pairs much lower than the pairs in SimLex-999 and built under less standard procedure, and thus supporting less reliable results, we evaluated our models over the Wordsmith353-S and RG1965 data sets. Wnet2vec showed competitive performance when put side by side with word2vec even though their scores were not superior. With these smaller alternative data sets, the results for the specific 13k model were slightly superior to the results for the random 60k model.

Additional task: The relation "semantic relatedness" is broader and less well defined than the relation "semantic similarity". Experiments with a second task of determining semantic relatedness showed that word2vec performs clearly better on this task than on the task of semantic similarity, while wnet2vec in general performs worst on it. Wnet2vec is thus less prone than word2vec to get fooled by words that are just semantically related by not necessarily similar. This indicates that the superiority of wnet2vec in the similarity task results from an enhanced discriminative capacity, with it being better both at judging as similar, words that are actually similar, and at judging as non similar, not only words that may be clearly non similar but also words that are semantically related, and thus may be close to be similar.

The results obtained with these experiments are displayed in Table 4.[12]

5 Related work

From semantic spaces to semantic networks: There has been a long research tradition on semantic networks enhanced with information extracted from text, including distributional vectors, which in the limit may encompass semantic networks obtained from semantic spaces. As a way of illustration, among many others, this includes the work on semantic relations determined from patterns based on regular expressions, either hand crafted (Hearst, 1992), or learned from corpora (Snow et al., 2005); work on semantic relations predicted by classifiers running over distributional vectors (Baroni et al., 2012; Roller et al., 2014; Weeds et al., 2014); work on semantic relations obtained with deep learning that integrates distributional information and patterns of grammatical dependency relations (Shwartz et al., 2016), including the hard task of distinguishing synonymy from antonymy (Nguyen et al., 2017); etc. While being highly relevant for a unified account of lexical semantics, this line of research addresses the conversion direction, from semantic spaces to semantic networks, that is not the major focus of this paper.

From semantic networks to semantic spaces: Work towards the conversion direction that is of interest here is more recent. As a way of illustration, among others, one can mention (Faruqui et al., 2015), which explored retrofitting to refine distributional representations using relational information, and (Yu and Dredze, 2014), which focused also on refining word embeddings with lexical knowledge, but which are not addressing the goal of obtaining semantic spaces solely on the basis of semantic networks as we do here.

That is the aim also of recent work like (Camacho-Collados et al., 2015) who improve the embeddings built from data sets made of selected Wikipedia pages by resorting to the local, one-edge relations of each relevant word in the WordNet graph.

Further recent works worth mentioning include (Vendrov et al., 2015) that resorted to order embeddings, which however do not preserve distance and/or do not preserve directionality under

---

[12]Pairs in the evaluation data set but not in the semantic space do not count to compute the evaluation score: proportion of vocabulary overlap does not affect the scoring.

data set	task	size	over-lap %	w2vec	n2vec 13k s	n2vec 60k r	w2vec	n2vec 13k s	n2vec 60k r
				Spearman coef			Pearson coef		
SimLex-999	simil	999	99.8	0.44	0.50	0.50	0.45	0.52	0.51
RG1965	simil	65	100.0	0.75	0.65	0.56	0.75	0.75	0.72
Wordsim353-S	simil	203	98.0	0.74	0.65	0.51	0.73	0.67	0.58
Wordsim353-R	relat	252	97.6	0.61	0.32	0.31	0.58	0.33	0.30
MEN	relat	3000	44.9	0.70	0.46	0.45	0.68	0.48	0.45
MTURK-771	relat	771	99.7	0.66	0.54	0.53	0.63	0.54	0.52

Table 4: Performance of different models in the semantic similarity (simil) and relatedness (relat) tasks over different data sets measured by Spearman's and Pearson's coefficients. Models used: word2vec (w2vec); wnet2vec with the random 60k subgraph (n2vec 60k r); and wnet2vec with the best specific 13k subgraph (n2vec 13k s), cf. Subsection 4.3. Overlap with the vocabulary of wnet2vec 60k random appears in the fourth column.

the relevant semantic relations; (Nickel and Kiela, 2017) that experimented with computing embeddings not in Euclidean but in hyperbolic space, namely the Poincaré ball model. A shortcoming with these proposals is that their outcome is not easily plugged into neural models. Also they are not fit to evaluation on external tasks, like the semantic similarity task, with their evaluation being rather based on their ability to complete missing edges from ontological graphs. In contrats, an example of the sutability of wnet2vec to be plugged into neural models and of its application in a downstream task is reported in (Rodrigues et al., 2018), where these embeddings support the predicition of brain activation based on neural networks.

There has been also a long tradition of research on learning vector embeddings from multi-relational data of which, among many others, one can refer (Bordes et al., 2013), (Lin et al., 2015), and (Nickel et al., 2016). Though to a large extent these are generic approaches for graph to vectors conversion, also here the major focus has been on exploring these models on their ability to complete missing relations in knowledge bases rather than to experiment them on natural language processing and lexical semantics.

Other related approaches worth of note are (De Deyne et al., 2016) and (Goikoetxea et al., 2015). While being based also on the iterative conversion procedure used here, the first concentrates however on converting, not a semantic network, but a fragment of the lexicon represented under a feature-based approach into a semantic space.

While seeking to obtain WordNet embeddings, the second resorts, however, not to a genuine conversion procedure, but to a lossy intermediate "textual" representation: it generates sequences of words by concatenating words visited by random walks over the WordNet; this "artificial text" is a partial and contingent reflection of the semantic network and is used to obtain distributional vectors by resorting to typical word embeddings techniques based on text.

Distances in a semantic graph:

The task of determining the semantic similarity between two words can be performed not only on the basis of the distance of their respective vectors in a semantic space, but also on the basis of the distance of the respective concepts in a lexical semantic network, like WordNet. There has been a long research tradition on this issue whose major proposals include (Jiang and Conrath, 1997), (Lin, 1998), (Leacock and Chodorow, 1998), (Hirst and St-Onge, 1998),(Resnik, 1999), among others, which received nice comparative assessments in (Ferlez and Gams, 2004) and (Budanitsky and Hirst, 2006), including their correlation with human judgments.

In this context, it is worth of note the work by (Hughes and Ramage, 2007), which resorts to random graph walks over WordNet edges. Differently from our approach, its goal is to obtain word-specific stationary probability distributions — such that the semantic affinity of two words is based on the similarity of their probability distributions —, rather than to obtain vectorial representations for words in a shared distributional semantic space.

The focus of the present paper is on an effective method to convert a semantic network into a semantic space, with the graph-based affinity obtained by the chaining of "local" one-edge distances ensured by the iteration in (1)-(2) being central for that goal.

It will be interesting to understand whether it will be possible to consider, as an alternative, those graph-based metrics of semantic similarity for any two nodes anywhere in the graph — resorting to the "non-local" multi-edge distance between the two input words. It remains to be understood whether they can be resorted to as the basis of an "all vs. all" type of procedures for an exhaustive screening of the graph that are computationally tractable — thus aiming at keeping up with an effective method for graph to matrix conversion of an entire lexical semantic network that resists the eventual exponential explosion.

6   Conclusions

In this paper, we offer a contribution towards a unified account of lexical semantics. We propose a methodology to convert from semantic networks, that are encoded in ontological graphs and empirically based on systematic linguistic intuitions (in their higher quality incarnations), to semantic spaces, that are encoded in distributional vectors and empirically based on very large collections of texts (in their higher quality implementations). This conversion methodology relies on a straightforward yet powerful intuition — the larger the number of paths and the shorter the paths connecting two nodes in an ontological graph the stronger is their semantic affinity —, with iteration (1) making it operative in order to generate a distributional matrix from an ontological graph.

We report also on the results of assessing this conversion methodology with a case study, namely by applying it to a subgraph of WordNet with less than half of its words (60k), randomly selected from the ones whose senses have a larger number of outgoing edges. The resulting distributional vectors wnet2vec were evaluated under the mainstream task of determining the semantic similarity of words arranged in pairs, against the mainstream gold standard SimLex-999, with very good results. The performance of wnet2vec was around 15% superior to the performance of word2vec, trained on a 100 billion token collection of texts. This in-

dicates that the proposed conversion procedure is very effective and that the WordNet embeddings are competitive when compared to text based embeddings.

It is nevertheless worth underlying that the research goal of this paper was not to search for word embeddings that outperform all previous proposals known in the literature in terms of intrinsic evaluation tasks, like semantic similarity, etc., or when they are embedded in larger systems. Its research goal was rather to demonstrate that it is feasible to create very effective word embeddings from semantic networks with a straightforward and yet powerful method of conversion from semantic networks to semantic spaces that, given its simplicity, offer the promise to generalize very well for more types of lexical networks and ontologies other than just WordNet, which was the case study used here.

The fact that less than half of the words in WordNet were used in the reported experiment reinforces this positive expectation with respect to the strength of the proposed approach, and point towards future work that will seek to use larger portions of WordNet, as computational limitation can be overcome.

The results reported in this paper thus hint at very promising research avenues, including, among others, experiments with further ontologies of different domains, empirical origins, etc.; with cross-lingual triangulation with aligned WordNets and aligned embeddings; with reciprocal reinforcement of ontological graphs and distributional vectors; with other metrics of semantic affinity in a graph, etc.

The wnet2vec data and software and their future updates are distributed at `https://github.com/nlx-group/WordNetEmbeddings`

Acknowledgments

The research results presented here were partly supported by PORTULAN/CLARIN Infrastructure for the Science and Technology of Language, by the National Infrastructure for Distributed Computing (INCD) of Portugal, and by the ANI/3279/2016 grant.

References

Eneko Agirre, Enrique Alfonseca, Keith Hall, Jana Kravalova, Marius Paşca, and Aitor Soroa. 2009. A study on similarity and relatedness using distributional and wordnet-based approaches. In *NAACL-HLT2009*, pages 19–27.

John Robert Anderson. 1974. Retrieval of propositional information from long-term memory. *Cognitive Psychology*, 6(4):451–474.

Marco Baroni, Raffaella Bernardi, Ngoc-Quynh Do, and Chung-chieh Shan. 2012. Entailment above the word level in distributional semantics. In *EACL2012*, pages 23–32.

Daniel G. Bobrow and Donald Arthur Norman. 1975. Some principles of memory schemata. In *Representation and Understanding: Studies in Cognitive Science*, page 131–149. Elsevier.

Antoine Bordes, Nicolas Usunier, Alberto Garcia-Duran, Jason Weston, and Oksana Yakhnenko. 2013. Translating embeddings for modeling multi-relational data. In *Advances in Neural Information Processing Systems 26*, pages 2787–2795.

Elia Bruni, Gemma Boleda, Marco Baroni, and Nam-Khanh Tran. 2012. Distributional semantics in technicolor. In *ACL2012*, pages 136–145.

Alexander Budanitsky and Graeme Hirst. 2006. Evaluating wordnet-based measures of lexical semantic relatedness. *Computational Linguistics*, 32(1):13–47.

José Camacho-Collados, Mohammad Taher Pilehvar, and Roberto Navigli. 2015. Nasari: a novel approach to a semantically-aware representation of items. In *NAACL-HLT2015*, pages 567–577.

Simon De Deyne, Daniel J Navarro, and Gert Storms. 2013. Better explanations of lexical and semantic cognition using networks derived from continued rather than single-word associations. *Behavior Research Methods*, 45(2):480–498.

Simon De Deyne, Amy Perfors, and Daniel J Navarro. 2016. Predicting human similarity judgments with distributional models: The value of word associations. In *COLING2016*, pages 1861–1870.

William K Estes. 1994. *Classification and Cognition.* Oxford University Press.

Manaal Faruqui, Jesse Dodge, Sujay Kumar Jauhar, Chris Dyer, Eduard Hovy, and Noah A. Smith. 2015. Retrofitting word vectors to semantic lexicons. In *AACL-HLT 2015*, pages 1606–1615.

Christiane Fellbaum, editor. 1998. *WordNet: An Electronic Lexical Database.* MIT Press.

Jure Ferlez and Matjaz Gams. 2004. Shortest-path semantic distance measure in wordnet v2.0. *Informatica*, 28:381–386.

Josu Goikoetxea, Aitor Soroa, and Eneko Agirre. 2015. Random walks and neural network language models on knowledge bases. In *NAACL-HLT25*, pages 1434–1439.

Andreas Grünauer and Markus Vincze. 2015. Using dimension reduction to improve the classification of high-dimensional data. *arXiv preprint arXiv:1505.06907.*

Guy Halawi, Gideon Dror, Evgeniy Gabrilovich, and Yehuda Koren. 2012. Large-scale learning of word relatedness with constraints. In *Proceedings of the 18th ACM SIGKDD International Conference on Knowledge Discovery and Data Mining*, pages 1406–1414. ACM.

Zellig S Harris. 1954. Distributional structure. *Word*, 10(2-3):146–162.

Marti A Hearst. 1992. Automatic acquisition of hyponyms from large text corpora. In *COLING1992*, pages 539–545.

Felix Hill, Roi Reichart, and Anna Korhonen. 2016. Simlex-999: Evaluating semantic models with (genuine) similarity estimation. *Computational Linguistics*, 41:665–695.

G. Hirst and D. St-Onge. 1998. Lexical chains as representations of context for the detection and correction of malapropisms. In C. Fellbaum, editor, *WordNet: An Electronic Lexical Database*, pages 305–332. MIT Press.

Keith J Holyoak and Kyunghee Koh. 1987. Surface and structural similarity in analogical transfer. *Memory & Cognition*, 15(4):332–340.

Thad Hughes and Daniel Ramage. 2007. Lexical semantic relatedness with random graph walks. In *EMNLP-CONLL2007*, Prague, Czech Republic.

Yangfeng Ji and Jacob Eisenstein. 2014. Representation learning for text-level discourse parsing. In *ACL2014*, pages 13–24.

J. Jiang and D. Conrath. 1997. Semantic similarity based on corpus statistics and lexical taxonomy. In *Proceedings on International Conference on Research in Computational Linguistics*.

Josh Kaufman. 2017. 10,000 most common english words in google's trillion word corpus. `https://github.com/first20hours/google-10000-english`.

C. Leacock and M. Chodorow. 1998. Combining local context and wordnet similarity for word sense identification. In C. Fellbaum, editor, *WordNet: An Electronic Lexical Database*, pages 265–285. MIT Press.

Jiwei Li and Dan Jurafsky. 2015. Do multi-sense embeddings improve natural language understanding? *arXiv preprint arXiv:1506.01070.*

D. Lin. 1998. An information-theoretic definition of similarity. In *Proceedings of 15th International Conference on Machine Learning*.

Yankai Lin, Zhiyuan Liu, Maosong Sun, Yang Liu, and Xuan Zhu. 2015. Learning entity and relation embeddings for knowledge graph completion. In *AAAI'15*, pages 2181–2187.

David E Meyer and Roger W Schvaneveldt. 1971. Facilitation in recognizing pairs of words: Evidence of a dependence between retrieval operations. *Journal of Experimental Psychology*, 90(2):227.

Tomas Mikolov, Kai Chen, Greg Corrado, and Jeffrey Dean. 2013a. Googlenews-vectors-negative300.bin.gz - efficient estimation of word representations in vector space. *arXiv preprint arXiv:1301.3781*. https://code.google.com/archive/p/word2vec/.

Tomas Mikolov, Ilya Sutskever, Kai Chen, Greg S Corrado, and Jeff Dean. 2013b. Distributed representations of words and phrases and their compositionality. In *Advances in Neural Information Processing Systems 26*, pages 3111–3119.

Marvin Minsky. 1975. A framework for representing knowledge. In *Psychology of Computer Vision*. McGraw-Hill.

Mark Newman. 2010. *Networks: An Introduction.* Oxford University Press.

Kim Anh Nguyen, Sabine Schulte im Walde, and Ngoc Thang Vu. 2017. Distinguishing antonyms and synonyms in a pattern-based neural network. *arXiv preprint arXiv:1701.02962*.

Maximilian Nickel, Lorenzo Rosasco, and Tomaso Poggio. 2016. Holographic embeddings of knowledge graphs. In *AAAI'16*, pages 1955–1961.

Maximillian Nickel and Douwe Kiela. 2017. Poincaré embeddings for learning hierarchical representations. In *Advances in Neural Information Processing Systems 30*, pages 6341–6350.

Charles E Osgood, George J Suci, and Percy H Tannenbaum. 1957. The measurement of meaning. *Urbana: University of Illinois Press*.

Francis Jeffrey Pelletier. 2016. Semantic compositionality. In *The Oxford Research Encyclopedia of Linguistics*. Oxford University Press.

M Ross Quillan. 1966. Semantic memory. Technical report, Bolt Beranek and Newman Inc., Cambridge MA.

Radim Řehůřek and Petr Sojka. 2010. Software framework for topic modelling with large corpora. In *Proceedings of the LREC 2010 Workshop on New Challenges for NLP Frameworks*, pages 45–50. European Language Resources Association.

P. Resnik. 1999. Semantic similarity in a taxonomy: An information-based measure and its application to problems of ambiguity in natural language. *Journal of Artificial Intelligence Research*, 11.

Lance J Rips. 1975. Inductive judgments about natural categories. *Journal of Verbal Learning and Verbal Behavior*, 14(6):665–681.

João António Rodrigues, Ruben Branco, João Ricardo Silva, Chakaveh Saedi, and António Branco. 2018. Predicting brain activation with wordnet embeddings. In *Proceedings of the 8th Workshop on Cognitive Aspects of Computational Language Learning and Processing (CogACLL2018), the 56th Annual Meeting of the Association for Computational Linguistics (ACL2018)*, Melbourne, Australia. Association for Computational Linguistics.

Stephen Roller, Katrin Erk, and Gemma Boleda. 2014. Inclusive yet selective: Supervised distributional hypernymy detection. In *COLING 2014*, pages 1025–1036.

Brian H Ross. 1984. Remindings and their effects in learning a cognitive skill. *Cognitive Psychology*, 16(3):371–416.

Herbert Rubenstein and John B Goodenough. 1965. Contextual correlates of synonymy. *Communications of the ACM*, 8(10):627–633.

Vered Shwartz, Yoav Goldberg, and Ido Dagan. 2016. Improving hypernymy detection with an integrated path-based and distributional method. In *ACL2016*, pages 2389–2398.

Rion Snow, Daniel Jurafsky, and Andrew Y Ng. 2005. Learning syntactic patterns for automatic hypernym discovery. In *Advances in Neural Information Processing systems 17*, pages 1297–1304.

Richard Socher, John Bauer, Christopher D Manning, and Andrew Y. Ng. 2013. Parsing with compositional vector grammars. In *ACL2013*, pages 455–465.

David G Underhill, Luke K McDowell, David J Marchette, and Jeffrey L Solka. 2007. Enhancing text analysis via dimensionality reduction. In *IEEE-IRI2007*, pages 348–353.

Ivan Vendrov, Ryan Kiros, Sanja Fidler, and Raquel Urtasun. 2015. Order-embeddings of images and language. *arXiv preprint arXiv:1511.06361*.

Julie Weeds, Daoud Clarke, Jeremy Reffin, David Weir, and Bill Keller. 2014. Learning to distinguish hypernyms and co-hyponyms. In *COLING 2014*, pages 2249–2259.

Wiktionary. 2017. Wiktionary: Frequency lists. https://en.wiktionary.org/wiki/Wiktionary:Frequency_lists.

Svante Wold, Kim Esbensen, and Paul Geladi. 1987. Principal component analysis. *Chemometrics and Intelligent Laboratory Systems*, 2(1-3):37–52.

Mo Yu and Mark Dredze. 2014. Improving lexical embeddings with semantic knowledge. In *ACL 2014*, pages 545–550.

Knowledge Graph Embedding with Numeric Attributes of Entities

Yanrong Wu, Zhichun Wang*

College of Information Science and Technology
Beijing Normal University, Beijing 100875, PR. China
yrwu@mail.bnu.edu.cn, zcwang@bnu.edu.cn

Abstract

Knowledge Graph (KG) embedding projects entities and relations into low dimensional vector space, which has been successfully applied in KG completion task. The previous embedding approaches only model entities and their relations, ignoring a large number of entities' numeric attributes in KGs. In this paper, we propose a new KG embedding model which jointly model entity relations and numeric attributes. Our approach combines an attribute embedding model with a translation-based structure embedding model, which learns the embeddings of entities, relations, and attributes simultaneously. Experiments of link prediction on YAGO and Freebase show that the performance is effectively improved by adding entities' numeric attributes in the embedding model.

1 Introduction

Recently, a number of Knowledge Graphs (KGs) have been created, such as DBpedia (Lehmann, 2015), YAGO (Mahdisoltani et al., 2015), and Freebase (Bollacker et al., 2008). KGs encode structured information of entities in the form of triplets (e.g. $\langle Microsoft, isLocatedIn, UnitedStates\rangle$), and have been successfully applied in many real-world applications. Although KGs contain a huge amount of triplets, most of them are incomplete. In order to further expand KGs, much work on KG completion has been done, which aims to predict new triplets based on the existing ones in KGs. A promising group of research for KG completion is known as KG embedding. KG embedding

approaches project entities and relations into a continuous vector space while preserving the original knowledge in the KG. KG embedding models achieve good performance in KG completion in terms of efficiency and scalability. TransE is a representative KG embedding approach (Bordes et al., 2013), which projects both entities and relations into the same vector space: if a triplet $\langle head\ entity, relation, tail\ entity\rangle$ (denoted as $\langle h, r, t\rangle$) holds, TransE wants that $h + r \approx t$. The embeddings are learned by minimizing a margin-based ranking criterion over the training set. TransE model is simple but powerful, and it gets promising results on link prediction and triple classification problems. There are several enhanced model of TransE, including TransR (Lin et al., 2015), TransH (Wang et al., 2014) and TransD (Ji et al., 2015) etc. By introducing new representations of relational translation, later approaches achieve better performance at the cost of increasing model complexity. Recent surveys (Wang et al., 2017; Nickel et al., 2016) give detailed introduction and comparison of various KG embedding approaches.

However, most of the existing KG embedding approaches only model relational triplets (i.e. triplets of entity relations), while ignoring a large number of attributive triplets (i.e. triplets of entity attributes, e.g. $\langle Microsoft, wasFoundedOnDate, 1975\rangle$) in KGs. attributive triplets describe various attributes of entities, such as ages of people or areas of a city. There are a huge number of attributive triplets in real KGs, and we believe that information encoded in these triplets is also useful for predicting entity relations. Having the above motivation, we propose a new KG embedding approach that jointly model entity relations and entities' numeric attributes. Our approach consists of two component models,

---

*Corresponding Author

132

Proceedings of the 3rd Workshop on Representation Learning for NLP, pages 132–136
Melbourne, Australia, July 20, 2018. ©2018 Association for Computational Linguistics

structure embedding model and attribute embedding model. The structure embedding model is a translational distance model that preserves the knowledge of entity relations; the attribute embedding model is a regression-based model that preserves the knowledge of entity attributes. Two component models are jointly optimized to get the embeddings of entities, relations, and attributes. Experiments of link prediction on YAGO and Freebase show that the performance is effectively improved by adding entities' numeric attributes in the embedding model.

2 Our Approach

To effectively utilize numeric attributes of entities in KG embedding, we propose **TransEA**, which combine a new attribute embedding model with the structure embedding model of TransE. Two component models in TransEA share the embeddings of entities, and they are jointly optimized in the training process.

2.1 Structure Embedding

The structure embedding directly adopts the translation-based method in TransE to model the relational triplets in KGs. Both Entities and relations in a KG are represented in the same vector space $\mathbb{R}^d$. In a triplet $\langle h, r, t \rangle$, the relation is considered as a translation vector $\mathbf{r}$, which connects the vector of entities $\mathbf{h}$ and $\mathbf{t}$ with low error, i.e. $\mathbf{h} + \mathbf{r} \approx \mathbf{t}$. The score function of a given triplet $\langle h, r, t \rangle$ is defined as

$$f_r(h, t) = -||\mathbf{h} + \mathbf{r} - \mathbf{t}||_{1/2} \qquad (1)$$

$||x||_{1/2}$ denotes either the $L1$ or $L2$ norm. For all the relational triplets in the KG, the loss function of the structure embedding is defined as:

$$L_R = \sum_{\langle h,r,t \rangle \in S} \sum_{\langle h',r,t' \rangle \in S'} [\gamma + f_r(h, t) - f_r(h', t')]_+ \qquad (2)$$

where $[x]_+ = \max\{0, x\}$, S' denotes the set of negative triplets constructed by corrupting $\langle h, r, t \rangle$, i.e. replacing h or t with a randomly chosen entity in KG; $\gamma > 0$ is a margin hyper-parameter separating positive and negative triplets.

2.2 Attribute Embedding

Attribute embedding model takes all the attributive triplets in a KG as input, and learns embeddings of entities and attributes. Both entities and attributes are represented as vectors in space $\mathbb{R}^d$. In an attributive triplet $\langle e, a, v \rangle$, e is an entity, a is an attribute, and v is the value of the entity's attribute. In our approach, we only consider attributive triplets containing numeric values or values can be easily converted into numeric ones. For a triplet $\langle e, a, v \rangle$, we define a score function as

$$f_a(e, v) = -||\mathbf{a}^\top \cdot \mathbf{e} + b_a - v||_{1/2} \qquad (3)$$

where $\mathbf{a}$ and $\mathbf{e}$ are vectors of attribute a and entity e, b_a is a bias for attribute a. The idea of this score function is to predict the attribute value by a linear regression model of attribute a; the vector $\mathbf{a}$ and bias b_a are the parameters of the regression model. For all the attributive triplets in the KG, the loss function of the attribute embedding is defined as:

$$L_A = \sum_{\langle e,a,v \rangle \in T} f_a(e, v) \qquad (4)$$

where T is the set of all attributive triplets with numeric values in the KG.

2.3 Joint Model

To combine the above two component models, TransEA minimizes the following loss function:

$$L = (1 - \alpha) \cdot L_R + \alpha \cdot L_A \qquad (5)$$

where α is a hyper-parameter that balances the importance of structure and attribute embedding. In the joint model, we let the embeddings of entities shared by two component models. Entities, relations, and attributes are all represented by vectors in $\mathbb{R}^d$. We implement our approach by using TensorFlow[1], and the loss function is minimized by performing stochastic gradient descent.

3 Experiments

3.1 Datasets

The following two datasets are used in the experiments, Table 1 shows their detail information.

YG58K. YG58K is a subset of YAGO3 (Mahdisoltani et al., 2015) which contains about 58K entities. YG58K is built by removing entities from YAGO3 that appear less than 25 times or have no attributive triplets. All the remaining triplets are then randomly split into training/validation/test sets.

---

[1] https://www.tensorflow.org

FB15K. FB15K is a subset of triplets extracted from Freebase[2]. This subset of Freebase was originally used in (Bordes et al., 2013), and then widely used for evaluating KB completion approaches. Since our approach consumes attributive triplets, we extract all the attributive triplets of entities in FB15K from Freebase to build the evaluation dataset.

Datasets	YG58K	FB15K
# Relational Triplets	497783	592213
# Attributive Triplets	130287	24034
# Entities	58130	14951
# Relations	32	1345
# Attributes	24	336
# Train Sets	399480	483142
# Valid Sets	49171	59071
# Test Sets	49132	50000

Table 1: Statistics of datasets

3.2 Experimental setup

In the experiments, Mean Rank (the mean rank of the original correct entity), Hits@k (the proportion of the original correct entity to the top k entities), and MRR (the mean reciprocal rank) are used as evaluation metrics. Given a testing triplet $\langle h, r, t \rangle$, we replace the head h by every entity in the KGs and calculate dissimilarity measures according to the score function f_r. Ranking the scores in ascending order, then we get the rank of the original correct triplet to compute the evaluation metrics. And we repeat the procedure when removing the tail t instead of the head h. We name the evaluation setting as **"Raw"**. While corrupted triplets that appear in the train/valid/test sets (except the original correct one) may underestimate the metrics, we also filter out those corrupted triplets before getting the rank of each testing triplet and we call this process **"Filter"**.

Because our approach is built based on TransE, we compare our approach with TransE to see whether adding attribute embedding in the model improves the performance of link prediction. For TransE and TransEA, we consider the learning rate λ among {0.1, 0.01, 0.001}, the margin γ among {1, 2, 4, 10}, the dimensions of embedding d among {20, 50, 100, 150}, the types of norm in two score functions among {L1, L2}, and α among {0.2, 0.3, 0.4, 0.5, 0.6}. Based on the mean rank in validation set, we select the best configurations for two approaches. On

the YG58K dataset, the best parameter configuration for TransE is $(\lambda = 0.1, \gamma = 4, d = 50, f_r = L1, f_a = L1)$, and for TransEA is $(\lambda = 0.001, \gamma = 4, d = 50, f_r = L1, f_a = L1, \alpha = 0.6)$. On the FB15K dataset, the best parameter configuration for TransE is $(\lambda = 0.01, \gamma = 1, d = 50, f_r = L1, f_a = L1)$, and for TransEA is $(\lambda = 0.001, \gamma = 2, d = 100, f_r = L1, f_a = L1, \alpha = 0.3)$.

3.3 Results

Table 2 shows the results of link prediction on YG58K and FB15K datasets. The results of predicting head and tail entities are outlined separately, and we also report the overall results by considering prediction of both head and tail entity. According to the overall results, TransEA outperforms TransE on both two datasets in terms of all the three metrics. TransEA gets lower Mean Ranks by about 10 on YG58K dataset; the MRR and Hits@k of two approaches are very close, TransEA gets slightly better results, the improvements of MRR and Hits@k are 0.1-0.2% and 0-0.3%. On FB15K dataset, TransEA gets lower Mean Ranks by 13, and it also gets better results than TransE according to MRR, Hits@10 and Hits@3.

Table 3 shows the results of different relational categories. In general, TransEA has superiority on two datasets, except one-to-many relation for replacing head entity on YG58K. And the improvements on FB15K are larger than YG58K.

In order to figure out which relations are predicted more accurately by TransEA, Table 4 lists the top 5 improved relations in terms of Hits@10 on YG58K. It shows the best improvement of Hits@10 is 25% for the relation `isInterestedIn`. The second one is 12.5% for `hasAcademicAdvisor`, and the third is 6.3% for `worteMusicFor`. Entities of these three relations have plenty of numeric attributes (`wasBornOnDate`, `diedOnDate`) describing people, we believe they are helpful to improving the embeddings of entity relations. Entities in relational triplets about `livesIn`, (e.g. $\langle HankAzaria, livesIn, NewYork \rangle$), also have some numeric attributes (`hasLatitude`, `hasLongtude`, `hasNumberOfPeople`, `etc`), therefore TransEA gets a 5% improvement of Hits@10.

On FB15K dataset, five relations have 100%

[2]https://everest.hds.utc.fr/doku.php?id=en:transe

Dataset	Entity	Model	Mean Rank		MRR(%)		Hits@10(%)		Hits@3(%)		Hits@1(%)	
			Raw	Filter	Raw	Filter	Raw	Filter	Raw	Filter	Raw	Filter
YG58K	Head	TransE	950	731	3.1	5.2	9.1	15.4	**4.1**	8.4	1.0	3.2
		TransEA	**944**	**723**	**3.1**	**5.4**	**9.4**	**16.0**	4.1	**8.5**	**1.1**	**3.4**
	Tail	TransE	240	234	8.4	10.2	27.0	31.9	12.2	17.0	4.5	6.5
		TransEA	**229**	**223**	**8.5**	**10.5**	**27.6**	**32.7**	**12.4**	**17.6**	**4.7**	**6.8**
	All	TransE	595	482	5.7	7.7	18.0	23.7	8.2	12.7	2.8	4.8
		TransEA	**586**	**473**	**5.8**	**7.9**	**18.5**	**24.3**	**8.2**	**13.0**	**2.9**	**5.1**
FB15K	Head	TransE	240	115	14.5	25.2	47.0	68.7	26.2	52.4	11.8	30.6
		TransEA	**225**	**100**	**15.1**	**28.1**	**49.5**	**74.0**	**28.0**	**60.1**	**11.8**	**34.8**
	Tail	TransE	168	87	17.6	28.2	54.8	75.1	32.8	58.9	**16.4**	35.7
		TransEA	**157**	**76**	**18.2**	**30.9**	**57.5**	**80.5**	**34.5**	**66.6**	16.3	**40.0**
	All	TransE	204	101	16.0	26.7	50.9	71.9	29.5	55.7	**14.1**	33.1
		TransEA	**191**	**88**	**16.7**	**29.5**	**53.5**	**77.3**	**31.3**	**63.3**	14.0	**37.4**

Table 2: Link prediction results

DATASETS	TASK	Predicting Head(Hits@10)				Prediction Tail(Hits@10)			
	REL.CAT	1-to-1	1-to-N	N-to-1	N-to-N	1-to-1	1-to-N	N-to-1	N-to-N
YG58K	TransE	61.4	**45.5**	15.4	15.5	62.0	18.2	31.9	31.1
	TransEA	**63.9**	36.4	**16.0**	**16.0**	**63.3**	**22.7**	**32.7**	**31.9**
FB15K	TransE	78.1	93.8	68.7	72.3	78.0	42.1	75.1	75.6
	TransEA	**84.3**	**95.5**	**74.0**	**77.6**	**83.3**	**52.4**	**80.5**	**81.1**

Table 3: Hits@10(%) by relational category in the filtered evaluation setting. (N. stand for MANY)

Relation	TransE	TransEA
isInterestedIn	50.0	75.0
hasAcademicAdvisor	31.3	43.8
wroteMusicFor	12.5	18.8
livesIn	23.8	28.8
hasNeighbor	48.1	52.8

Table 4: Top 5 relations of promoted Hits@10 and their Hits@10(%) on YG58K

Relation	TransE	TransEA
business/brand/company	24	2
base/celebrity/restaurant	249	4
base/celebrity/product	24	2
music/artists_supported	44	3
sports/competition/country	24	4

Table 5: Top 5 relations of promoted Hit@10 and their Mean Rank on FB15K

improvements of Hits@10, because TransE does not correctly predict any correct triplets in the top 10 ranked ones. We find that these relations only have one single sample in the test sets, so Table 5 lists the Mean Rank of them. Obviously, TransEA improves their Mean Rank a lot. Entities in triplets of the five relations have only a few attributes. For example, the relation `business/brand/company` only has one numeric attributive triplet about `organization/dateFounded`. And the relation `music/artists supported` has two triplets with numeric attributes `person/dateOfBirth` and one triplet with `person/heightMeters`. Therefore, the quality of predicted links can be improved as well even with only a small number of entities numeric attributes.

4 Conclusion

In this paper, we propose TransEA, an embedding approach which jointly models relational and attributive triplets in KGs. TransEA combines an attribute embedding model with the translation-based embedding model in TransE. Experiments on YAGO and Freebase show that TransEA achieves better performance than TransE in link prediction task. In the future, we will study how to predict missing attribute values in KGs based on KG embedding.

Acknowledgments

The work is supported by the National Key Research and Development Program of China (No. 2017YFC0804004) and the National Natural Science Foundation of China (No. 61772079).

References

Kurt Bollacker, Colin Evans, Praveen Paritosh, Tim Sturge, and Jamie Taylor. 2008. Freebase: a collaboratively created graph database for structuring human knowledge. *SIGMOD 08 Proceedings of the 2008 ACM SIGMOD international conference on Management of data*, pages 1247–1250.

Antoine Bordes, Nicolas Usunier, Alberto Garcia-Duran, Jason Weston, and Oksana Yakhnenko. 2013. Translating embeddings for modeling multi-relational data. In *Proceedings of Advances in neural information processing systems (NIPS2013)*, pages 2787–2795.

Guoliang Ji, Shizhu He, Liheng Xu, Kang Liu, and Jun Zhao. 2015. Knowledge graph embedding via dynamic mapping matrix. In *Proceedings of the 53rd Annual Meeting of the Association for Computational Linguistics and the 7th International Joint Conference on Natural Language Processing*, volume 1, pages 687–696.

J. Lehmann. 2015. Dbpedia: A large-scale, multilingual knowledge base extracted from wikipedia. *Semantic Web*, 6(2):167–195.

Yankai Lin, Zhiyuan Liu, Maosong Sun, Yang Liu, and Xuan Zhu. 2015. Learning entity and relation embeddings for knowledge graph completion. In *Proceedings of the Twenty-Ninth AAAI Conference on Artificial Intelligence (AAAI2015)*, volume 15, pages 2181–2187.

Farzaneh Mahdisoltani, Joanna Asia Biega, and Fabian M. Suchanek. 2015. YAGO3: A Knowledge Base from Multilingual Wikipedias . *7th Biennial Conference on Innovative Data Systems Research*.

Maximilian Nickel, Kevin Murphy, Volker Tresp, and Evgeniy Gabrilovich. 2016. A review of relational machine learning for knowledge graphs. *Proceedings of the IEEE*, 104(1):11–33.

Quan Wang, Zhendong Mao, Bin Wang, and Li Guo. 2017. Knowledge graph embedding: A survey of approaches and applications. *IEEE Transactions on Knowledge and Data Engineering*, 29(12):2724–2743.

Zhen Wang, Jianwen Zhang, Jianlin Feng, and Zheng Chen. 2014. Knowledge graph embedding by translating on hyperplanes. In *Proceedings of the Twenty-eighth AAAI Conference on Artificial Intelligence (AAAI2014)*, volume 14, pages 1112–1119.

Injecting Lexical Contrast into Word Vectors by Guiding Vector Space Specialisation

Ivan Vulić and **Anna Korhonen**
Language Technology Lab, University of Cambridge, UK
`{iv250,alk23}@cam.ac.uk`

Abstract

Word vector space specialisation models offer a portable, light-weight approach to fine-tuning arbitrary distributional vector spaces to discern between synonymy and antonymy. Their effectiveness is drawn from external linguistic constraints that specify the exact lexical relation between words. In this work, we show that a careful selection of the external constraints can steer and improve the specialisation. By simply selecting appropriate constraints, we report state-of-the-art results on a suite of tasks with well-defined benchmarks where modeling lexical contrast is crucial: 1) true semantic similarity, with highest reported scores on SimLex-999 and SimVerb-3500 to date; 2) detecting antonyms; and 3) distinguishing antonyms from synonyms.

1 Introduction

Representation models grounded in the distributional hypothesis (Harris, 1954) generally fail to distinguish highly contrasting words (*antonyms*) from highly similar ones (*synonyms*), due to similar word co-occurrence signatures in text corpora (Turney and Pantel, 2010; Mohammad et al., 2013).[1] In addition to antonymy and synonymy being fundamental lexical relations that are central to the organisation of the mental lexicon (Miller and Fellbaum, 1991; Murphy, 2010), this undesirable property of distributional word vector spaces has grave implications on their application in NLP reasoning and understanding tasks. As shown in prior work (Pham et al., 2015; Mrkšić et al., 2016; Kim et al.,

2016; Nguyen et al., 2017b; Mrkšić et al., 2017, *i.a.*), explicitly modeling the *lexical contrast* benefits text entailment, dialogue state tracking, spoken language understanding, language generation, etc.[2]

A popular solution to address the limitation concerning lexical contrast is to move beyond standalone unsupervised learning. Post-processing procedures have been designed that leverage external lexical knowledge available in human- and automatically-constructed lexical resources (e.g., PPDB, WordNet): these methods *fine-tune* input word vectors to satisfy *linguistic constraints* from the external resources (Faruqui et al., 2015; Jauhar et al., 2015; Rothe and Schütze, 2015; Wieting et al., 2015; Mrkšić et al., 2016; Mrkšić et al., 2017; Vulić et al., 2017b, *i.a.*). This process has been termed *retrofitting* or *vector space specialisation*.

As one advantage, the post-processing methods are applicable to arbitrary input vector spaces. They are also "light-weight", that is, they do not require large corpora for (re-)training, as opposed to *joint specialisation models* (Yu and Dredze, 2014; Kiela et al., 2015; Pham et al., 2015; Nguyen et al., 2016) which integrate lexical knowledge directly into distributional training objectives.[3]

The main driving force of the retrofitting models are the external constraints, which specify which words should be close to each other in the specialised vector space (i.e., the so-called ATTRACT constraints), and which words should be far apart in the space (REPEL). By manipulating the constraints, one can steer the specialisation goal: e.g., Vulić et al. (2017a) use verb relations from VerbNet (Kipper, 2005) to accentuate VerbNet-style syntactic-semantic relations in the vector space.

---

[1] As pointed out by Cruse (1986), antonyms have a paradoxical nature: on the one hand, they constitute the two opposites of a meaning continuum, and therefore could be seen as semantically remote; on the other hand, they are paradigmatically similar, having almost identical distributions.

[2] Using a simple example, users asking for *a cheap pub in northern Seattle* do not want a virtual personal assistant to recommend *an expensive restaurant in southern Portland*.

[3] An additional advantage of post-processors is their better overall performance across a range of tasks when compared to the "heavy-weight" joint models (Mrkšić et al., 2016).

Proceedings of the 3rd Workshop on Representation Learning for NLP, pages 137–143
Melbourne, Australia, July 20, 2018. ©2018 Association for Computational Linguistics

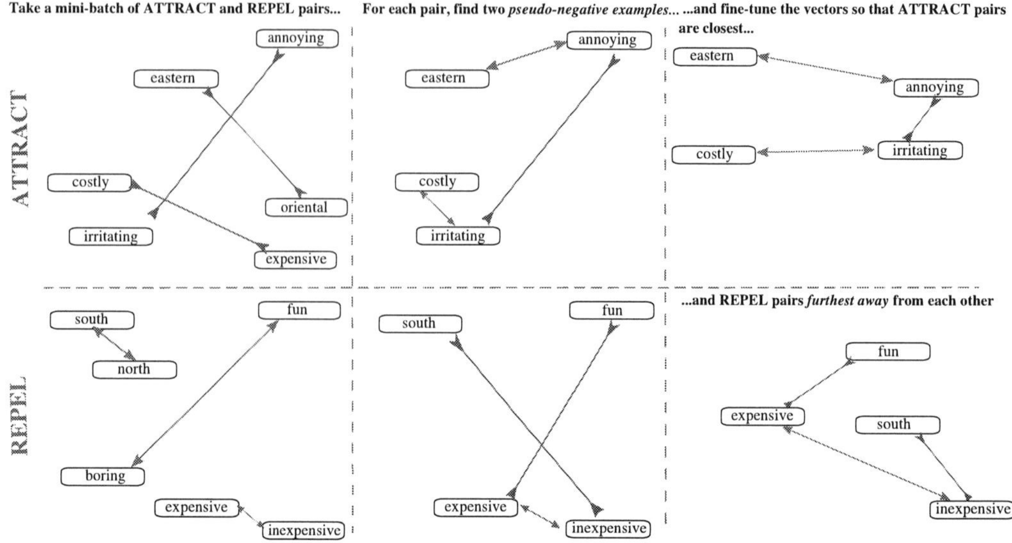

Figure 1: An illustration of specialisation for lexical contrast with toy examples. The specialisation model operates with two sets of external linguistic constraints: 1) ATTRACT word pairs, which have to be as close as possible in the fine-tuned vector space (e.g., *irritating* and *annoying*); and 2) REPEL word pairs, which have to be as far away from each other as possible (e.g., *expensive* and *inexpensive*).

Contributions. In this work, we investigate how different constraints affect specialisation. We show that a careful selection of external constraints can guide specialisation models to emphasise lexical contrast in the fine-tuned vector space: e.g., we indicate that direct (i.e., 1-step) WordNet hypernymy-hyponymy pairs are useful for boosting lexical contrast. Our specialised word vector spaces yield state-of-the-art results on a range of tasks where modeling lexical contrast is crucial: **1)** true semantic similarity; **2)** antonymy detection; and **3)** distinguishing antonyms from synonyms. Our SimLex-999 (Hill et al., 2015) and SimVerb-3500 (Gerz et al., 2016) scores are the highest reported results on these datasets to date: the result on SimLex-999 is the first result on the dataset surpassing the ceiling of mean inter-annotator agreement.

2 Methodology

Specialisation Model. Post-processing models are generally guided by two broad sets of constraints: **1)** ATTRACT constraints (AC) specify which words should be close to each other in the fine-tuned vector space; **2)** REPEL (RC) constraints describe which words should be pulled away from each other. The nomenclature is adopted from Mrkšić et al. (2017). Earlier post-processors (Faruqui et al., 2015; Jauhar et al., 2015; Wieting et al., 2015) operate only with ATTRACT con-

syn (AC)	hyp1 (AC)	antexp (RC)
(outburst, outbreak)	(discordance, dissonance)	(smooth, shake)
(safe, secure)	(postmen, deliverymen)	(clear, obscurity)
(cordial, warmhearted)	(employee, worker)	(relief, pressure)
(answer, response)	(swap, exchange)	(half, full)

Table 1: Examples of linguistic constraints.

straints, and are therefore not suited to model both aspects of lexical contrast. In this work, we employ the state-of-the-art specialisation model of Mrkšić et al. (2017) which integrates both sets of constraints into its fine-tuning process. Here, we provide only a high-level description of the model, also illustrated by Figure 1, while we refer the interested reader to the original paper for a full (technical) description.

In short, the model trains over batches of AT-TRACT and REPEL pairs and contains three terms in its objective function. First, the ATTRACT term pushes two words from each ATTRACT constraint closer to each other (in terms of the cosine similarity) than to any other word present in the current batch by a margin δ_{att}. Second, the REPEL term pulls away two words from each REPEL constraint so that they are further away from each other than from any other word present in the current batch (again, by a margin δ_{rpl}): see Figure 1 again. Third, a regularisation term is used to preserve the useful semantic content originally present in the distributional space, as long as this information does not contradict the injected external knowledge.

Linguistic Constraints. The constraints are in fact word pairs (x_i, x_j), $x_i, x_j \in V$, where V is the vocabulary represented in the input distributional space. First, the conflation of synonymy and antonymy relations in the input space can be obviously mitigated by assigning synonymy pairs (syn) to the ATTRACT set, and antonymy pairs (ant) to the REPEL set. Further, similar to Ono et al. (2015), it is possible to extend the (typically less exhaustive) list of antonyms by combining the available knowledge from syn and ant word pairs. If (x_i, x_j) are a pair of synonyms, and (x_i, x_k) are a pair of antonyms, one can add another pair (x_j, x_k) to the expanded list of antonyms: this yields a larger set (antexp) to serve as REPEL constraints.

Finally, as the analysis of Hill et al. (2015) shows, the taxonomic hypernymy-hyponymy IS-A relation is often mistaken by true synonymy by humans. Therefore, we also experiment with direct (i.e. 1-step) IS-A pairs (hyp1) from Wordnet as another set included in the ATTRACT pairs for lexical contrast specialisation. To the best of our knowledge, the hyp1 pairs were not used before for lexical contrast modeling. A selection of constraints from different sets is shown in Table 1. In what follows, we test how these different configurations of constraints influence the specialisation process.

3 Experimental Setup

Training Setup and Constraints. We train the state-of-the-art specialisation model of Mrkšić et al. (2017) using suggested settings:[4] Adagrad (Duchi et al., 2011) is used for stochastic optimisation, batch size is 50, and we train for 15 epochs. To emphasise lexical contrast in the specialised space we set the respective ATTRACT and REPEL margins δ_{att} and δ_{rpl} to the same value: 1.0. We use large 300-dim skip gram vectors with bag-of-words contexts and negative sampling (SGNS-GN) (Mikolov et al., 2013), pre-trained on the 100B Google News corpus. As all other components of the model are kept fixed, the difference in performance can be attributed to the difference in the constraints used.

We experiment with external constraints employed in prior work (Zhang et al., 2014; Ono et al., 2015): these were extracted from WordNet (Fellbaum, 1998) and the Roget thesaurus

(Kipfer, 2009), and comprise 1,023,082 synonymy (syn) pairs and 380,873 ant pairs. The expanded antexp set of antonyms contains a total of 10,334,811 word pairs. Finally, the hyp1 set extracted from WordNet contains 326,187 word pairs.

We evaluate all specialised spaces in three standard tasks with well-defined benchmarks where modeling lexical contrast is beneficial: **1)** semantic similarity, **2)** antonymy detection, and **3)** distinguishing antonyms from synonyms. For each task, we compare against a representative selection of baselines, currently holding peak scores on the respective benchmarks. Due to a large space of models in our comparison, we refer the interested reader to the original papers for their full descriptions.

Task 1: Word Similarity. We evaluate all models on the SimLex-999 dataset (Hill et al., 2015), and SimVerb-3500 (Gerz et al., 2016), a recent verb pair similarity dataset with 3,500 verb pairs.[5] The evaluation metric is Spearman's ρ rank correlation.

Task 2: Antonymy Detection. For this task, we rely on the widely used Graduate Record Examination (GRE) dataset (Mohammad et al., 2008, 2013). The task, given an input cue word, is to select the best antonym from five options. Given a word vector space, we take the word with the largest cosine distance to the cue as the best antonym. The GRE dataset contains 950 questions in total. We report balanced F_1 scores on the entire dataset.

Task 3: Synonymy vs. Antonymy. In this binary classification task, the system must decide whether the relation between two words is synonymy or antonymy. We use the recent dataset of Nguyen et al. (2017b), comprising 1,020 noun (N) test pairs, 908 verb (V) pairs, and 1,986 adjective (A) pairs, with the equal number of synonymy and antonymy pairs in each test subset. A classification threshold decides on the relation: all word pairs with their cosine similarity above the threshold are considered synonyms, all the others are antonyms.[6]

---

[4]https://github.com/nmrksic/attract-repel

[5]Unlike WordSim-353 (Finkelstein et al., 2002) or MEN (Bruni et al., 2014), SimLex and SimVerb provide explicit guidelines to discern between true semantic similarity and (more broad) conceptual relatedness, so that related but non-similar words (e.g. *tiger* and *jungle*) have a low rating.

[6]Similar to the work on hypernymy detection (Santus et al., 2014; Nguyen et al., 2017a; Vulić and Mrkšić, 2018), we tune the threshold on a validation set of 206 N pairs, 182 V pairs, and 398 A pairs, also used by Nguyen et al. (2017b).

MODEL	SimLex	SimVerb
SGNS-GN (Mikolov et al., 2013)	0.414	0.348
Symmetric Patterns (Schwartz et al., 2015)	0.563	0.328
Non-distributional (Faruqui and Dyer, 2015)	0.578	0.596
Joint Specialisation (Nguyen et al., 2016)	0.590	0.516
Paragram-SL999 (Wieting et al., 2015)	0.690	0.540
Counter-fitting (Mrkšić et al., 2016)	0.740	0.628
AR: BabelNet (Mrkšić et al., 2017)	0.751	0.674
RC: `ant`	0.596	0.589
RC: `antexp`	0.606	0.551
AC: `syn`	0.748	0.728
AC: `hyp1`	0.546	0.387
AC: `syn`, RC: `ant`	0.778	0.767
AC: `syn`, RC: `antexp`	0.736	0.708
AC: `syn+hyp1`, RC: `ant`	**0.791**	**0.770**
AC: `syn+hyp1`, RC: `antexp`	0.751	0.710
Mean inter-annotator agreement	0.779	0.864

Table 2: **Task 1.** Results on two word similarity benchmarks (Spearman's ρ). Best-scoring baseline models from the literature are reported. The dashed line separates purely distributional models from the ones leveraging external lexical knowledge.

MODEL	GRE: F_1
Constraints Lookup (ANT)	0.62
SGNS-GN (Mikolov et al., 2013)	0.48
Polarity LSA (Yih et al., 2012)	0.81
Bayesian Tensor Factor. (Zhang et al., 2014)	0.82
Joint Specialisation Model (Ono et al., 2015)	0.89
RC: `ant`	0.79
RC: `antexp`	0.80
AC: `syn`	0.33
AC: `hyp1`	0.44
AC: `syn`, RC: `ant`	0.90
AC: `syn`, RC: `antexp`	0.83
AC: `syn+hyp1`, RC: `ant`	**0.92**
AC: `syn+hyp1`, RC: `antexp`	0.85

Table 3: **Task 2.** Results (F_1 scores) on the full GRE multiple-choice antonymy detection dataset.

4 Results and Discussion

Task 1: Word Similarity. A summary of the results is provided in Table 2. The most striking findings are new state-of-the-art correlation scores on both benchmarks: both are obtained by combining `syn` and `hyp1` into ATTRACT constraints, and using the unexpanded list of antonyms as REPEL constraints. This suggests that: **1)** both ATTRACT and REPEL constraints are required to provide the synergistic effect during specialisation; **2)** a larger (and noisier) set of antonymy pairs is not necessarily more effective; **3)** the `hyp1` pairs are useful for modeling lexical contrast. When included as ATTRACT constraints, these pairs lead to small but consistent gains across all three tasks (see also Tables 3-4).

MODEL	A	V	N
Symmetric Patterns (Schwartz et al., 2015)	0.718	0.584	0.482
(Roth and Schulte im Walde, 2014)	0.717	0.788	0.832
AntSynNET (Nguyen et al., 2017b)	0.784	0.777	0.855
RC: `ant`	0.956	0.938	0.854
RC: `antexp`	0.899	0.915	0.809
AC: `syn`	0.876	0.845	0.773
AC: `hyp1`	0.678	0.678	0.681
AC: `syn`, RC: `ant`	0.959	0.969	0.872
AC: `syn`, RC: `antexp`	0.951	0.955	0.871
AC: `syn+hyp1`, RC: `ant`	**0.969**	**0.975**	**0.879**
AC: `syn+hyp1`, RC: `antexp`	0.953	0.947	0.872

Table 4: **Task 3.** Results (F_1) on the synonymy-vs-antonymy evaluation set (Nguyen et al., 2017b).

The reported high score on SimLex of **0.791** is the first correlation score moving beyond mean human performance on the dataset (0.779), thus questioning the further usability of the benchmark in semantic modeling evaluation. The gain on SimVerb is even more substantial: from the previous high score of 0.674 (Mrkšić et al., 2017) to **0.770**.[7] The difference is again attributed to the use of higher-quality constraints: Mrkšić et al. (2017) relied on a noisier and smaller set from BabelNet, verifying the importance of guiding specialisation by the correct choice of constraints. In short, the specialisation model simply encodes the provided external knowledge into the input vector space, and as such it is critically tied to the constraints.

Task 2: Antonymy Detection. A summary of the results is provided in Table 3. The results suggest that antonymous REPEL constraints are more beneficial for this task, which is easily explained by the nature of the task, but the synergistic effect is again observed: both types of constraints are essential to boost the scores. The best performing configuration of constraints outperforms two strong baselines (Zhang et al., 2014; Ono et al., 2015) which also rely on the same external lexical knowledge (minus `hyp1` pairs). Importantly, the results also suggest that the specialisation model indeed learns useful relationships in the specialised space beyond a simple baseline model that lookups into constraints: large gains over this baseline are reported with a variety of configurations. Distributional SGNS-GN vectors coalesce antonymy and synonymy: as a consequence, they are not a competitive baseline in any of the three evaluation tasks.

---

[7] We have also verified that the specialisation process is robust to the chosen distributional vector space. The best configuration of constraints from Table 2 with two other starting spaces, GLOVE (Pennington et al., 2014) and FASTTEXT (Bojanowski et al., 2017), yields respective correlation scores of 0.787 and 0.774 on SimLex and 0.764 and 0.744 on SimVerb.

The model which uses a large set of ANTEXP again cannot match performance of the model which relies on the original ANT. We see this as an interesting finding which suggests that the massive expansion of lexical constraints decreases the strength of originally provided word relationships, which were hand-crafted by linguistic experts.

Task 3: Synonymy vs. Antonymy. A summary of the results with strongest baselines from prior work is provided in Table 4: specialisation again outperforms the competitors.[8] The score differences between best-performing configurations are not as pronounced as in the other two tasks: we attribute this to the reduced task complexity. However, the results again indicate that: **1)** both types of constraints are important for distinguishing between the coalesced relations of synonymy and antonymy, with the synergistic effect again observed; **2)** the noisy and large ANTEXP set of antonyms falls short of the smaller, more accurate ANT set; and **3)** the same configuration as in the two other tasks (AC: SYN+HYP1, RC: ANT) again leads to peak performance.

5   Conclusion

We have demonstrated that post-processing specialisation models serve as a powerful tool for injecting lexical contrast knowledge into distributional word vector spaces. We have verified the hypothesis that a careful selection of external constraints is crucial for guiding the specialisation by improving state-of-the-art scores on three standard tasks used for evaluation of lexical contrast modeling: detecting antonyms, distinguishing antonyms from synonyms, and word similarity.

The post-processing specialisation models such as ATTRACT-REPEL fine-tune only vectors of words present in the external constraints. In the follow-up work, we have proposed a method which can propagate the useful external signal also to the full vocabulary (Vulić et al., 2018), leading to additional gains with specialised vectors in downstream language understanding applications. In future work, we will further investigate the full-vocabulary specialisation approaches.

---

[8]However, note that the specialization model cannot be directly and fairly compared to the baselines in this task, which do not use any supervision signal. The reported performance of the specialisation model can be seen as an upper bound to such distributional approaches.

Acknowledgments

This work is supported by the ERC Consolidator Grant LEXICAL (no 648909). The authors would like to thank the anonymous reviewers for their helpful suggestions.

References

Piotr Bojanowski, Edouard Grave, Armand Joulin, and Tomas Mikolov. 2017. Enriching word vectors with subword information. *Transactions of the ACL*, 5:135–146.

Elia Bruni, Nam-Khanh Tran, and Marco Baroni. 2014. Multimodal distributional semantics. *Journal of Artificial Intelligence Research*, 49:1–47.

Alan D. Cruse. 1986. *Lexical Semantics*. Cambridge University Press.

John C. Duchi, Elad Hazan, and Yoram Singer. 2011. Adaptive subgradient methods for online learning and stochastic optimization. *Journal of Machine Learning Research*, 12:2121–2159.

Manaal Faruqui, Jesse Dodge, Sujay Kumar Jauhar, Chris Dyer, Eduard Hovy, and Noah A. Smith. 2015. Retrofitting word vectors to semantic lexicons. In *Proceedings of NAACL-HLT*, pages 1606–1615.

Manaal Faruqui and Chris Dyer. 2015. Non-distributional word vector representations. In *Proceedings of ACL*, pages 464–469.

Christiane Fellbaum. 1998. *WordNet*.

Lev Finkelstein, Evgeniy Gabrilovich, Yossi Matias, Ehud Rivlin, Zach Solan, Gadi Wolfman, and Eytan Ruppin. 2002. Placing search in context: The concept revisited. *ACM Transactions on Information Systems*, 20(1):116–131.

Daniela Gerz, Ivan Vulić, Felix Hill, Roi Reichart, and Anna Korhonen. 2016. SimVerb-3500: A large-scale evaluation set of verb similarity. In *Proceedings of EMNLP*, pages 2173–2182.

Zellig S. Harris. 1954. Distributional structure. *Word*, 10(23):146–162.

Felix Hill, Roi Reichart, and Anna Korhonen. 2015. SimLex-999: Evaluating semantic models with (genuine) similarity estimation. *Computational Linguistics*, 41(4):665–695.

Sujay Kumar Jauhar, Chris Dyer, and Eduard Hovy. 2015. Ontologically grounded multi-sense representation learning for semantic vector space models. In *Proceedings of NAACL-HLT*, pages 683–693.

Douwe Kiela, Felix Hill, and Stephen Clark. 2015. Specializing word embeddings for similarity or relatedness. In *Proceedings of EMNLP*, pages 2044–2048.

Joo-Kyung Kim, Gokhan Tur, Asli Celikyilmaz, Bin Cao, and Ye-Yi Wang. 2016. Intent detection using semantically enriched word embeddings. In *Proceedings of SLT*.

Barbara Ann Kipfer. 2009. *Roget's 21st Century Thesaurus (3rd Edition)*. Philip Lief Group.

Karin Kipper. 2005. *VerbNet: A broad-coverage, comprehensive verb lexicon*. Ph.D. thesis.

Tomas Mikolov, Ilya Sutskever, Kai Chen, Gregory S. Corrado, and Jeffrey Dean. 2013. Distributed representations of words and phrases and their compositionality. In *Proceedings of NIPS*, pages 3111–3119.

George A. Miller and Christiane Fellbaum. 1991. Semantic networks of English. *Cognition*, 41(1):197 – 229.

Saif Mohammad, Bonnie J. Dorr, and Graeme Hirst. 2008. Computing word-pair antonymy. In *Proceedings of EMNLP*, pages 982–991.

Saif Mohammad, Bonnie J. Dorr, Graeme Hirst, and Peter D. Turney. 2013. Computing lexical contrast. *Computational Linguistics*, 39(3):555–590.

Nikola Mrkšić, Diarmuid Ó Séaghdha, Blaise Thomson, Milica Gašić, Lina Maria Rojas-Barahona, Pei-Hao Su, David Vandyke, Tsung-Hsien Wen, and Steve Young. 2016. Counter-fitting word vectors to linguistic constraints. In *Proceedings of NAACL-HLT*, pages 142–148.

Nikola Mrkšić, Ivan Vulić, Diarmuid Ó Séaghdha, Ira Leviant, Roi Reichart, Milica Gašić, Anna Korhonen, and Steve Young. 2017. Semantic specialization of distributional word vector spaces using monolingual and cross-lingual constraints. *Transactions of the ACL*, 5:309–324.

M. Lynne Murphy. 2010. *Lexical Meaning*. Cambridge University Press.

Kim Anh Nguyen, Maximilian Köper, Sabine Schulte im Walde, and Ngoc Thang Vu. 2017a. Hierarchical embeddings for hypernymy detection and directionality. In *Proceedings of EMNLP*, pages 233–243.

Kim Anh Nguyen, Sabine Schulte im Walde, and Ngoc Thang Vu. 2016. Integrating distributional lexical contrast into word embeddings for antonym-synonym distinction. In *Proceedings of ACL*, pages 454–459.

Kim Anh Nguyen, Sabine Schulte im Walde, and Ngoc Thang Vu. 2017b. Distinguishing antonyms and synonyms in a pattern-based neural network. In *Proceedings of EACL*, pages 76–85.

Masataka Ono, Makoto Miwa, and Yutaka Sasaki. 2015. Word embedding-based antonym detection using thesauri and distributional information. In *Proceedings of NAACL-HLT*, pages 984–989.

Jeffrey Pennington, Richard Socher, and Christopher Manning. 2014. Glove: Global vectors for word representation. In *Proceedings of EMNLP*, pages 1532–1543.

Nghia The Pham, Angeliki Lazaridou, and Marco Baroni. 2015. A multitask objective to inject lexical contrast into distributional semantics. In *Proceedings of ACL*, pages 21–26.

Michael Roth and Sabine Schulte im Walde. 2014. Combining word patterns and discourse markers for paradigmatic relation classification. In *Proceedings of ACL*, pages 524–530.

Sascha Rothe and Hinrich Schütze. 2015. AutoExtend: Extending word embeddings to embeddings for synsets and lexemes. In *Proceedings of ACL*, pages 1793–1803.

Enrico Santus, Alessandro Lenci, Qin Lu, and Sabine Schulte im Walde. 2014. Chasing hypernyms in vector spaces with entropy. In *Proceedings of EACL*, pages 38–42.

Roy Schwartz, Roi Reichart, and Ari Rappoport. 2015. Symmetric pattern based word embeddings for improved word similarity prediction. In *Proceedings of CoNLL*, pages 258–267.

Peter D. Turney and Patrick Pantel. 2010. From frequency to meaning: vector space models of semantics. *Journal of Artifical Intelligence Research*, 37(1):141–188.

Ivan Vulić, Goran Glavaš, Nikola Mrkšić, and Anna Korhonen. 2018. Post-specialisation: Retrofitting vectors of words unseen in lexical resources. In *Proceedings of NAACL-HLT*.

Ivan Vulić and Nikola Mrkšić. 2018. Specialising word vectors for lexical entailment. In *Proceedings of NAACL-HLT*.

Ivan Vulić, Nikola Mrkšić, and Anna Korhonen. 2017a. Cross-lingual induction and transfer of verb classes based on word vector space specialisation. In *Proceedings of EMNLP*, pages 2546–2558.

Ivan Vulić, Nikola Mrkšić, Roi Reichart, Diarmuid Ó Séaghdha, Steve Young, and Anna Korhonen. 2017b. Morph-fitting: Fine-tuning word vector spaces with simple language-specific rules. In *Proceedings of ACL*, pages 56–68.

John Wieting, Mohit Bansal, Kevin Gimpel, and Karen Livescu. 2015. From paraphrase database to compositional paraphrase model and back. *Transactions of the ACL*, 3:345–358.

Wen-tau Yih, Geoffrey Zweig, and John Platt. 2012. Polarity inducing Latent Semantic Analysis. In *Proceedings of EMNLP*, pages 1212–1222.

Mo Yu and Mark Dredze. 2014. Improving lexical embeddings with semantic knowledge. In *Proceedings of ACL*, pages 545–550.

Jingwei Zhang, Jeremy Salwen, Michael Glass, and Alfio Gliozzo. 2014. Word semantic representations using bayesian probabilistic tensor factorization. In *Proceedings of EMNLP*, pages 1522–1531.

Characters or Morphemes: How to Represent Words?

Ahmet Üstün   **Murathan Kurfalı**
Cognitive Science Department
Informatics Institute
Middle East Technical University, Turkey
{ustun.ahmet,kurfali}@metu.edu.tr

Burcu Can
Department of Computer Engineering
Hacettepe University
Turkey
burcucan@cs.hacettepe.edu.tr

Abstract

In this paper, we investigate the effects of using subword information in representation learning. We argue that using syntactic subword units effects the quality of the word representations positively. We introduce a morpheme-based model and compare it against to word-based, character-based, and character n-gram level models. Our model takes a list of candidate segmentations of a word and learns the representation of the word based on different segmentations that are weighted by an attention mechanism. We performed experiments on Turkish as a morphologically rich language and English with a comparably poorer morphology. The results show that morpheme-based models are better at learning word representations of morphologically complex languages compared to character-based and character n-gram level models since the morphemes help to incorporate more syntactic knowledge in learning, that makes morpheme-based models better at syntactic tasks.

1   Introduction

The distributional hypothesis of Harris (1954) has been used to motivate work on vector space models to learn word representations. Deep learning models learn another kind of vector space model for building word representations, which shows superior performance in representing words.

Although deep neural networks have been very successful in representing words via such vectors, those models have not been very successful at estimating the representations of rare words since they do not appear often enough to allow us to collect reliable statistics about their context. Morpholog-

ically complex words are also rare by definition. Cao and Rei (2016) state that a word like *unbelievableness* does not exist in the first 17 million words of Wikipedia. Some methods have been proposed to deal with the sparsity issue in learning word representations. One approach is to utilize the subword information such as characters, character n-grams, or morphemes rather than learning distinct word representations without considering the inner structure of words.

Character-based models usually learn better word representations compared to word-based models since they capture the regularities inside the words so that it mitigates the sparsity in representation learning. However, those models learn the representations through the characters that do not correspond to a syntactic or semantic unit. In Turkish, two words can have similar word representations under a character-based model just because of their common suffixes. For example, character-based models such as (Bojanowski et al., 2017) generate similar word representations for words that have common character n-grams such as *kitaplardan* (from the books) and *kasaplardan* (from the butchers) (where *lar* and *dan* are suffixes, *kitap* and *kasap* are the roots) although the two words are semantically not related at all.

Another problem we observed for the character-based models is that such models estimate distant representations for words that are semantically related but involve different forms of the same morpheme so called allomorphs. This is one of the consequences of vowel harmony in some languages like Turkish. We observed this through several semantic similarity tasks performed on semantically similar but orthographically different words by using the word representations obtained from character n-gram level models such as fasttext (Bojanowski et al., 2017). For example, Turkish words such as *mavililerinki* (of the ones with

Proceedings of the 3rd Workshop on Representation Learning for NLP, pages 144–153
Melbourne, Australia, July 20, 2018. ©2018 Association for Computational Linguistics

the blue color) and *sarılılarınki* (of the ones with the yellow color) with allomorphs *li* and *lı*; *ler* and *lar*; *in* and *ın* are asserted to be distant from each other in regard to their word representations under a character n-gram level model such as fast-text (Bojanowski et al., 2017), although the two words are semantically similar and both referring to colors.

In this paper, we argue that learning word representations through morphemes rather than characters lead to more accurate word vectors especially in morphologically complex languages. Such character-based models are strongly affected by the orthographic commonness of words, that governs orthographically similar words to have similar word representations.

We introduce a model to learn morpheme and word representations especially for morphologically very complex words without using an external supervised morphological segmentation system. Instead, we use an unsupervised segmentation model to initialize our model with a list of candidate morphological segmentations of each word in the training data. We do not provide a single segmentation per word like others (Botha and Blunsom, 2014; Qiu et al., 2014), but instead we provide a list of potential segmentations of each word. Therefore, our model relaxes the requirement of an external segmentation system in morpheme-based representation learning. To our knowledge, this will be the first attempt in co-learning of morpheme representations and word representations in an unsupervised framework without assuming a single morphological segmentation per word.

Our model is mostly similar to that of Lazaridou et al. (2013) and Botha and Blunsom (2014) since we also aim to learn morpheme and word representations. Our model is akin to that of Pinter et al. (2017) from the training perspective since they infer the out-of-vocabulary word embeddings from pre-trained word embeddings. Here, we also try to mimic the word2vec (Mikolov et al., 2013) embeddings (i.e. that are the expected outputs of the model) to learn the rare word representations with a complex morphology.

Our model shows some architectural similarities to that of Cao and Rei (2016). Both models use the attention mechanism to up-weight the correct morphological segmentation of a word. However, their model is character-based and our model

is morpheme-based where different segmentations of each word contribute to the resulting vector. It should be noted that our main concern is to investigate what character-based models cannot learn that the morpheme-based models learn. As for the experimental setting, we have chosen Turkish language that has a complex morphology and severe allomorphy.

The results show that a morpheme-based model is better at estimating word representations of morphologically complex words (with at least 2-3 suffixes) compared to other word-based and character-based models. We present experimental results on Turkish as an agglutinative language and English as a morphologically poor language.

2 Related Work

Classical word representation models such as word2vec (Mikolov et al., 2013) have been successful in learning word representations for frequent words. Since these classical models are based on collecting contextual information in a very large corpus, they estimate deficient word representations for rare words due to insufficient contextual information. This has a negative consequence in some natural language processing tasks that make use of the word representations.

One approach to overcome this deficiency in estimating rare word representations is to apply compositional methods. Each word comprises of different subword units, such as characters, character n-grams, or morphemes. Lazaridou et al. (2013) apply compositional methods by having the stem and affix representations in order to estimate the distributional representation of morphologically complex words. Bojanowski et al. (2017) introduce an extension to word2vec (Mikolov et al., 2013) by representing each word in terms of the vector representations of its n-grams, which was earlier applied by Schütze (1993) that learns the representations of fourgrams by applying singular value decomposition (SVD). Analogously, Alexandrescu and Kirchhoff (2006) represent each character n-gram with a vector representation and words are estimated by the summation of the subword representations. Their results show that compositional methods that are originally proposed for estimating the meaning of phrases can also be used for estimating the meaning of a word by combining the information coming from different subword units. Botha and Blunsom (2014) introduce

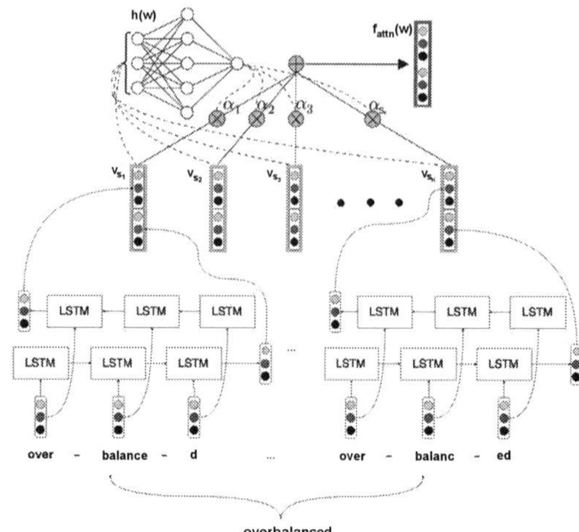

Figure 1: The neural network architecture of the morph2vec model.

a log-bilinear language model that integrates morphology with compositional methods, that is applied to translation task for morphologically rich languages.

Compositional models that use character-level features show that the representations of rare words can be estimated more accurately (in both semantic and syntactic tasks) than the word-based models since the character-level models share more features across different words that helps to mitigate sparsity. Cotterell and Schütze (2015) encode morphological tags within word embeddings by using a log-bilinear model, thereby leading morphologically similar words to have closer word representations in the embedding space. Luong et al. (2013) learn word representations based on morphemes that are obtained from an external morphological segmentation system. Collobert et al. (2011) enhance word vectors with some character-level features such as capitalization. Bhatia et al. (2016) incorporate morphological information as a prior distribution to improve word embeddings. They use Morfessor (Creutz and Lagus, 2002) as an external morphological segmentation system to extract the inner structure of words.

3 The morph2vec Model

In our morpheme-based model, a word is encoded by a sequence of morphemes. Each word w_{s_i} with a particular morphological segmentation s_i is represented by a list of morphemes $\mathbf{m} =$ $\{m_0, m_1, \ldots, m_n\}$ as follows:

$$w_{s_i} = m_0 m_1 \ldots m_n$$

We assume that the correct morphological segmentation of a word is not known a priori by assuming a completely unsupervised learning model. We use an unsupervised neural segmentation algorithm (Üstün and Can, 2016) that generates a list of candidate segmentations for a given word (see Section 4 for the details).

Each distinct morpheme is defined by a column vector in a morpheme embedding matrix $W_m \in \mathbb{R}^{d_{morph} \times |M|}$ where d_{morph} is the vector dimension for the morphemes and M is the set of all pseudo morphemes.

Word representations are coupled with a particular morphological segmentation of each word. In other words, each segmentation of a single word has its own representation. Word representation for each particular segmentation is learned by a sequential function f that takes a sequence of morphemes and generates the word representation with a dimension of d_{word}. The word embedding that is to be estimated compositionally via its morphemes that belong to segmentation s_i is denoted by v_{s_i} and estimated by a function f as follows:

$$v_{s_i} = f(w_{s_i}) = f(v_{m_0}, v_{m_1}, \ldots, v_{m_n}) \quad (1)$$

where v_{m_0} denotes the vector of m_0.

We use bidirectional LSTMs (Bi-LSTM) (Hochreiter and Schmidhuber, 1997) to estimate a trainable function f in our neural network architecture that is illustrated in Figure 1. In the forward LSTMs, morphemes from the beginning till the end of the word are given sequentially, whereas in the backward LSTMs, morphemes from the end till the beginning of the word are given in the reverse order. Each output of Bi-LSTM which is the concatenation of the outputs of the forward and backward LSTMs represents a particular segmentation of a given word.

Therefore, we train the model with a list of potential segmentations of each word in training data. Since a word is represented by different morpheme sequences that refer to different segmentations of the same word, we use an attention model over these sequences that are learned by the Bi-LSTMs. Attention model learns a weight α_i for each segmentation, such that $\sum_i^{S_w} \alpha_i = 1$ where S_w denotes all potential morphological segmentations of w. The final word representation is the

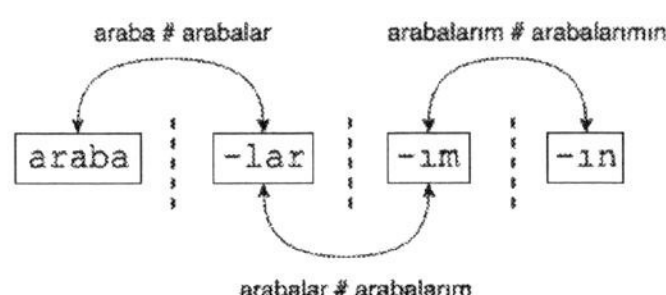

Figure 2: An illustration of generating potential segmentations for words in the training set.

weighted sum of the embeddings of all candidate segmentations:

$$f_{attn}(w) = \sum_i \alpha_i v_{s_i} \qquad (2)$$

where v_{s_i} is the vector for segmentation s_i that is the output of a Bi-LSTM. The weight α_i is estimated as follows (Bahdanau et al., 2014):

$$\alpha_i = \frac{\exp(v^T \tanh(W \cdot v_{s_i}))}{\sum_j \exp(v^T \tanh(W \cdot v_{s_j}))} \qquad (3)$$

Here, a feed-forward layer is used with a softmax function that is applied over the outputs of Bi-LSTMs. $W \cdot v_{s_i}$ denotes the corresponding column in the weight matrix of the feed-forward layer in the attention.

For training, we use the pre-trained word2vec (Mikolov et al., 2013) vectors in order to minimize the cost between the learned and pre-trained vectors with the following objective function:

$$J(\Theta) = \sum_{i=k}^{N} h(w_k) + \frac{\lambda}{2} \|\Theta\|_2^2 \qquad (4)$$

where $h(w_k)$ is the cost for the kth word w_k in a training set of size N with a L2 regularization term on the model parameters θ. We use the cosine proximity loss between the learned and the pre-trained vector.

4 Neural Morphological Segmentation

Although it is possible to train the model by providing all the potential segmentations of each word, we utilize an unsupervised segmentation algorithm to make the model computationally more efficient by reducing the search space. The segmentation algorithm is based on the neural model by Üstün and Can (2016) that uses the semantic similarity between substrings of a word to detect the potential morpheme boundaries. This algorithm is based on the idea that the meaning of a word is preserved especially through inflection

s_0	araba - larım - ın
s_1	arabalar - ı - mın
s_2	arabalar - ım - ın
s_3	araba - lar - ı - mın
s_4	**araba - lar - ım - ın**

Table 1: Some candidate segmentations of the Turkish word *arabalarımın*. The bold one is the correct segmentation for this word.

Parent	Child	Sim.
araba	araba-**lar**	0.65
arabalar	araba-**lar-ım**	0.41
arabalarım	araba-**lar-ım-ın**	0.26

Table 2: The cosine similarities between the substrings (parent-child) of the Turkish word *arabalarımın* (of my cars). 0.25 is assigned for the cosine similarity threshold and only the splits above the threshold are listed.

and it benefits from the word representations to utilize this preservation. The parent-child relations such as (respect,respectful) are defined similar to that of Narasimhan et al. (2015).

The algorithm begins by generating all possible segmentations where there are at most K segments[1] (see Table 1). Then, the algorithm checks the semantic similarity at each split point (between the parent and its child) whether it is greater than a threshold[2]. If the condition is satisfied for all split points in a segmentation, the segmentation is added to the segmentations list that will be passed to a Bi-LSTM. Figure 2 illustrates an example for the segmentation algorithm on the Turkish word *arabalarımın (of my cars)*. # denotes a function that takes two words and returns true if the cosine similarity between two substrings is above the threshold value. The cosine similarities between the substrings of the word *arabalarımın* are given in Table 2.

Here we use the segmentation algorithm for mainly training purposes because the accuracy of the algorithm has a strong impact on generating word representations. Since all possible morphemes are not generated in training, if the segmentation algorithm generates an unknown morpheme in testing, the representation for that word involving the unknown suffix cannot be generated. In order to ensure that all morphemes have a rep-

---

[1] K is defined as 4 in all experiments.
[2] The threshold is assigned 0.25 in all experiments.

resentation, we use an external supervised segmentation system for only testing purposes. Another reason is that due to incorrect segmentations suggested by the unsupervised segmentation algorithm, two words (semantically related) involving the same set of suffixes cannot benefit from the syntactic similarity and therefore the representations of those words might diverge in testing.

5 Experiments

We performed several experiments to assess the quality of our morpheme and word embeddings. We did experiments on Turkish as a highly agglutinative language with a very complex morphology and English with a comparably poor morphology.

5.1 Experimental Setting

In all experiments, morpheme vectors have a dimension of $d_{morph} = 75$, while the forward and backward LSTMs have a dimension of $d_{LSTM} = 300$. Since the output of the Bi-LSTMs is the concatenation of the forward and backward LSTMs, the Bi-LSTM output has a dimensionality of $d_{biLSTM} = 600$. The output of the Bi-LSTMs is reduced to half after feeding the output through a feed-forward layer that results with a word vector dimension of $d_{word} = 300$. Our model is implemented in Keras, and publicly available[3].

For the pre-trained word vectors, we used the word vectors of dimension 300 that were obtained by training word2vec (Mikolov et al., 2013). For Turkish, we trained word2vec on Boun corpus (Sak et al., 2008) that contains 361 million word tokens. For English, we used the Google's pre-trained word2vec model[4] that was trained on 100 billion words with a vocabulary size of 3M. For training of our model, we used the most frequent 200K words from the pre-trained vocabularies to filter out the noise for both languages.

In order to compare the quality of our embeddings against the embeddings obtained from character n-gram level model fasttext (Bojanowski et al., 2017), we used the pre-trained word vectors trained on Wikipedia (Bojanowski et al., 2017) and we used the Google's pre-trained word vectors[5]. In order to compare our model with the character-based model by Cao and Rei (2016), we used Text8 corpus[6].

Model	en	tr
word2vec (Mikolov et al., 2013)	0.69	0.483
fasttext (Bojanowski et al., 2017)	**0.71**	0.208
morph2vec	0.38	**0.529**

Table 3: The comparison of the Spearman correlation between the human judgments and the word similarities obtained by computing the cosine similarity between the learned word embeddings for English and Turkish.

Only for testing reasons, we used PC-KIMMO (Koskenniemi, 1984) for English and the two-level Turkish morphology (Akın and Akın, 2007) for Turkish in order to segment test sets to obtain the actual morphemes for generating word representations from the morpheme vectors that are learned in a fully unsupervised setting. Unsupervised segmentation system also could be used for the evaluation step, but we wanted to minimize the effect of incorrect segmentations to be able to evaluate the embeddings properly. Yet, we discuss the effect of the supervised vs unsupervised segmentations in Section 5.5.

We did only intrinsic evaluation with a set of experiments that assess the quality of the word and morpheme representations.

5.2 Evaluation of Word Representations: Word Similarity Results

In order to evaluate the quality of the word vectors, we did experiments on a list of word pairs. We computed the cosine similarity between the learned vectors of each word pair and compared the similarity scores against to human judgments.

We used the Set 2 in WordSim353 dataset (Finkelstein et al., 2001) for the semantic similarity experiments that already involves the human judgment scores from 1 to 10 for 200 English word pairs. Since there is no available word-pair list for Turkish, we prepared *WordSimTr*[7] that involves 138 word pairs and asked 15 human annotators to judge how similar two words are on a fixed scale from 1 to 10 where 1 shows a poor semantic similarity between the two words. Our Turkish word pair list involves two groups of words. The first group involves 81 semantically similar words that have at least two suffixes (possibly allomorphs). An example pair is *televizyonlarda* (on the televi-

---

[3]http://nlp.cs.hacettepe.edu.tr/projects/morph2vec/
[4]https://code.google.com/archive/p/word2vec/
[5]https://code.google.com/archive/p/word2vec/
[6]Available at mattmahoney.net/dc/text8
[7]http://nlp.cs.hacettepe.edu.tr/projects/morph2vec/

Model	WordSim353	RW
char2vec		
(Cao and Rei, 2016)	0.345	0.284
morph2vec	**0.386**	**0.297**

Table 4: The comparison of the Spearman correlation between the human judgments and the word similarities obtained by computing the cosine similarity between the learned word embeddings for English on Text8 corpus.

sions) and *radyolarda* (on the radios) that have *lar* (for the plural) and *da* (for the locative case) with a semantically similar stem pair. The second group involves 57 semantically unrelated word pairs that are orthographically similar through their suffixes. An example word pair in this group is *kitaplardan* (from the books) and *kasaplardan* (from the butchers) with two suffixes *lar* (for the plural) and *dan* (for the ablative case) with semantically unrelated two stems *kitap* (the book) and *kasap* (the butcher). Some other example word pairs in the Turkish word pair list is given in Table 5. As seen on the table, our morpheme-based model is better at learning word representations with multiple suffixes.

The results are given in Table 3. English words mostly do not involve any suffixes, which hinders our model's performance. However, our model performs better than both fasttext (Bojanowski et al., 2017) and word2vec (Mikolov et al., 2013) on Turkish despite the highly agglutinative morphological structure of the language. It shows that our model learns better word representations for morphologically complex words, whereas words with no suffixes are not estimated as good as the complex ones.

We also compared our model against the character-based model char2vec (Cao and Rei, 2016). For this purpose, we trained our model on the same dataset and parameters as char2vec to be able to compare with their reported results. The dataset is called Text8 corpus and consists of the first 100mb of a cleaned-up dumb of Wikipedia in 2006. For the evaluation, we tested our word embeddings on Rare Words (RW) (Luong et al., 2013) and Wordsim353 (Finkelstein et al., 2001) datasets. The results are given in Table 4. Our results outperform char2vec (Cao and Rei, 2016) on both word similarity test sets. This shows that our model learns better word embeddings for

both in-vocabulary and rare words compared to char2vec (Cao and Rei, 2016).

5.3 Evaluation of Word Representations: Analogy Results

We performed experiments for the analogy task in order to test whether the suffixes make a linear numerical change on the word vectors in the embedding space. The analogy experiments are usually performed for a triple of words such that A is to B so C is to ?, where A-B+C is expected to be equal to the questioned word. The analogy can be semantical such as *cat* is to *meow*, so *dog* is to *bark*, or syntactic such as *go* is to *gone*, so *have* is to *had*.

Here, we tested only the syntactic analogy on a list of word tuples since our focus is especially morphologically complex languages. For English, we used the syntactic relations section provided in the Google analogy dataset (Mikolov et al., 2013) that involves 10675 questions. Since there is no analogy dataset for Turkish, we prepared a Turkish analogy set *SynAnalogyTr*[8] with 206 syntactic questions that involves inflected word forms. The syntactic word tuples are judged by 40 human annotators in a scale from 1 to 10, where 1 shows a weak word analogy. Most words involve more than one suffix to test the morphological regularity in the analogy task.

The results are given in Table 6 and Table 7 for English and Turkish. The results show that our model outperforms both word2vec (Mikolov et al., 2013) and fasttext (Bojanowski et al., 2017) on both Turkish and English languages. Additionally, some examples to analogy results are given in Table 9 and the nearest neighbors of the Turkish word *kitap-lar-dan-mış* (it was from the books) are given in Table 8.

5.4 Evaluation of Morpheme Representations: Allomorph Results

In addition to the evaluation of the word vectors, we also evaluated the morpheme vectors that are the input embeddings to the neural network to be estimated during training. In order to evaluate how well our morpheme vectors represent the morphemes, we used the allomorphs. Allomorphs can be considered as *true synonyms* as they convey the same meaning with each other but with a different orthography.

---

[8]http://nlp.cs.hacettepe.edu.tr/projects/morph2vec/

Word Pair	Human Score	morph2vec	word2vec	fasttext
kitap-lar-dan / kasap-lar-dan (from the books) / (from the butchers)	0.12	0.07	0.19	0.55
kağıt-ta-ki-ler / bardak-ta-ki-ler (the ones on the paper) / (the ones in the glass)	0.22	0.12	OOW	0.64
şirket-ler-de / firma-lar-da (in the companies) / (in the firms)	0.87	0.82	0.46	0.76
kazanan-lar-dı / yenilen-ler-di (they were the winners) / (they were the defeated ones)	0.64	0.60	OOW	0.43

Table 5: Example Turkish word pairs and their similarities based on human judgements, morph2vec, word2vec (Mikolov et al., 2013), and fasttext (Bojanowski et al., 2017). - denotes the morpheme boundaries.

Model	Accuracy (%)
word2vec (Mikolov et al., 2013)	74.0
fasttext (Bojanowski et al., 2017)	74.9
morph2vec	**80.5**

Table 6: Analogy results on English Google syntactic analogy dataset.

Model	Accuracy (%)
word2vec (Mikolov et al., 2013)	16.0
fasttext (Bojanowski et al., 2017)	65.5
morph2vec	**71.3**

Table 7: Analogy results on Turkish syntactic analogy dataset *SynAnalogyTr*.

kitap-lar-dan-mış (it was from the books)	Cosine sim.
yazılmış (it was written)	0.669
hikaye-ler-den (from the stories)	0.667
kitap-lar (the books)	0.661
kitap-lar-dan (from the books)	0.639
kitap-lar-da (in the books)	0.635
roman-lar-dan (from the novels)	0.625

Table 8: Nearest neighbors of the word *kitap-lar-dan-mış* and the cosine similarity between the word and the neighbor that are obtained from morph2vec word vectors.

In Turkish, there is a common use of allomorphs due to the vowel and consonant harmony in the language. For example, the morpheme *dı* has got 8 allomorphs one of which is chosen depending on the last vowel and the consonant in the word, that are *di, du, dü, ti, tu, tü,* and *tı*. For example, *-ti* (the past tense of the third person singular) is chosen, for the verb *git-(mek)* (to go), whereas *du* is chosen for the verb *solu-(mak)* (to breathe).

We prepared a Turkish dataset that involves 108 morphemes[9] that are allomorphs of 33 unique morpheme types including tense and case markers as well as derivations. For the evaluation of allomorphs, we used the MAP metric that is often used in information retrieval tasks. For each allomorph set in the data, we calculated the MAP@k where k is the number of allomorphs for the given morpheme. If the allomorph of a morpheme exists in the k nearest neighbours, then it is regarded as correct, otherwise it is incorrect. We averaged the MAP@k scores for all allomorph sets. The results are given in Table 10. Our model can learn the morpheme representations better than fasttext (Bojanowski et al., 2017) since allomorphs in our model are closer to each other in the embedding space compared to fasttext. Some of the allomorphs obtained from our model and fasttext (Bojanowski et al., 2017) are given in Table 11. As seen on the table, our model can capture the allomorphs better than fasttext (Bojanowski et al., 2017). Additionally, all Turkish allomorphs learned by our model are given in Figure 3. As can be seen from the figure, the allomorphs fall into similar regions in the vector space. Apart from some infrequent morphemes, the rest has similar representations.

5.5 The Effect of Supervision

In our experiments, the model training is performed in a fully unsupervised setting in terms of

[9]http://nlp.cs.hacettepe.edu.tr/projects/morph2vec/

Word 1	Word 2	Word 3	Expected	morph2vec	word2vec	fasttext
gel-dim (I came)	gel-me-dim (I did not come)	duy-dum (I heard)	duy-ma-dım (I did not hear)	**0.80**	0.43	0.63
çöz-müş (she solved)	çöz-müş-tü (she had solved)	bul-muş (she found)	bul-muş-tu (she had found)	**0.73**	0.18	0.66
aç-mak (to open)	aç-ıl-mak (to be opened)	ört-mek (to cover)	ört-ün-mek (to cover himself)	**0.89**	0.36	0.52

Table 9: Example Turkish analogy questions and the cosine similarities between the expected words and the learned word representations obtained from morph2vec, word2vec and fasttext.

Model	MAP
fasttext (Bojanowski et al., 2017)	0.504
morph2vec	**0.618**

Table 10: MAP scores for the allomorph coverage in fasttext (Bojanowski et al., 2017) and the morph2vec.

morph	morph2vec	fasttext
iyor	ıyor yor uyor üyor	ıyor yor uyor üyor
mı	mu mi mü	mi mu **ıyor**
dı	tı di du tu dü ti **duk**	**dır** tı dü di **ın tır ı**
mış	müş muş	müş **yor dık**

Table 11: Some allomorphs of the given morpheme on the left that are found by our model and fasttext (Bojanowski et al., 2017). The bold font indicates the non-allomorphs for the given morpheme type.

Model	Spearman
Unsupervised (Üstün and Can, 2016)	0.517
Supervised (Akın and Akın, 2007)	**0.529**

Table 12: Word similarity Spearman correlation scores obtained when a supervised and unsupervised segmentation algorithm is used for the test sets.

the segmentation algorithm. However, we used supervised methods for segmenting test sets in evaluation to generate word representations from the actual morphemes that are learned in the training. We conducted another set of experiments with both supervised and unsupervised segmentation algorithms to show the effect of the segmentation algorithm used to generate the word embeddings in the word similarity test sets. Table 12 demonstrates the effect of the segmentation algorithm. Here, we employed the neural unsupervised model by Üstün and Can (2016) and the supervised segmentation system *Zemberek* (Akın and Akın, 2007).

The results show that we can generate better word embeddings when the morphemes are extracted by a supervised segmentation algorithm beforehand although the difference is not significant. Therefore the supervised segmentation algorithm used in testing can be replaced with an unsupervised segmentation algorithm.

However, it should be noted that when an unsupervised algorithm used, the possibility to come across with a segment that is not present in our model increases, hence we cannot generate the word embeddings for such words. Therefore, the results for the unsupervised setting is limited to only in-vocabulary words (i.e the words for which we can create a word embedding).

6 Conclusion and Future Work

Recent work shows that character level models learn more representative word embeddings for rare words (including morphologically complex words) compared to word level models, which is a sign that incorporating subword information improves the word representations. However, in this paper, we argued that morpheme-based representation models can learn better word embeddings (especially for the syntactic tasks) since they incorporate the syntactic and semantic information through the morphemes better compared to character level models. We pointed to the poor representation of allomorphs in complex words where the character-level models estimate a low word similarity between semantically similar words with different forms of the same morpheme, i.e. allomorphs. Moreover, we pointed to the character level models that assign a high word similar-

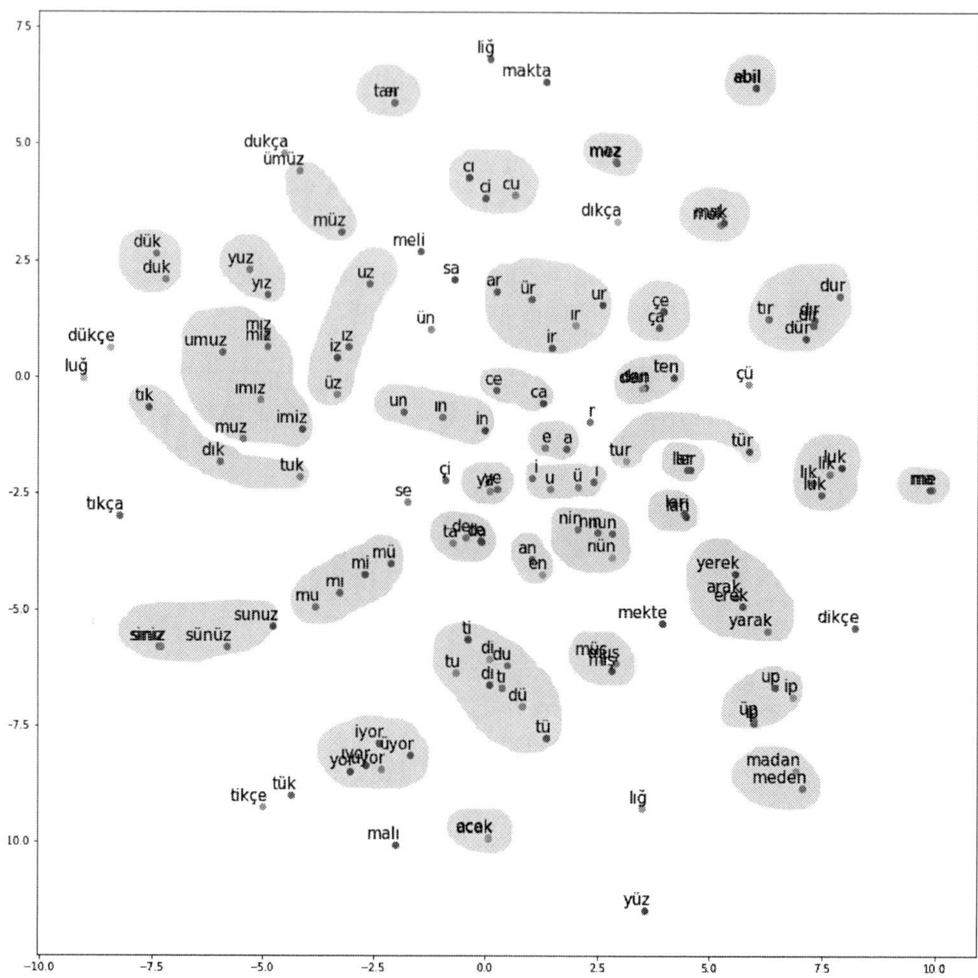

Figure 3: Turkish allomorph vectors learned by morph2vec. Some morphemes are blurry because of the overlapping of a few allomorphs.

ity to the words that are orthographically similar but semantically unrelated.

We introduce a morpheme-based representation model that learns word embeddings through the morphemes that are obtained from a list of morphological segmentations for each word. Therefore, our work introduces the idea of releasing the need for using an external morphological segmentation system in such representation learning models that are based on subword information. Our morpheme-based model *morph2vec* learns better word representations for morphologically complex words compared to the word-based model word2vec (Mikolov et al., 2013), character-based model char2vec (Cao and Rei, 2016), and the character n-gram level model fasttext (Bojanowski

et al., 2017). Our results are also competitive for the English language.

We leave other languages and experiments such as morphological segmentation task for the future work. Another goal is to perform extrinsic evaluation on a different task such as part-of-speech tagging using the learned word embeddings.

Acknowledgments

This research was supported by TUBITAK (The Scientific and Technological Research Council of Turkey) grant number 115E464. We thank all the anonymous people for helping us to collect the human judgment scores for our word similarity and syntactic analogy datasets. We thank Suresh Manandhar for his valuable feedback.

References

Ahmet Afsin Akın and Mehmet Dündar Akın. 2007. Zemberek, an open source NLP framework for Turkic languages. *Structure* 10:1–5.

Andrei Alexandrescu and Katrin Kirchhoff. 2006. Factored neural language models. In *Proceedings of the Human Language Technology Conference of the NAACL, Companion Volume: Short Papers*. Association for Computational Linguistics, Stroudsburg, PA, USA, NAACL-Short '06, pages 1–4.

Dzmitry Bahdanau, Kyunghyun Cho, and Yoshua Bengio. 2014. Neural machine translation by jointly learning to align and translate. *CoRR* abs/1409.0473.

Parminder Bhatia, Robert Guthrie, and Jacob Eisenstein. 2016. Morphological priors for probabilistic neural word embeddings. In *Proceedings of the 2016 Conference on Empirical Methods in Natural Language Processing*. Association for Computational Linguistics, pages 490–500.

Piotr Bojanowski, Edouard Grave, Armand Joulin, and Tomas Mikolov. 2017. Enriching word vectors with subword information. In *Transactions of the Association of Computational Linguistics*. TACL, pages 135–146.

Jan A. Botha and Phil Blunsom. 2014. Compositional morphology for word representations and language modelling. In *Proceedings of the 31st International Conference on International Conference on Machine Learning - Volume 32*. JMLR.org, ICML'14, pages II–1899–II–1907.

Kris Cao and Marek Rei. 2016. A joint model for word embedding and word morphology. *CoRR* abs/1606.02601.

Ronan Collobert, Jason Weston, Léon Bottou, Michael Karlen, Koray Kavukcuoglu, and Pavel Kuksa. 2011. Natural language processing (almost) from scratch. *Journal of Machine Learning Research* 12:2493–2537.

Ryan Cotterell and Hinrich Schütze. 2015. Morphological word embeddings. In *Proceedings of the Human Language Technologies: The 2015 Annual Conference of the North American Chapter of the ACL*. ACL'15, pages 1287–1292.

Mathias Creutz and Krista Lagus. 2002. Unsupervised discovery of morphemes. In *Proceedings of the ACL-02 Workshop on Morphological and Phonological Learning - Volume 6*. Association for Computational Linguistics, Stroudsburg, USA, pages 21–30.

Lev Finkelstein, Evgeniy Gabrilovich, Yossi Matias, Ehud Rivlin, Zach Solan, Gadi Wolfman, and Eytan Ruppin. 2001. Placing search in context: The concept revisited. In *Proceedings of the 10th International Conference on World Wide Web*. ACM, New York, NY, USA, WWW '01, pages 406–414.

Zellig Harris. 1954. *Distributional Structure*. Word.

Sepp Hochreiter and Jürgen Schmidhuber. 1997. Long short-term memory. *Neural computation* 9(8):1735–1780.

Kimmo Koskenniemi. 1984. A general computational model for word-form recognition and production. In *Proceedings of the 10th International Conference on Computational Linguistics and 22nd Annual Meeting on Association for Computational Linguistics*. Association for Computational Linguistics, Stroudsburg, PA, USA, ACL '84, pages 178–181.

Angeliki Lazaridou, Marco Marelli, Roberto Zamparelli, and Marco Baroni. 2013. Compositional-ly derived representations of morphologically complex words in distributional semantics. In *ACL 2013 - 51st Annual Meeting of the Association for Computational Linguistics, Proceedings of the Conference*. pages 1517–1526.

Thang Luong, Richard Socher, and Christopher Manning. 2013. Better word representations with recursive neural networks for morphology. In *Proceedings of the Seventeenth Conference on Computational Natural Language Learning*. Association for Computational Linguistics, pages 104–113.

Tomas Mikolov, Kai Chen, Greg Corrado, and Jeffrey Dean. 2013. Efficient estimation of word representations in vector space. *CoRR* abs/1301.3781.

Karthik Narasimhan, Regina Barzilay, and Tommi S. Jaakkola. 2015. An unsupervised method for uncovering morphological chains. *TACL* 3:157–167.

Yuval Pinter, Robert Guthrie, and Jacob Eisenstein. 2017. Mimicking word embeddings using subword RNNs. In *Proceedings of the Empirical Methods in Natural Language Processing*. Association for Computational Linguistics, pages 102–112.

Siyu Qiu, Qing Cui, Jiang Bian, Bin Gao, and Tie-Yan Liu. 2014. Co-learning of word representations and morpheme representations. In *Proceedings of COLING 2014, the 25th International Conference on Computational Linguistics: Technical Papers*. Dublin City University and Association for Computational Linguistics, pages 141–150.

Haşim Sak, Tunga Güngör, and Murat Saraçlar. 2008. Turkish language resources: Morphological parser, morphological disambiguator and Web corpus. In *Advances in natural language processing*, Springer, pages 417–427.

Hinrich Schütze. 1993. Word space. In *Advances in Neural Information Processing Systems 5, [NIPS Conference]*. Morgan Kaufmann Publishers Inc., San Francisco, CA, USA, pages 895–902.

Ahmet Üstün and Burcu Can. 2016. Unsupervised morphological segmentation using neural word embeddings. In *International Conference on Statistical Language and Speech Processing*. Springer, pages 43–53.

Learning Hierarchical Structures On-The-Fly with a Recurrent-Recursive Model for Sequences

Athul Paul Jacob[*][†]
MILA
University of Waterloo

Zhouhan Lin[*][†]
MILA
University of Montréal
AdeptMind Scholar

Alessandro Sordoni
Microsoft Research
Montréal, Canada

Yoshua Bengio
MILA
University of Montréal, CIFAR

Abstract

We propose a hierarchical model for sequential data that learns a tree on-the-fly, i.e. while reading the sequence. In the model, a *recurrent* network adapts its structure and reuses recurrent weights in a *recursive* manner. This creates adaptive skip-connections that ease the learning of long-term dependencies. The tree structure can either be inferred without supervision through reinforcement learning, or learned in a supervised manner. We provide preliminary experiments in a novel Math Expression Evaluation (MEE) task, which is explicitly crafted to have a hierarchical tree structure that can be used to study the effectiveness of our model. Additionally, we test our model in a well-known propositional logic and language modelling tasks. Experimental results show the potential of our approach.

1 Introduction

Many kinds of sequential data such as language or math expressions naturally come with a hierarchical structure. Sometimes the structure is hidden deep in the semantics of the sequence, like the syntax tree in natural language; Other times the structure is more explicit, as in math expressions, where the tree is determined by the parentheses.

Recurrent neural networks (RNNs) have shown tremendous success in modeling sequential data, such as natural language (Mikolov et al., 2010; Merity et al., 2017). However, RNNs process the observed data as a linear sequence of observations:

the length of the computational path between any two words is a function of their position in the observed sequence, instead of their semantic or syntactic roles, leading to the appearance of difficult-to-learn long-term dependencies and stimulating research on strategies to deal with that (Bengio et al., 1994; El Hihi and Bengio, 1996; Hochreiter and Schmidhuber, 1997). Hierarchical, tree-like structures may alleviate this problem by creating shortcuts between distant inputs and by simulating compositionality of the sequence, compressing the sequence into higher-level abstractions. Models that use tree as prior knowledge (e.g. (Socher et al., 2013; Tai et al., 2015; Bowman et al., 2016)) have shown improved performances over sequential models, validating the value of tree structure. For example, TreeLSTM (Tai et al., 2015) learns a bottom-up encoder, but requires the model to have access to the entire sentence as well as its parse tree before encoding it, which limits its application in some cases, e.g. language modeling. There has been various efforts to learn the tree structure as a supervised training target (Dyer et al., 2016; Socher et al., 2010; Zhou et al., 2017; Zhang et al., 2015), which free the model from relying on an external parser.

More recent efforts learn the best tree structure without supervision, by minimizing the log likelihood of the observed corpus, or by optimizing over a downstream task (Williams et al., 2017). These models usually take advantage of a binary tree assumption on the inferred tree, which imposes restrictions on the flexibility of inferred tree structure, for example, Gumbel TreeLSTM (Choi et al., 2017; Yogatama et al., 2016).

We propose a model that reads sequences using a hierarchical, tree-structured process (Fig. 1): it creates a tree on-the-fly, in a top-down fashion. Our model sits in between fully recursive models that have access to the whole sequence, such as

---

[*] Equal contribution (Ordering determined by coin flip). Corresponding authors: zhouhan.lin@umontreal.ca, apjacob@edu.uwaterloo.ca

[†] Work done while at Microsoft Research, Montreal.

Proceedings of the 3rd Workshop on Representation Learning for NLP, pages 154–158
Melbourne, Australia, July 20, 2018. ©2018 Association for Computational Linguistics

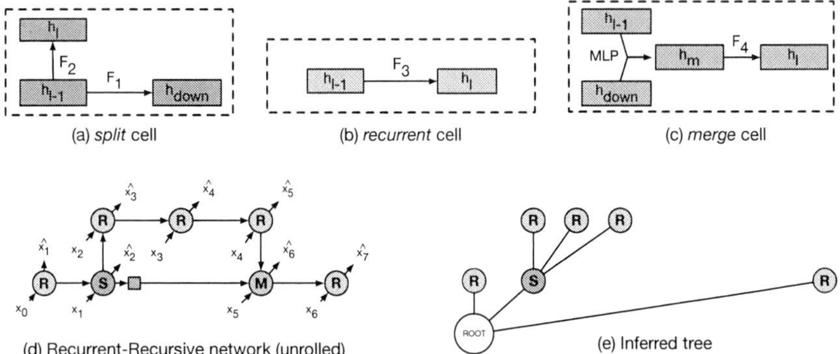

Figure 1: (a) - (c) are the 3 different cells. (d) is a sample model structure resulted from a sequence of decisions. "R", "S" and "M" stand for recurrent cell, split cell, and merge cell, respectively. Note that the "S" and "M" node can take inputs in datasets where splitting and merging signals are part of the sequence. For example, in math data the splitting signal are related to the brackets. (e) is the tree inferred from (d).

TreeLSTMs (Tai et al., 2015), and vanilla recurrent models that "flatten" input sequence, such as LSTMs (Schmidhuber, 1992). At each time-step in the sequence, the model chooses either to create a new sub-tree (split), to return and merge information into the parent node (merge), or to predict the next word in the sequence (recur). On split, a new sub-tree is created which takes control on which operation to perform. Merge operations end the current computation and return a representation of the current sub-tree to the parent node, which composes it with the previously available information on the same level. Recurrent operations use information from the siblings to perform predictions. Operations at every level in the tree use shared weights, thus sharing the recursive nature of TreeLSTMs. In contrast to TreeLSTMs however, the tree is created on-the-fly, which establishes skip-connections with previous tokens in the sequence and forms compositional representations of the past. The branching decisions can either be trained through supervised learning, by providing the true branching signals, or by policy gradients (Williams, 1992) which maximizes the log-likelihood of the observed sequence. As opposed to previous models, these three operations constantly change the structure of the model in an online manner.

Experimental evaluation aims to analyze various aspects of the model such as: how does the model generalize on sequences of different lengths than those seen during training? how hard is the tree learning problem? To answer those questions, we propose a novel multi-operation math expression evaluation (MEE) dataset, with a standard set of tasks with varying levels of difficulty, where the difficulty scales up with respect to the length of the sequence.

2 Model

Similar to a standard RNN, our model modifies a hidden state h_l for each step of the input sequence $x = \{x_1, \ldots, x_N\}$ by means of split, merge and recurrent operations. Denote the sequence of operations by $z = \{z_1, \ldots, z_L\}$, where L may be greater than the number of tokens N since only recurrent operations consume input tokens (see Fig. 1). Each operation is parametrized by a different "cell". A policy network controls which operation to perform during sequence generation.

split (S) The split cell creates a sub-tree by taking the previous state h_{l-1} as input and generating two outputs h_l and h_{down}. h_l is used for further computation, while h_{down} (the small blue rectangle in Fig. 1(d)) is pushed into a stack for future use. In our model, $h_{down} = F_1(h_{l-1}, x_t)$ and $h_l = F_2(h_{l-1}, x_t)$ where the F_1 and F_2 are LSTM units (Hochreiter and Schmidhuber, 1997), and x_t is the current input.

recurrent (R) This cell is a standard LSTM unit that takes as input the previous state h_{l-1} and the current token x_t, and outputs the hidden state h_l, which will be used to predict the next output $\hat{x}_{t+1}$. After application of this cell, the counter t is incremented and input x_t is consumed.

merge (M)   The merge cell closes a sub-tree and returns control to its parent node. It does so by merging the previous hidden state h_{l-1} with the top of the stack h_{down} into a new hidden state $h_m = MLP(h_{l-1}, h_{down})$ (Fig. 1(c)). h_m is then used as input to another LSTM unit (F_4) to yield $h_l = F_4(x_t, h_m)$, the new hidden state of the overall network. Intuitively, h_{l-1} summarizes the contents within the sub-tree. This is merged with information obtained before the model entered the sub-tree h_{down} into the new state h_l.

Policy Network   We consider the decision at each timestep $z_t \in \{S, M, R\}$ as a categorical variable sampled from a policy network p_π, conditioned on the hidden state h_t and the input embedding e_t of the current input x_t. In the supervised setting, $p_\pi(z_t|e_t, h_t)$ is trained by maximizing the likelihood of the true branching labels, while in the unsupervised setting, we resort to the REINFORCE algorithm using $-\log p(y_t|C)$ as a reward, where y_t is the task target (i.e. the next word in language modeling), and C is the representation learnt by the model up until time t.

3   Experimental Results

We conduct our experiments on a math induction task, a propositional logic inference task (Bowman et al., 2016) and language modelling. First of all, we aim to investigate whether a) our hierarchical model may help in tasks that explicitly exhibit hierarchical structure, and then b) whether the trees learned without supervision correspond to the ground-truth trees, c) how our model fare with respect to hierarchical models that have access to the whole sequence with a pre-determined tree structure and finally, d) are there any limitations for models that are not capable of learning hierarchical structures on-the-fly.

3.1   Math Induction

Our math expression evaluation dataset (MEE) consists of parenthesized mathematical expressions and their corresponding evaluations. The math expressions contain bracketing symbols ("()"), four different kinds of operations, "+-*%", where "%" is the modulo operation, and digits from 0 to 9. The "length" of an expression is the number of operations in the expression and its result is restricted to be a positive, two-digit integer (Table 1). We randomly generate expressions of different lengths and for each length the resulting

Length	Expression	Value
4	((9+(2+6))+(1*3))	20
5	(((7-2)%((3%1)+6))*9)	45
6	((((3-0)+(7-6))*(0+9))-7)	29
7	((4*(6+(7*(2*8))))%(9+(3+7)))	16

Table 1: Sample expressions from MEE dataset

sub-dataset is divided into 100,000, 10,000 and 10,000 expressions as training, valid and test sets. We make sure that there is no overlap between the splits and every expression is made unique across the whole dataset.

We use an encoder-decoder approach where the encoder reads the characters in the expression and produces the encoding as input to the decoder, which in turn sequentially generates 2 digits as the predicted value. We experiment on various encoders, including our model, and compare their performances. We use the same decoder architecture to ensure a fair comparison. The output of the encoder is provided as the initial hidden state of the decoder LSTM. To test the generalization of our model, for all the experiments shown in this subsection, we train the model on expressions of length 4 and 5, and evaluate on expressions of length 4 to 7 in the test sets.

For this task, our baseline is a simple *LSTM* encoder (which corresponds to our model with only recur operations). We compare two versions of our *RRNet* encoder. In the supervised setting, we force the model to split and merge when it reads "(" and ")", respectively, and recur otherwise. This gives us an idea on how well the model would perform if it had access to the ground-truth tree. In the unsupervised setting, we learn the tree using policy gradient, where the reward is the accuracy of the math result prediction.

The results are in Table 2. The *supervised RRNet* yields the best performance showing that (a) it is important to exploit the hierarchical structure of the observed data, corroborating previous work (Williams et al., 2017), and (b) our model is effective at capturing that information. The *unsupervised RRNet* model also outperforms the baseline LSTM: the model learn to exploit branching operations to achieve better performance. We observe that the trees produced by the model do not correspond to the ground-truth trees. In order to assess whether the additional parameters of split and merge operations, rather than the learned tree

Model	Train	Test			
		L=4	L=5	L=6	L=7
LSTM	75.80	81.32	67.65	52.70	41.35
Uns RRNet	86.00	89.42	77.96	61.34	50.46
Sup RRNet	93.70	93.28	86.69	79.09	72.70

Table 2: Prediction accuracy on MEE dataset.

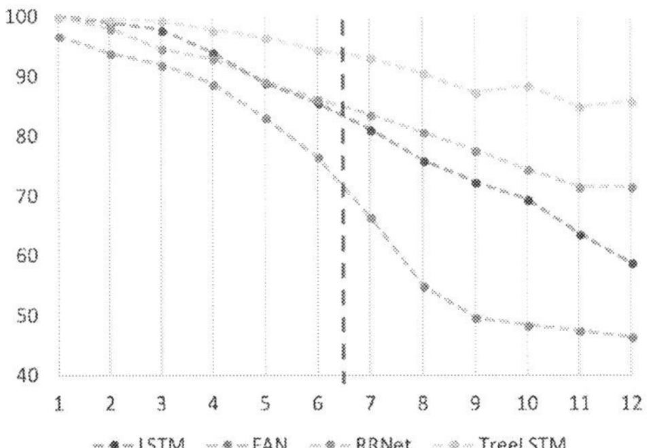

Figure 2: Test accuracy of the models, trained on sequences of length ≤ 6 in logic data. The horizontal axis indicates the length of the sequence, and the vertical axis indicates the accuracy of model's performance on the corresponding test set.

structure, produce better results, we measured the performance of our model trained with "random" deterministic policies (associating each of the input characters to either a split, merge or recur operation). We see that "random" policies perform worse than a "learnt" policy on the task, effectively similar to the baseline LSTM. In turn, the model with the learnt policy underperforms the model trained with ground-truth trees. Even in this seemingly easy task, it has appeared difficult for the model to learn the optimal branching policy.

3.2 Logical inference

In the next task, we analyze performance on the artificial language as described in Bowman et al. (2015b). This language has six word types {*a, b, c, d, e, f*} and three logical operations {*or, and, not*}. There are seven mutually exclusive logical relations that describe the relationship between two sentences: entailment ($\sqsubset$, $\sqsupset$), equivalence ($\equiv$), exhaustive and non-exhaustive contradiction ($^\wedge$, $|$), and two types of semantic independence ($\#$, $\smile$). The train/dev/test dataset ratios are set to 0.8/0.1/0.1 as described [1] with the number of logical operations ranging from 1 to 12.

From Figure 2, we report the performance of our model when trained with ground-truth trees as input. It is encouraging to see that our recurrent-recursive encoder improves performance over Transformer (FAN) (Tran et al., 2018) and LSTM, especially for long sequences. The best performance on this dataset is given by TreeLSTM, which has access to the whole sequence (Bowman et al., 2015b) and does not encode sequences on-the-fly.

3.3 Language Modelling

In language modeling, architectures such as TreeLSTM aren't directly applicable since their structure isn't computed on-the-fly, while reading the sentence. We perform preliminary experiments using the Penn Treebank Corpus dataset (Marcus et al., 1993), which has a vocabulary of 10,000 unique words and 929k, 73k and 82k words in training, validation and test set respectively. Our cells use one layer and the hidden dimensionality is 350. Our model yields test perplexity of 107.28 as compared to the LSTM baseline which gets 113.4 (Dyer et al., 2016). This preliminary result shows that the endeavor to exploit explicit hierarchical structures for language modeling, although challenging, may be promising.

4 Final Considerations

In this work, we began exploring properties of a recurrent-recursive neural network architecture that learns to encode the sequence on-the-fly, i.e. while reading. We argued this may be an important feature for tasks such as language modeling. We additionally proposed a new mathematical expression evaluation dataset (MEE) as a toy problem for validating the performance of sequential models to learn from hierarchical data. We empirically observed that, in this task, our model performs better than a standard LSTM architecture with no explicit structure and also outperforms the baseline LSTM and FAN architectures on the propositional logic task.

We hope to further study the properties of this model by either more thorough architecture search (recurrent dropouts, layer norm, hyper-parameter sweeps), different variation of RL algorithms such

[1]`https://github.com/sleepinyourhat/`
`vector-entailment`

as deep Q-learning (Mnih et al., 2013) and employing this model on various other tasks such as SNLI (Bowman et al., 2015a) and semi-supervised parsing.

Acknowledgement

The authors would like to thank Compute Canada for providing the computational resources. Zhouhan Lin would like to thank AdeptMind for generously supporting his research via scholarship.

References

Yoshua Bengio, Patrice Simard, and Paolo Frasconi. 1994. Learning long-term dependencies with gradient descent is difficult. *IEEE transactions on neural networks* 5(2):157–166.

Samuel R. Bowman, Gabor Angeli, Christopher Potts, and Christopher D. Manning. 2015a. A large annotated corpus for learning natural language inference. In *Proceedings of the 2015 Conference on Empirical Methods in Natural Language Processing (EMNLP)*. Association for Computational Linguistics.

Samuel R Bowman, Jon Gauthier, Abhinav Rastogi, Raghav Gupta, Christopher D Manning, and Christopher Potts. 2016. A fast unified model for parsing and sentence understanding .

Samuel R. Bowman, Christopher D. Manning, and Christopher Potts. 2015b. Tree-structured composition in neural networks without tree-structured architectures. *CoRR* abs/1506.04834.

Jihun Choi, Kang Min Yoo, and Sang-goo Lee. 2017. Learning to compose task-specific tree structures. *arXiv preprint arXiv:1707.02786* .

Chris Dyer, Adhiguna Kuncoro, Miguel Ballesteros, and Noah A Smith. 2016. Recurrent neural network grammars. *Proceedings of ACL* .

Salah El Hihi and Yoshua Bengio. 1996. Hierarchical recurrent neural networks for long-term dependencies. In *Proceedings of NIPS*.

Sepp Hochreiter and Jürgen Schmidhuber. 1997. Long short-term memory. *Neural computation* 9(8):1735–1780.

Mitchell P Marcus, Mary Ann Marcinkiewicz, and Beatrice Santorini. 1993. Building a large annotated corpus of english: The penn treebank. *Computational linguistics* 19(2):313–330.

Stephen Merity, Nitish Shirish Keskar, and Richard Socher. 2017. Regularizing and optimizing lstm language models. *arXiv preprint arXiv:1708.02182* .

Tomas Mikolov, Martin Karafit, Luks Burget, Jan Cernock, and Sanjeev Khudanpur. 2010. Recurrent neural network based language model. In Takao Kobayashi, Keikichi Hirose, and Satoshi Nakamura, editors, *INTERSPEECH*. ISCA, pages 1045–1048.

Volodymyr Mnih, Koray Kavukcuoglu, David Silver, Alex Graves, Ioannis Antonoglou, Daan Wierstra, and Martin Riedmiller. 2013. Playing atari with deep reinforcement learning. *arXiv preprint arXiv:1312.5602* .

Jürgen Schmidhuber. 1992. Learning complex, extended sequences using the principle of history compression. *Neural Computation* 4(2).

Richard Socher, Christopher D Manning, and Andrew Y Ng. 2010. Learning continuous phrase representations and syntactic parsing with recursive neural networks. In *Proceedings of the NIPS-2010 Deep Learning and Unsupervised Feature Learning Workshop*. pages 1–9.

Richard Socher, Alex Perelygin, Jean Wu, Jason Chuang, Christopher D Manning, Andrew Ng, and Christopher Potts. 2013. Recursive deep models for semantic compositionality over a sentiment treebank. In *Proceedings of the 2013 conference on empirical methods in natural language processing*. pages 1631–1642.

Kai Sheng Tai, Richard Socher, and Christopher D Manning. 2015. Improved semantic representations from tree-structured long short-term memory networks. *arXiv preprint arXiv:1503.00075* .

K. Tran, A. Bisazza, and C. Monz. 2018. The Importance of Being Recurrent for Modeling Hierarchical Structure. *ArXiv e-prints* .

Adina Williams, Andrew Drozdov, and Samuel R Bowman. 2017. Learning to parse from a semantic objective: It works. is it syntax? *arXiv preprint arXiv:1709.01121* .

Ronald J Williams. 1992. Simple statistical gradient-following algorithms for connectionist reinforcement learning. *Machine learning* 8(3-4):229–256.

Dani Yogatama, Phil Blunsom, Chris Dyer, Edward Grefenstette, and Wang Ling. 2016. Learning to compose words into sentences with reinforcement learning. *arXiv preprint arXiv:1611.09100* .

Xingxing Zhang, Liang Lu, and Mirella Lapata. 2015. Top-down tree long short-term memory networks. *arXiv preprint arXiv:1511.00060* .

Ganbin Zhou, Ping Luo, Rongyu Cao, Yijun Xiao, Fen Lin, Bo Chen, and Qing He. 2017. Generative neural machine for tree structures. *arXiv preprint arXiv:1705.00321* .

Limitations of cross-lingual learning from image search

Mareike Hartmann
Department of Computer Science
University of Copenhagen
Denmark
hartmann@di.ku.dk

Anders Søgaard
Department of Computer Science
University of Copenhagen
Denmark
soegaard@di.ku.dk

Abstract

Cross-lingual representation learning is an important step in making NLP scale to all the world's languages. Previous work on bilingual lexicon induction suggests that it is possible to learn cross-lingual representations of words based on similarities between images associated with these words. However, that work focused (almost exclusively) on the translation of nouns only. Here, we investigate whether the meaning of other parts-of-speech (POS), in particular adjectives and verbs, can be learned in the same way. Our experiments across five language pairs indicate that previous work does not scale to the problem of learning cross-lingual representations beyond simple nouns.

1 Introduction

Typically, cross-lingual word representations are learned from word alignments, sentence alignments, from aligned, comparable documents (Levy et al., 2017), or from monolingual corpora using seed dictionaries (Ammar et al., 2016).[1] However, for many languages such resources are not available.

Bergsma and Van Durme (2011) introduced an alternative idea, namely to learn bilingual representations from image data collected via web image search. The idea behind their approach is to represent words in a visual space and find valid translations between words based on similarities between their visual representations. Representations of words in the visual space are built by rep-

resenting a word by a set of images that are associated with that word, i.e., the word is a semantic tag for the images in the set.

Kiela et al. (2015) improve performance for the same task using a feature representation extracted from convolutional networks. However, both works only consider nouns, leaving open the question of whether learning cross-lingual representations for other POS from images is possible.[2]

In order to evaluate whether this work scales to verbs and adjectives, we compile wordlists containing these POS in several languages. We collect image sets for each image word and represent all words in a visual space. Then, we rank translations computing similarities between image sets and evaluate performance on this task.

Another field of research that exploits image data for NLP applications is the induction of multi-modal embeddings, i.e. semantic representations that are learned from textual and visual information jointly (Kiela et al., 2014; Hill and Korhonen, 2014; Kiela and Bottou, 2014; Lazaridou et al., 2015; Silberer et al., 2017; Kiela et al., 2016; Vulić et al., 2016). The work presented in our paper differs from these approaches, in that we do not use image data to improve semantic representations, but use images as a resource to learn cross-lingual representations. Even though lexicon induction from text resources might be more promising in terms of performance, we think that lexicon induction from visual data is worth exploring as it might give insights in the way that language is grounded in visual context.

---

[1] Recent work by Lample et al. (2018) introduces unsupervised bilingual lexicon induction from monolingual corpora, however, it was shown that this approach has important limitations (Søgaard et al., 2018).

[2] Kiela et al. (2016) induce English-Italian word translations from image data for the Simlex-999 dataset which contains adjectives and verbs, but they do not evaluate the performance for these POS compared to nouns.

Proceedings of the 3rd Workshop on Representation Learning for NLP, pages 159–163
Melbourne, Australia, July 20, 2018. ©2018 Association for Computational Linguistics

1.1 Contributions

We evaluate the approaches by Bergsma and Van Durme (2011) and Kiela et al. (2015) on an extended data set, which apart from nouns includes both adjectives and verbs. Our results suggest that none of the approaches involving image data are directly applicable to learning cross-lingual representations for adjectives and verbs.

2 Data

Wordlists We combined 3 data sets of English words to compile the wordlists for our experiments: the original wordlist used by Kiela et al. (2015), the Simlex-999 data set of English word pairs (Hill et al., 2014) and the MEN data set (Bruni et al., 2014). Whereas the first wordlist contains only nouns, the latter two datasets contain words of three POS classes (nouns, adjectives and verbs). We collect all distinct words and translate the final wordlist into 5 languages (German, French, Russian, Italian, Spanish) using the Google translation API[3], choosing the most frequent translation with the respective POS tag. Table 1 shows the POS distribution in the datasets.

	MEN	Simlex	Bergsma	Combined
N	656	751	500	1406
V	38	170	0	206
A	57	107	0	159

Table 1: Distribution of POS tags in the datasets used to compile the final wordlist.

Image Data Sets We use the Google Custom Search API[4] to represent each word in a wordlist by a set of images. We collect the first 50 jpeg images returned by the search engine when querying the words specifying the target language.[5] This way, we compile image data sets for 6 languages.[6] Figure 1 shows examples for images associated with a word in two languages.

---

[3] https://translate.google.com/

[4] https://developers.google.com/custom-search/

[5] Even though we get the search results for the first 50 images, some of them cannot be downloaded. On average, we collect 42 images for each image word.

[6] The wordlists and image datasets are available at https://github.com/coastalcph/cldi_from_image_search/

3 Approach

The assumption underlying the approach is that semantically similar words in two languages are associated with similar images. Hence, in order to find the translation of a word, e.g. from English to German, we compare the images representing the English word with all the images representing German words, and pick as translation the German word represented by the most similar images. To compute similarities between images, we compute cosine similarities between their feature representations.

3.1 Convolutional Neural Network Feature Representations

Following Kiela et al. (2015), we compute convolutional neural network (CNN) feature representations using a model pre-trained on the ImageNet classification task (Russakovsky et al., 2015). For each image, we extract the pre-softmax layer representation of the CNN. Instead of an AlexNet (Krizhevsky et al., 2012) as used by Kiela et al. (2015), we use the Keras implementation of the VGG19 model as described in Simonyan and Zisserman (2014), which was shown to achieve similar performance for word representation tasks by Kiela et al. (2016). Using this model, we represent each image by a 4069-dimensional feature vector.

Similarities Between Individual Images Bergsma and Van Durme (2011) determine similarities between image sets based on similarities between all individual images. For each image in image set 1, the maximum similarity score for any image in image set 2 is computed. These maximum similarity scores are then either averaged (AVGMAX) or their maximum is taken (MAXMAX).

Similarities Between Aggregated Representations In addition to the above described methods, Kiela et al. (2015) generate an aggregated representation for each image set and then compute the similarity between image sets by computing the similarity between the aggregated representations. Aggregated representations for image sets are generated by either taking the component-wise average (CNN-MEAN) or the component-wise maximum (CNN-MAX) of all images in the set.

K-Nearest Neighbor For each image in an image set in language 1, we compute its nearest

(a) Images associated with the English noun *cow* (left) and the German translation *Kuh* (right).

(b) Images associated with the English verb *discuss* (left) and the German translation *diskutieren* (right).

(c) Images associated with the English adjective *sad* (left) and the German translation *traurig* (right).

Figure 1: Examples for images associated with equivalent words in two languages (English and German).

neighbor across all image sets in language 2. Then, we find the image set in language 2 that contains the highest number of nearest neighbors. The image word is translated into the image word that is associated with that image 2 set. Ties between image sets containing an equivalent number of nearest neighbors are broken by computing the average distance between all members. We refer to the method as KNN. Whereas the other approaches described above provide a ranking of translations, this method determines only the one translation that is associated with the most similar image set.

Clustering Image Sets As we expect the retrieved image sets for a word to contain images associated with different senses of the word, we first cluster images into k clusters. This way, we hope to group images representing different word senses. Then, we apply the KNN method as described above. We refer to this method as KNN-C.

3.2 Evaluation Metrics

Ranking performance is evaluated by computing the Mean Reciprocal Rank (MRR) as $MRR = \frac{1}{M}\sum_{i=1}^{M}\frac{1}{rank(w_s, w_t)}$ M is the number of words to be translated and $rank(w_s, w_t)$ is the position the correct translation w_t for source word w_s is ranked on.

In addition to MRR, we also evaluate the cross-lingual representations by means of precision at k (P@k).

4 Experiments and Results

We run experiments for 5 language pairs English–German, English–Spanish, English–French, English–Russian and English–Italian. We evaluate the representations computed from image data and compare the different methods for similarity computation described in 3. For each English

word, we rank all the words in the corresponding target languages based on similarities between image sets and evaluate the models' ability to identify correct translations, i.e. to rank the correct translation on a position near the top. We compare 4 settings that differ in the set of English words that are translated. In the setting ALL, all English words in the wordlist are translated. NN, VB and ADJ refer to the settings where only nouns, verbs and adjectives are translated.

4.1 Results

Comparison of similarity computation methods for visual representations Table 2 displays results averaged over all language pairs.[7] First, comparing the different methods to compute similarities between image sets, AVGMAX outperforms the other methods in almost all cases. Most importantly, we witness a very significant drop in performance when moving from nouns to verbs and adjectives. For verbs, we rarely pick the right translation based on the image-based word representations. This behavior applies across all methods for similarity computation. Further, we see small improvements if we cluster the image sets prior to applying the KNN method, which might indicate that the clustering helps in finding translations for polysemous words.

4.2 Analysis

If we try to learn translations from images, integrating verbs and adjectives into the dataset worsens results compared to a dataset that contains only nouns. One possible explanation is that images associated with verbs and adjectives are less suited to represent the meaning of a concept than images associated with nouns.

Kiela et al. (2015) suppose that lexicon induction via image similarity performs worse for

---

[7] We also evaluate our visual representations on the set of 500 nouns used by Kiela et al. (2015), which results in P@1=0.6 and MRR=0.63 averaged over 5 language pairs for the AVGMAX method.

	ALL			NN			VB			ADJ		
	MRR	P@1	P@10	MRR	P@1	P@10	MRR	P@1	P@10	MRR	P@1	P@10
AVGMAX	0.53	0.49	0.60	0.60	0.56	0.67	0.20	0.15	0.30	0.28	0.22	0.37
MAXMAX	0.44	0.38	0.54	0.49	0.43	0.61	0.19	0.15	0.24	0.23	0.18	0.31
CNNMEAN	0.49	0.44	0.57	0.56	0.52	0.64	0.15	0.10	0.26	0.24	0.20	0.32
CNNMAX	0.47	0.43	0.55	0.55	0.50	0.63	0.15	0.10	0.24	0.19	0.15	0.27
KNN	–	0.42	–	–	0.50	–	–	0.06	–	–	0.13	–
KNN-C ($k = 3$)	–	0.47	–	–	0.56	–	–	0.10	–	–	0.16	–

Table 2: Results for translation ranking with images represented by CNN features averaged over 5 language pairs. KNN and KNN-C do not produce a ranking, hence we only provide P@1 values.

datasets containing words that are more abstract. In order to approximate the degree of abstractness of a concept, they compute the *image dispersion* d for a word w as the average cosine distance between all image pairs in the image set $\{i_j, \ldots, i_n\}$ associated with word w according to

$$d(w) = \frac{2}{n(n-1)} \sum_{k<j\leq n} 1 - \frac{i_j \cdot i_k}{|i_j||i_k|}$$

In their analysis, Kiela et al. (2015) find that their model performs worse on datasets with a higher average image dispersion. Kiela et al. (2014) introduce a dispersion-based filtering approach for learning multi-modal representations of nouns. They show that the quality of their representations with respect to a monolingual word-similarity prediction task improves, if they include visual information only in cases where the dispersion of the visual data is low.

Computing the average image dispersion for our data across languages shows that image sets associated with verbs and adjectives have a higher average image dispersion than image sets associated with nouns (nouns: $d = 0.60$, verbs: $d = 0.68$, adjectives: $d = 0.66$).

Table 3 shows the image words associated with the image sets that have the highest and lowest dispersion values in the English image data. For nouns and adjectives, we observe that the words with lowest dispersion values express concrete concepts, whereas the words with highest dispersion values express more abstract concepts that can be displayed in many variants. Manually inspecting the dataset, we find e.g. that the images associated with the noun *animal* display many different animals, such as birds, dogs, etc, whereas the images for *mug* all show a prototypical mug.

Besides the dispersion values, we also analyze the number of word senses per POS using Word-Net[8]. We find that the verbs in our dataset have a higher average number of word senses ($n = 9.18$) than the adjectives ($n = 6.88$) and the nouns ($n = 5.08$). That we get worst results for the words with highest number of different word senses is in agreement with Gerz et al. (2016), who find that in a monolingual word similarity prediction task, models perform worse for verbs with more different senses than for less polysemous verbs.

	Lowest dispersion		Highest dispersion	
	Word	d	Word	d
NN	mug	0.31	animal	0.78
	oscilloscope	0.32	companion	0.78
	padlock	0.33	mammal	0.78
VB	vanish	0.43	differ	0.76
	shed	0.43	hang	0.76
	divide	0.47	arrange	0.75
ADJ	yellow	0.39	huge	0.79
	white	0.40	large	0.79
	fragile	0.43	big	0.78

Table 3: English image words associated with the image sets with highest and lowest dispersion scores d.

5 Conclusion

We showed that existing work on learning cross-lingual word representations from images obtained via web image search does not scale to other POS than nouns. It is possible that training convolutional networks on different resources than ImageNet data will provide better features represent-

[8]https://wordnet.princeton.edu/

ing verbs and adjectives. Finally, it would be interesting to extend the approach to multi-modal input, combining images and texts, e.g. from comparable corpora with images such as Wikipedia.

References

Waleed Ammar, George Mulcaire, Yulia Tsvetkov, Guillaume Lample, Chris Dyer, and Noah A. Smith. 2016. Massively multilingual word embeddings. *CoRR* abs/1602.01925.

Elia Bruni, Nam Khanh Tran, and Marco Baroni. 2014. Multimodal distributional semantics. *Journal of Artificial Intelligence Research* 49(1):1–47.

Daniela Gerz, Ivan Vulić, Felix Hill, Roi Reichart, and Anna Korhonen. 2016. SimVerb-3500: A Large-Scale Evaluation Set of Verb Similarity. In *Proceedings of EMNLP*.

Felix Hill and Anna Korhonen. 2014. Learning abstract concept embeddings from multi-modal data: Since you probably can't see what I mean. In *Proceedings of EMNLP*.

Felix Hill, Roi Reichart, and Anna Korhonen. 2014. Simlex-999: Evaluating semantic models with (genuine) similarity estimation. *CoRR* abs/1408.3456. http://arxiv.org/abs/1408.3456.

Douwe Kiela and Léon Bottou. 2014. Learning image embeddings using convolutional neural networks for improved multi-modal semantics. In *Proceedings of EMNLP*.

Douwe Kiela, Felix Hill, Anna Korhonen, and Stephen Clark. 2014. Improving multi-modal representations using image dispersion: Why less is sometimes more. In *Proceedings of ACL*. Baltimore, Maryland.

Douwe Kiela, Anita Lilla Verő, and Stephen Clark. 2016. Comparing data sources and architectures for deep visual representation learning in semantics. In *Proceedings of EMNLP*.

Douwe Kiela, Ivan Vulic, and Stephen Clark. 2015. Visual bilingual lexicon induction with transferred convnet features. In *Proceedings of EMNLP*.

Alex Krizhevsky, Ilya Sutskever, and Geoffrey E. Hinton. 2012. Imagenet classification with deep convolutional neural networks. In *Proceedings of NIPS*.

Guillaume Lample, Alexis Conneau, Marc'Aurelio Ranzato, Ludovic Denoyer, and Herv Jgou. 2018. Word translation without parallel data. In *Proceedings of ICLR*.

Angeliki Lazaridou, Nghia The Pham, and Marco Baroni. 2015. Combining language and vision with a multimodal skip-gram model. In *Proceedings of NAACL HLT*.

Omer Levy, Yoav Goldberg, and Anders Søgaard. 2017. A strong baseline for learning cross-lingual word embeddings from sentence alignments. In *Proceedings of EACL*.

Olga Russakovsky, Jia Deng, Hao Su, Jonathan Krause, Sanjeev Satheesh, Sean Ma, Zhiheng Huang, Andrej Karpathy, Aditya Khosla, Michael Bernstein, Alexander C. Berg, and Li Fei-Fei. 2015. ImageNet Large Scale Visual Recognition Challenge. *International Journal of Computer Vision (IJCV)* 115(3).

Shane Bergsma and Benjamin Van Durme. 2011. Learning Bilingual Lexicons using the Visual Similarity of Labeled Web Images. In *Proceedings of IJCAI*. Barcelona, Spain, IJCAI '11.

Carina Silberer, Vittorio Ferrari, and Mirella Lapata. 2017. Visually grounded meaning representations. *IEEE Transactions on Pattern Analysis and Machine Intelligence* 39.

K. Simonyan and A. Zisserman. 2014. Very deep convolutional networks for large-scale image recognition. *CoRR* abs/1409.1556.

Anders Søgaard, Sebastian Ruder, and Ivan Vulić. 2018. On the limitations of unsupervised bilingual dictionary induction. In *Proceedings of ACL*.

Ivan Vulić, Douwe Kiela, S. Clark, and M.F Moens. 2016. Multi-modal representations for improved bilingual lexicon learning. In *Proceedings of ACL*.

Learning Semantic Textual Similarity from Conversations

Yinfei Yang[a], Steve Yuan[c], Daniel Cer[a], Sheng-yi Kong[a], Noah Constant[a], Petr Pilar[c],
Heming Ge[a], Yun-Hsuan Sung[a], Brian Strope[a], Ray Kurzweil[a]

[a]Google AI
Mountain View, CA, USA

[b]Google
Cambridge, MA, USA

[c]Google
Zurich, Switzerland

Abstract

We present a novel approach to learn representations for sentence-level semantic similarity using conversational data. Our method trains an unsupervised model to predict conversational responses. The resulting sentence embeddings perform well on the Semantic Textual Similarity (STS) Benchmark and SemEval 2017's Community Question Answering (CQA) question similarity subtask. Performance is further improved by introducing multi-task training, combining conversational response prediction and natural language inference. Extensive experiments show the proposed model achieves the best performance among all neural models on the STS Benchmark and is competitive with the state-of-the-art feature engineered and mixed systems for both tasks.

1 Introduction

We propose a novel approach to sentence-level semantic similarity based on unsupervised learning from conversational data. We observe that semantically similar sentences have a similar distribution of potential conversational responses, and that a model trained to predict conversational responses should implicitly learn useful semantic representations. As illustrated in Figure 1, "How old are you?" and "What is your age?" are both questions about age, which can be answered by similar responses such as "I am 20 years old". In contrast, "How are you?" and "How old are you?" use similar words but have different meanings and lead to different responses.

Deep learning models have been shown to predict conversational responses with increasingly good accuracy (Henderson et al., 2017; Kannan

Figure 1: Sentences have similar meanings if they can be answered by a similar distribution of conversational responses.

et al., 2016). The internal representations of such models resolve the semantics necessary to predict the correct response across a broad selection of input messages. Meaning similarity between sentences then can be obtained by comparing the sentence-level representations learned by such models. We follow this approach, and assess the quality of the resulting similarity scores on the Semantic Textual Similarity (STS) Benchmark (Cer et al., 2017) and a question similarity subtask from SemEval 2017's Community Question Answering (CQA) evaluation. The STS benchmark scores sentence pairs based on their degree of meaning similarity. The Community Question Answering (CQA) subtask B (Nakov et al., 2017) ranks questions based on their similarity with a target question.

We first assess representations learned from unsupervised conversational input-response pairs. We then explore augmenting our model with multi-task training over a combination of unsupervised conversational response prediction and supervised training on Natural Language Inference (NLI) data, as training to NLI has been shown to independently yield useful general purpose representations (Conneau et al., 2017). Unsupervised training over conversational data yields represen-

Proceedings of the 3rd Workshop on Representation Learning for NLP, pages 164–174
Melbourne, Australia, July 20, 2018. ©2018 Association for Computational Linguistics

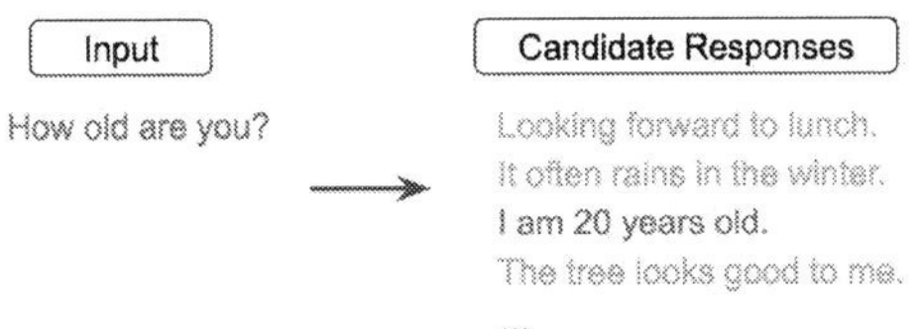

Figure 2: The conversational response selection problem attempts to identify the correct response from a collection of candidate responses. We train using batch negatives with each candidate response serving as a positive example for one input and a negative sample for the remaining inputs.

tations that perform well on STS and CQA question similarity. The addition of supervised SNLI data leads to further improvements and reaches state-of-the-art performance for neural STS models, surpassing training on NLI data alone.

2 Approach

This section describes the conversational learning task and our architecture for predicting conversational responses. We detail two encoding methods for converting sentences into sentence embeddings and describe multitask learning over conversational and NLI data.

2.1 Conversational Response Prediction

We formulate the conversational learning task as response prediction given an input (Kannan et al., 2016; Henderson et al., 2017). Following prior work, the prediction task is cast as a response selection problem. As shown in Figure 2, the model $P(y|x)$ attempts to identify the correct response y from $K - 1$ randomly sampled alternatives.

2.2 Model Architecture

Our model architecture encodes input and response sentences into fixed-length vectors u and v, respectively. The preference of an input described by u for a response described by v is scored by the dot product of the two vectors. The dot product scores are converted into probabilities using a softmax over the scores from all other candidate responses. Model parameters are trained to maximize the log-likelihood of the correct responses.

Figure 3 illustrates the input-response scoring model architecture. Tied parameters are used for the input and response encoders. In order to model the mapping between inputs and their expected

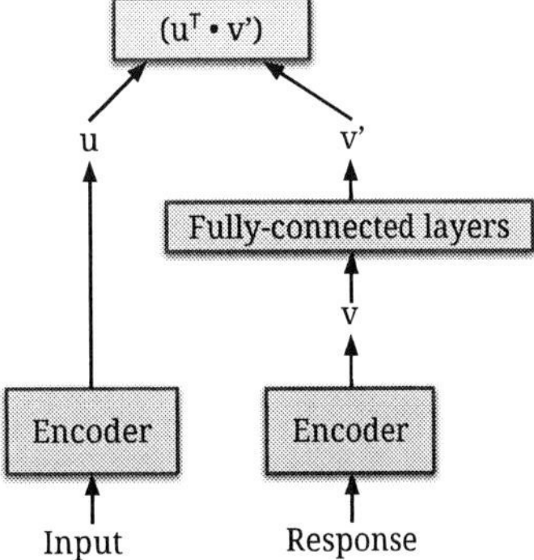

Figure 3: Conversational response prediction model. The sentence encoders are in red and use shared parameters. Fully connected DNN layers perform the mapping between the semantics of the input sentence and the candidate response.

responses, the response embeddings are passed through an additional feed-forward network to get the final response vector v' before computing the dot product with the input sentence embedding.[1]

Training is performed using batches of K randomly shuffled input-response pairs. Within a batch, each response serves as the correct answer to its corresponding input and the incorrect response to the remaining $K - 1$ inputs in the batch. In the remaining sections, this architecture is referred to as the *input-response model*.

2.3 Encoders

Figure 4 illustrates the encoders we explore for obtaining sentence embeddings: DANs (Iyyer et al., 2015) and Transformer (Vaswani et al., 2017).[2]

2.3.1 DAN

Deep averaging networks (DAN) compute sentence-level embeddings by first averaging word-level embeddings and then feeding the averaged representation to a deep neural network (DNN) (Iyyer et al., 2015). We provide our encoder with input embeddings for both words and bigrams in the sentence being encoded. This simple architecture has been found to outperform LSTMs on email response prediction (Henderson et al., 2017). The embeddings for words and

---

[1] While feed-forward layers could have been added to the input encoder as well, early experiments suggested it was sufficient to add additional layers to only one of the encoders.

[2] We tried other encoder architectures, notably LSTM (Hochreiter and Schmidhuber, 1997) and Bi-LSTM (Graves and Schmidhuber, 2005), but found they performed worse than transformer in preliminary experiments.

bigrams are learned during training of the input-response model. Our implementation sums the input embeddings and then divides by $sqrt(n)$, where n is the sentence length.[3] The resulting vector is passed as input to the DNN.

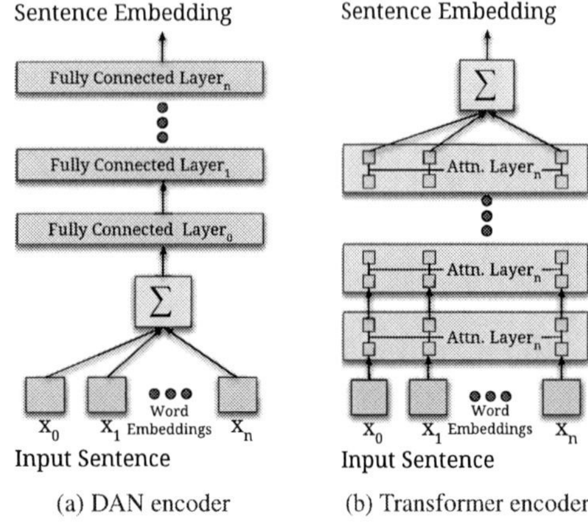

Figure 4: Model architectures for the DAN and Transformer sentence encoders.

DANs perform well in practice on sentence-level prediction and encoding tasks (Iyyer et al., 2015; Henderson et al., 2017). However, they lack any explicit network structure for encoding long range relationships between words.

2.3.2 Transformer

Transformer (Vaswani et al., 2017) is a recent network architecture that makes use of attention mechanisms to explicitly capture relationships between words appearing at any position in a sentence. The architecture is able to achieve state-of-the-art performance on translation tasks and is available as open-source.[4]

While the original transformer architecture contains an encoder and decoder, we only need the encoder component in our training procedure. The encoder is constructed as a series of attention layers consisting of a multi-headed self-attention operation over all input positions followed by a feedforward layer that processes each position independently (see figure 4b). Positional information is captured by injecting a "timing signal" into the

input embeddings based on sine/cosine functions at different frequencies.

The transformer encoder output is a variable-length sequence. We reduce it to fixed length by averaging across all sequence positions. Intuitively, this is similar to building a bag-of-words representation, except that the words have had a chance to interact with their contexts through the attention layers. In practice, we see that the learned attention masks focus largely on nearby words in the first layer, and attend to progressively more distant context in the higher layers.

2.4 Multitask Encoder

We anticipate that learning good semantic representations may benefit from the inclusion of multiple distinct tasks during training. Multiple tasks should improve the coverage of semantic phenomenon that are critical to one task but less essential to another. We explore multitask models that use a shared encoder for learning conversational response prediction and natural language inference (NLI). The NLI data are from the Stanford Natural Language Inference (SNLI) (Bowman et al., 2015) corpus. The sentences are mostly non-conversational, providing a complementary learning signal.

Figure 5 illustrates the multitask model with SNLI. We keep the input-response model the same, and build another two encoders for SNLI pairs, sharing parameters with the input-response encoders. Following Conneau et al. (2017), we encode a sentence pair into vectors u_1, u_2 and construct a feature vector $(u_1, u_2, |u_1 - u_2|, u_1 * u_2)$. The feature vector is fed into a 3-way classifier consisting of a feedforward network culminating in a softmax layer. Following prior work, we use a single 512 unit hidden layer for our experiments.

3   Conversational Data

Our unsupervised model relies on structured conversational data. The data for our experiments are drawn from Reddit conversations spanning 2007 to 2016, extracted by Al-Rfou et al. (2016). This corpus contains 133 million posts and a total of 2.4 billion comments. The comments are mostly conversational and well structured, making it a good resource for training conversational models.

Figure 6 provides an example of a Reddit comment chain. Comment B is a child of comment A if comment B is a reply to comment A. We extract

---

[3] `sqrtn` is one of TensorFlow's built-in embedding combiners. The intuition behind dividing by $sqrt(n)$ is as follows: We want our input embeddings to be sensitive to length. However, we also want to ensure that for short sequences the relative differences in the representations are not dominated by sentence length effects.

[4] https://github.com/tensorflow/tensor2tensor

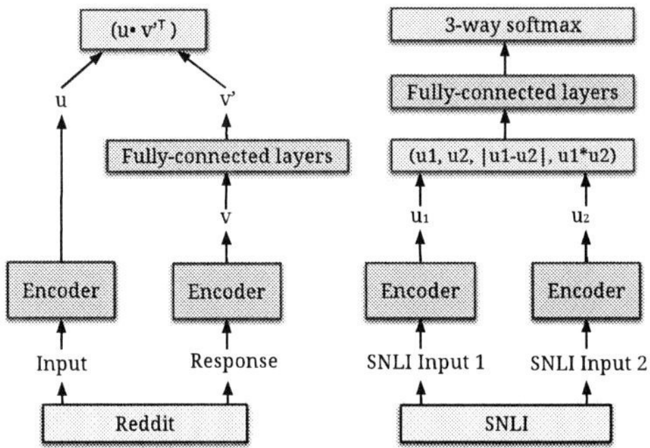

Figure 5: Architecture of the multitask model. Sentence encoders are in red and share parameters.

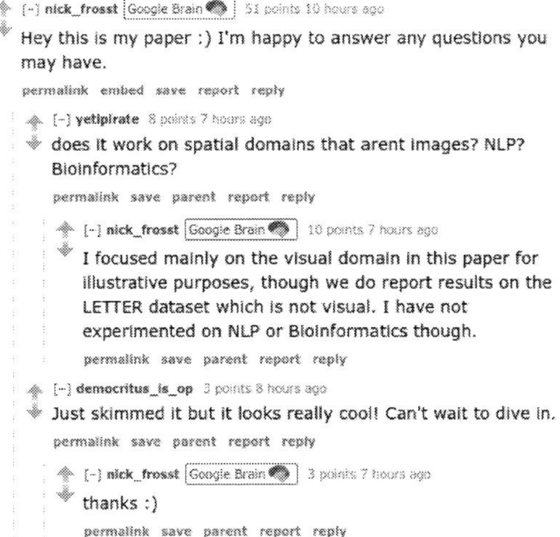

Figure 6: Reddit comment chain.

comments and their children to form the input-response pairs described above. Several rules are applied to filter out the noisy data. A comment is removed if any of the following conditions holds: number of characters ≥ 350, percentage of alphabetic characters $\leq 70\%$, starts with "https", "/r/" or "@", author's name contains "bot". The total number of extracted pairs is around 600 million.

3.1 Model Configuration

Model configuration and hyperparameters are set based on prior experiments on Reddit response prediction and performance of the multi-task model on SNLI. All inputs are tokenized and normalized before being fed into model. For all experiments, we use SGD with a batch size of 128 and a learning rate of 0.01. The total training steps are 40 million steps for the Reddit model and 30 million steps for the Reddit+SNLI model. We

	P@1	P@3	P@10
Transformer	**65.7**	**78.7**	**89.8**
DAN	56.1	70.2	83.6

Table 1: Precision at N (P@N) results on the Reddit response predication test set for models built using the DAN and Transformer encoders. Models attempt to select the true response for an input against 99 randomly selected negatives.

adjust the batch size to 256 and learning rate to 0.001 after 30 million and 20 million steps for the Reddit and the Reddit+SNLI models, respectively. When training the multitask model, we initialize the shared parameters with a pretrained Reddit model. We employ a distributed training system with multiple workers, where 95% of workers are used to continue training the Reddit task and 5% of workers are used to train the SNLI task. We use a sentence embedding size of 500 in all experiments, and normalize sentence embeddings prior to use in subsequent network layers. The parameters were only lightly tuned to prevent overfitting on the SNLI task.

The encoder configurations are taken from the default parameters from previous work. For DAN, we employ a 3-layer DNN with layers containing 300, 300, and 500 hidden units. For the transformer encoder, our experiments make use of 6 attention layers (`num_hidden_layers`) and 8 attentions heads (`num_heads`). Within each attention layer, the feedforward network applied to each head has an input and output size of 512 (`hidden_size`) and makes use of a 2048 unit inner-layer (`filter_size`).

4 Experiments

We first evaluate the different encoders on the response prediction task. For the multitask models, we then examine their performance on SNLI. Finally, we evaluate the encoders on the STS Benchmark (Cer et al., 2017) and on SemEval 2017 Community Question Answering (CQA) subtask B (Nakov et al., 2017). We refer to the model trained over Reddit input-response pairs as *Reddit* and the multitask model as *Reddit+SNLI*.

4.1 Response Prediction

Following Henderson et al. (2017), we use precision at N (P@N) as an evaluation metric for the conversational response prediction task. Given an

167

	Accuracy
Reddit+SNLI	84.1
InferSent	**84.5**
KIM Ensemble	**89.0**
Gumbel TreeLSTM	86.0

Table 2: SNLI classification performance for the Reddit+SNLI model using the transformer encoder with reference evaluation numbers from prior work. We note that similar to InferSent, our goal is to use SNLI to obtain better sentence representations rather than achieving state-of-the-art performance on the SNLI task itself.

input, the task is to select the true response (positive) from 99 randomly selected responses (negatives). We rank all 100 candidate responses by their dot-product scores from the input-response model. The P@N score evaluates if the true response (positive) appears in the top N responses. For the evaluation, the Reddit data is randomly split into train (90%) and test (10%) sets.

Table 1 shows the P@N results of Reddit models trained with different encoders, for N=1, 3, 10. The DAN encoder (with n-grams), as investigated by Henderson et al. (2017), provides a strong baseline. We observe the transformer encoder outperforms DAN for all values of N. The transformer encoder achieves a P@1 metric of 65.7% while DAN achieves only 56.1%. Given its greater performance, we use a transformer encoder for the remainder of the experiments reported in this work.

4.2 SNLI

SNLI (Bowman et al., 2015) annotates the inferential relationship between paired sentences as entailment, contradiction, or neural. One sentence is entailed by another sentence if its meaning can be inferred from the other. Sentences contradict each other if the meaning of one implies that the other is not true. The sentence pairs in the dataset are partitioned into train (550,152), dev (10,000), and test (10,000). Model performance is evaluated based on classification accuracy.

Our multitask model learns a shared encoder for the conversational response prediction and SNLI tasks. We report evaluation results on the SNLI task in order to facilitate better comparison with InferSent (Conneau et al., 2017), which served as the inspiration for the inclusion of the SNLI task within a multitask model. For reference, we pro-

vide the results of Gumbel TreeLSTM (Williams et al., 2017), which is the best sentence encoder based model, and KIM Ensemble (Chen et al., 2017), which is the current state-of-the-art.

Sentence encoder based models first encode the two sentences in an SNLI input pair separately, and then feed the encodings into a classifier. By comparison, other models explicitly consider word-level interactions between the paired sentences (e.g., using cross-attention). We note that our model is sentence encoder based.

Table 2 shows the accuracy on the test set of the joint model and baselines. The multitask model achieves 84.1% accuracy and is close to the performance of InferSent. There are two significant differences between our model and prior work. First, the proposed model learns all model parameters from scratch, including the word embeddings. Due in part to the size of the SNLI training set, InferSent uses a large pre-trained word embedding model fit via GloVe (Pennington et al., 2014) on 840 billion tokens of web crawl data, which results in fewer out-of-vocabulary words. For our multitask model, the Reddit dataset is large enough that we do not necessarily require pre-trained word embeddings. However, it is possible the pretrained GloVe embeddings provide slightly better performance on the SNLI task.[5] Secondly, our multi-task model learns two tasks simultaneously, balancing performance between them, while InferSent only optimizes performance on SNLI. As will be presented below, our multi-task model performs better on STS. We suspect multi-task training both increases coverage of different language phenomenon and acts as a regularizer across tasks that prevents the resulting sentence embeddings from overfitting any particular task, thus improving transfer performance to new tasks.[6]

4.3 STS Benchmark

The proposed models encode text into a sentence-level embedding space. We evaluate the extent to which the embeddings accurately encode sentence-level meaning using the Semantic Tex-

---

[5] Preliminary experiments with pre-trained embeddings on a P@N Reddit response prediction evaluation revealed no performance advantage over embeddings learned directly from the data.

[6] We note that, if our model is reduced to just training on SNLI without multitask training on Reddit, it would be equivalent to InferSent but without the use of pretrained sentence embeddings. We do not provide results for this configuration as preliminary experiments suggested it performed poorly.

	dev	test
Reddit+SNLI tuned	**0.835**	**0.808**
Reddit+SNLI	0.814	0.782
Reddit tuned	0.809	0.781
Reddit	0.762	0.731
Neural representation models		
CNN (HCTI)	**0.834**	**0.784**
InferSent	0.801	0.758
Sent2Vec	0.787	0.755
SIF	0.801	0.720
PV-DBOW	0.722	0.649
C-PHRASE	0.743	0.639
Feature engineered and mixed systems		
ECNU	<u>**0.847**</u>	<u>**0.810**</u>
BIT	0.829	0.809

Table 3: Pearson's r on the STS Benchmark.

tual Similarity (STS) Benchmark. The benchmark includes English datasets from the SemEval/*SEM STS shared tasks between 2012 and 2017 (Cer et al., 2017; Agirre et al., 2016, 2015, 2014, 2013, 2012). The data include 8,628 sentence pairs from three categories: *captions*, *news* and *forums*. Each pair is annotated with a human-labeled degree of meaning similarity, ranging from 0 to 5. The dataset is divided into train (5,749), dev (1,500) and test (1,379).

We report results using two configurations for the evaluation of the Reddit and Reddit+SNLI models. The first configuration is "out-of-the-box" with no adaptation for the STS task. Rather, we take the original sentence embeddings u, v and directly score the sentence pair similarity based on the angular distance between the two vectors, $-\arccos\left(\frac{uv}{\|u\|\,\|v\|}\right)$.[7] We suspect the original sentence embeddings from the Reddit and Reddit+SNLI models will not necessary weight all semantic distinctions in a way that is consistent with the annotations for STS. The second configuration for evaluating the two models uses a single transformation matrix to fine-tune the sentence embedding representations for the STS task. The matrix, which is parameterized using the STS training data, transforms the original sentence embedding vectors u, v to u^*, v^*.

Table 3 presents results on the dev and test sets of the STS Benchmark. For model comparisons, we include the state-of-the-art neural STS

model CNN (HCTI) (Shao, 2017) and other systems in Cer et al. (2017).[8] The untuned Reddit model is competitive with many of the other neural representation models, demonstrating that the sentence embeddings learned on Reddit conversations do keep text with similar semantics close in embedding space. The "out-of-the-box" multitask model, Reddit+SNLI, achieves an r of 0.814 on the dev set and 0.782 on test. Using a transformation matrix to adapt the Reddit model trained without SNLI to STS, we achieve Pearson's r of 0.809 on dev and 0.781 on test. This surpasses InferSent and is close to the performance of the best neural representation approach, CNN (HCTI).[9]

The adapted multitask model achieves the best performance among all neural models, with an r of 0.835 on the dev data and 0.808 on test. The results are competitive with state-of-the-art feature engineered and mixed systems, e.g. ECNU and BIT. However, our models are simpler and require no feature engineering.[10]

4.4 CQA Subtask B

To further validate the effectiveness of sentence representations learned from conversational data, we assess the proposed models on subtask B of SemEval Community Question Answering (CQA) (Nakov et al., 2017). In this task, given an "original" question Q, and the top ten related questions from a forum $(Q_1, \ldots, Q_{10})$ as retrieved by a search engine, the goal is to rank the related questions according to their similarity with respect

---

[7]arccos is used to convert the cosine similarity scores into angular distances that obey the triangle inequality.

[8]InferSent (Conneau et al., 2017), Sent2Vec (Pagliardini et al., 2017), SIF (Arora et al., 2017), PV-DBOW (Lau and Baldwin, 2016), C-PHRASE (Kruszewski et al., 2015), ECNU (Tian et al., 2017) and BIT (Wu et al., 2017).

[9]For both the STS shared task and the STS benchmark leaderboard, systems are allowed to use external datasets as long as they do not make use of supervised annotations on data that overlap with the evaluation sets. InferSent introduced the use of SNLI for STS. However, we discovered 4 out of the 1,379 pairs within the STS Benchmark dev set and 5 out of the 1,500 pairs in the STS Benchmark test set overlap with the SNLI training set. We do not believe this minimal overlap had a meaningful impact on the results presented here.

[10]As summarized by Cer et al. (2017), ENCU makes use of a large feature set that includes: n-gram overlap; edit distance; longest common prefix/suffix/substring; tree kernels; word alignment based similarity; summarization and MT evaluation metrics; kernel similarity of bags-of-words and bags-of-dependency triples; and pooled word embeddings. The manually engineered features are combined with scores from DAN and LSTM based deep learning models. BIT relies primarily on a measure of sentence information content (IC) with a non-trivial derivation that is optionally combined with either an alignment based similarity score or the cosine similarity of IDF weighed summed word embeddings.

	dev				test			
	all	captions	forums	news	all	captions	forums	news
Reddit+SNLI	**0.814**	**0.885**	**0.756**	**0.646**	**0.782**	**0.891**	**0.764**	**0.585**
Reddit	0.762	0.815	0.751	0.632	0.731	0.816	0.759	0.578
Reddit+SNLI tuned	**0.835**	**0.888**	**0.759**	**0.731**	**0.808**	**0.894**	**0.767**	0.667
Reddit tuned	0.809	0.843	0.754	0.721	0.781	0.843	0.762	**0.668**

Table 4: Pearson's r of the proposed models on the STS Benchmark with a breakdown by category.

	Score	Label	STS Input Sentences
Good	-0.51	4.2	S1: a small bird sitting on a branch in winter. S2: a small bird perched on an icy branch.
Good	-1.23	0.0	S1: microwave would be your best bet. S2: your best bet is research.
Bad	-0.42	2.2	S1: a little boy is singing and playing a guitar. S2: a man is singing and playing the guitar.
Bad	-0.45	1.0	S1: yes, you have to file a tax return in canada. S2: you are not required to file a tax return in canada if you have no taxable income.

Table 5: Example model and human similarity scores on pairs from the STS Benchmark. System scores are reported as the negative angular distance between the sentence embeddings. The scores can range from 0 to $-\pi$, but in practice are typically between 0 and $-\frac{1}{2}\pi$.

	MAP
Reddit+SNLI	**47.42**
Reddit	47.07
KeLP-contrastive1	**49.00**
SimBow-contrastive2	47.87
SimBow-primary	47.22

Table 6: Mean Average Precision (MAP) on Community Question Answering (CQA) subtask B.

to the original question. Mean average precision (MAP) is used to evaluate candidate models.

Each pairing of an original question and a related question (Q, Q_i) is labeled "PerfectMatch", "Relevant" or "Irrelevant". Both "PerfectMatch" and "Relevant" are considered as *good questions*, which should rank above "Irrelevant" ones.

Similar to the STS experiments, we use cosine similarity between the original question and related questions, without considering any other interaction between the two questions.[11] Given a related question Q_i and its original question Q, we first encode them into vectors u_i and u. Then the related questions are ranked based on the cosine similarity with respect to the original question,

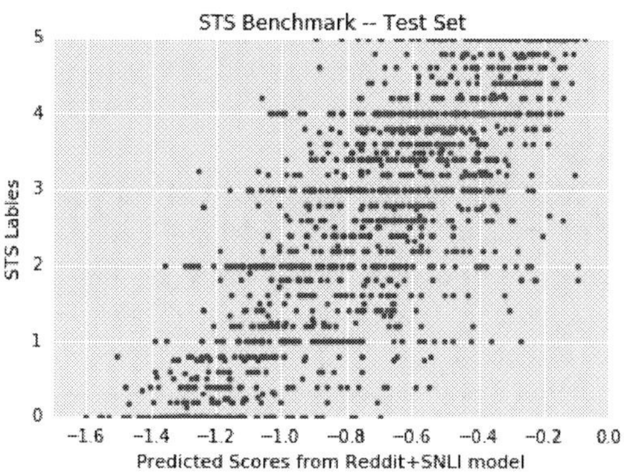

Figure 7: Predicted semantic similarity scores vs. ground truth on the STS Benchmark.

$cos(u_i, u)$. Results are shown in table 6. SimBow (Charlet and Damnati, 2017) and KeLP (Filice et al., 2017), which are the best systems on the 2017 task, are used as baselines.[12] Even without tuning on the training data provided by the task, our models show competitive performance. Reddit+SNLI outperforms SimBow-primary, which official ranked first during the 2017 shared task.

---

[11] Our model also excludes the use of comments and user profiles provided by CQA as optional contextual features.

[12] In the competition, each team can submit one primary run and two contrastive runs. Only the primary run is used for the official ranking.

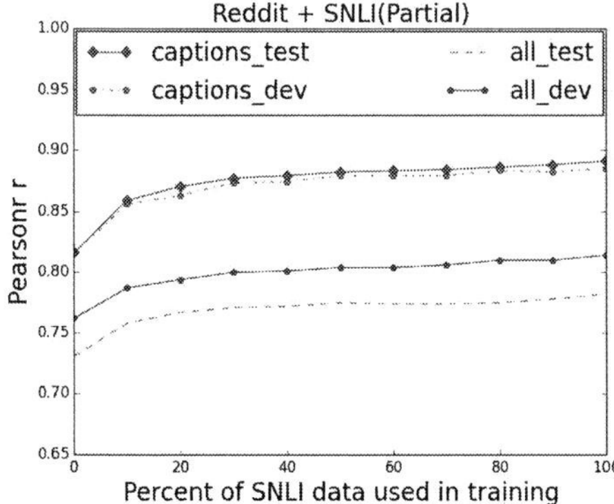

Figure 8: Pearson's r on the STS Benchmark for the multitask model trained with Reddit and varying amounts of SNLI data.

5 Analysis

Model performance on the STS Benchmark can be partition by sentence pair source. The test set contains 625 sentence pairs drawn from *captions*, 500 pairs from *news* data, and 254 from online *forums*.

Table 4 provides results on each sub-group. For the *captions* category, adding the SNLI data improves the baseline Reddit model by about 8% absolute. Even with tuning to STS, mixing in SNLI data still helps dramatically on *captions*, as the STS tuned Reddit+SNLI model is 5% absolute higher than the STS tuned Reddit model on this category. The improvement is likely attributed to the fact that the SNLI sentences are from image captions, while Reddit doesn't contain much caption-style data. Training with the SNLI data has a smaller impact on performance for the other categories, with even a slight decrease for the STS tuned models on *news* test.

We observe that the STS tuned models have only modest performance improvements on the forum data over the untuned models, with much larger improvements for *captions* and *news*. Moreover, for the Reddit+SNLI models, tuning produces a large performance increase for *news* with smaller increases for both *captions* and *forums*. This suggests tuning is impart compensating for domain limitations within the training data.[13] Further improvements on the STS Benchmark could likely be achieved by including additional encoder training data sourced from news data.

Figure 7 plots predicted similarity scores

---

against the ground truth labels within the STS Benchmark test data. The figure shows that while the predicted scores are correlated with human judgment, there is still a sizable range of predicted similarity values for any given gold STS label. We provide examples of good and bad similarity predictions in table 5. For the two good examples, the model correctly has a relatively high similarity score for the first pair, and a relatively low score for the second. For the first bad example, the model fails to penalize its similarity score based on the semantic distinction between "boy" and "man" as much as human raters did. For the second bad example, apparently being on the topic of whether it is necessary to file Canadian tax returns was enough for the model to assign a high similarly score. Human raters correctly assigned a low similarity score since the two sentences are making very different claims.

5.1 Quantity of SNLI data and Performance

The experiments in the previous section show that supervised in-domain data, SNLI's image captions, can be used to improve the semantic representations of in-domain (*caption*) sentences. However, supervised data is difficult to obtain, especially on the order of SNLI's 570,000 sentence pairs. In order to learn how much supervised data is needed, we train multitask models with Reddit and varying amounts of SNLI data, ranging from 10% to 90% of the full dataset.

Figure 8 shows the STS Benchmark results for all data and for caption data only, on both dev and test sets. When first adding the SNLI data into the training task, Pearson's r increases rapidly across all measures. Even with only 10% of the SNLI data, r reaches around 0.85 for captions data on both dev and test. The curves mostly flatten out after using 40% of the data, with performance only improving slightly past this point. This suggests encoders trained primarily on Reddit data can be efficiently adapted to perform well on other domains using a small sample of in-domain data.

6 Related Work

The STS task was first introduced by Agirre et al. (2012). Early methods focused on lexical semantics, surface form matching and basic syntactic similarity (Bär et al., 2012; Jimenez et al., 2012). More recently, deep learning based methods became competitive (Shao, 2017; Tai et al., 2015).

---

[13]e.g., the Reddit+SNLI model is trained on image caption and discussion forum data but not news.

One approach to this task is to encode sentences into sentence-level embeddings and then calculate the cosine similarity between the encoded representations of the sentence pair. The encoding model can be directly trained on the STS task (Shao, 2017) or it can be trained on an alternative supervised (Conneau et al., 2017) or unsupervised (Pagliardini et al., 2017) task. The primary contribution of the work described in this paper falls into the latter category, introducing a new unsupervised task based on conversational data that achieves good performance on predicting semantic similarity scores. Training on input-response data has been previously shown to be effective at email response prediction (Kannan et al., 2016; Henderson et al., 2017). We extend prior work by exploring the effectiveness of representations learned from conversations in capturing general-purpose semantic information. The approach is similar to Skip-Thought (Kiros et al., 2015), which learns sentence-level representations through prior and next sentence prediction within a document. However, within our work, the adjacent sentences are pulled from turns in a conversation.

7 Conclusion

In this paper, we propose using conversational response prediction models to obtain sentence-level embeddings. We find that encodings learned for conversational response prediction perform well on sentence-level semantic similarity. Sentence embeddings extracted from a model trained on conversational data can be used to obtain results on the STS Benchmark that are competitive with well performing models based on sentence-level encoders. A multitask model trained on response prediction and SNLI achieves state-of-the-art performance for sentence encoding based models on the STS Benchmark, and surpasses prior work that trained on SNLI alone (InferSet). Finally, even without any task-specific training, the sentence embeddings obtained from both the conversational response prediction model and the multitask model that includes SNLI are competitive on CQA subtask B.

Acknowledgments

We thank the anonymous reviewers and our teammates from Descartes and other Google groups for their feedback and suggestions, particularly Dan Gillick and Raphael Hoffman.

References

Eneko Agirre, Carmen Banea, Claire Cardie, Daniel Cer, Mona Diab, Aitor Gonzalez-Agirre, Weiwei Guo, Inigo Lopez-Gazpio, Montse Maritxalar, Rada Mihalcea, German Rigau, Larraitz Uria, and Janyce Wiebe. 2015. Semeval-2015 task 2: Semantic textual similarity, english, spanish and pilot on interpretability. In *Proceedings of the 9th International Workshop on Semantic Evaluation (SemEval 2015)*, pages 252–263.

Eneko Agirre, Carmen Banea, Claire Cardie, Daniel Cer, Mona Diab, Aitor Gonzalez-Agirre, Weiwei Guo, Rada Mihalcea, German Rigau, and Janyce Wiebe. 2014. Semeval-2014 task 10: Multilingual semantic textual similarity. In *Proceedings of the 8th International Workshop on Semantic Evaluation (SemEval 2014)*, pages 81–91.

Eneko Agirre, Carmen Banea, Daniel Cer, Mona Diab, Aitor Gonzalez-Agirre, Rada Mihalcea, German Rigau, and Janyce Wiebe. 2016. Semeval-2016 task 1: Semantic textual similarity, monolingual and cross-lingual evaluation. In *Proceedings of the 10th International Workshop on Semantic Evaluation (SemEval-2016)*, pages 497–511.

Eneko Agirre, Daniel Cer, Mona Diab, and Aitor Gonzalez-Agirre. 2012. Semeval-2012 task 6: A pilot on semantic textual similarity. In **SEM 2012: The First Joint Conference on Lexical and Computational Semantics – Volume 1: Proceedings of the main conference and the shared task, and Volume 2: Proceedings of the Sixth International Workshop on Semantic Evaluation (SemEval 2012)*, pages 385–393.

Eneko Agirre, Daniel Cer, Mona Diab, Aitor Gonzalez-Agirre, and Weiwei Guo. 2013. *sem 2013 shared task: Semantic textual similarity. In *Second Joint Conference on Lexical and Computational Semantics (*SEM), Volume 1: Proceedings of the Main Conference and the Shared Task: Semantic Textual Similarity*, pages 32–43.

Rami Al-Rfou, Marc Pickett, Javier Snaider, Yunhsuan Sung, Brian Strope, and Ray Kurzweil. 2016. Conversational contextual cues: The case of personalization and history for response ranking. *arXiv preprint arXiv:1606.00372*.

Sanjeev Arora, Yingyu Liang, and Tengyu Ma. 2017. A simple but tough-to-beat baseline for sentence embeddings. In *5th International Conference on Learning Representations (ICLR)*.

Daniel Bär, Chris Biemann, Iryna Gurevych, and Torsten Zesch. 2012. Ukp: Computing semantic textual similarity by combining multiple content similarity measures. In *Proceedings of the First Joint Conference on Lexical and Computational Semantics-Volume 1: Proceedings of the main conference and the shared task, and Volume 2: Proceedings of the Sixth International Workshop on Semantic Evaluation*, pages 435–440. Association for Computational Linguistics.

Samuel R. Bowman, Gabor Angeli, Christopher Potts, and Christopher D. Manning. 2015. A large annotated corpus for learning natural language inference. In *Proceedings of the 2015 Conference on Empirical Methods in Natural Language Processing (EMNLP)*. Association for Computational Linguistics.

Daniel Cer, Mona Diab, Eneko Agirre, Inigo Lopez-Gazpio, and Lucia Specia. 2017. Semeval-2017 task 1: Semantic textual similarity multilingual and cross-lingual focused evaluation. In *Proceedings of the 11th International Workshop on Semantic Evaluation (SemEval-2017)*, pages 1–14.

Delphine Charlet and Geraldine Damnati. 2017. Simbow at semeval-2017 task 3: Soft-cosine semantic similarity between questions for community question answering. In *Proceedings of the 11th International Workshop on Semantic Evaluation (SemEval-2017)*, pages 315–319.

Qian Chen, Xiaodan Zhu, Zhen-Hua Ling, Diana Inkpen, and Si Wei. 2017. Natural language inference with external knowledge. *arXiv preprint arXiv:1711.04289*.

Alexis Conneau, Douwe Kiela, Holger Schwenk, Loïc Barrault, and Antoine Bordes. 2017. Supervised learning of universal sentence representations from natural language inference data. In *Proceedings of the 2017 Conference on Empirical Methods in Natural Language Processing*, pages 681–691, Copenhagen, Denmark. Association for Computational Linguistics.

Simone Filice, Giovanni Da San Martino, and Alessandro Moschitti. 2017. Kelp at semeval-2017 task 3: Learning pairwise patterns in community question answering. In *Proceedings of the 11th International Workshop on Semantic Evaluation (SemEval-2017)*, pages 326–333.

Alex Graves and Jürgen Schmidhuber. 2005. Framewise phoneme classification with bidirectional LSTM and other neural network architectures. *Neural Networks*, 18(5):602 – 610. IJCNN 2005.

Matthew Henderson, Rami Al-Rfou, Brian Strope, Yun-Hsuan Sung, László Lukács, Ruiqi Guo, Sanjiv Kumar, Balint Miklos, and Ray Kurzweil. 2017. Efficient natural language response suggestion for smart reply. *CoRR*, abs/1705.00652.

Sepp Hochreiter and Jürgen Schmidhuber. 1997. Long short-term memory. *Neural Computation*, 9(8):1735–1780.

Mohit Iyyer, Varun Manjunatha, Jordan Boyd-Graber, and Hal Daumé III. 2015. Deep unordered composition rivals syntactic methods for text classification.

In *Proceedings of the 53rd Annual Meeting of the Association for Computational Linguistics and the 7th International Joint Conference on Natural Language Processing (Volume 1: Long Papers)*, pages 1681–1691, Beijing, China. Association for Computational Linguistics.

Sergio Jimenez, Claudia Becerra, and Alexander Gelbukh. 2012. Soft cardinality: A parameterized similarity function for text comparison. In *Proceedings of the First Joint Conference on Lexical and Computational Semantics-Volume 1: Proceedings of the main conference and the shared task, and Volume 2: Proceedings of the Sixth International Workshop on Semantic Evaluation*, pages 449–453. Association for Computational Linguistics.

Anjuli Kannan, Karol Kurach, Sujith Ravi, Tobias Kaufman, Balint Miklos, Greg Corrado, Andrew Tomkins, Laszlo Lukacs, Marina Ganea, Peter Young, and Vivek Ramavajjala. 2016. Smart reply: Automated response suggestion for email. In *Proceedings of the ACM SIGKDD Conference on Knowledge Discovery and Data Mining (KDD) (2016)*.

Ryan Kiros, Yukun Zhu, Ruslan R Salakhutdinov, Richard Zemel, Raquel Urtasun, Antonio Torralba, and Sanja Fidler. 2015. Skip-thought vectors. In C. Cortes, N. D. Lawrence, D. D. Lee, M. Sugiyama, and R. Garnett, editors, *Advances in Neural Information Processing Systems 28*, pages 3294–3302. Curran Associates, Inc.

German Kruszewski, Angeliki Lazaridou, Marco Baroni, et al. 2015. Jointly optimizing word representations for lexical and sentential tasks with the c-phrase model. In *Proceedings of the 53rd Annual Meeting of the Association for Computational Linguistics and the 7th International Joint Conference on Natural Language Processing (Volume 1: Long Papers)*, volume 1, pages 971–981.

Jey Han Lau and Timothy Baldwin. 2016. An empirical evaluation of doc2vec with practical insights into document embedding generation. In *Processings of ACL Workshop on Representation Learning for NLP*, page 78.

Preslav Nakov, Doris Hoogeveen, Lluís Màrquez, Alessandro Moschitti, Hamdy Mubarak, Timothy Baldwin, and Karin Verspoor. 2017. SemEval-2017 task 3: Community question answering. In *Proceedings of the 11th International Workshop on Semantic Evaluation*, SemEval '17, Vancouver, Canada. Association for Computational Linguistics.

Matteo Pagliardini, Prakhar Gupta, and Martin Jaggi. 2017. Unsupervised learning of sentence embeddings using compositional n-gram features. *arXiv preprint arXiv:1703.02507*.

Jeffrey Pennington, Richard Socher, and Christopher D. Manning. 2014. Glove: Global vectors for word representation. In *Empirical Methods in Natural Language Processing (EMNLP)*, pages 1532–1543.

Yang Shao. 2017. Hcti at semeval-2017 task 1: Use convolutional neural network to evaluate semantic textual similarity. In *Proceedings of the 11th International Workshop on Semantic Evaluation (SemEval-2017)*, pages 130–133.

Kai Sheng Tai, Richard Socher, and Christopher D Manning. 2015. Improved semantic representations from tree-structured long short-term memory networks. *arXiv preprint arXiv:1503.00075.*

Junfeng Tian, Zhiheng Zhou, Man Lan, and Yuanbin Wu. 2017. Ecnu at semeval-2017 task 1: Leverage kernel-based traditional nlp features and neural networks to build a universal model for multilingual and cross-lingual semantic textual similarity. In *Proceedings of the 11th International Workshop on Semantic Evaluation (SemEval-2017)*, pages 191–197.

Ashish Vaswani, Noam Shazeer, Niki Parmar, Jakob Uszkoreit, Llion Jones, Aidan N Gomez, Ł ukasz Kaiser, and Illia Polosukhin. 2017. Attention is all you need. In I. Guyon, U. V. Luxburg, S. Bengio, H. Wallach, R. Fergus, S. Vishwanathan, and R. Garnett, editors, *Advances in Neural Information Processing Systems 30*, pages 6000–6010. Curran Associates, Inc.

Adina Williams, Andrew Drozdov, and Samuel R Bowman. 2017. Learning to parse from a semantic objective: It works. is it syntax? *arXiv preprint arXiv:1709.01121.*

Hao Wu, Heyan Huang, Ping Jian, Yuhang Guo, and Chao Su. 2017. Bit at semeval-2017 task 1: Using semantic information space to evaluate semantic textual similarity. In *Proceedings of the 11th International Workshop on Semantic Evaluation (SemEval-2017)*, pages 77–84.

Multilingual seq2seq training with similarity loss for cross-lingual document classification

Katherin Yu
Facebook AML
yukatherin@fb.com

Haoran Li
Facebook AML
aimeeli@fb.com

Barlas Oguz
Facebook AML
barlaso@fb.com

Abstract

In this paper we continue the line of work where neural machine translation training is used to produce joint cross-lingual fixed-dimensional sentence embeddings. In this framework we introduce a simple method of adding a loss to the learning objective which penalizes distance between representations of bilingually aligned sentences. We evaluate cross-lingual transfer using two approaches, cross-lingual similarity search on an aligned corpus (Europarl) and cross-lingual document classification on a recently published benchmark Reuters corpus, and we find the similarity loss significantly improves performance on both. Our cross-lingual transfer performance is competitive with state-of-the-art, even while there is potential to further improve by investing in a better in-language baseline. Our results are based on a set of 6 European languages.

1 Introduction

Many real-world services collect data in many languages, and machine learning models on text need to support these languages. In practice, however, it is often only the top one or two dominant languages (usually English) which are supported because it is expensive to collect labeled training data for the task in every language. It is desirable, therefore, to obtain a representation of sequences of text that is joint across all languages, which allows for cross-lingual transfer on the languages without labeled data.

These representations typically take the form of a fixed-size embedding representing a complete sentence or document. Previous work has focused on several approaches in this setting, all of which rely on parallel corpora. In (AP et al., 2013), a predictive auto-encoder is used to reconstruct the featurized representation of a pair of sentences. (Hermann and Blunsom, 2014) constructs a bilingual sentence embedding by minimizing the squared distance between the embeddings of parallel sentences. (Pham et al., 2015) learns a common representation by simultaneously predicting n-grams in both languages from a common vector. In (Mogadala and Rettinger, 2016), a similarity measure is used to minimize distance on both the sentence embeddings, and the average of the word embeddings of a pair of sentences. A method is also proposed to apply this approach to label-aligned corpora in the absence of sentence-aligned corpora by doing a pre-alignment.

Finally, multilingual representations can be learned using a sequence-to-sequence encoder-decoder neural machine translation (NMT) architecture, such as the one introduced in (Sutskever et al., 2014). Multilingual encoders have been successfully demonstrated in the NMT setting (Dong et al., 2015; Firat et al., 2017, 2016; Johnson et al., 2016). Recently (Schwenk et al., 2017) has proposed using this framework for generating multilingual sentence representations and apply it to cross-lingual document classification.

In this paper, we combine this NMT approach with the pairwise similarity approach to obtain better representations. In section 2 we describe our framework. Then in section 4 we present an evaluation of our method based on measuring similarity on the multiply aligned Europarl corpus (Koehn, 2005). Section 5 contains our cross-lingual document classification experiments on the balanced version of the Reuters Corpus Volume 2 dataset (RCV2b), recently published by resampling from the Reuters Corpus Volume 2 to have a balanced distribution of languages and a similar label distribution for each language (Schwenk and Li, 2018).

Proceedings of the 3rd Workshop on Representation Learning for NLP, pages 175–179
Melbourne, Australia, July 20, 2018. ©2018 Association for Computational Linguistics

Table 1: SentEval results: performance as a sentence encoder in English

Method	SST	MR	CR	MPQA	SUBJ	TREC	Average
(Conneau et al., 2017) BLSTM, maxpool	81.1	86.3	92.4	90.2	84.6	88.2	87.1
ours, with similarity, meanpool	80.3	73.9	77.5	85.6	90.9	88.0	82.7
ours, with similarity, maxpool	80.4	75.0	79.6	87.3	91.1	88.0	83.56
ours, with similarity, self-attention	80.2	74.3	84.3	88.0	91.8	93.1	85.28

2 Multilingual encoder with similarity loss

We build mostly on the work of (Schwenk et al., 2017) of training an encoder to produce a fixed-dimensional vector representation based on an aggregation over the encoder hidden states. Our setup involves a single shared encoder and decoder with six languages: English, German, French, Spanish, Italian, and Portuguese. We pair languages with English and Spanish, giving 10 unique pairings. The shared vocabulary is of size 85k.

The encoder consists of a two-layer LSTM with hidden sizes 512 and 1024, where the first layer is bidirectional. The decoder is an LSTM without attention, with hidden size 1024. Sentence representations will thus be 1024-dimensional.

We follow the method of prepending a token representing the target language as a first input for the decoder (Johnson et al., 2016). This avoids target-language specific encoder representations since the target language token is not an input to the encoder. We use gradient clipping with max norm 5. We use multi-cca trained word embeddings (Ammar et al., 2016) and allow trainable word embeddings.

2.1 Bilingual batch sampling

Our approach relies on bilingually aligned data. We do not assume multiply aligned (n-way parallel) data, even though we have it in training corpora such as Europarl. Inspired by the m:1 approach in (Schwenk et al., 2017), we train translation in both directions in each batch of bilingually aligned data.

2.2 Translation and similarity loss

We use the average over encoder hidden states to initialize the decoder, and also as a constant input to the decoder at each position, without using attention. The decoder then produces a probability distribution $p_d(t|h)$ on the space of output sequences conditioned on the output of the encoder. Given a set of translation pairs (s, t), let $h(s)$ be the sentence embedding, an elementwise mean of the hidden states of the encoder. The translation loss penalizes the negative log likelihood of the target sequence, given the source:

$$L_{NMT} = \frac{1}{n_t} \sum_{j=1}^{n_t} - \log p_d(t_j | t_1, \cdots, t_{j-1}; h(s))$$

Meanwhile the similarity loss directly minimizes the distance between the embeddings of s and t:

$$L_{sim} = \| h(s) - h(t) \|_2^2$$

We combine these into our final loss term, adding weight regularization on the encoder:

$$L = (L_{NMT}^{src \to tgt} + L_{NMT}^{tgt \to src}) + \alpha L_{sim},$$

where α needs to be chosen to balance the contributions from each term. Note that similarity loss by itself would have a degenerate solution, which is to map all inputs to a constant embedding vector. Introducing negative sampling or a contrastive loss would improve this situation. Note also that both the similarity loss has a regularization effect on the encoder weights. We also try replacing similarity loss term with an L2 norm on the encoder weights. We believe that regularizing encoder weights is important for cross-lingual transfer in that it helps prevent the encoder from "splitting" its output space by source language distribution.

The choice of α depends on relative batch / weight normalization, the distribution of initial word embeddings, hidden size, and other factors. We find that starting with the two terms having comparable value is a good place to start tuning. We tune these parameters to one cross-lingual transfer task (Europarl similarity between De, En, Es).

Training takes about 1.5 days on 4 GPUs for 6 languages with 10 directions. All results are using a single trained encoder in with- and without-similarity loss settings.

Table 2: Europarl (5k) similarity retrieval accuracy from training { without encoder regularization / with encoder weight regularization / with similarity loss }. Some combinations are omitted for space.

| | Retrieved language | | | | | | |
	De	En	Es	Fr	It	Pt	All
De	(96.9 / 96.9 / 96.8)	87.0 / 89.2 / 89.8	86.7 // 90.0	85.3 // 89.4	83.2 // 87.2	85.8 // 90.1	87.5 / 89.4 / 90.6
En	85.5 / 89.1 / 88.3	(97.2 / 97.1 / 97.2)	89.9 // 92.4	88.3 // 91.3	86.1 // 89.9	89.4 // 92.0	89.4 / 91.6 / 91.9
Es	85.4 / 87.8 / 87.8	90.2 / 92.0 / **92.4**	(97.1 // 97.0)	88.8 // 91.6	87.5 // **90.9**	91.1 // **93.2**	90.0 / 91.9 / 92.2
Fr	83.8 / 87.4 / 87.8	88.9 / 91.1 / 91.9	89.0 // 92.1	(97.0 // 97.0)	86.2 // 89.8	89.1 // 91.8	89.0 / 91.4 / 91.8
It	82.2 / 85.3 / 85.9	86.7 / 89.4 / 90.3	87.7 // 90.8	86.6 // 90.0	(97.0 // 97.1)	86.9 // 90.9	87.8 / 90.3 / 90.8
Pt	84.5 / 87.6 / **87.9**	90.0 / 91.2 / 92.2	91.0 // **93.0**	88.8 // **91.7**	86.6 // 90.1	(97.3 // 97.3)	89.7 / 91.6 / 92.0
All	86.4 / 89.0 / 89.2	90.0 / 91.7 / 92.3	90.2 // 92.6	89.1 // 91.8	87.8 // 90.8	89.9 // 92.6	88.9 / 91.0 / 91.6

Table 3: Example top 3 retrieved sentences in Europarl 5k: the correctly retrieved sentence is omitted.

Retrieving sentence	*Retrieved (It)*	*Retrieved (Fr)*
Mr President, as it is now Christmas, I would be grateful if you would allow me to speak for a moment.	Signor Presidente, resto in Aula perché mi è stato fatto sapere che, per poter presentare una dichiarazione di voto, occorre essere presenti. Signora Presidente, prendo la parola soltanto per chiedere che, per ragioni ovvie, sia messo a verbale che mi asterrò in questa votazione, visto che mi riguarda in modo diretto.	Monsieur le Président, je reste ici parce que l'on m'a expliqué qu'il fallait être présent dans l'hémicycle pour être autorisé à déposer des explications de vote. Puisque M. Prodi est présent, je vais lui donner la parole en premier, s'il accepte.

3 English performance

We first evaluate our sentence embeddings on a set of English transfer tasks (SentEval). We compare mean pooling, max pooling, and self-attention (Lin et al., 2017) as aggregation methods, with an MLP with one hidden layer of size 128. Our results are several points lower than current best SentEval results.

4 Cross-lingual similarity search

As one of our evaluation methods, we follow (Schwenk et al., 2017) in validating that the closest sentence in an aligned corpus based on our sentence embeddings is the aligned sentence. We use cosine similarity. We use a Europarl development set of 5k sentences across 6 languages and report the accuracy of retrieval in each direction. Note that the corpus has duplicates, thus retrieval cannot be perfect, as reflected in the in-language results. We notice that Portuguese is best for retrieving Spanish sentences and Spanish is best for retrieving Italian and Portuguese sentences.

The results are shown in table 2. As a baseline, we take our setup with NMT loss only, and compare the results with similarity loss added. We see that both encoder weight regularization and similarity loss significantly improve retrieval performance, with similarity loss possibly slightly better.

5 Cross-lingual document classification

One of the main motivations for pursuing multilingual sentence embeddings is to achieve cross-lingual transfer on NLP tasks such as document classification. The multilingual Reuters News Corpus has been adopted as a standard dataset for this task. We will be using a version of this dataset that has been subsampled to obtain even label distribution prior across languages (Schwenk and Li, 2018), to make the interpretation of transfer results easier.

For these tests, we use a linear classifier (logistic regression) and tune the regularization parameter to the development set defined in RCV2Balanced.

5.1 Document segmentation

Method	Mean accuracy
Punctuation, meanpool	74.6
Punctuation, maxpool	67.0
Fixed window, meanpool	73.5
Fixed window, maxpool	68.2

Table 5: Comparison of aggregation methods for document embedding (RCV2Balanced)

Documents in the Reuters corpus are composed of many sentences. In principle, it is possible consider each document as a long sequence and use the resulting embedding from our encoder as-is;

Table 4: Cross-lingual document classification results (RCV2Balanced): from training { without encoder regularization / with similarity loss }. Zero-shot paradigm. Bold indicates best result for target language.

	De	En	Es	Fr	It	Ru	All
De	(91.1 / 90.5)	76.8 / 77.1	67.2 / 76.4	75.3 / **81.7**	63.5 / 71.8	49.5 / 60.5	70.5 / 73.3
En	72.9 / 80.2	(89.0 / 89.4)	72.2 / 74.1	73.0 / 81.0	63.4 / 70.8	60.9 / **65.7**	71.9 / 76.8
Es	76.4 / 79.5	74.1 / 73.4	(92.0 / 92.4)	78.1 / 78.9	68.2 / 72.0	58.7 / 58.0	74.6 / 75.7
Fr	79.5 / **82.5**	79.0 / **80.8**	77.1 / 76.5	(87.5 / 89.9)	68.1 / **72.7**	63.4 / 59.4	75.7 / 77.0
It	76.6 / 78.3	74.8 / 71.2	**76.8** // 75.5	66.8 / 74.0	(81.3 / 81.8)	63.8 / 55.9	73.3 / 72.8
Ru	74.2 / 70.0	72.3 / 71.3	56.3 / 61.8	69.5 / 66.5	64.9 / 60.9	(82.2 / 84.0)	69.9 / 69.1
All	78.4 / 80.2	77.6 / 77.2	73.6 / 76.1	75.0 / 78.7	68.2 / 71.7	63.1 / 63.9	72.7 / 74.6
LOO	- / 78.5	- / (89.4)	- / 73.0	- / 80.5	- / 70.0	- / 65.6	- / (76.2)

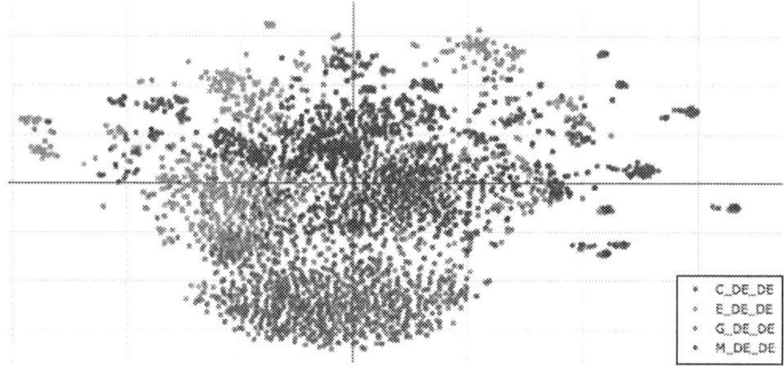

Figure 1: t-SNE projection of document embeddings in RCV2Balanced, De test set

however, our encoder would have problems representing such long input sequences with fixed dimensional embeddings, especially because no attention mechanism is present. As a result, we need a method to split a document into smaller sequences, and an aggregation method to go from short sequence embeddings to a document embedding. For splitting we consider simply using the sentences, delimited by punctuation (the characters [.!?]). We also try splitting by a fixed window size (128 words) and fixed stride (64 words). For aggregation, we try elementwise mean- and max-pooling. We find that splitting on punctuation and using mean pooling works best (Table 5).

5.2 Evaluation paradigms

Evaluation paradigm	Mean accuracy
Zero-shot transfer	74.6
Targeted transfer	75.6

Table 6: Comparison of tuning to source- versus target-language development data

Following (Schwenk and Li, 2018), we use two transfer learning paradigms: zero-shot learning and targeted transfer. In zero-shot learning, we tune regularization hyperparameters to the development set in the training/source language and test on the transfer/target language, and the trained model is the same for all directions with the same source; in targeted transfer, we tune these paramaters to the target development set and each model is unique for each dialect direction.

Results are compiled in table 4. It can be seen that adding similarity loss significantly improves over our baseline on average by nearly 2 points. Our best results per target language are better than best results per target language in the zero-shot paradigm in (Schwenk and Li, 2018) using word embeddings and sentence embeddings; however, these are not directly comparable given we are using significantly more training data. Finally, Figure 1 shows a t-SNE representation of the document embeddings over the four classes on a sample of RCVBalanced dataset.

We also try "leaving one out" (LOO) where we pool training data over all languages except the target to augment training data, while tuning to the English development set. However results do not improve over the best single-language transfer numbers (last row in table 4).

6   Conclusion

We presented an improved method for training multi-lingual sentence embeddings, including higher benchmark results for the RCV2 balanced dataset. We showed that including an explicit similarity loss combined with the encoder-decoder framework improves the quality of multilingual representations. We demonstrated that our representations allow better transfer from one language to another of document classification performance.

We note that although we have shown improvements in RCV2Balanced, our English-only SentEval results are lagging state-of-the-art by at least 2 points. For future work, it is conceivable that starting from a fixed state-of-the-art English encoder (possibly with multitask training with a fixed decoder joint with the English encoder), the similarity loss method could be used to produce the same relative cross-lingual quality while preserving strong in-language performance.

Acknowledgments

We wish to thank Veselin Stoyanov for his mentorship, and our anonymous reviewers for their insightful comments. We look forward to improving this work.

References

Waleed Ammar, George Mulcaire, Yulia Tsvetkov, Guillaume Lample, Chris Dyer, and Noah A Smith. 2016. Massively multilingual word embeddings. *arXiv preprint arXiv:1602.01925.*

Sarath Chandar AP, Mitesh M Khapra, Balaraman Ravindran, Vikas Raykar, and Amrita Saha. 2013. Multilingual deep learning. *NIPS DL workshop.*

Alexis Conneau, Douwe Kiela, Holger Schwenk, Loic Barrault, and Antoine Bordes. 2017. Supervised learning of universal sentence representations from natural language inference data. *arXiv preprint arXiv:1705.02364.*

Daxiang Dong, Hua Wu, Wei He, Dianhai Yu, and Haifeng Wang. 2015. Multi-task learning for multiple language translation. *Proceedings of ACL-IJNLP.*

Orhan Firat, Kyunghyun Cho, Baskaran Sankaran, Fatos T Yarman Vural, and Yoshua Bengio. 2017. Multi-way, multilingual neural machine translation. *Computer Speech & Language*, 45:236–252.

Orhan Firat, Baskaran Sankaran, Yaser Al-Onaizan, Fatos T Yarman Vural, and Kyunghyun Cho. 2016. Zero-resource translation with multilingual neural machine translation. *arXiv preprint arXiv:1606.04164.*

Karl Moritz Hermann and Phil Blunsom. 2014. Multilingual models for compositional distributed semantics. *arXiv preprint arXiv:1404.4641.*

Melvin Johnson, Mike Schuster, Quoc V Le, Maxim Krikun, Yonghui Wu, Zhifeng Chen, Nikhil Thorat, Fernanda Viégas, Martin Wattenberg, Greg Corrado, et al. 2016. Google's multilingual neural machine translation system: enabling zero-shot translation. *arXiv preprint arXiv:1611.04558.*

Philipp Koehn. 2005. Europarl: A Parallel Corpus for Statistical Machine Translation. In *Conference Proceedings: the tenth Machine Translation Summit*, pages 79–86, Phuket, Thailand. AAMT, AAMT.

Zhouhan Lin, Minwei Feng, Cicero Nogueira dos Santos, Mo Yu, Bing Xiang, Bowen Zhou, and Yoshua Bengio. 2017. A structured self-attentive sentence embedding. *eprint arXiv:1703.03130.*

Aditya Mogadala and Achim Rettinger. 2016. Bilingual word embeddings from parallel and non-parallel corpora for cross-language text classification. In *Proceedings of the 2016 Conference of the North American Chapter of the Association for Computational Linguistics: Human Language Technologies*, pages 692–702.

Hieu Pham, Thang Luong, and Christopher Manning. 2015. Learning distributed representations for multilingual text sequences. In *Proceedings of the 1st Workshop on Vector Space Modeling for Natural Language Processing*, pages 88–94.

Holger Schwenk and Xian Li. 2018. A corpus for multilingual document classification in eight languages. In *Eleventh International Conference on Language Resources and Evaluation (LREC'18)*. European Language Resources Association (ELRA).

Holger Schwenk, Ke Tran, Orhan Firat, and Matthijs Douze. 2017. Learning joint multilingual sentence representations with neural machine translation. *arXiv preprint arXiv:1704.04154.*

Ilya Sutskever, Oriol Vinyals, and Quoc V Le. 2014. Sequence to sequence learning with neural networks. In *Advances in neural information processing systems*, pages 3104–3112.

LSTMs Exploit Linguistic Attributes of Data

Nelson F. Liu[♠◇]   **Omer Levy**[♠]   **Roy Schwartz**[♠♣]   **Chenhao Tan**[♡]   **Noah A. Smith**[♠]

[♠]Paul G. Allen School of Computer Science & Engineering, University of Washington, Seattle, WA, USA
[◇]Department of Linguistics, University of Washington, Seattle, WA, USA
[♣]Allen Institute for Artificial Intelligence, Seattle, WA, USA
[♡]Department of Computer Science, University of Colorado, Boulder, CO, USA
`{nfliu,omerlevy,roysch,nasmith}@cs.washington.edu`,
`chenhao.tan@colorado.edu`

Abstract

While recurrent neural networks have found success in a variety of natural language processing applications, they are general models of sequential data. We investigate how the properties of natural language data affect an LSTM's ability to learn a nonlinguistic task: recalling elements from its input. We find that models trained on natural language data are able to recall tokens from much longer sequences than models trained on non-language sequential data. Furthermore, we show that the LSTM learns to solve the memorization task by explicitly using a subset of its neurons to count timesteps in the input. We hypothesize that the patterns and structure in natural language data enable LSTMs to learn by providing approximate ways of reducing loss, but understanding the effect of different training data on the learnability of LSTMs remains an open question.

1 Introduction

Recurrent neural networks (RNNs; Elman, 1990), especially variants with gating mechanisms such as long short-term memory units (LSTM; Hochreiter and Schmidhuber, 1997) and gated recurrent units (GRU; Cho et al., 2014), have significantly advanced the state of the art in many NLP tasks (Mikolov et al., 2010; Vinyals et al., 2015; Bahdanau et al., 2015, among others). However, RNNs are general models of sequential data; they are not explicitly designed to capture the unique properties of language that distinguish it from generic time series data.

In this work, we probe how linguistic properties such as the hierarchical structure of language (Everaert et al., 2015), the dependencies between tokens, and the Zipfian distribution of token frequencies (Zipf, 1935) affect the ability of LSTMs to learn. To do this, we define a simple memorization task where the objective is to recall the identity of the token that occurred a fixed number of timesteps in the past, within a fixed-length input. Although the task itself is not linguistic, we use it because (1) it is a generic operation that might form part of a more complex function on arbitrary sequential data, and (2) its simplicity allows us to unfold the mechanism in the trained RNNs.

To study how linguistic properties of the training data affect an LSTM's ability to solve the memorization task, we consider several training regimens. In the first, we train on data sampled from a uniform distribution over a fixed vocabulary. In the second, the token frequencies have a Zipfian distribution, but are otherwise independent of each other. In another, the token frequencies have a Zipfian distribution but we add Markovian dependencies to the data. Lastly, we train the model on natural language sequences. To ensure that the models truly memorize, we evaluate on uniform samples containing *only rare words*.[1]

We observe that LSTMs trained to perform the memorization task on natural language data or data with a Zipfian distribution are able to memorize from sequences of greater length than LSTMs trained on uniformly-sampled data. Interestingly, increasing the length of Markovian dependencies in the data does not significantly help LSTMs to learn the task. We conclude that linguistic properties can help or even enable LSTMs to learn the memorization task. Why this is the case remains an open question, but we propose that the additional structure and patterns within natural language data provide additional noisy, approximate

---

[1]This distribution is adversarial with respect to the Zipfian and natural language training sets.

Proceedings of the 3rd Workshop on Representation Learning for NLP, pages 180–186
Melbourne, Australia, July 20, 2018. ©2018 Association for Computational Linguistics

paths for the model to minimize its loss, thus offering more training signal than the uniform case, in which the only way to reduce the loss is to learn the memorization function.

We further inspect *how* the LSTM solves the memorization task, and find that some hidden units count the number of inputs. Shi et al. (2016a) analyzed LSTM encoder-decoder translation models and found that similar counting neurons regulate the length of generated translations. Since LSTMs better memorize (and thus better count) on language data than on non-language data, and counting plays a role in encoder-decoder models, our work could also lead to improved training for sequence-to-sequence models in non-language applications (e.g., Schwaller et al., 2017).

2 The Memorization Task

To assess the ability of LSTMs to retain and use information, we propose a simple memorization task. The model is presented with a sequence of tokens and is trained to recall the identity of the middle token.[2] We predict the middle token since predicting items near the beginning or the end might enable the model to avoid processing long sequences (e.g., to perfectly memorize the last token, simply set the forget gate to 0 and the input gate to 1).[3] All input sequences at train and test time are of equal length. To explore the effect of sequence length on LSTM task performance, we experiment with different input sequence lengths $(10, 20, 40, 60, \ldots, 300)$.

3 Experimental Setup

We modify the linguistic properties of the training data and observe the effects on model performance. Further details are found in Appendix A, and we release code for reproducing our results.[4]

Model. We train an LSTM-based sequence prediction model to perform the memorization task. The model embeds input tokens with a randomly initialized embedding matrix. The embedded inputs are encoded by a single-layer LSTM and the final hidden state is passed through a linear projection to produce a probability distribution over the

vocabulary.

Our goal is to evaluate the memorization ability of the LSTM, so we freeze the weights of the embedding matrix and the linear output projection during training. This forces the model to rely on the LSTM parameters (the only trainable weights), since it cannot gain an advantage in the task by shifting words favorably in either the (random) input or output embedding vector spaces. We also tie the weights of the embeddings and output projection so the LSTM can focus on memorizing the timestep of interest rather than also transforming input vectors to the output embedding space.[5] Finally, to examine the effect of model capacity on memorization ability, we experiment with different hidden state size values.

Datasets. We experiment with several distributions of training data for the memorization task. In all cases, a 10K vocabulary is used.

- In the *uniform* setup, each token in the training dataset is randomly sampled from a uniform distribution over the vocabulary.

- In the *unigram* setup, we modify the *uniform* data by integrating the Zipfian token frequencies found in natural language data. The input sequences are taken from a modified version of the Penn Treebank (Marcus et al., 1993) with randomly permuted tokens.

- In the *5gram*, *10gram*, and *50gram* settings, we seek to augment the *unigram* setting with Markovian dependencies. We generate the dataset by grouping the tokens of the Penn Treebank into 5, 10, or 50-length chunks and randomly permuting these chunks.

- In the *language* setup, we assess the effect of using real language. The input sequences here are taken from the Penn Treebank, and thus this setup further extends the *5gram*, *10gram*, and *50gram* datasets by adding the remaining structural properties of natural language.

We evaluate each model on a test set of uniformly sampled tokens from the 100 rarest words in the vocabulary. This evaluation setup ensures that, regardless of the data distribution the models were trained on, they are forced to generalize in

---

[2]Or the $(\frac{n}{2} + 1)$th token if the sequence length n is even.

[3]We experimented with predicting tokens at a range of positions, and our results are not sensitive to the choice of predicting *exactly* the middle token.

[4]http://nelsonliu.me/papers/
lstms-exploit-linguistic-attributes/

[5]Tying these weights constrains the embedding size to always equal the LSTM hidden state size.

order to perform well on the test set. For instance, in a test on data with a Zipfian token distribution, the model may do well by simply exploiting the training distribution (e.g., by ignoring the long tail of rare words).

4 Results

We first observe that, in every case, the LSTM is able to perform the task perfectly (or nearly so), up to some input sequence length threshold. Once the input sequence length exceeds this threshold, performance drops rapidly.

How does the training data distribution affect performance on the memorization task? Figure 1 compares memorization performance of an LSTM with 50 hidden units on various input sequence lengths when training on each of the datasets. Recall that the test set of only rare words is fixed for each length, regardless of the training data. When trained on the *uniform* dataset, the model is perfect up to length 10, but does no better than the random baseline with lengths above 10. Training on the *unigram* setting enables the model to memorize from longer sequences (up to 20), but it begins to fail with input sequences of length 40; evaluation accuracy quickly falls to 0.[6] Adding Markovian dependencies to the *unigram* dataset leads to small improvements, enabling the LSTM to successfully learn on inputs of up to length 40 (in the case of *5gram* and *10gram*) and inputs of up to length 60 (in the case of *50gram*). Lastly, training on *language* significantly improves model performance, and it is able to perfectly memorize with input sequences of up to 160 tokens before any significant degradation. These results clearly indicate that training on data with linguistic properties helps the LSTM learn the non-linguistic task of memorization, even though the test set has an adversarial non-linguistic distribution.

How does adding hidden units affect memorization performance? Figure 2 compares memorization performance on each dataset for LSTMs with 50, 100, and 200 hidden units. When training on the *uniform* dataset, increasing the number of LSTM hidden units (and thus also the embedding size) to 100 or 200 does not help it memorize longer sequences. Indeed, even at 400

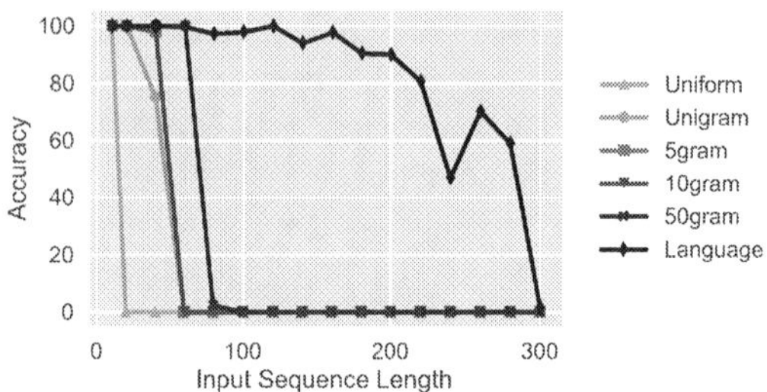

Figure 1: Test set accuracy of LSTMs with 50 hidden units trained on the *uniform*, *gram*, and *language* datasets with various input sequence lengths. *5gram* and *10gram* perform nearly identically, so the differences may not be apparent in the figure. *unigram* accuracy plateaus to 0, and *uniform* accuracy plateaus to ≈0.01% (random baseline). Best viewed in color.

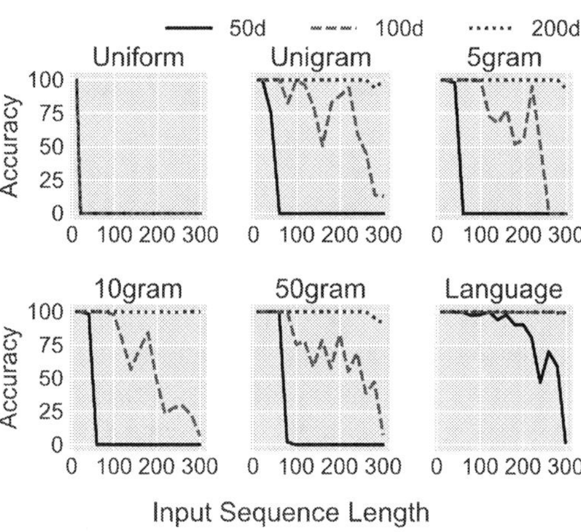

Figure 2: Test set accuracy of LSTMs with 50, 100 or 200 hidden units trained on each dataset with various input sequence lengths.

and 800 we saw no improvement (not shown in Figure 2). When training on any of the other datasets, adding more hidden units eventually leads to perfect memorization for all tested input sequence lengths. We take these results as a suggestion that successful learning for this task requires sufficiently high capacity (dimensionality in the LSTM). The capacity need is diminished when the training data is linguistic, but LSTMs trained on the *uniform* set cannot learn the memorization task even given high capacity.

---

[6]Manual inspection of the trained models reveals that they predict the most frequent words in the corpus. Since the evaluation set has only the 100 rarest types, performance (0% accuracy) is actually worse than in the *uniform* setting.

5 Analysis

Throughout this section, we analyze an LSTM with 100 hidden units trained with the *language* setting with an input sequence length of 300. This setting is a somewhat closer simulation of current NLP models, since it is trained on real language and recalls perfectly with input sequence lengths of 300 (the most difficult setting tested).

How do LSTMs solve the memorization task? A simple way to solve the memorization task is by counting. Since all of the input sequences are of equal length and the timestep to predict is constant throughout training and testing, a successful learner could maintain a counter from the start of the input to the position of the token to be predicted (the middle item). Then, it discards its previous cell state, consumes the label's vector, and maintains this new cell state until the end of the sequence (i.e., by setting its forget gate near 1 and its input gate near 0).

While LSTMs clearly have the expressive power needed to count and memorize, whether they can learn to do so from data is another matter. Past work has demonstrated that the LSTMs in an encoder-decoder machine translation model learn to increment and decrement a counter to generate translations of proper length (Shi et al., 2016a) and that representations produced by auto-encoding LSTMs contain information about the input sequence length (Adi et al., 2017). Our experiments isolate the counting aspect from other linguistic properties of translation and autoencoding (which may indeed be correlated with counting), and also test this ability with an adversarial test distribution and much longer input sequences.

We adopt the method of Shi et al. (2016a) to investigate whether LSTMs solve the memorization task by learning to count. We identify the neurons that best predict timestep information by fitting a linear regression model to predict the number of inputs seen from the hidden unit activation. When evaluating on the test set, we observe that the LSTM cell state as a whole is very predictive of the timestep, with $R^2 = 0.998$.

While no single neuron perfectly records the timestep, several of them are strongly correlated. In our model instance, neuron 77 has the highest correlation ($R^2 = 0.919$), and neuron 61 is next ($R^2 = 0.901$). The activations of these neurons over time for a random correctly classified test in-

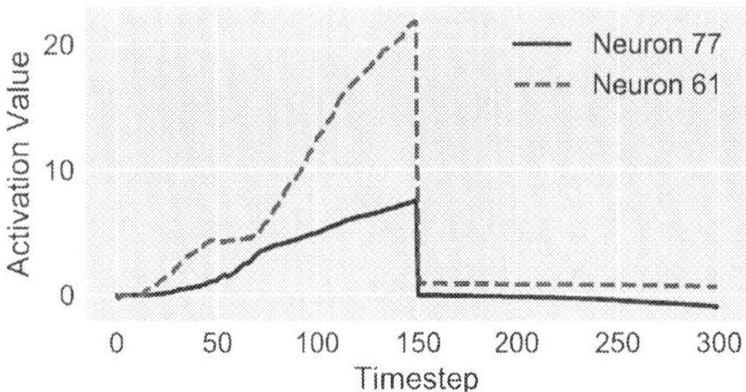

Figure 3: Activations of the neurons at indices 77 and 61 over time, showing counter-like behavior up to the target timestep to be remembered.

put linearly increase up to the target token, after which the activations falls to nearly 0 (Figure 3).

One hypothesis for why linguistic data helps. During training, the LSTM must: (1) determine what the objective is (here, "remember the middle token") and (2) adjust its weights to minimize loss. We observed that adding hidden units to LSTMs trained on *unigram* or *language* sets improves their ability to learn from long input sequences, but does not affect LSTMs trained on the *uniform* dataset. One explanation for this disparity is that LSTMs trained on *uniform* data are simply not learning what the task is—they do not realize that the label always matches the token in the middle of the input sequence, and thus they cannot properly optimize for the task, even with more hidden units. On the other hand, models trained on *unigram* or *language* can determine that the label is always the middle token, and can thus learn the task. Minimizing training loss ought to be easier with more parameters, so adding hidden units to LSTMs trained on data with linguistic attributes increases the length of input sequences that they can learn from.

But why might LSTMs trained on data with linguistic attributes be able to effectively learn the task for long input sequences, whereas LSTMs trained on the *uniform* dataset cannot? We conjecture that linguistic data offers more reasonable, if approximate, pathways to loss minimization, such as counting frequent words or phrases. In the *uniform* setting, the model has only one path to success: true memorization, and it cannot find an effective way to reduce the loss. In other words, linguistic structure and the patterns of language may provide additional signals that correlate with the label and facilitate learning the memorization task.

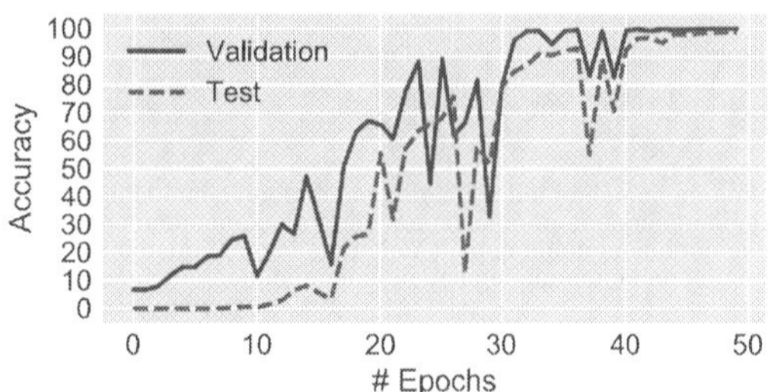

Figure 4: Model validation and test accuracy over time during training. Validation improves faster than test, indicating that the model exploits linguistic properties of the data during training.

Figure 4 shows that models trained on the *unigram* and *language* datasets converge to high validation accuracy faster than high test accuracy. This suggests that models trained on data with linguistic attributes first learn to do well on the training data by exploiting the properties of language and not truly memorizing. Perhaps the model generalizes to actually recalling the target token later, as it refines itself with examples from the long tail of infrequent tokens.

Figure 4 may show this shift from exploiting linguistic properties to true memorization. The validation and test accuracy curves are quite synchronized from epoch 37 onward, indicating that the model's updates affect both sets identically. The model clearly learns a strategy that works well on both datasets, which strongly suggests that it has learned to memorize. In addition, when the model begins to move toward true memorization, we'd expect validation accuracy to momentarily falter as it moves away from the crutches of linguistic features—this may be the dip at around epoch 35 from perfect validation accuracy to around 95% accuracy.

6   Related Work

To our knowledge, this work is the first to study how linguistic properties in training data affect the ability of LSTMs to learn a general, non-linguistic, sequence processing task.

Previous studies have sought to better understand the empirical capabilities of LSTMs trained on natural language data. Linzen et al. (2016) measured the ability of LSTMs to learn syntactic long range dependencies commonly found in language, and Gulordava et al. (2018) provide evidence that LSTMs can learn the hierarchical struc-

ture of language. Blevins et al. (2018) show that the internal representations of LSTMs encode syntactic information, even when trained without explicit syntactic supervision.

Also related is the work of Weiss et al. (2018), who demonstrate that LSTMs are able to count infinitely, since their cell states are unbounded, while GRUs cannot count infinitely since the activations are constrained to a finite range. One avenue of future work could compare the performance of LSTMs and GRUs on the memorization task.

Past studies have also investigated what information RNNs encode by directly examining hidden unit activations (Karpathy et al., 2016; Li et al., 2016; Shi et al., 2016a, among others) and by training an auxiliary classifier to predict various properties of interest from hidden state vectors (Shi et al., 2016b; Adi et al., 2017; Belinkov et al., 2017, among others).

7   Conclusion

In this work, we examine how linguistic attributes in training data can affect an LSTM's ability to learn a simple memorization task. We find that LSTMs trained on uniformly sampled data are only able to learn the task with the sequence length of 10, whereas LSTMs trained with language data are able to learn on sequences of up to 300 tokens.

We further investigate how the LSTM learns to solve the task, and find that it uses a subset of its hidden units to track timestep information. It is still an open question why LSTMs trained on linguistic data are able to learn the task whereas LSTMs trained on uniformly sampled data cannot; based on our observations, we hypothesize that the additional patterns and structure in language-based data may provide the model with approximate paths of loss minimization, and improve LSTM trainability as a result.

Acknowledgments

We thank the ARK as well as the anonymous reviewers for their valuable feedback. NL is supported by a Washington Research Foundation Fellowship and a Barry M. Goldwater Scholarship. This work was supported in part by a hardware gift from NVIDIA Corporation and a UW High Performance Computing Club Cloud Credit Award.

References

Yossi Adi, Einat Kermany, Yonatan Belinkov, Ofer Lavi, and Yoav Goldberg. 2017. Fine-grained analysis of sentence embeddings using auxiliary prediction tasks. In *Proc. of ICLR*.

Dzmitry Bahdanau, Kyunghyun Cho, and Yoshua Bengio. 2015. Neural machine translation by jointly learning to align and translate. In *Proc. of ICLR*.

Yonatan Belinkov, Nadir Durrani, Fahim Dalvi, Hassan Sajjad, and James Glass. 2017. What do neural machine translation models learn about morphology? In *Proc. of ACL*.

Terra Blevins, Omer Levy, and Luke Zettlemoyer. 2018. Deep RNNs learn hierarchical syntax. In *Proc. of ACL*.

Kyunghyun Cho, Bart van Merrienboer, Çaglar Gülçehre, Dzmitry Bahdanau, Fethi Bougares, Holger Schwenk, and Yoshua Bengio. 2014. Learning phrase representations using RNN encoder-decoder for statistical machine translation. In *Proc. of EMNLP*.

Jeffrey L. Elman. 1990. Finding structure in time. *Cognitive Science*, 14:179–211.

Martin B.H. Everaert, Marinus A.C. Huybregts, Noam Chomsky, Robert C. Berwick, and Johan J. Bolhuis. 2015. Structures, not strings: linguistics as part of the cognitive sciences. *Trends in Cognitive Sciences*, 19(12):729–743.

Kristina Gulordava, Piotr Bojanowski, Edouard Grave, Tal Linzen, and Marco Baroni. 2018. Colorless green recurrent networks dream hierarchically. In *Proc. of NAACL*.

Sepp Hochreiter and Jürgen Schmidhuber. 1997. Long short-term memory. *Neural Computation*, 9 8:1735–80.

Andrej Karpathy, Justin Johnson, and Li Fei-Fei. 2016. Visualizing and understanding recurrent networks. In *Proc. of ICLR*.

Diederik P. Kingma and Jimmy Ba. 2015. Adam: a method for stochastic optimization. In *Proc. of ICLR*.

Jiwei Li, Xinlei Chen, Eduard Hovy, and Dan Jurafsky. 2016. Visualizing and understanding neural models in NLP. In *Proc. of NAACL*.

Tal Linzen, Emmanuel Dupoux, and Yoav Goldberg. 2016. Assessing the ability of LSTMs to learn syntax-sensitive dependencies. *Transactions of the Association of Computational Linguistics*, 4(1):521–535.

Mitchell P. Marcus, Mary Ann Marcinkiewicz, and Beatrice Santorini. 1993. Building a large annotated corpus of English: the Penn Treebank. *Computational Linguistics*, 19(2):313–330.

Tomáš Mikolov, Martin Karafiát, Lukás Burget, Jan Cernocký, and Sanjeev Khudanpur. 2010. Recurrent neural network based language model. In *Proc. of INTERSPEECH*.

Tomáš Mikolov, Stefan Kombrink, Lukáš Burget, Jan Černocký, and Sanjeev Khudanpur. 2011. Extensions of recurrent neural network language model. In *Proc of. ICASSP*.

Philippe Schwaller, Theophile Gaudin, David Lanyi, Costas Bekas, and Teodoro Laino. 2017. "found in translation": predicting outcomes of complex organic chemistry reactions using neural sequence-to-sequence models. In *Proc. of NIPS Machine Learning for Molecules and Materials Workshop*.

Xing Shi, Kevin Knight, and Deniz Yuret. 2016a. Why neural translations are the right length. In *Proc. of EMNLP*.

Xing Shi, Inkit Padhi, and Kevin Knight. 2016b. Does string-based neural MT learn source syntax? In *Proc. of EMNLP*.

Oriol Vinyals, Lukasz Kaiser, Terry Koo, Slav Petrov, Ilya Sutskever, and Geoffrey E. Hinton. 2015. Grammar as a foreign language. In *Proc. of NIPS*.

Gail Weiss, Yoav Goldberg, and Eran Yahav. 2018. On the practical computational power of finite precision RNNs for language recognition. In *Proc. of ACL*.

George Kingsley Zipf. 1935. *The Psycho-biology of Language*. Houghton, Mifflin.

Appendices

A   Experimental Setup Details

Penn Treebank Processing   Our experiments use a preprocessed version of the Penn Treebank commonly used in the language modeling community and first introduced by Mikolov et al. (2011). This dataset has 10K types, hence why we use this vocabulary size for all experiments. We generate examples by concatenating the sentences together and taking subsequences of the desired input sequence length.

Training   The model is trained end-to-end to directly predict the tokens at a particular timestep in the past; it is optimized with Adam (Kingma and Ba, 2015) with an initial learning rate of 0.001, which is halved whenever the validation dataset (a held-out portion of the training dataset) loss fails to improve for three consecutive epochs. The model is trained for a maximum of 240 epochs or until it converges to perfect validation performance. We do not use dropout; we included it in initial experiments, but it severely hampered model performance and does not make much sense for a task where the goal is to explicitly memorize. We ran each experiment three times with different random seeds and evaluate the model with the highest validation accuracy on the test set. We take the best since we are interested in whether the LSTMs *can* be trained for the task.

Learning Distributional Token Representations from Visual Features

Samuel Broscheit   **Rainer Gemulla**   **Margret Keuper**
University of Mannheim, Mannheim, Germany
`{lastname}@informatik.uni-mannheim.de`

Abstract

In this study, we compare token representations constructed from visual features (i.e., pixels) with standard lookup-based embeddings. Our goal is to gain insight about the challenges of encoding a text representation from low-level features, e.g. from characters or pixels. We focus on Chinese, which—as a logographic language—has properties that make a representation via visual features challenging and interesting. To train and evaluate different models for the token representation, we chose the task of character-based neural machine translation (NMT) from Chinese to English. We found that a token representation computed only from visual features can achieve competitive results to lookup embeddings. However, we also show different strengths and weaknesses in the models' performance in a part-of-speech tagging task and also a semantic similarity task. In summary, we show that it is possible to achieve a *text representation* only from pixels. We hope that this is a useful stepping stone for future studies that exclusively rely on visual input, or aim at exploiting visual features of written language.

1 Introduction

Language representation beyond the word level can be advantageous for words from the tail of the distribution, as has been shown in recent neural approaches for various tasks (Schütze, 2017; Kim et al., 2016; Lee et al., 2017; Wu et al., 2016; Sennrich et al., 2016). In these approaches, a neural model represents an input text based on its sequence of characters or character n-grams (instead

of its words). This helps the model to handle out-of-vocabulary tokens and avoids the need of text segmentation or tokenization, which remains an unsolved problem for many languages. For some applications, e.g. language processing for social media, models should be able to capture the creative use of language. However, a disadvantage is that we loose the certainty of a known vocabulary. Also, regarding computational complexity, there is a trade-off between the memory that is required for large embedding lookup tables and the additional computational cost that is required to compose representations from low-level features.

In contrast to the characters of languages based on the Latin alphabet, the Chinese written language is defined over a set of ≈ 8000 characters that already carry meaning. The characters can either appear in a traditional or simplified form, and many share visual components that can indicate a related meaning. Thus, it is reasonable to hypothesize that encoding Chinese characters directly from their visual components might improve their token representation in a neural network model.

In recent studies, Liu et al. (2017) evaluated character encodings from visual features by classifying Wikipedia titles into 12 categories and Su and Lee (2017) evaluated such encodings by measuring correlation with human similarity judgments. Both studies found that using character encodings from visual input did not outperform or were equal to lookup-based embeddings. No support for the hypothesis above is thus provided.

In this study, we aim to explore the question of whether and when visual-feature representations are beneficial or detrimental. We make the following contributions: (i) Since the evaluation tasks from prior studies did not test the capabilities of the visual features for *text representation*, we propose to employ the task of neural machine trans-

187

Proceedings of the 3rd Workshop on Representation Learning for NLP, pages 187–194
Melbourne, Australia, July 20, 2018. ©2018 Association for Computational Linguistics

lation (NMT) for training and evaluation. We argue that NMT requires the token representation to serve as a reliable syntactic and semantic signal. (ii) Prior work reported evaluations for one architecture to encode the visual features. In this paper, we evaluate different settings and argue for architecture choices that performed well in our experiments. (iii) We provide evidence for the possibility to compute token representations from visual features that perform on-par with lookup-based embeddings in NMT. (iv) Finally, we revisit two of the tasks from prior work that use visual features: measuring correlation with semantic similarity judgments by humans as well as joint segmentation and part-of-speech tagging. We use the best models from the NMT evaluation in these two tasks. For semantic similarity, we find that token representation from pixels are clearly beneficial for unseen characters, while a lookup embedding performs better for seen characters. For joint segmentation and part-of-speech tagging we find no clear difference between lookup embeddings and character representation from pixels.

2   Related Work

We start by summarizing prior work, in which token representations were obtained from bitmaps of Chinese characters.

Su and Lee (2017) propose several embedding models for Chinese, including one from visual features. For the evaluation they create a dataset with Chinese word pairs in traditional Chinese. In their evaluation, they measure the correlation of the cosine similarity of embedded word pairs against human similarity judgments for those word pairs. In their experiments, they found that the representation from visual features was not competitive to an embedding lookup model, but a combination of lookup embeddings with visual features was. For their model, they train a 5-layer CNN auto-encoder on bitmaps of Chinese characters. The auto-encoder character representation is fed into two GRU layers and two fully connected layers with ELU activation to encode the characters into a word. The model was trained to predict the Skip-Gram objective (Mikolov et al., 2013) or the Glove objective (Pennington et al., 2014).

Liu et al. (2017) evaluate the classification of Chinese Wikipedia titles into 12 categories. They found that the representation from visual features representations was not competitive to embedding lookup models. They did find, however, that a combination of lookup-based embeddings and visual features can be beneficial. Their character encoder is a convolutional neural network (CNN). The CNN consists of 3 convolutional layers with max-pooling followed by a fully connected transformation layer with ReLU activation. The character encodings are fed as input to a recurrent neural network (RNN) that encodes the Wikipedia title. Both, character encoder and classifier were trained jointly.

Costa-jussà et al. (2017) investigate the neural machine translation from Chinese to Spanish. To investigate the helpfulness of visual features they augmented lookup embeddings by concatenating the corresponding bitmap features of the characters. They showed that this approach improved the performance of both, their character-based and their word-based NMT system. They did not study the exclusive use of visual features.

Shao et al. (2017) investigate joint part-of-speech tagging and segmentation for Chinese. In contrast to the studies mentioned above, they found that the inclusion of visual features did not help. However, in their study, the CNN encoder was not pre-trained and only a small amount of training data was available, which may explain this finding. In their approach, they augmented character and n-gram embeddings with visual features. The model is a 2-layer CNN with max-pooling and a consecutive fully-connected transformation layer. They concatenated the CNN-based character embeddings to the lookup embeddings and fed them to a BI-LSTM-CRF.

Other related approaches with regards to encoding symbols from visual features are: Deng et al. (2017) proposed to translate from images to a markup language; e.g.; images of mathematical expressions to LaTeX code. While their system performed remarkably well on those regular languages, they did not discuss their approach in the context of natural language. Remotely related is optical character recognition (OCR) and multi-model machine translation. While OCR could benefit from this study, its main goal is character recognition under noisy conditions. Multi-modal machine translation augments a main task with additional features or when the translation is from a non-textual source, e.g. images, to text (Elliott et al., 2017). In contrast, our goal is to study text representation from low-level features.

Model	transformation	activation	transformation	activation
CNN+FC+ReLU	CNN(484 → F),	BN+ReLU	FC(F → 512)	BN+ReLU
CNN+SM+FC	CNN(484 → F)	Softmax	FC(F → 512)	
CNN+ReLU	CNN(484 → 512)	BN+ReLU		
FC 1L	FC(484 → 512)			
FC 2L	FC(484 → 512)	BN+ReLU	FC(512 → 512)	

Table 1: Character encoder architectures. Abbreviations: FC = fully connected, SM = softmax, BN = Batchnorm (Ioffe and Szegedy, 2015), F = CNN output size (see Table 2).

	in	out	kernel	stride
(0): Conv2d	1	32	(3, 3)	(1, 1)
(1): ReLU				
(2): MaxPool2d			(2, 2)	(2, 2)
(3): Conv2d	32	32	(3, 3)	(1, 1)
(4): ReLU				
(5): MaxPool2d			(2, 2)	(2, 2)
(6): Conv2d	32	F	(4, 4)	(1, 1)

Table 2: Configuration of the CNN layers. F is the CNN output feature size and takes values in $[256, 512, 1024, 2048, 4096]$.

3 Character Encoding

In this section, we first describe how a tokenized text is mapped to vector representations of its tokens. Then, we describe the character encoders that we have evaluated.

3.1 Preliminaries

Neural approaches that compute a function from text input commonly map each token t_i (e.g., a word) from the input text T to a dense vector representation $\mathbf{t}_i \in \mathbb{R}^d$ via some function $D(t_i) \rightarrow \mathbf{t}_i$. Lookup-based models associate each token of a fixed vocabulary V with its own dense representation (embedding). In particular, lookup-based models use (or learn) an embedding matrix $\mathbf{E} \in \mathbb{R}^{n \times d}$, where $n = |V|$. The j-th row of $\mathbf{E}$ holds the embedding of the j-th token in the vocabulary. Thus $D(t_i) = \mathbf{e}_j^T \mathbf{E}$, where j is the token number of token t_i in V and $\mathbf{e}_j$ denotes the j-th standard basis vector.

If we represent each character from its visual features—i.e., the pixels of its bitmap image—, we compute the embedding instead of performing a lookup in an embedding matrix. In particular, $D(t_i)$ computes a dense representation of token t_i from its pixels $p(t_i)$ via a character encoder C. Therefore, there is no fixed vocabulary of tokens any more. We have $D(t_i) = C(p(t_i))$.

3.2 Character Encoders

As discussed in Section 2, most of the prior related work—except Costa-jussà et al. (2017)—used CNNs to learn position-invariant features of the character image. In Table 2, we report the configuration of the convolutional layers that was used in our models. All studies report different numbers of layers and different numbers of CNN features, therefore, we vary the CNN feature size F as a hyper-parameter. In Table 1 we report the character encoder architectures, that roughly cover the architectures from previous work. After the CNN, Liu et al. (2017) and Shao et al. (2017) use fully connected layers (*CNN+FC+ReLU*), while Su and Lee (2017) directly feed the CNN features into a recurrent neural network encoder (*CNN+ReLU*). We also consider a similar setup as Costa-jussà et al. (2017) by including two settings with one or two fully connected layers, (*FC 1L* and *FC 2L*). In addition to previous work, we also evaluated a model architecture that computes a softmax activation over the image features (*CNN+SM+FC*). Our hypothesis is that the sparse activation from the softmax may act like a soft lookup (in an $F \times 512$ embedding matrix).

4 Experimental Study

In this section, we describe the results of our experimental study. First, we report how the character images were created, followed by the experiments for the neural machine translation task. To expand on these results, we describe experiments and results for joint segmentation and part-of-speech tagging, as well as for measuring correlation with semantic similarity judgments.

4.1 Character Images

We convert each character from the source vocabulary into a 22×22 binary representation of its glyph.[1] This was the lowest resolution that did not collapse nearby strokes into indistinguishable clusters.

4.2 Experiments for Machine Translation

For the machine translation experiments, we trained a NMT model to translate from Chinese to English. In the following sections, we describe the model, the data and the training settings, followed by the results.

NMT Model We used a standard sequence-to-sequence model with a recurrent encoder and attention-based decoder (Luong et al., 2015). This architecture does not represent the state of the art in neural machine translation. However, due to its wide adoption in empirical research, there is broad knowledge about suitable hyper-parameters, which makes it a preferred choice for our study.

The coarse architecture of this model can be described by an encoder enc and a decoder dec. The encoder enc is a function that takes a tokenized text T in a source vocabulary as input and computes a representation that is the input for the subsequent decoder. The decoder dec then creates a sequence of tokens in the target vocabulary. The final output is $\mathrm{dec}(\mathrm{enc}(T))$.

The input of the encoder enc is first transformed to a dense vector representation, i.e., each input token is transformed by function D of Section 3.1. In the following experiments, we evaluate different choices for D.

Data For training the translation model, we used a subset of the available data from the WMT 2017 Workshop on Machine Translation (Bojar et al., 2017),[2] namely the *News Commentary v12* corpus as well as *Casia2015* and *Neu2017* from the *CWMT Corpus*. Overall, these datasets yielded 3,277,330 sentences. For development and evaluation, we used WMT 2017 dev and test data, respectively.

Training For Chinese, we use characters as input. For English, we use byte pair encoding (Sennrich et al., 2016) with $\approx$32,000 sym-

	Encoder	Decoder
Emb. size	512	512
Layers	bi-dir + uni-dir	uni-dir + uni-dir
Hid. size	512 + 1024	512 + 1024
Voc. size	8457	32413
Voc. type	character	byte pair enc.

Table 3: Hyperparameters of the sequence-to-sequence model for the NMT task.

bols. We implemented the model in PyTorch (Version 0.3.1) (Paszke et al., 2017). The recurrent neural networks in the encoder and decoder are LSTMs (Hochreiter and Schmidhuber, 1997). Table 3 summarizes the hyper-parameters of the NMT model.

For training, we used Adam (Kingma and Ba, 2014) with the standard parameters of PyTorch. We used a learning rate of 10^{-3} for 4 epochs, then we halved the learning rate every epoch until we reached 10^{-5}. For regularization, we used dropout with probability 0.2 in both encoder and decoder RNNs. We pretrained the decoder for 20 epochs to a perplexity of 108.21 on the validation data. This did result in: faster convergence, improved fluency of translations, and less variance of evaluation results. We trained all the models for 10 epochs. We selected the models by the best batch-based approximate BLEU score on the development set. This worked slightly better than selecting them by the best perplexity. We perform translation via beam search with a beam-size of 10 and length normalization of 0.9.

We trained the NMT models with each of the character encoders of Table 1 as well as with lookup-based embeddings (*EMB*) as a baseline.

Results Table 4 summarizes the results of the machine translation experiments. We include the result from a WMT 2017 system to give context for the expected BLEU score in this task. This result is from a baseline NMT system for Chinese to English (Wang et al., 2017), which is most comparable to our approach (i.e., no reranking, no ensembles, no special treatment of names and numbers). However, a crucial difference is that the WMT 2017 system uses pre-segmented text, which yields a vocabulary size of 300k on the

---

[1] We use ImageMagick's convert command together with the open source font NotoSansCJK-Regular.

[2] See `http://www.statmt.org/wmt17/translation-task.html`

---

[2] We use the BLEU implementation sacrebleu, `https://github.com/awslabs/sockeye/tree/master/contrib/sacrebleu`.

Model	F	BLEU
EMB	-	**16.63**
CNN+FC+ReLU	256	16.34
	512	16.33
	1024	**16.60**
	2048	16.40
	4096	16.20
CNN+SM+FC	512	15.85
	1024	15.49
	2048	15.36
	4096	**16.03**
CNN+ReLU	512	16.22
FC 1L	512	15.75
FC 2L	512	**16.32**
Word-segmented	-	19.4

Table 4: BLEU scores for translation zh-en on the WMT17 test data. Result for a word-segmented baseline model reported by Wang et al. (2017).

Model	full	low	mid	high
EMB	**16.63**	**15.60**	17.17	16.03
CNN+SM+FC	16.03	13.91	16.86	15.41
CNN+FC+R	**16.60**	14.47	17.11	**16.91**
FC 2L	16.32	15.10	**17.20**	16.37

Table 5: BLEU scores on the WMT17 test data for sentence buckets with low, medium and high frequency characters.

source side, while our system is character-based.

Our results indicate that using only one fully connected transformation layer *FC 1L* for character encoding is possible but does not yield comparable results to the best-performing convolutional architectures. However, the *FC 2L* comes close to the CNN models. Note that *CNN+SM+FC 4096* needs a larger number of CNN features to perform comparable to *CNN+FC+ReLU 1024*. In terms of BLEU score, the best character encoders perform equal to a standard lookup embedding.

To gain insight into the differences between the models, we split the test data into three buckets. Each sentence is scored with $1/n \sum_{i=1}^{n} \#t_i$, where $\#t_i$ is the training data frequency of character t_i. We partition the test data into a *low* and *high* bucket with the sentences scored in the lower and upper quartile, respectively, and a *mid* bucket with the remaining 2nd and 3rd quartile. Table 5

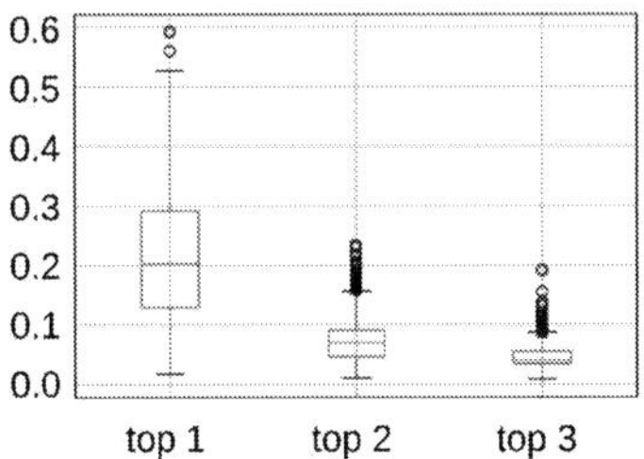

Figure 1: Distributions of the top-3 softmax activation magnitudes per character.

shows the results per bucket for *CNN+FC+ReLU 1024*, *CNN+SM+FC 4096*, *FC 2L* and *EMB*. Interestingly, the *CNN+FC+ReLU 1024* and *EMB* perform differently well in the frequency buckets. The *CNN+FC+ReLU 1024* model, surprisingly, performs better than *EMB* for high-frequency characters, while this is inversed for the low-frequency characters.

For the *CNN+SM+FC* encoders, our hypothesis was that the sparse activation of the softmax could act like a soft lookup function; i.e., it selects only few rows for the subsequent fully connected layer. We measured the top-3 softmax activation magnitudes per character from a random sample of 350 sentences from the training data (a total of 11234 words). As shown in Figure 1, the activations are indeed spiked, which supports our hypothesis. However, in our evaluation, we found no advantage over *CNN+FC+ReLU* encoders.

4.3 Experiments for Joint Part-of-Speech Tagging and Segmentation

In the translation experiment we evaluated the token representations for a syntactic *and* semantic signal. In this experiment, we want to investigate the *morpho-syntactic* information in the representations. To evaluate this, we employ the task of joint part-of-speech tagging and segmentation.

Model We used a Linear-Chain-CRF with a CNN encoder (Strubell et al., 2017) to compute the emissions. The encoder is a three-layer CNN with kernel size 3, iteratively growing dilations, residual connections, ReLU activations, and a hidden size of 512. We do not report numbers for a BI-RNN-CRF similar to Shao et al. (2017), because our implementation did not yield their results for unigrams which is most likely caused by the different embeddings.

Model	F1	
	adapt	fix
EMB	91.42	92.18
CNN+FC+ReLU 1024	91.99	90.75
FC2L 512	88.45	91.32
CNN+SM+FC 4096	71.54	87.63
1-gram BI-RNN-CRF*/**	*92.45*	
3-gram BI-RNN-CRF*	94.07	

Table 6: Results for joint segmentation and POS tagging on the test set of CTB-5.0. (*) 1-gram and 3-gram BI-RNN-CRF reported by Shao et al. (2017), (**) the 1-gram BI-RNN-CRF result was reported on the development set.

Data   The Chinese Treebank 5.0 (Xue et al., 2005) has joint annotations for word segmentation and part-of-speech tags. The commonly used cross validation split was reported by Jiang et al. (2008). Instead of the BIES tagging scheme (begin, inside, end, single), we used the BI scheme, which worked better for our models.

Training   We use the parameters from the *EMB*, *CNN+FC+ReLU 1024*, *FC2L 512* and *CNN+SM+FC 4096* of the NMT task. We either adjust these parameters during training (*adapt*) or keep them fixed (*fix*). For training, we used Adagrad (Duchi et al., 2010) with an initial learning rate of 0.1, and dropout for regularization with probability 0.1 for the encoder and 0.5 for the output classifier. We trained the models for 50 epochs and selected the model with the best accuracy on the development set.

Results   Our results reported in Table 6 are averaged over two distinct runs each. For comparison, we show results reported for the 1-gram and 3-gram lookup model of Shao et al. (2017). Our models correspond to the 1-gram model, as they are character-based. We find no clear difference between lookup-based and the best character encoder models. Interestingly, *CNN+SM+FC 4096* (softmax) is the weakest model. The sparseness in the in the signal apparently removes syntactic information. Comparing the *adapt* and the *fix* setting, we see that adapting the character encoder during training is —in most cases— not helpful. This is most likely due to the small amount of training data.

4.4   Experiments for Word Similarity

In our final experiment, we evaluated the representation of semantic information. The task is to compute a similarity score for pairs of words. The evaluation is the Spearman's correlation between the scores and numerical similarity judgments by humans. The words in this data set are translated into traditional Chinese. The training data from the NMT task is mostly from news and web sources, which is why our vocabulary contains many but not all Chinese characters. The characters in the modern simplified Chinese sometimes can be visually similar to their predecessors in traditional Chinese, i.e. they share visual components with a related meaning. Therefore, we can also evaluate the capability of the models to generalize to unseen characters.

Data and Experimental Setup   For the experiments we use the WordSim-240, WordSim-296 and SimLex-999 datasets provided and described by Su and Lee (2017). Due to the use of traditional Chinese we are missing at least one character in 430 out of 1536 test examples. On average, we are missing 1.1 characters per word, where each word has in average 2.13 characters. We split the data into word pairs in which all characters are completely covered (*seen words*), and into word pairs where at least one character is not seen (*unseen words*). We evaluate *unseen words* in two settings: either we remove the unseen characters (*seen chars*) or not (*all chars*).

We did not train any model for this experiments. Most of the words in the dataset are composed of multiple characters, therefore, we average the output of the character encoder into a single wordvector. Subsequently, we compute the cosine similarity between these vectors of word pairs.

Results   The results in Table 7 show that, for words with *seen* characters, the lookup embeddings correlate better with human judgments of similarity than the embeddings based on character encoders. However, especially the results for *unseen* words in WordSim-240 show that the character encoders can generalize to *all characters*. Surprisingly, the *FC2L* model, the model without CNNs, yields the best results. In the results reported by Su and Lee (2017), the lookup embedding model *SG-EMB* performs much better than *EMB*. However, they learn a RNN-based character composition, while we average the embeddings.

| Model | WordSim-240 | | | WordSim-297 | | | SimLex-999 | | |
| | seen | unseen | | seen | unseen | | seen | unseen | |
Characters		all	seen		all	seen		all	seen
EMB	**0.33**	n/a	0.06	**0.47**	n/a	0.15	**0.32**	n/a	**0.32**
CNN+SM+FC 4096	0.09	0.11	0.07	0.22	0.23	0.16	0.25	0.29	0.26
CNN+FC+R 1024	0.24	0.17	0.07	0.35	0.28	0.25	0.26	**0.30**	0.25
FC 2L 512	0.21	**0.26**	**0.15**	0.36	**0.29**	**0.30**	**0.33**	0.28	0.19
SG-EMB	0.59	n/a	n/a	0.59	n/a	n/a	0.36	n/a	n/a
SG-CNN	0.34	n/a	n/a	0.36	n/a	n/a	0.24	n/a	n/a

Table 7: Results for semantic similarity on the WordSim-240, WordSim-296 and SimLex-999 data. Lookup SkipGram (*SG-EMB*) and SkipGram char. encoder (*SG-CNN*) reported by Su and Lee (2017).

5 Conclusion

We have shown that it is possible to compute useful text representations from visual features, i.e., pixels of Chinese characters. We used neural machine translation as a framework for training and evaluating token representations. In the NMT experiment, we found that representations from visual features are competitive to lookup embeddings in a standard NMT model. In contrast to our expectations, the visual features outperform lookup embeddings on high-frequency characters, but are weaker in low-frequency characters. We conjecture that one of the reasons is that shared visual features between characters *can* have related meanings or related syntactic functions, but also the opposite can be true. For example, 沐 is the reflexive verb of "washing" and it contains the phonetic component 木 , which can also mean "tree". Therefore, the visual information for rare characters introduces probably as many difficulties as it can be helpful.

We performed additional experiments akin to prior studies and could show that the advantage of a representation by visual features is the ability to generalize to unseen Chinese characters. Also, we could show that joint part-of-speech tagging and segmentation achieved similar results with representation from visual features.

With regard to the character encoder architecture, we find only a slight advantage of using CNNs to simply using two fully connected layers in the NMT experiment, while 2 fully connected layers outperform CNNs in the similarity experiment. Whether or not there is an advantage could only be answered by an exhaustive hyperparameter search.

Future work is to explore how we can create a model that can distinguish helpful from unhelpful visual information for rare characters.

References

Ondrej Bojar, Christian Buck, Rajen Chatterjee, Christian Federmann, Yvette Graham, Barry Haddow, Matthias Huck, Antonio Jimeno-Yepes, Philipp Koehn, and Julia Kreutzer, editors. 2017. *Proceedings of the Second Conference on Machine Translation, Copenhagen, Denmark, September 7-8, 2017*, WMT 2017.

Marta R. Costa-jussà, David Aldón, and José A. R. Fonollosa. 2017. Chinese–Spanish neural machine translation enhanced with character and word bitmap fonts. *Machine Translation*, 31(1):35–47.

Yuntian Deng, Anssi Kanervisto, Jeffrey Ling, and Alexander M. Rush. 2017. Image-to-Markup Generation with Coarse-to-Fine Attention. In *Proceedings of the 34th International Conference on Machine Learning, Sydney, NSW, Australia, 6-11 August 2017*, ICML 2017, pages 980–989.

John Duchi, Elad Hazan, and Yoram Singer. 2010. Adaptive Subgradient Methods for Online Learning and Stochastic Optimization. Technical Report UCB/EECS-2010-24, EECS Department, University of California, Berkeley.

Desmond Elliott, Stella Frank, Loïc Barrault, Fethi Bougares, and Lucia Specia. 2017. Findings of the Second Shared Task on Multimodal Machine Translation and Multilingual Image Description. In *Proceedings of the Second Conference on Machine Translation, Volume 2: Shared Task Papers, Copenhagen, Denmark, September 7-8, 2017*, WMT 2017, pages 215–233, Copenhagen, Denmark.

Sepp Hochreiter and Jürgen Schmidhuber. 1997. Long Short-Term Memory. *Neural Computation*, 9(8):1735–1780.

Sergey Ioffe and Christian Szegedy. 2015. Batch Normalization: Accelerating Deep Network Training by Reducing Internal Covariate Shift. In *Proceedings of the 32nd International Conference on Machine Learning, Lille, France, 6-11 July 2015*, ICML 2015, pages 448–456.

Wenbin Jiang, Liang Huang, Qun Liu, and Yajuan Lü. 2008. A Cascaded Linear Model for Joint Chinese Word Segmentation and Part-of-Speech Tagging. In *Proceedings of the 46th Annual Meeting of the Association for Computational Linguistics, June 15-20, 2008, Columbus, Ohio, USA*, ACL 2008, pages 897–904.

Yoon Kim, Yacine Jernite, David Sontag, and Alexander M. Rush. 2016. Character-aware Neural Language Models. In *Proceedings of the Thirtieth AAAI Conference on Artificial Intelligence*, AAAI 2016, pages 2741–2749, Phoenix, Arizona. AAAI Press.

Diederik P. Kingma and Jimmy Ba. 2014. Adam: A Method for Stochastic Optimization. *CoRR*, abs/1412.6980.

Jason Lee, Kyunghyun Cho, and Thomas Hofmann. 2017. Fully Character-Level Neural Machine Translation without Explicit Segmentation. *TACL*, 5:365–378.

Frederick Liu, Han Lu, Chieh Lo, and Graham Neubig. 2017. Learning Character-level Compositionality with Visual Features. In *Proceedings of the 55th Annual Meeting of the Association for Computational Linguistics, Vancouver, Canada, July 30 - August 4, Volume 1: Long Papers*, ACL 2017, Vancouver, Canada.

Thang Luong, Hieu Pham, and Christopher D. Manning. 2015. Effective Approaches to Attention-based Neural Machine Translation. In *Proceedings of the 2015 Conference on Empirical Methods in Natural Language Processing, Lisbon, Portugal, September 17-21, 2015*, EMNLP 2015, pages 1412–1421.

Tomas Mikolov, Ilya Sutskever, Kai Chen, Gregory S. Corrado, and Jeffrey Dean. 2013. Distributed Representations of Words and Phrases and their Compositionality. In *Advances in Neural Information Processing Systems 26: 27th Annual Conference on Neural Information Processing Systems 2013. Proceedings of a meeting held December 5-8, 2013, Lake Tahoe, Nevada, United States.*, NIPS 2013, pages 3111–3119.

Adam Paszke, Sam Gross, Soumith Chintala, Gregory Chanan, Edward Yang, Zachary DeVito, Zeming Lin, Alban Desmaison, Luca Antiga, and Adam Lerer. 2017. Automatic differentiation in PyTorch.

Jeffrey Pennington, Richard Socher, and Christopher D. Manning. 2014. GloVe: Global Vectors for Word Representation. In *Proceedings of the 2014 Conference on Empirical Methods in Natural Language Processing, October 25-29, 2014, Doha, Qatar*, EMNLP 2014, pages 1532–1543.

Hinrich Schütze. 2017. Nonsymbolic Text Representation. In *Proceedings of the 15th Conference of the European Chapter of the Association for Computational Linguistics: Volume 1, Long Papers*, EACL 2017, pages 785–796.

Rico Sennrich, Barry Haddow, and Alexandra Birch. 2016. Neural Machine Translation of Rare Words with Subword Units. In *Proceedings of the 54th Annual Meeting of the Association for Computational Linguistics, August 7-12, 2016, Berlin, Germany, Volume 1: Long Papers*, ACL 2016.

Yan Shao, Christian Hardmeier, Jörg Tiedemann, and Joakim Nivre. 2017. Character-based Joint Segmentation and POS Tagging for Chinese using Bidirectional RNN-CRF. In *Proceedings of the Eighth International Joint Conference on Natural Language Processing, Taipei, Taiwan, November 27 - December 1, 2017 - Volume 1: Long Papers*, IJCNLP 2017, pages 173–183.

Emma Strubell, Patrick Verga, David Belanger, and Andrew McCallum. 2017. Fast and Accurate Entity Recognition with Iterated Dilated Convolutions. In *Proceedings of the 2017 Conference on Empirical Methods in Natural Language Processing, Copenhagen, Denmark, September 9-11, 2017*, EMNLP 2017, pages 2670–2680.

Tzu-ray Su and Hung-yi Lee. 2017. Learning Chinese Word Representations From Glyphs Of Characters. In *Proceedings of the 2017 Conference on Empirical Methods in Natural Language Processing, Copenhagen, Denmark, September 9-11, 2017*, EMNLP 2017, pages 264–273, Copenhagen, Denmark.

Yuguang Wang, Shanbo Cheng, Liyang Jiang, Jiajun Yang, Wei Chen, Muze Li, Lin Shi, Yanfeng Wang, and Hongtao Yang. 2017. Sogou Neural Machine Translation Systems for WMT17. In *Proceedings of the Second Conference on Machine Translation*, WMT 2017, pages 410–415, Copenhagen, Denmark.

Yonghui Wu, Mike Schuster, Zhifeng Chen, Quoc V. Le, Mohammad Norouzi, Wolfgang Macherey, Maxim Krikun, Yuan Cao, Qin Gao, Klaus Macherey, Jeff Klingner, Apurva Shah, Melvin Johnson, Xiaobing Liu, Lukasz Kaiser, Stephan Gouws, Yoshikiyo Kato, Taku Kudo, Hideto Kazawa, Keith Stevens, George Kurian, Nishant Patil, Wei Wang, Cliff Young, Jason Smith, Jason Riesa, Alex Rudnick, Oriol Vinyals, Greg Corrado, Macduff Hughes, and Jeffrey Dean. 2016. Google's Neural Machine Translation System: Bridging the Gap between Human and Machine Translation. *CoRR*, abs/1609.08144.

Naiwen Xue, Fei Xia, Fu-dong Chiou, and Marta Palmer. 2005. The Penn Chinese TreeBank: Phrase Structure Annotation of a Large Corpus. *Natural Language Engineering*, 11(2):207–238.

Jointly Embedding Entities and Text with Distant Supervision

Denis Newman-Griffis[♣,♠], Albert M Lai[♠,♦], and **Eric Fosler-Lussier[♣]**

[♣]Department of Computer Science and Engineering, The Ohio State University, Columbus, OH
[♠]Rehabilitation Medicine Department, Clinical Center, National Institutes of Health, Bethesda, MD
[♦]Institute for Informatics, Washington University in St. Louis, St. Louis, MO
{newman-griffis.1, fosler-lussier.1}@osu.edu   amlai@wustl.edu

Abstract

Learning representations for knowledge base entities and concepts is becoming increasingly important for NLP applications. However, recent entity embedding methods have relied on structured resources that are expensive to create for new domains and corpora. We present a distantly-supervised method for jointly learning embeddings of entities and text from an unnanotated corpus, using only a list of mappings between entities and surface forms. We learn embeddings from open-domain and biomedical corpora, and compare against prior methods that rely on human-annotated text or large knowledge graph structure. Our embeddings capture entity similarity and relatedness better than prior work, both in existing biomedical datasets and a new Wikipedia-based dataset that we release to the community. Results on analogy completion and entity sense disambiguation indicate that entities and words capture complementary information that can be effectively combined for downstream use.

1 Introduction

Distributed representations of knowledge base entities and concepts have become key elements of many recent NLP systems, for applications from document ranking (Jimeno-Yepes and Berlanga, 2015) and knowledge base completion (Toutanova et al., 2015) to clinical diagnosis code prediction (Choi et al., 2016a,b). These works have taken two broad tacks for the challenge of learning to represent entities, each of which may have multiple unique surface forms in text. Knowledge-based approaches learn entity representations based on

the structure of a large knowledge base, often augmented by annotated text resources (Yamada et al., 2016; Cao et al., 2017). Other methods utilize explicitly annotated data, and have been more popular in the biomedical domain (Choi et al., 2016a; Mencia et al., 2016). Both approaches, however, are often limited by ignoring some or most of the available textual information. Furthermore, such rich structures and annotations are lacking for many specialized domains, and can be prohibitively expensive to obtain.

We propose a fully text-based method for jointly learning representations of words, the surface forms of entities, and the entities themselves, from an unannotated text corpus. We use distant supervision from a *terminology*, which maps entities to known surface forms. We augment the well-known log-linear skip-gram model (Mikolov et al., 2013) with additional term- and entity-based objectives, and evaluate our learned embeddings in both intrinsic and extrinsic settings.

Our joint embeddings clearly outperform prior entity embedding methods on similarity and relatedness evaluations. Entity and word embeddings capture complementary information, yielding improved performance when they are combined. Analogy completion results further illustrate these differences, demonstrating that entities capture domain knowledge, while word embeddings capture morphological and lexical information. Finally, we see that an oracle combination of entity and text embeddings nearly matches a state of the art unsupervised method for biomedical word sense disambiguation that uses complex knowledge-based approaches. However, our embeddings show a significant drop in performance compared to prior work in a newswire disambiguation dataset, indicating that knowledge graph structure contains entity information that a purely text-based approach does not capture.

Proceedings of the 3rd Workshop on Representation Learning for NLP, pages 195–206
Melbourne, Australia, July 20, 2018. ©2018 Association for Computational Linguistics

2 Related Work

Knowledge-based approaches to entity representation are well-studied in recent literature. Several approaches have learned representations from knowledge graph structure alone (Grover and Leskovec, 2016; Yang et al., 2016; Wang et al., 2017). Wang et al. (2014), Yamada et al. (2016), and Cao et al. (2017) all use a joint embedding method, learning representations of text from a large corpus and entities from a knowledge graph; however, they rely on the disambiguated entity annotations in Wikipedia to align their models. Fang et al. (2016) investigate heuristic methods for joint embedding without annotated entity mentions, but still rely on graph structure for entity training.

The robust terminologies available in the biomedical domain have been instrumental to several recent annotation–based approaches. De Vine et al. (2014) use string matching heuristics to find possible occurrences of known biomedical concepts in literature abstracts, and use the sequence of these noisy concepts (without the document text) as input for skip-gram training. Choi et al. (2016c) and Choi et al. (2016a) use sequences of structured medical observations from patients' hospital stays for context-based learning. Finally, Mencia et al. (2016) take documents tagged with Medical Subject Heading (MeSH) topics, and use their texts to learn representations of the MeSH headers. These methods are able to draw on rich structured and semi-structured data from medical databases, but discard important textual information, and empirically are limited in the scope of the vocabularies they can embed.

3 Methods

In order to jointly learn entity and text representations from an unannotated corpus, we use distant supervision (Mintz et al., 2009) based on known *terms*, strings which can represent one or more entities. The mapping between terms and entities is many-to-many; for example, the same infection can be expressed as "cold" or "acute rhinitis", but "cold" can also describe the temperature or refer to chronic obstructive lung disease.

Mappings between terms and entities are defined by a terminology.[1] We extracted terminologies from two well-known knowledge bases:

	UMLS	Wikipedia
# entities	3,590,353	9,723,785
# terms	7,558,254	17,147,756
Max terms	495	7,077
# entities represented by n terms		
$n = 1$	1,823,569 (51%)	6,828,958 (70%)
$n = 2$	894,932 (25%)	1,565,109 (16%)
$3 \leq n \leq 10$	831,494 (23%)	1,143,452 (12%)
$n > 10$	40,358 (1%)	186,266 (2%)
# terms mapping to n entities		
$n = 1$	7,473,902 (98%)	16,127,138 (94%)
$n = 2$	69,816 (1%)	958,242 (5%)
$3 \leq n \leq 10$	14,366 (< 1%)	62,062 (< 1%)
$n > 10$	170 ($\ll$ 1%)	15 ($\ll$ 1%)

Table 1: Statistics of the many-to-many mapping between terms and entities in our terminologies, including the maximum # of terms per entity.

The Unified Medical Language System (UMLS; Bodenreider, 2004); we use the mappings between concepts and strings in the MRCONSO table as our terminology. This yields 3.5 million entities, represented by 7.6 million strings in total.

Wikipedia; we use page titles and redirects as our terminology. This yields 9.7 million potential entities (pages), represented by 17.1 million total strings. Table 1 gives further statistics about the mapping between entities and surface forms in each of these terminologies.

While iterating through the training corpus, we identify any exact matches of the terms in our terminologies.[2] We allow for overlapping terms: thus, "in New York City" will include an occurrence of both the terms "New York" and "New York City." Each matched term may refer to one or more entities; we do not use a disambiguation model in preprocessing, but rather assign a probability distribution over the possible entities.

3.1 Model

We extend the skip-gram model of Mikolov et al. (2013), to jointly learn vector representations of words, terms, and entities from shared textual contexts. For a given target word, term, or entity v, let $C_v = c_{-k} \ldots c_k$ be the observed contexts in a window of k words to the left and right of v, and let $N_v = n_{-k,1} \ldots n_{k,d}$ be the d random negative samples for each context word. Then, the context-based objective for training v is

$$O(v, C_v, N_v) = \sum_{c \in C_v} \log\sigma(\vec{c} \cdot \vec{v}) + \sum_{n \in N_v} \log\sigma(-\vec{n} \cdot \vec{v}) \quad (1)$$

---

[1] *Terminology* is overloaded with both biomedical and lexical senses; we use it here strictly to mean a mapping between terms and entities.

[2] We lowercase and strip special characters and punctuation from both terms and corpus text, and then find all exact matches for the terms.

	Pubmed	Wikipedia	Gigaword
# tokens	2.6B	1.9B	4.3B
# mentions	1.5B	1.4B	3.2B
Avg CP	2.54	1.01	1.01
% of entities by polysemy impact			
$CP \geq 1$	99.1%	98.6%	98.8%
$CP \geq 2$	9.3%	3.5%	2.2%
$CP \geq 10$	0.3%	0%	$\ll 0.1\%$

Table 2: Statistics of our embedding training corpora. # mentions is the number of exact matches found for terms in the relevant terminology. CP = corpus polysemy of a given entity. B = billion.

where σ is the logistic function.

We use a sliding context window to iterate through our corpus. At each step, the word w at the center of the window C_w is updated using $O(w, C_w, N_w)$, where N_w are the randomly-selected negative samples.

As terms are of variable token length, we treat each term t as an atomic unit for training, and set C_t to be the context words prior to the first token of the term and following the final token. Negative samples N_t are sampled independently of N_w.

Finally, each term t can represent a set of entities E_t. Vectors for these entities are updated using the same C_t and N_t from t. Since the entities are latent, we weight updates with uniform probability $|E_t|^{-1}$; attempts to learn this probability did not produce qualitatively different results from the uniform distribution. Thus, letting T be the set of terms completed at w, the full objective function to maximize is:

$$\hat{O} = O(w, C_w, N_w) + \\ \sum_{t \in T} \left[O(t, C_t, N_t) + \sum_{e \in E_t} \frac{1}{|E_t|} O(e, C_t, N_t) \right] \quad (2)$$

Term and entity updates are only calculated when the final token of one or more terms is reached; word updates are applied at each step. To assign more weight to near contexts, we subsample the window size at each step from $[1, k]$.

3.2 Training corpora

We train embeddings on three corpora. For our biomedical embeddings, we use 2.6 billion tokens of biomedical abstract texts from the 2016 PubMed baseline (1.5 billion noisy annotations). For comparison to previous open-domain work, we use English Wikipedia (5.5 million articles from the 2018-01-20 dump); we also use the Gigaword 5 newswire corpus (Parker et al., 2011), which does not have gold entity annotations.

As our model does not include a disambiguation module for handling ambiguous term mentions, we also calculate the expected effect of polysemous terms on each entity that we embed using a given corpus. We call this the entity's *corpus polysemy*, and denote it with $CP(e)$. For entity e with corresponding terms T_e, $CP(e)$ is given as

$$CP(e) = \sum_{t \in T_e} \frac{f(t)}{Z} \text{polysemy}(t) \quad (3)$$

where $f(t)$ is the corpus frequency of term t, Z is the frequency of all terms in T_e, and polysemy(t) is the number of entities that t can refer to.

Table 2 breaks down expected polysemy impact for each corpus. The vast majority of entities experience some polysemy effect in training, but very few have an average ambiguity per mention of 50% or greater. Most entities with high corpus polysemy are due to a few highly ambiguous generic strings, such as *combinations* and *unknown*. However, some specific terms are also high ambiguity: for example, *Washington County* refers to 30 different US counties.

3.3 Hyperparameters

For all of our embeddings, we used the following hyperparameter settings: a context window size of 2, with 5 negative samples per word; initial learning rate of 0.05 with a linear decay over 10 iterations through the corpus; minimum frequency for both words and terms of 10, and a subsampling coefficient for frequent words of 1e-5.

3.4 Baselines

We compare the words, terms,[3] and entities learned in our model against two prior biomedical embedding methods, using pretrained embeddings from each. De Vine et al. (2014) use sequences of automatically identified ambiguous entities for skip-gram training, and Mencia et al. (2016) use texts of documents tagged with MeSH headers to represent the header codes. The most recent comparison method for Wikipedia entities is MPME (Cao et al., 2017), which uses link anchors and graph structure to augment textual contexts. We also include skip-gram vectors as a final baseline; for Pubmed, we use pretrained embeddings with optimized hyperparameters from Chiu et al. (2016a), and we train our own embeddings with word2vec for both Wikipedia and Gigaword.

---

[3] Unknown terms were handled by backing off to words.

Method	Full		Filtered	
	Sim	Rel	Sim	Rel
Prior work				
word2vec	0.559	0.496		
DeVine'14	0.455	0.422	0.534	0.482
Mencia'16	0.565	0.534	0.573	0.536
Proposed				
Word	0.561	0.490		
Term	0.619	0.557*		
Entity	0.633*	0.563*	0.614*	0.567*
Entity+Word	0.653*	0.586*	0.615*	**0.583***
+Cross	**0.662***	**0.588***	**0.622***	0.573*

Table 3: Spearman's ρ for similarity/relatedness predictions in UMNSRS. Filtered results indicate performance on the shared-vocabulary subset. *=significantly better ($p < 0.05$) than word baseline (full), DeVine et al (filtered).

Method	Wikipedia		Gigaword	
	Sim	Rel	Sim	Rel
Prior work				
word2vec	0.630	0.630	0.624	0.623
MPME	0.506	0.567	–	–
Proposed				
Word	0.646	0.655	0.615	0.600
Term	0.607	0.667	0.625	0.673
Entity	0.594	0.648	0.634	0.686
Entity+Word	**0.718**	**0.754***	**0.701***	**0.722***
+Cross	0.697*	0.753*	0.695*	0.729*

Table 4: Spearman's ρ for similarity/relatedness predictions in WikiSRS, training on two corpora. All Proposed results are significantly better than MPME; *=significantly better than strongest word-level baseline ($p < 0.05$).

4 Evaluations

Following Chiu et al. (2016b), Cao et al. (2017), and others, we evaluate our embeddings on both intrinsic and extrinsic tasks. To evaluate the semantic organization of the space, we use the standard intrinsic evaluations of similarity and relatedness and analogy completion. To explore the applicability of our embeddings to downstream applications, we apply them to named entity disambiguation. Results and analyses for each experiment are discussed in the following subsections.

4.1 Similarity and relatedness

We evaluate our biomedical embeddings on the UMNSRS datasets (Pakhomov et al., 2010), consisting of pairs of UMLS concepts with judgments of similarity (566 pairs) and relatedness (587 pairs), as assigned by medical experts. For evaluating our Wikipedia entity embeddings, we created WikiSRS, a novel dataset of similarity and relatedness judgments of paired Wikipedia entities (people, places, and organizations), as assigned by Amazon Mechanical Turk workers. We followed the design procedure of Pakhomov et al. (2010) and produced 688 pairs each of similarity and relatedness judgments; for further details on our released dataset, please see the Appendix.

For each labeled entity pair, we calculated the cosine similarity of their embeddings, and ranked the pairs in order of descending similarity. We report Spearman's ρ on these rankings as compared to the ranked human judgments: Table 3 shows results for UMNSRS, and Table 4 for WikiSRS.

As the dataset includes both string and disambiguated entity forms for each pair, we evaluate

each type of embeddings learned in our model. Additionally, as words and entities are embedded in the same space (and thus directly comparable), we experiment with two methods of combining their information. Entity+Word sums the cosine similarities calculated between the entity embeddings and word embeddings for each pair; the Cross setting further adds comparisons of each entity in the pair to the string form of the other.

4.1.1 Results

Our proposed method clearly outperforms prior work and text-based baselines on both datasets. Further, we see that the words and entities learned by our model include complementary information, as combining them further increases our ranking performance by a large margin. As the results on UMNSRS could have been due to our model's ability to embed many more entities than prior methods, we also filtered the dataset to the 255 similarity pairs and 260 relatedness pairs that all evaluated entity-level methods could represent;[4] Table 3 shows similar gains on this even footing. We follow Rastogi et al. (2015) in calculating significance, and use their statistics to estimate the minimum required difference for significant improvements on our datasets.

In UMNSRS, we found that cosine similarity of entities consistently reflected human judgments of similarity better than of relatedness; this reflects previous observations by Agirre et al. (2009) and Muneeb et al. (2015). Interestingly, we see the opposite behavior in WikiSRS, where relatedness is captured better than similarity in all settings. In fact, we see a number of errors of relatedness

---

[4]For WikiSRS, all methods covered all pairs.

Dataset	Words	Entities	Entity+Word+Cross
UMNSRS	Iron/Iron Nausea/Vomiting Lipitor/Zocor	Iron/Iron Sinemet/Sinemet Enalapril/Lisinopril	Levaquin/Avelox Enalapril/Lisinopril Carboplatin/Cisplatin
WikiSRS	Minas Tirith/Minas Morgul Moscow/Moscow Kremlin Norway/Denmark	Real Madrid/FC Barcelona Minas Tirith/Minas Morgul Charlize Theron/Screen Actor's Guild	Ferrari/Lamborghini Moscow/Moscow Kremlin Toshiro Mifune/Akira Kurosawa

Table 5: Top 3 pairs in the Relatedness datasets, as ranked by different embedding methods.

in WikiSRS predictions, e.g., "Hammurabi I" and "Syria" are marked highly similar, while the composers "A.R. Rahman" and "John Phillip Sousa" are marked dis-similar. MPME embeddings tend towards over-relatedness as well (e.g., ranking "Richard Feynman" and "Paris-Sorbonne University" much more highly than gold labels). Despite better similarity performance, this trend of over-relatedness also holds in biomedical embeddings: for example, *C0027358* (Narcan) and *C0026549* (morphine) are consistently marked highly similar across embedding methods, even though Narcan blocks the effects of opioids like morphine.

4.1.2 Comparing entities and words

We observe clear differences in the rankings made by entity vs word embeddings. As shown in Table 5, highly related entities tend to have high cosine similarity, while word embeddings are more sensitive to lexical overlap and direct cooccurrence. Combining both sources often gives the most inuitive results, balancing lexical effects with relatedness. For example, while the top three pairs by combination in WikiSRS are likely to co-occur, the top three in UMNSRS are pairs of drug choices (antibiotics, ACE inhibitors, and chemotherapy drugs, respectively), only one of which is likely to be prescribed to any given patient at once.

These differences also play out in erroneous predictions. Entity embeddings often fix the worst misrankings by words: for example, "Tony Blair" and "United Kingdom" (gold rank: 28) are ranked highly unrelated (position 633) by words, but entities move this pair back up the list (position 86). However, errors made by entity embeddings are often also made by words: e.g., *C0011175* (dehydration) and *C0017160* (gastroenteritis) are erroneously ranked as highly unrelated by both methods. Interestingly, we find no correlation between the corpus polysemy of entity pairs and ranking performance, indicating that ambiguity of term mentions is not a significant confound for this task.

Method	B3	H1	C6	L1	L6
Words	2.9	0.4	**7.9**	**51.5**	**69.3**
Entities	**18.3**	**22.4**	4.5	10.6	10.0
Oracle	20.7	22.9	12.1	55.0	70.9

Table 6: Accuracy % on 5 of the relations in BMASS with greatest absolute difference in word performance vs entity performance: B3 (*gene-encodes-product*), H1 (*refers-to*), C6 (*associated-with*), L1 (*form-of*), and L6 (*has-free-acid-or-base-form*). The better of word and entity performance is highlighted; all entity vs word differences are significant (McNemar's test; $p \ll 0.01$).

4.2 Analogy completion

We use analogy completion to further explore the properties of our joint embeddings. Given analogy $a : b :: c : d$, the task is to guess d given (a, b, c), typically by choosing the word or entity with highest cosine similarity to $b - a + c$ (Levy and Goldberg, 2014). We report accuracy using the top guess (ignoring a, b, and c as candidates, per Linzen, 2016).

4.2.1 Biomedical analogies

To compare between word and entity representations, we use the entity-level biomedical dataset BMASS (Newman-Griffis et al., 2017), which includes both entity and string forms for each analogy. In order to test if words and entities are capturing complementary information, we also include an oracle evaluation, in which an analogy is counted as correct if either words or entities produce a correct response.[5] We do not compare against prior biomedical entity embedding methods on this dataset, due to their limited vocabulary.

Table 6 contrasts the performance of different jointly-trained representations for five relations with the largest performance differences from this dataset. For *gene-encodes-product* and *refers-to*, both of which require structured domain knowledge, entity embeddings significantly

---

[5] We use the Multi-Answer setting for our evaluation (a single (a, b, c) triple, but a set of correct values for d).

outperform word-level representations. Many of the errors made by word embeddings in these relations are due to lexical over-sensitivity: for example, in the renaming analogy *spinal epidural hematoma:epidural hemorrhage::canis familiaris:___*, words suggest latinate completions such as *latrans* and *caballus*, while entities capture the correct *C1280551* (dog). However, on more morphological relations such as *has-free-acid-or-base-form*, words are by far the better option.

The success of the oracle combination method for entity and word predictions clearly indicates that not only are words and entities capturing different knowledge, but that it is complementary. In the majority of the 25 relations in BMASS, oracle results improved on words and entities alone by at least 10% relative. In some cases, as with *has-free-acid-or-base-form*, one method does most of the heavy lifting. In several others, including the challenging (and open-ended) *associated-with*, entities and words capture nearly orthogonal cases, leading to large jumps in oracle performance.

4.2.2 General-domain analogies

No entity-level encyclopedic analogy dataset is available, so we follow Cao et al. (2017) in evaluating the effect of joint training on words using the Google analogy set (Mikolov et al., 2013). As shown in Table 7, our Wikipedia embeddings roughly match MPME embeddings (which use annotated entity links) on the semantic portion of the dataset, but our ability to train on unannotated Gigaword boosts our results on all relations except *city-in-state*.[6] Overall, we find that jointly-trained word embeddings split performance with word-only skipgram training, but that word-only training tends to get consistently closer to the correct answer. This suggests that terms and entities may conflict with word-level semantic signals.

4.3 Entity disambiguation

Finally, to get a picture of the impact of our embedding method on downstream applications, we investigated entity disambiguation.[7] Given a named entity occurrence in context, the task is to assign a canonical identifier to the entity being referred to: e.g., to mark that "New York" refers to

---

[6]We failed to precisely replicate the analogy numbers reported by Cao et al. (2017); we attribute this primarily to the different training corpus and slightly different preprocessing.

[7]This task is also referred to as entity linking and entity sense disambiguation.

Method	Capital (common)	Capital (all)	Currency	City in State	Family
word2vec (W)	89.1	86.0	15.0	**55.5**	**82.4**
word2vec (G)	90.9	89.7	**18.4**	38.4	81.0
MPME (W)	83.6	80.5	11.9	50.6	78.9
Proposed (W)	90.1	78.7	9.1	42.5	75.5
Proposed (G)	**92.7**	**92.3**	16.4	31.3	81.6

Table 7: Analogy completion accuracy % on the semantic relations in the Google analogy dataset. W=Wikipedia, G=Gigaword.

the city in the sentence, "The mayor of New York held a press conference." It bears noting that in unambiguous cases, a terminology alone is sufficient to link the correct entity: for example, "Barack Obama" can only refer to a single entity, regardless of context. However, many entity strings (e.g., "cold", "New York") are ambiguous, necessitating the use of alternate sources of information such as our embeddings to assign the correct entity.

4.3.1 Biomedical abstracts

We evaluate on the MSH WSD dataset (Jimeno-Yepes et al., 2011), a benchmark for biomedical word sense disambiguation. MSH WSD consists of mentions of 203 ambiguous terms in biomedical literature, with over 30,000 total instances. Each sample is annotated with the set of UMLS entities the term could refer to. We adopt the unsupervised method of Sabbir et al. (2016), which combines cosine similarity and projection magnitude of an entity representation e to the averaged word embeddings of its contexts C_{avg} as follows:

$$f(e, C_{avg}) = \cos(C_{avg}, e) \cdot \frac{||P(C_{avg}, e)||}{||e||} \quad (4)$$

The entity maximizing this score is predicted.

We compare against concept embeddings learned by Sabbir et al. (2016). They used MetaMap (Aronson and Lang, 2010) with the disambiguation module enabled on a curated corpus of 5 million Pubmed abstracts to create a UMLS concept cooccurrence corpus for word2vec training. As shown in Table 8, our method lags behind theirs, though it clearly beats both random (49.7% accuracy) and majority class (52%) baselines. In addition, we leverage our jointly-embedded entities and words by adding in the definition-based model used by Pakhomov et al. (2016), which calculates an entity's embedding as the average of definitions of its neighbors in the UMLS hierarchy (McInnes et al., 2011). We use this alternate

Method	Accuracy %
Baselines	
Sabbir et al. (2016) (entities; +MetaMap)	89.3
Sabbir et al. (2016) (+MetaMap, UMLS)	**92.2**
Pakhomov et al. (2016) (words)	77.7
Proposed	
Entities	76.4
Definitions (joint words)	80.8
Entities+Definitions	82.7
Oracle (Entities—Definitions)	90.9

Table 8: MSH WSD disambiguation accuracy. Definitions is comparable to Pakhomov et al. (2016), using jointly-embedded words. All differences are significant (McNemar's test, $p \ll 0.01$).

entity embedding in Equation 4 to calculate a second score that we add to the direct entity embedding score. This yields a large performance boost of over 6% absolute, indicating that using entities and words together makes up much of the gap between our distantly supervised embeddings and the external resources used by Sabbir et al. (2016). Using the definition-based method alone with our jointly-embedded words, we see a significant increase over Pakhomov et al. (2016), indicating the benefits of joint training. However, the combined entity and definition model still yields a significantly different 2% boost in accuracy over definitions alone. Finally, we evaluate an oracle combination that reports correct if either entity or definition embeddings achieve the correct result; as shown in the last row of Table 8, this combination outperforms the entity-only method of Sabbir et al. (2016), and approaches their state-of-the-art result that combines entity embeddings with a knowledge-based approach from the structure of the UMLS.

Specific errors shed more light on these differences. The definition-based method performs better in many cases where the surface form is a common word, such as *coffee* (68% definition accuracy vs 28% entity accuracy) and *iris* (93% definition accuracy vs 35% entity accuracy). Entities outperform on some more technical cases, such as *potassium* (74% entity accuracy vs 49% definition accuracy). Combining both approaches in the joint model recovers performance on several cases of low entity accuracy; for example, joint accuracy on *coffee* is 68%, and on *lupus* (53% entity accuracy), joint performance is 60%.

Method	Accuracy %
MPME (entities; +graph structure)	**89.0**
Wikipedia	40.9
Wikipedia + mentions	44.6
Gigaword	58.0
Gigaword + mentions	63.9

Table 9: AIDA linking accuracy, using entity embeddings trained on Wikipedia and Gigaword. All differences are significant (McNemar's test, $p \ll 0.01$).

4.3.2 Newswire entities

AIDA (Hoffart et al., 2011) is a standard dataset for entity linking in newswire, consisting of approximately 30,000 entities linked to Wikipedia page IDs. To reduce the search space, Pershina et al. (2015) provided a set of candidate entities for each mention, which we use for our experiments. The MPME model of Cao et al. (2017) achieves near state-of-the-art performance accuracy on AIDA with this candidate set, using the mention sense distributions and full document context included in the model. As our embeddings are trained without explicit entity annotations, we instead use the same cosine similarity and projection model discussed in Section 4.3.1 for this task. In contrast to our results on the biomedical data, we see performance far below the baseline on these data, as shown in Table 9.

However, we improve this performance slightly by multiplying by the similarity between the entity embedding and the average word embedding of the mention itself; this gives us roughly a further 4% accuracy for both Wikipedia and Gigaword embeddings. Using the surface form recovers several cases where entities alone yield unlikely options, e.g. Roman-era Britain instead of the United Kingdom for *Britain*. However, it also introduces lexical errors: for example, *British* in several cases refers to the United Kingdom, but the British people are often selected instead. We note that this extra score actually hurts performance on MSH WSD, where the terms are curated to be highly ambiguous, in contrast to the shorter contexts and clearer terms used in AIDA.

Two other issues bear consideration in this evaluation. Prior approaches to the AIDA dataset, including MPME, make use of the global context of entity mentions within a document to improve predictions; by using local context only, we observe some inconsistent predictions, such as selecting the cricket world cup instead of the FIFA com-

Entity	Words	Terms	Entities	Joint
C0009443 (common cold)	k(+)-grown	cold	C0041912 (upper respiratory infections)	C0041912 (upper respiratory infections)
	legionella-contaminated	short periods	C0234192 (cold sensation)	C0234192 (cold sensation)
	hyperinflating	changed	C0719425 ("Cold" pharmaceutical brand)	C0719425 ("Cold" pharmaceutical brand)
C0242797 (home health aides)	homemaker-home	home health aide	C1553498 (home health encounter)	home health aide
	voluntary-sector	home health aides	C0019855 (home care services)	home health aides
	health/social	home health	C1317851 (home health care specialty)	C1553498 (home health encounter)

Table 10: Top 3 nearest neighbors to two UMLS entities, using words, terms, entities, or all three.

petition for *world cup*, in a document discussing football. Additionally, in contrast to the MSH WSD dataset, many instances in AIDA have several highly-related candidates that introduce some confusion in our results. For example, *Ireland* could refer to the United Kingdom of Great Britain and Ireland, the island of Ireland, or the Republic of Ireland. As our embedding training does not include gold entity links, cases like this are often errors in our predictions.

5 Analysis of joint embeddings

To get a more detailed picture of our joint embedding space, we investigate nearest neighbors for each point by cosine similarity. As entities in the UMLS are assigned one or more of over 120 semantic types, we first examine how intermixed these types are in our biomedical embeddings. Figure 1 shows how often an entity's nearest neighbor shares at least one semantic type with it, across the three biomedical embedding methods we evaluated. As each set of embeddings has a different vocabulary, we also restrict to the entities

that all three can embed (approximately 11,000).

We see that our method puts entities of the same type together nearly 40% of the time, despite embedding over 270 thousand entities. On an even footing, our method puts types together significantly more often Mencia et al. (2016) (McNemar's; $p < 0.05$), and equivalently with De Vine et al. (2014), despite using less entity-level information in training. Within our embeddings, major biological types such as bacteria, eukaryotes, mammals, and viruses all have more than 60% of neighbors with the same type, while less structured clinical types such as Clinical Attribute and Daily or Recreational Activity are in the 10-20% range. Corpus polysemy does not appear to have any effect on this type matching (mean polysemy of 1.5 for both matched and non-matched entities).

Expanding to include the words and terms in the joint embedding space, however, we see definite qualitative effects of corpus polysemy on entity nearest neighbors. Table 10 gives nearest word, term, entity, and joint neighbors to two biomedical entities: *C0009443* (the common cold; $CP = 6.71$) and *C0242797* (home health aides; $CP = 1$). For the more polysemous *C0009443*, where 95% of its mentions are of the word "cold" (polysemy=7), word-level neighbors are mostly nonsensical, while term neighbors are more logical, and entity neighbors reflect different senses of "cold". By contrast, the non-polysemous *C0242797*, which is represented by 14 different unambiguous strings, words, terms, and entities are all very clearly in line with the theme of home health aides. Notably, the common and unambiguous terms for *C0242797* are its nearest neighbors out of all points, while only two of the top 10 neighbors to *C0009443* are terms.

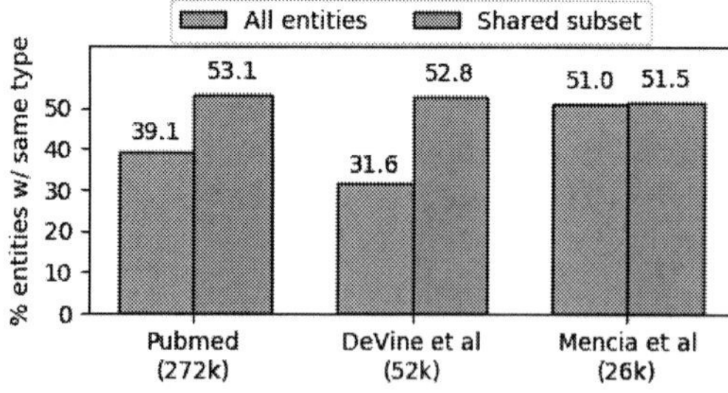

Figure 1: Percentage of UMLS entities whose nearest neighbor shares a semantic type, with no vocabulary restriction (vocab size in parentheses) and in a shared vocabulary subset.

6 Discussion

Faruqui et al. (2016) observe that similarity and relatedness are not clearly distinguished in semantic embedding evaluations, and that it is unclear exactly how vector-space models should capture them. We see more evidence of this, as cosine similarity seems to be capturing a mix of the two properties in our data. This mix is clearly informative, but it empirically favors relatedness judgments, and cosine similarity is insufficient to separate the two properties.

Corpus polysemy plays a qualitative role in our embedding model, but less of a quantitative one. It does not correlate with similarity and relatedness judgments or entity disambiguation decisions, but it clearly affects the organization of the embedding space, by embedding entities with high corpus polysemy in less coherent areas than those with low polysemy. Linzen (2016) points out that for analogy completion, local neighborhood structure can interfere with standard methods; how this neighborhood structure affects predictions in more complex tasks is an open question.

Overall, we find two main advantages to our model over prior work. First, by only using a terminology and an unannotated corpus, we are able to learn entity embeddings from larger and more diverse data; for example, embeddings learned from Gigaword (which has no entity annotations) outperform embeddings learned on Wikipedia in most of our experiments. Second, by embedding entities and text into a joint space, we are able to leverage complementary information to get higher performance in both intrinsic and extrinsic tasks; an oracle model nearly matches a state-of-the-art ensemble vector and knowledge-based model for biomedical word sense disambiguation. However, our other entity disambiguation results demonstrate that there is additional entity-level information that we are not yet capturing. In particular, it is unclear whether our low performance on disambiguating newswire entities is due to a disambiguation model mismatch, a lack of information in our embeddings, or a combination of both.

7 Conclusions

We present a method for jointly learning embeddings of entities and text from an arbitrary unannotated corpus, using only a terminology for distant supervision. Our learned embeddings better capture both biomedical and encyclopedic similarity and relatedness than prior methods, and approach state-of-the-art performance for unsupervised biomedical word sense disambiguation. Furthermore, entities and words learned jointly with our model capture complementary information, and combining them improves performance in all of our evaluations. We make an implementation of our method available at `github.com/OSU-slatelab/JET`, along with the source code used for our evaluations and our pretrained entity embeddings. Our novel Wikipedia similarity and relatedness datasets are available at the same source.

Acknowledgments

We would like to thank Chaitanya Shivade for helpful discussions, and all of our anonymous reviewers for their invaluable advice. This research was supported in part by the Intramural Research Program of the National Institutes of Health, Clinical Research Center and through an Inter-Agency Agreement with the US Social Security Administration.

References

Eneko Agirre, Enrique Alfonseca, Keith Hall, Jana Kravalova, Marius Paca, and Aitor Soroa. 2009. A study on similarity and relatedness using distributional and WordNet-based approaches. In *Proceedings of Human Language Technologies: The 2009 Annual Conference of the North American Chapter of the Association for Computational Linguistics on - NAACL '09*, pages 19–27, Boulder, Colorado. Association for Computational Linguistics.

Alan R Aronson and François-Michel Lang. 2010. An overview of MetaMap: historical perspective and recent advances. *Journal of the American Medical Informatics Association : JAMIA*, 17(3):229–36.

Olivier Bodenreider. 2004. The Unified Medical Language System (UMLS): integrating biomedical terminology. *Nucleic Acids Research*, 32(90001):D267–D270.

Yixin Cao, Lifu Huang, Heng Ji, Xu Chen, and Juanzi Li. 2017. Bridge Text and Knowledge by Learning Multi-Prototype Entity Mention Embedding. In *Proceedings of the 55th Annual Meeting of the Association for Computational Linguistics (Volume 1: Long Papers)*, pages 1623–1633, Vancouver, Canada. Association for Computational Linguistics.

Billy Chiu, Gamal Crichton, Anna Korhonen, and Sampo Pyysalo. 2016a. How to Train Good Word Embeddings for Biomedical NLP. *Proceedings of the 15th Workshop on Biomedical Natural Language Processing*, pages 166–174.

Billy Chiu, Anna Korhonen, and Sampo Pyysalo. 2016b. Intrinsic Evaluation of Word Vectors Fails to Predict Extrinsic Performance. *Proceedings of the 1st Workshop on Evaluating Vector Space Representations for NLP*, pages 1–6.

Edward Choi, Mohammad Taha Bahadori, Andy Schuetz, Walter F Stewart, and Jimeng Sun. 2016a. RETAIN: Interpretable Predictive Model in Healthcare using Reverse Time Attention Mechanism. In *NIPS*, pages 1–15.

Edward Choi, Mohammad Taha Bahadori, Elizabeth Searles, Catherine Coffey, Michael Thompson, James Bost, Javier Tejedor-Sojo, and Jimeng Sun. 2016b. Multi-layer Representation Learning for Medical Concepts. *Proceedings of the 22nd ACM SIGKDD International Conference on Knowledge Discovery and Data Mining - KDD '16*, pages 1495–1504.

Youngduck Choi, Chill Yi-I Chiu, and David Sontag. 2016c. Learning Low-Dimensional Representations of Medical Concepts. In *AMIA Joint Summits on Translational Science Proceedings*, pages 41–50.

Lance De Vine, Guido Zuccon, Bevan Koopman, Laurianne Sitbon, and Peter Bruza. 2014. Medical semantic similarity with a neural language model. In *Proceedings of the 23rd ACM International Conference on Information and Knowledge Management - CIKM '14*, CIKM '14, pages 1819–1822, Shanghai, China. ACM.

Wei Fang, Jianwen Zhang, Dilin Wang, Zheng Chen, and Ming Li. 2016. Entity Disambiguation by Knowledge and Text Jointly Embedding. In *Proceedings of the 20th SIGNLL Conference on Computational Language Learning (CoNLL)*, pages 260–269. Association for Computational Linguistics.

Manaal Faruqui, Yulia Tsvetkov, Pushpendre Rastogi, and Chris Dyer. 2016. Problems With Evaluation of Word Embeddings Using Word Similarity Tasks. In *Proceedings of the 1st Workshop on Evaluating Vector-Space Representations for NLP*, pages 30–35, Berlin, Germany. Association for Computational Linguistics.

Aditya Grover and Jure Leskovec. 2016. Node2Vec: Scalable Feature Learning for Networks. In *Proceedings of the 22Nd ACM SIGKDD International Conference on Knowledge Discovery and Data Mining*, KDD '16, pages 855–864, New York, NY, USA. ACM.

Johannes Hoffart, Mohamed Amir Yosef, Ilaria Bordino, Hagen Fürstenau, Manfred Pinkal, Marc Spaniol, Bilyana Taneva, Stefan Thater, and Gerhard Weikum. 2011. Robust Disambiguation of Named Entities in Text. In *Proceedings of the 2011 Conference on Empirical Methods in Natural Language Processing*, pages 782–792, Edinburgh, Scotland, UK. Association for Computational Linguistics.

Antonio Jimeno-Yepes and Rafael Berlanga. 2015. Knowledge based word-concept model estimation and refinement for biomedical text mining. *Journal of Biomedical Informatics*, 53:300–307.

Antonio J Jimeno-Yepes, Bridget T McInnes, and Alan R Aronson. 2011. Exploiting MeSH indexing in MEDLINE to generate a data set for word sense disambiguation. *BMC Bioinformatics*, 12:223.

Omer Levy and Yoav Goldberg. 2014. Linguistic Regularities in Sparse and Explicit Word Representations. In *Proceedings of the Eighteenth Conference on Computational Natural Language Learning*, pages 171–180, Ann Arbor, Michigan. Association for Computational Linguistics.

Tal Linzen. 2016. Issues in evaluating semantic spaces using word analogies. In *Proceedings of the 1st Workshop on Evaluating Vector-Space Representations for NLP*, pages 13–18.

Farzaneh Mahdisoltani, Joanna Biega, and Fabian M Suchanek. 2015. YAGO3: A Knowledge Base from Multilingual Wikipedias. In *Conference on Innovative Data Systems Research (CIDR)*.

Bridget T McInnes, Ted Pedersen, Ying Liu, Serguei V Pakhomov, and Genevieve B Melton. 2011. Using second-order vectors in a knowledge-based method for acronym disambiguation. *CoNLL 2011 - Fifteenth Conference on Computational Natural Language Learning, Proceedings of the Conference*, (June):145–153.

Eneldo Loza Mencia, Gerard de Melo, and Jinseok Nam. 2016. Medical Concept Embeddings via Labeled Background Corpora. In *Proceedings of the Tenth International Conference on Language Resources and Evaluation (LREC 2016)*, pages 4629–4636. European Language Resources Association (ELRA).

Tomas Mikolov, Kai Chen, Greg Corrado, and Jeffrey Dean. 2013. Efficient Estimation of Word Representations in Vector Space. *arXiv preprint arXiv:1301.3781*, pages 1–12.

Mike Mintz, Steven Bills, Rion Snow, and Dan Jurafsky. 2009. Distant supervision for relation extraction without labeled data. In *Proceedings of the Joint Conference of the 47th Annual Meeting of the ACL and the 4th International Joint Conference on Natural Language Processing of the AFNLP*, pages 1003–1011, Suntec, Singapore. Association for Computational Linguistics.

T H Muneeb, Sunil Kumar Sahu, and Ashish Anand. 2015. Evaluating distributed word representations for capturing semantics of biomedical concepts. In *Proceedings of the 2015 Workshop on Biomedical Natural Language Processing (BioNLP 2015)*, pages 158–163, Beijing, China. Association for Computational Linguistics.

Denis Newman-Griffis, Albert M Lai, and Eric Fosler-Lussier. 2017. Insights into Analogy Completion from the Biomedical Domain. In *BioNLP 2017*, pages 19–28, Vancouver, Canada. Association for Computational Linguistics.

Serguei Pakhomov, Bridget McInnes, Terrence Adam, Ying Liu, Ted Pedersen, and Genevieve B Melton. 2010. Semantic Similarity and Relatedness between Clinical Terms: An Experimental Study. In *AMIA Annual Symposium Proceedings*, pages 572–576. American Medical Informatics Association.

Serguei V S Pakhomov, Greg Finley, Reed McEwan, Yan Wang, and Genevieve B Melton. 2016. Corpus domain effects on distributional semantic modeling of medical terms. *Bioinformatics*, 32(August):btw529.

Robert Parker, David Graff, Junbo Kong, Ke Chen, and Kazuaki Maeda. 2011. English Gigaword Fifth Edition LDC2011T07. *Linguistic Data Consortium*.

Maria Pershina, Yifan He, and Ralph Grishman. 2015. Personalized Page Rank for Named Entity Disambiguation. In *Proceedings of the 2015 Conference of the North American Chapter of the Association for Computational Linguistics: Human Language Technologies*, pages 238–243, Denver, Colorado. Association for Computational Linguistics.

Pushpendre Rastogi, Benjamin Van Durme, and Raman Arora. 2015. Multiview LSA : Representation Learning via Generalized CCA. *Proceedings of the 2015 Annual Conference of the North American Chapter of the ACL*, (1961):556–566.

A. K. M. Sabbir, Antonio Jimeno Yepes, and Ramakanth Kavuluru. 2016. Knowledge-Based Biomedical Word Sense Disambiguation with Neural Concept Embeddings.

Kristina Toutanova, Danqi Chen, Patrick Pantel, Hoifung Poon, Pallavi Choudhury, and Michael Gamon. 2015. Representing Text for Joint Embedding of Text and Knowledge Bases. In *Proceedings of the 2015 Conference on Empirical Methods in Natural Language Processing*, pages 1499–1509, Lisbon, Portugal. Association for Computational Linguistics.

Quan Wang, Zhendong Mao, Bin Wang, and Li Guo. 2017. Knowledge Graph Embedding: A Survey of Approaches and Applications. *IEEE Transactions on Knowledge and Data Engineering*, 29(12):2724–2743.

Zhen Wang, Jianwen Zhang, Jianlin Feng, and Zheng Chen. 2014. Knowledge Graph and Text Jointly Embedding. In *Proceedings of the 2014 Conference on Empirical Methods in Natural Language Processing (EMNLP)*, pages 1591–1601, Doha, Qatar. Association for Computational Linguistics.

Ikuya Yamada, Hiroyuki Shindo, Hideaki Takeda, and Yoshiyasu Takefuji. 2016. Joint Learning of the Embedding of Words and Entities for Named Entity Disambiguation. In *Proceedings of The 20th SIGNLL Conference on Computational Natural Language Learning (CoNLL)*, pages 250–259, Berlin, Germany. Association for Computational Linguistics.

Zhilin Yang, William Cohen, and Ruslan Salakhudinov. 2016. Revisiting Semi-Supervised Learning with Graph Embeddings. In *Proceedings of The 33rd International Conference on Machine Learning*, volume 48 of *Proceedings of Machine Learning Research*, pages 40–48, New York, New York, USA. PMLR.

A WikiSRS construction details

We followed a similar process to Pakhomov et al. (2010) in selecting the entity pairs to be used in our dataset. We first filtered the full list of Wikipedia pages to the subset that we learned embeddings for, and then used the entity types assigned to these pages in YAGO (Mahdisoltani et al., 2015) to restrict to only entities labeled with WordNet types organization or person, or with the YAGO type geoEntity. For each pairing of these categories (Organization-Organization, Organization-Place, Organization-Person, Place-Place, Place-Person, and Person-Person), we manually selected 30 pairs of entities for each of the following relatedness categories: Completely Unrelated, Somewhat Unrelated, Somewhat Related, and Highly Related. These produced the list of 720 entity pairs we used for our Mechanical Turk surveys.

We augmented each survey of 30 questions with 4 manually-created validation pairs using common entities (e.g., London, New York), each of which was categorized as Highly Related or Completely Unrelated. We included these validation questions at random indices in our surveys. To evaluate if participants were reading the questions, we binned their ratings on these validation questions into 0-25 (Completely Unrelated), 26-50 (Somewhat Unrelated), 51-75 (Somewhat Related), and 76-100 (Highly Related). If a participant's ratings disagreed with ours on multiple validation questions, we discarded their data (we allowed disagreement on a single question, as some validation questions had high variance in responses among reliable annotators).

We recruited 6 participants for each survey, for a total of 34 unique participants across the 48 HITs. Participants were presented with a message describing the survey and stating that by clicking the button at the bottom of the message to begin the survey, they were providing informed consent to participate. Identifying participant data was not collected, and we used only the anonymous worker IDs provided by the Mechanical Turk interface to collate our data and remunerate workers. Participants were asked optional demographic questions about their age bracket and native language at the end of the survey; we did not end up using age information, but filtered our participants for those that self-reported English reading proficiency. The majority responded to a single HIT,

# of raters	Similarity		Relatedness	
	ICC	# pairs	ICC	# pairs
4	0.531	419	0.467	180
5	0.520	267	0.540	207
6			0.560	299
> 6	–	2	–	2
Total		688		688

Table 11: The intraclass correlation coefficient (ICC) among Amazon Mechanical Turk worker judgments of similarity and relatedness of pairs of Wikipedia entities. As ICC requires a fixed number of raters, but we had variable numbers of responses to each HIT, we break down the datasets by the number of workers who rated each item.

while 3 completed more than 20. We discarded all submissions from 3 participants, as they did not report English reading proficiency (1) or did not satisfy the validation questions (2). All participants were paid state minimum wage at the time of the study for their time, regardless of whether they answered demographic questions or if we used their data in the final sample. Collection of this data was approved under Ohio State University IRB protocol 2017E0050.

To generate the final dataset, we assessed each participant's responses to the validation questions in each survey. We kept surveys for which we had at least 4 participants with satisfactory answers to the validation questions; this resulted in discarding 1 of the 24 HITs for each task. Due to 2 repeated pairs, this gave us final dataset sizes of 688 pairs for each of similarity and relatedness, 658 of which were shared between the tasks.

Following Pakhomov et al. (2010), we assessed inter-annotator agreement using the intraclass correlation coefficient (ICC). Table 11 gives the values for our datasets. The numbers reported are within the moderate range, and they correspond to the ICC numbers reported by Pakhomov et al. on the UMNSRS datasets.

The source code of our Mechanical Turk interface and data files used to generate the tasks are available at `github.com/OSU-slatelab/WikiSRS`.

A Sequence-to-Sequence Model for Semantic Role Labeling

Angel Daza and Anette Frank
Leibniz ScienceCampus "Empirical Linguistics and Computational Language Modeling"
Department of Computational Linguistics
Heidelberg University
69120 Heidelberg, Germany
`{daza,frank}@cl.uni-heidelberg.de`

Abstract

We explore a novel approach for Semantic Role Labeling (SRL) by casting it as a sequence-to-sequence process. We employ an attention-based model enriched with a copying mechanism to ensure faithful regeneration of the input sequence, while enabling interleaved generation of argument role labels. Here, we apply this model in a monolingual setting, performing PropBank SRL on English language data. The constrained sequence generation set-up enforced with the copying mechanism allows us to analyze the performance and special properties of the model on manually labeled data and benchmarking against state-of-the-art sequence labeling models. We show that our model is able to solve the SRL argument labeling task on English data, yet further structural decoding constraints will need to be added to make the model truly competitive. Our work represents a first step towards more advanced, generative SRL labeling setups.

1 Introduction

Semantic Role Labeling (SRL) is the task of assigning semantic argument structure to constituents or phrases in a sentence, to answer the question: *Who* did *what* to *whom*, *where* and *when*? This task is normally accomplished in two steps: first, identifying the predicate and second, labeling its arguments and the roles that they play with respect to the predicate. SRL has been formalized in different frameworks, the most prominent being FrameNet (Baker et al., 1998) and PropBank (Palmer et al., 2005). In this work we focus on *argument identification and labeling* using the PropBank (PB) annotation scheme.

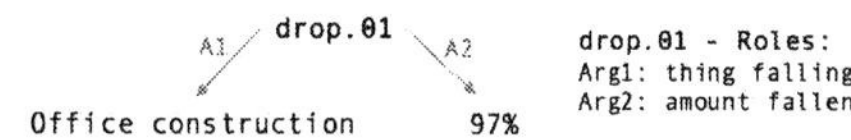

Figure 1: An input sentence (top), its PropBank predicate-argument structure (middle) and its linearized labeled sequence produced by our system.

Recent end-to-end neural models considerably improved the state-of-the-art results for SRL in English (He et al., 2017; Marcheggiani and Titov, 2017). In general, such models treat the problem as a supervised sequence labeling task, using deep LSTM architectures that assign a label to each token within the sentence.

SRL training resources for other languages are more restricted in size and thus, models suffer from sparseness problems because specific predicate-role instances occur only a handful of times in the training set. Since annotating SRL data in larger amounts is expensive, the use of a generative neural network model could be beneficial for automatically obtaining more labeled data in low-resource settings. The model that we present in this paper is a first step towards a joint label and language generation formulation for SRL, using the sequence-to-sequence architecture as a starting point.

We explore a sequence-to-sequence formulation of SRL that we apply, as a first step, in a classical monolingual setting on PropBank data, as illustrated in Figure 1. This constrained monolingual setting will allow us to analyze the suitablility of a sequence-to-sequence architecture for SRL, by benchmarking the system performance against existing sequence labeling models for SRL on well known labeled evaluation data.

Proceedings of the 3rd Workshop on Representation Learning for NLP, pages 207–216
Melbourne, Australia, July 20, 2018. ©2018 Association for Computational Linguistics

Sequence-to-sequence (seq2seq) models were pioneered by Sutskever et al. (2014), and later enhanced with an attention mechanism (Bahdanau et al., 2014; Luong et al., 2015). They have been successfully applied in many related structure prediction tasks such as syntactic parsing (Vinyals et al., 2015), parsing into Abstract Meaning Representation (Konstas et al., 2017), semantic parsing (Dong and Lapata, 2016), and cross-lingual Open Information Extraction (Zhang et al., 2017).

When applying a seq2seq model with attention in a monolingual SRL labeling setup, we need to restrict the decoder to reproduce the original input sentence, while in addition inserting PropBank labels into the target sequence in the decoding process (see Figure 1). To achieve this, we encode each input sentence into a suitable representation that will be used by the decoder to regenerate word tokens as given in the source sentence and introducing SRL labels in appropriate positions to label argument spans with semantic roles. In order to avoid lexical deviations in the output string, we add a copying mechanism (Gu et al., 2016) to the model. This technique was originally proposed to deal with rare words by copying them directly from the source when appropriate. We apply this mechanism in a novel way, with the aim of guiding the decoder to reproduce the input as closely as possible, while otherwise giving it the option of generating role labels in appropriate positions in the target sequence.

Our main contributions in this work are:

(i) We propose a novel neural architecture for SRL using a seq2seq model enhanced with attention and copying mechanisms.

(ii) We evaluate this model in a monolingual setting, performing PropBank-style SRL on standard English datasets, to assess the suitability of this model type for the SRL labeling task.

(iii) We compare the performance of our model to state-of-the-art sequence labeling models, including detailed (also comparative) error analysis.

(iv) We show that the seq2seq model is suited for the task, but still lags behind sequence labeling systems that include higher-level constraints.

2   Model

We propose an extension to the Sequence-to-Sequence model of (Bahdanau et al., 2014) to perform SRL.[1] The model will learn to map an unla-

beled source sequence of words $(x_1...x_{T_x})$ into a target sequence $(y_1...y_{T_y})$ consisting of word tokens and SRL label tokens (see Figure 2). The source sentence, represented as a sequence of dense word vectors, is fed to an LSTM encoder to produce a series of hidden states that represent the input. This information is used by the decoder to recursively generate tokens step-by-step, conditioned on the previous generated tokens and the source by attending the encoder's hidden states as proposed in Bahdanau et al. (2014). On top of this architecture, we add the copying mechanism (Gu et al., 2016), which helps the model to avoid lexical deviations in the output while still having the freedom of generating words and SRL labels based on the context. The attention-based generation and copying mechanism will be competing with each other so that the model learns when to copy directly from the source and when to generate the next token.

In our current setup we restrict role labeling to a single predicate per sentence. If a sentence has more than one predicate, we create a separate copy for each predicate; the same setting was applied in Zhou and Xu (2015). In each sentence copy the predicate whose roles are to be labeled is preceded by a special token <PRED> that marks the position of the predicate under consideration. This helps the decoder to focus on generating argument labels for that specific predicate (see Table 1.)

2.1   Vocabulary

We assume a unique vocabulary for both encoder and decoder that comprises the words occurring during training, the out-of-vocabulary token, and the special symbol used to mark the position of the predicate, thus $\mathcal{V} = \{v_1, ..., v_N\} \cup \{UNK, < PRED >\}$. In addition, we employ a set $\mathcal{L} = \{l_1, ..., l_M\}$ with all the possible labeled brackets and a set $\mathcal{X} = \{x_1..., x_{T_x}\}$, a per-instance set containing the T_x words from the current source sequence. Thus, our total vocabulary is defined for each instance as $\mathcal{V} \cup \mathcal{L} \cup \mathcal{X}$.

The label set $\mathcal{L}$ contains one common opening bracket *(#* for all argument types to indicate the beginning of an argument span, and several label-specific closing brackets, such as *P0:A1)*, which indicates in this case that the span for argument *A1* is ending (see also Table 1).

---

[1] In this work we restrict ourselves to argument labeling.

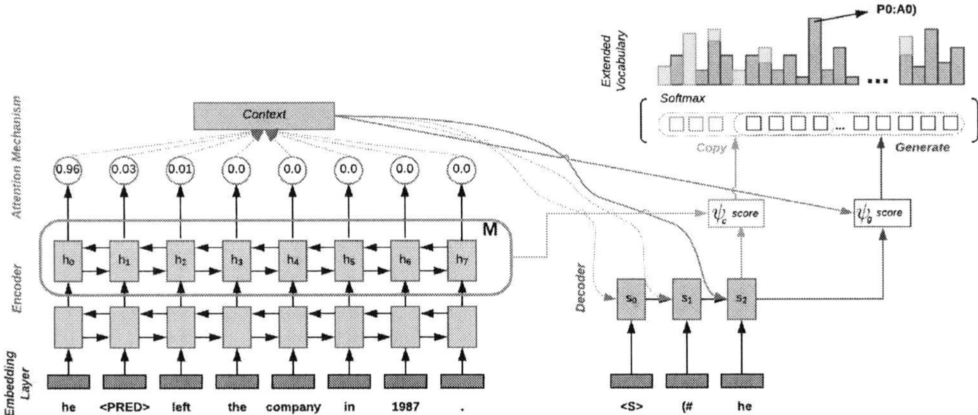

Figure 2: A sequence-to-sequence model for SRL. A score for copying and a score for generating tokens is computed at each time step and a joint softmax determines the probability of the next token over the extended vocabulary of words $\mathcal{V}$, labels $\mathcal{L}$ and current instance words $\mathcal{X}$.

2.2 Encoder

We use a two-layer bi-RNN encoder with LSTM cells (Hochreiter and Schmidhuber, 1997) that outputs a series of hidden states $h_j = \left[\overrightarrow{h_j}; \overleftarrow{h_j} \right]$ where each h_j contains information about the surrounding context of the word x_j. We refer to the complete matrix of encoder hidden states as $\mathbf{M}$, since it acts as a memory that the decoder can use to copy words directly from the source.

2.3 Attention Mechanism

We use the global dot product attention from Luong et al. (2015) to compute the context vector c_i:

$$c_i = \sum_{j=1}^{T_x} \alpha_{ij} h_j \quad ; \quad \alpha_{ij} = \frac{\exp(e_{i,j})}{\sum_{k=1}^{T_x} \exp(e_{i,k})} \quad (1)$$

where $e_{i,j}$ is the dot product function between decoder state s_{i-1} and each encoder hidden state h_j.

2.4 Decoder

The role of the decoder (a single-layer recurrent unidirectional LSTM) is to emit an output token y_t from a learned distribution over the vocabulary at each time step t given its state s_t, the previous output token y_{t-1}, the attention context vector c_t, and the memory $\mathbf{M}$. To get this distribution it is necessary to compute two separate modes: one for generating and one for copying.

To obtain the probability of generating y_t we use the context vector produced by the attention to learn a score ψ_g for each possible token v_i of

being the next generated token. We define ψ_g as:

$$\psi_g(y_t = v_i) = W_o[s_t; c_t], \quad v_i \epsilon \mathcal{V} \cup \mathcal{L} \quad (2)$$

where $W_o \epsilon \mathbb{R}^{N \times 2d_s}$ is a learnable parameter and s_t, c_t are the current decoder state and context vector respectively. This means that the model computes a generation score for both words and labels, based on what it is attending on at the current step.

For the probability of copying y_t we compute the score ψ_c of copying a token directly from the source as:

$$\psi_c(y_t = x_j) = \sigma(h_j^T W_c) s_t, \quad x_j \epsilon \mathcal{X} \quad (3)$$

where $W_c \epsilon \mathbb{R}^{d_h \times d_s}$ is a learnable parameter, h_j is the encoder hidden state representing x_j, s_t is the current decoder state, and σ is a non-linear transformation; we used `tanh` for our experiments.

Using the two scoring methods, the decoder will have two competing modes: the generation mode, used to generate the most probable subsequent token based on attention; and the copying, used to choose the next token directly from the encoder memory $\mathbf{M}$, which holds both positional and content information of the source. A final mixed distribution is calculated by adding the probability of generating y_t and the probability of copying y_t:

$$p(y_t|s_t, y_{t-1}, c_t, \mathbf{M}) = p(y_t, \mathbf{g}|s_t, y_{t-1}, c_t) +$$
$$p(y_t, \mathbf{c}|s_t, y_{t-1}, \mathbf{M}) \quad (4)$$

We use a *softmax* layer to convert the two scores into a joint distribution that represents the mixed

Source-1:	The trade figures *<PRED>* **turn out** well , and all those recently unloaded bonds spurt in price .
Target-1:	*(# The trade figures P0:A1) (# **turn out** P0:V) (# well P0:A2) , and all those recently unloaded bonds spurt in price .*
Source-2:	The trade figures turn out well , and all those recently *<PRED>* **unloaded** bonds spurt in price .
Target-2:	The trade figures turn out well , and all those *(# recently P0:AM-TMP) (# **unloaded** P0:V) (# bonds P0:A1)* spurt in price .
Source-3:	The trade figures turn out well , and all those recently unloaded bonds *<PRED>* **spurt** in price .
Target-3:	The trade figures turn out well , and *(# all those recently unloaded bonds P0:A1) (# **spurt** P0:V) (# in price P0:AM-ADV)* .

Table 1: A single sentence with three labeled predicates is converted into three different source-target pairs. The symbol *<PRED>* in each source marks the predicate for which the model is expected to generate a correct predicate-argument structure.

likelihood of generating and copying y_t. Again following Gu et al. (2016), we define this as:

$$
p(y_t, \mathbf{g}|\cdot) = \begin{cases} \frac{1}{Z} e^{\psi_g(y_t)} & y_t \epsilon \mathcal{V} \cup \mathcal{L} \\ 0 & otherwise \end{cases}
$$

$$
p(y_t, \mathbf{c}|\cdot) = \begin{cases} \frac{1}{Z} \sum_{j:x_j=y_t} e^{\psi_c(x_j)} & y_t \epsilon \mathcal{X} \\ 0 & otherwise \end{cases}
\tag{5}
$$

where Z is the normalization term shared by the two modes, $Z = \sum_{v\epsilon\mathcal{V}} e^{\psi_g(v)} + \sum_{x\epsilon\mathcal{X}} e^{\psi_c(x)}$. Since a single *softmax* is applied over the copying and generating modes, the network learns by itself when it is proper to copy a word from the source and when it needs to generate a label.

During training, the objective is to minimize the negative log-likelihood of the target token y_t for each time-step for both generate mode (given previous generated tokens) and copy mode (given source sequence X). We calculate the loss for the whole sequence as:

$$
loss = -\frac{1}{T_y} \sum_{t=0}^{T_y} \log P(y_t|y_{<t}, X)
\tag{6}
$$

3 Experimental Setup

3.1 Datasets and Evaluation Measures

We test the performance of our system on the span-based SRL datasets CoNLL-05[2] and CoNLL-12.[3] These datasets provide the gold predicate as part of the input. Since we focus on argument identification and classification, we provide this information in the input to the system. We use the standard training, development and test splits and use the official CoNLL-05 evaluation script on both datasets. We compare our results with Collobert et al. (2011); FitzGerald et al. (2015); Zhou and Xu (2015) and He et al. (2017) who use the same datasets and evaluation script. We show results separately for the Brown and WSJ portion of the CoNLL-05 test dataset.

The CoNLL-05 Shared Task[4] evaluation script computes precision, recall and F1 measure (the harmonic mean of precision and recall) for the predicted arguments. The script expects prediction-gold pairs that have the same number of words in order to consider them comparable, and only if this is the case, it computes a score. Furthermore, an argument is only considered correct if the words spanning the argument as well as its role label match with gold (Carreras and Màrquez, 2005). This means that it is essential to predict perfect argument spans besides the correct role label.

3.2 Pre-processing

For our seq2seq model we need to provide sources and targets in a linearized manner. The sequences are sentences with zero or more predicates. Following Zhou and Xu (2015), if a sentence has n_p predicates we process the sentence n_p times, each one with its corresponding predicate-argument structure. As shown in Table 1, we linearize the target side by converting the CoNLL format into sequences of tokens that include brackets indicating the span of the argument and the argument label on the closing bracket. We inform the model about the predicate that it should focus on by adding the special token *<PRED>* to the source sequence immediately before the predicate word. This process is entirely reversible and thus we convert the system outputs back to CoNLL format and evaluate the results with the official script.

---

[2] http://www.lsi.upc.edu/~srlconll/home.html

[3] http://conll.cemantix.org/2012/data.html

[4] http://www.lsi.upc.edu/~srlconll/soft.html

| | CoNLL-05 | | | CoNLL-12 | |
	Dev	WSJ	Brown	Dev	Test
Seq2seq (attention-only)					
same length	29.19	29.98	32.24	-	-
brackets	95.25	94.93	94.24	-	-
Seq2seq (w/ Attention & Copying)					
same length	96.71	97.15	97.24	97.46	96.07
brackets	99.91	99.82	99.88	99.97	99.93

Table 2: Quality of reproducing words and SRL brackets with seq2seq: Attention-only vs. Attention & Copying, on CoNLL-05 and CoNLL-12 datasets: percentage of correctly reproduced sentence length and percentage of balanced brackets.

3.3 Training

Since we process as many copies of sentences as it has predicates, the final amount of sequences is approximately 94K for CoNLL-05 and 185K for CoNLL-12 training sets. We keep linearized sequences up to 100 tokens long and lowercase all tokens. Given this limit, we omit 30 (CoNLL-05) and 900 (CoNLL-12) sequences from training. We initialize the model with pre-trained 100-dimensional GloVe embeddings (Pennington et al., 2014) and update them during training.[5] All the tokens that are not covered by GloVe or that appear less frequently than a given threshold[6] in the training dataset are mapped to the UNK embedding. We keep track of this mapping to be able to post-process the sequence and recover the rare tokens. Our vocabulary size is set to $|\mathcal{V}| \approx 20K$ words for CoNLL-05 and $|\mathcal{V}| \approx 18K$ words for CoNLL-12.

We use Adam optimizer (Kingma and Ba, 2014), a learning rate $l_r = 0.001$ and gradient clipping at 5.0. Both encoder and decoder have hidden layer of 512 LSTMs. We use dropout (Srivastava et al., 2014) of 0.4 and train for 4 epochs with batch size of 6.

4 Evaluation and Results

Initially, we trained a model using attention only, and it learned to generate balanced brackets (every opening bracket has a corresponding closing

---

[5]We also experimented with word2vec word embeddings (Mikolov et al., 2013) but found GloVe6B (trained on Wikipedia2014+Gigaword5) embeddings to perform better. Available at https://nlp.stanford.edu/projects/glove/

[6]We used a threshold of 10 for CoNLL-05 and 15 for CoNLL-12.

| | CoNLL-05 | | | | CoNLL-12 | |
	dev	test	WSJ	Brown	dev	test
Collobert	72.29	74.15	-	-	-	-
FitzGerald	78.3	-	79.4	71.2	79.2	79.6
Zhou & Xu	79.55	81.27	82.84	69.41	81.07	81.27
He	81.6	81.6	83.1	72.1	81.5	81.7
Ours (min)	76.05	76.7	78.13	66.28	73.4	73.61
Ours (max)	77.29	77.87	79.23	68.39	75.05	75.43

Table 3: F1 measure for argument role labeling of our seq2seq model w/ Attention & Copying on CoNLL-05 and CoNLL-12 dev and test sets, compared to Collobert w/o parser, FitzGerald single model, Zhou & Xu, and He single model .

bracket within the sequence) without further constraints. Yet, due to its generative nature, many target sequences diverged from the source in both length and token sequences. This was expected, because the system has to learn to generate not only the labels at the correct time-step but also to re-generate the complete sentence accurately. This is a disadvantage compared to the sequence labeling models where the words are already given.

By adding copying mechanism the model successfully regenerates the source sentence in the majority (up to 99%) of cases, as shown in Table 2. Such behavior also enables us to measure the performance of the model as an argument role classifier against the gold standard. Thus, we can benchmark its labeling performance against previous architectures built to solve the SRL task.

Table 3 displays the overall labeling performance of our copying-enhanced seq2seq model in comparison to previous neural sequence labeling architectures. For sequences that do not fully reproduce the input, we cannot compute appropriate scores against the gold standard. We compute two alternative scores for these cases: *oracle-min*, by setting the score for these sentences to 0.0 F1, and *oracle-max*, by setting their results to the scores we would obtain with perfect (= gold) labels. With these scores, we can better estimate the loss we are experiencing by non-perfectly reproduced sequences (see Table 2.)

As seen in Table 3, our model achieves an F1 score of 76.05 on the CoNLL-05 development set, and 73.4 on CoNLL-12 (min-oracle), and 77.29 and 75.05 (max-oracle), respectively. While these scores are still low compared to the latest neural SRL architectures, they are above the relatively simple model of Collobert et al. (2011). Note also

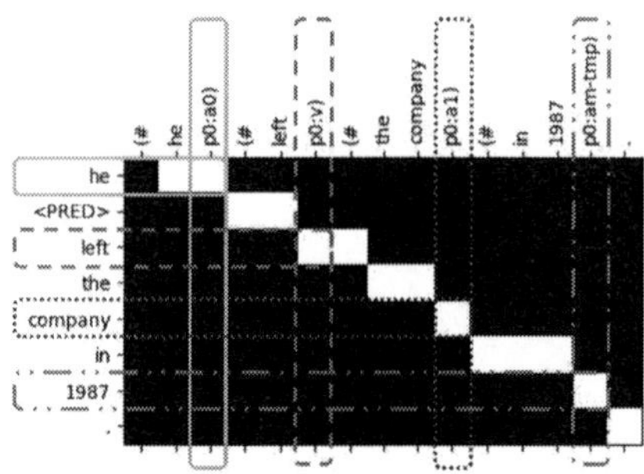

Figure 3: Example of the alignments learned by the attention mechanism.

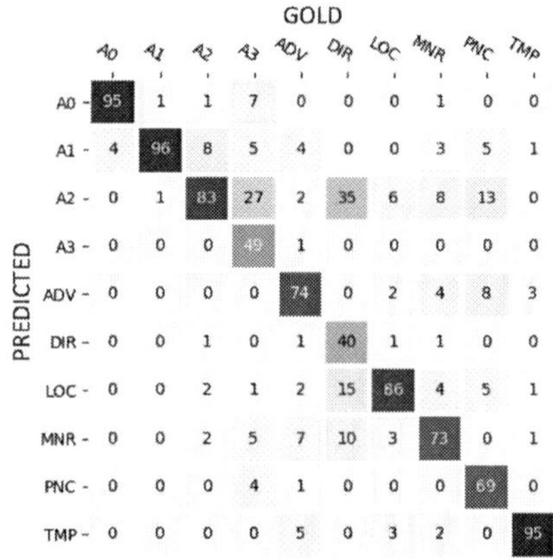

Figure 4: Confusion matrix showing percentage of predicted labels compared to the gold labels on the CoNLL-05 development set.

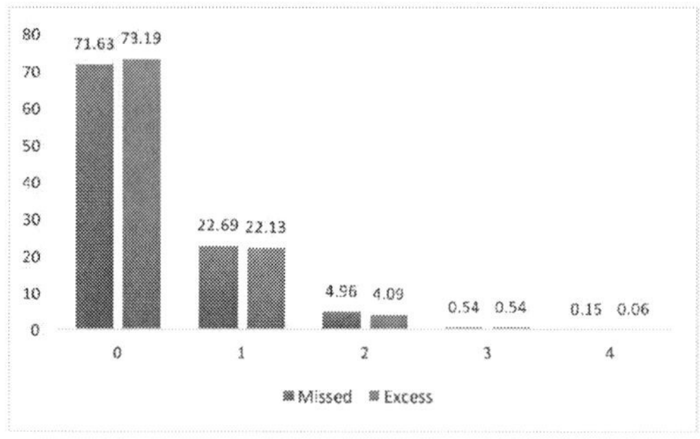

Figure 5: Percentage of sentences with 0,1,2 or more missing (blue) or excess (orange) arguments (seq2seq w/Copying, CoNLL-05, dev set).

that in contrast to the stronger models of FitzGerald et al. (2015); Zhou and Xu (2015) and He et al. (2017), our architecture is very lean and does not (yet) employ structured prediction (e.g. Conditional Random Field), to impose structural constraints on the label assignment. While this is certainly an extension we are going to explore in future work, here we will conduct deeper investigation to learn more about the kind of errors that our unconstrained seq2seq model makes. We report the analysis on CoNLL-05 development set.

4.1 Analysis

Argument Spans The model needs to generate labeled brackets at the appropriate time-step, in other words, the prediction of correct spans for arguments. To verify how well it is doing this, we measure how much overlap exists between the generated spans and the gold ones. This is equivalent to computing unlabeled argument assignment. We found that 77.5% of the spans match the gold spans completely, 21.2% of spans are partially overlapping with gold spans, and only 1.2% of the spans do not overlap at all with gold.

Argument Labels Recall from Section 2 that our model is labeling the sentences as in a translation task. It learns to use information from relevant words in the source sequence, aligning the labels to the argument words via learned attention weights as it is shown in Figure 3. This allows us to see where the model is looking when generating the labeled bracket. The confusion matrix in Figure 4 shows predicted vs. gold labels for all correctly assigned argument spans (i.e., the spans that match the gold boundaries). We observe that the model does very well for A0 and A1 gold roles, and that it causes only few misclassifications for A2. However, it frequently predicts core ar-

gument roles A0–A3 for non-argument roles, and also tends to mix predictions among non-core arguments. Since A0 and A1 roles are most frequent in the data, this indicates that the seq2seq model would benefit from more training data, particularly for less frequent roles, to better differentiate roles, and this is more prominent for the ones that are marked with prepositions.

Role co-occurrence and role set constraints Despite the absence of more refined decoding constraints, our model learns to avoid generating duplicated argument labels in most of the sequences. We find duplicated argument labels in less than 1% of the sequences. Figure 5 shows that the majority (about 70%) of sentences do not involve any missing or excess arguments; about 24/20% of sentences experience a single missing/excess role, and only 5/4% of the sentences experience a higher amount of missed/excess roles. Overall,

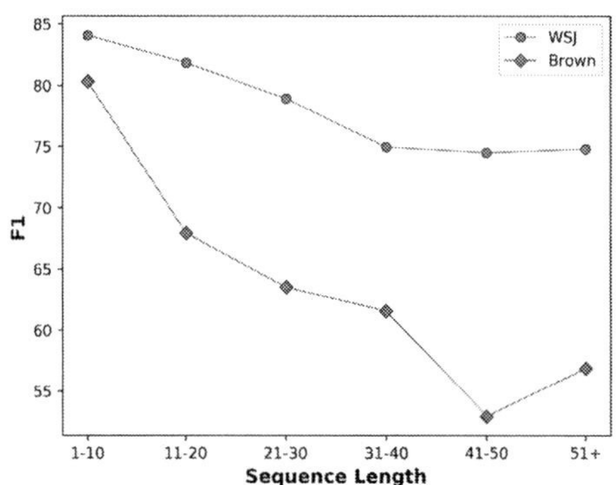

Figure 6: Performance of the model based on the number of tokens that the sequence has.

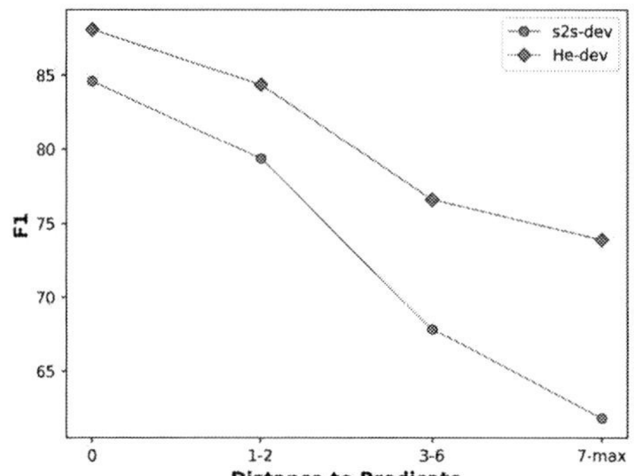

Figure 7: F1 score of arguments in buckets of increasing distances from their predicate, with distance normalized by sentence length (CoNLL-05, dev). We compare our model with He et al. (2017).

missed vs. excess arguments are balanced.

Sequence Length Another characteristic of the seq2seq model is that it encodes within a single sequence both words and labeled brackets. This increases the length of the sequences that need to be processed, and it is a well known problem that sequence length affects performance of recurrent neural models, even with the use of attention.

To measure the labeling performance difficulty with increasing sequence length, we partitioned the system outputs in six different bins containing groups of sentences of similar length (see Figure 6). As expected, the F1 score degrades proportionally to the length of the sequence, especially in sentences with more than 30 tokens.

Distance to predicate He et al. (2017) show

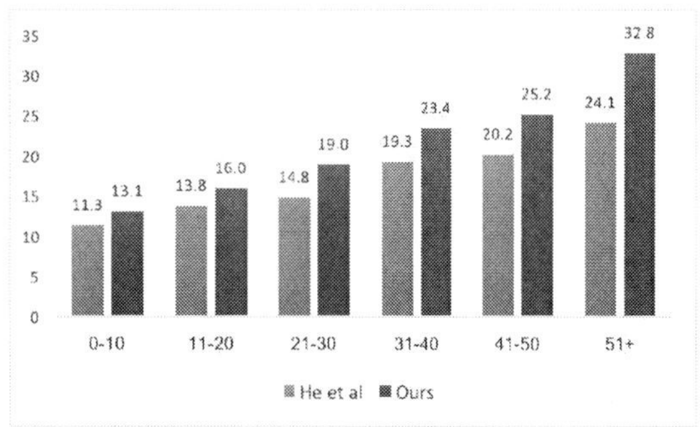

Figure 8: Error ratio of arguments in different regions of the sequences (CoNLL-05, dev).

that the surface distance between the argument and the predicate is also proportional to the amount of labeling errors. In our model, the distance between argument words and the predicate is even longer because of labeled brackets embedded in the sequence. Figure 7 displays the F1 score for different token distances between predicate and the respective argument. We see that the seq2seq model follows the same trend as the sequence labeling model, despite the fact that our model has access to the hidden states from the encoded input sentence; however, the real distance between predicate and argument in the decoder is also bigger.

Distance from sentence beginning. With each token that the model generates in decoding, the distance to the end position of the encoded sentence representation grows. While intuitively we would expect the model performance to degrade with larger distance to the input, it is also true that the model could be more prone to making mistakes at the beginning of the sequence, when the decoder has not yet generated enough context. To investigate this, we traced the ratio of errors that occur in several ranges of the sequence. We can see in Figure 8 that the first intuition was correct, the distance to the encoded representation is proportional to the mistakes that the model makes. We compare the error ratio to He et al. (2017) and show that the seq2seq system follows a similar trend but degrades faster with sequence length.

5   Related Work

Semantic Role Labeling. Traditional approaches to SRL relied on carefully designed features and expensive techniques to achieve global consistency such as Integer Linear Programming (Punyakanok et al., 2008) or dynamic programming

(Täckström et al., 2015). First neural SRL attempts tried to mix syntactic features with neural network representations. For example, FitzGerald et al. (2015) created argument and role representations using a feed-forward NN, and used a graphical model to enforce global constraints. Roth and Lapata (2016), on the other hand, proposed a neural classifier using dependency path embeddings to assign semantic labels to syntactic arguments.

Collobert et al. (2011) proposed the first SRL neural model that did not depend on hand-crafted features and treated the task as an IOB sequence labeling problem. Later, Zhou and Xu (2015) proposed a deep bi-directional LSTM model with a CRF layer on top. This model takes only the original text as input and assigns a label to each individual word in the sentence. He et al. (2017) also treat SRL as a IOB tagging problem, and use again a deep bi-LSTM incorporating highway connections, recurrent dropout and hard decoding constraints together with an ensemble of experts. This represents the best performing system on two span-based benchmark datasets so far (namely, CoNLL-05 and CoNLL-12). Marcheggiani et al. (2017) show that it is possible to construct a very accurate dependency-based SRL system without using any kind of explicit syntactic information. In subsequent work, Marcheggiani and Titov (2017) combine their LSTM model with a graph convolutional network to encode syntactic information at word level, which improves their LSTM classifier results on the dependency-based benchmark dataset (CoNLL-09).

Sequence-to-sequence models. Seq2seq models were first discovered as powerful models for Neural Machine Translation (Sutskever et al., 2014; Cho et al., 2014) but soon proved to be useful for any kind of problem that could be represented as a mapping between source and target sequences. Vinyals et al. (2015) demonstrate that constituent parsing can be formulated as a seq2seq problem by linearizing the parse tree. They obtain close to state-of-the-art results by using a large automatically parsed dataset. Dong and Lapata (2016) built a model for a related problem, semantic parsing, by mapping sentences to logical form. Seq2seq models have also been widely used for language generation (e.g. Karpathy and Li (2015); Chisholm et al. (2017)) given their ability to produce linguistic variation in the output sequences.

More closely related to SRL is the AMR parsing and generation system proposed by Konstas et al. (2017). This work successfully constructs a two-way mapping: generation of text given AMR representations as well as AMR parsing of natural language sentences. Finally, Zhang et al. (2017) went one step further by proposing a cross-lingual end-to-end system that learns to encode natural language (i.e. Chinese source sentences) and to decode them into sentences on the target side containing open semantic relations in English, using a parallel corpus for training.

6 Conclusions

In this paper we explore the properties of a Sequence-to-Sequence model for identifying and labeling PropBank roles. This is motivated by the fact that using a seq2seq model gives more flexibility for further tasks such as constrained generation and cross-lingual label projection. Another advantage is that our model is a very lean architecture compared to the deep Bi-LSTM of the recent SRL models.

To our knowledge, this is the first attempt to perform SRL using a seq2seq approach. Specific challenges emerged by formulating the problem in this way, such as: (i) the decoding of labels and words within a single sequence; (ii) generating balanced labeled brackets at the correct position; (iii) avoiding repetition of tokens, and especially, (iv) generating labeled sequences that perfectly match the source sentence in order to make the labeled sequence absolutely comparable.

Despite these difficulties, we could show that a sequence-to-sequence model with attention and copying achieves quite respectable labeling performance with a lean architecture and without yet considering structural constraints. For future work we consider extensions towards joint semantic role labeling and constrained generation, to produce new variations of existing labeled data.

Acknowledgements

We thank the reviewers for their insightful comments. We are also grateful to Éva Mújdricza-Maydt for assistance with the PropBank labeling scheme and CoNLL datasets. This research is funded by the Leibniz ScienceCampus Empirical Linguistics & Computational Language Modeling, supported by Leibniz Association grant no. SAS2015-IDS-LWC and by the Ministry of Science, Research, and Art of Baden-Wurttemberg.

References

Dzmitry Bahdanau, Kyunghyun Cho, and Yoshua Bengio. 2014. Neural Machine Translation by Jointly Learning to Align and Translate.

Collin F. Baker, Charles J. Fillmore, John B. Lowe, Collin F. Baker, Charles J. Fillmore, and John B. Lowe. 1998. The berkeley framenet project. In *Proceedings of the 17th international conference on Computational linguistics*, volume 1, page 86, Morristown, NJ, USA. Association for Computational Linguistics.

Xavier Carreras and Lluís Màrquez. 2005. Introduction to the conll-2005 shared task: Semantic role labeling. In *Proceedings of the Ninth Conference on Computational Natural Language Learning*, CONLL '05, pages 152–164, Stroudsburg, PA, USA. Association for Computational Linguistics.

Andrew Chisholm, Will Radford, and Ben Hachey. 2017. Learning to generate one-sentence biographies from wikidata. In *Proceedings of the 15th Conference of the European Chapter of the Association for Computational Linguistics: Volume 1, Long Papers*, pages 633–642. Association for Computational Linguistics.

Kyunghyun Cho, Bart van Merriënboer, Çalar Gülçehre, Dzmitry Bahdanau, Fethi Bougares, Holger Schwenk, and Yoshua Bengio. 2014. Learning phrase representations using rnn encoder–decoder for statistical machine translation. In *Proceedings of the 2014 Conference on Empirical Methods in Natural Language Processing (EMNLP)*, pages 1724–1734, Doha, Qatar. Association for Computational Linguistics.

Ronan Collobert, Jason Weston, Lon Bottou, Michael Karlen, Koray Kavukcuoglu, and Pavel P. Kuksa. 2011. Natural language processing (almost) from scratch. *Journal of Machine Learning Research*, 12:2493–2537.

Li Dong and Mirella Lapata. 2016. Language to logical form with neural attention. In *Proceedings of the 54th Annual Meeting of the Association for Computational Linguistics (Volume 1: Long Papers)*, pages 33–43. Association for Computational Linguistics.

Nicholas FitzGerald, Oscar Täckström, Kuzman Ganchev, and Dipanjan Das. 2015. Semantic role labeling with neural network factors. In *Proceedings of the 2015 Conference on Empirical Methods in Natural Language Processing (EMNLP '15)*.

Jiatao Gu, Zhengdong Lu, Hang Li, and Victor O.K. Li. 2016. Incorporating copying mechanism in sequence-to-sequence learning. In *Proceedings of the 54th Annual Meeting of the Association for Computational Linguistics (Volume 1: Long Papers)*, pages 1631–1640, Berlin, Germany. Association for Computational Linguistics.

Luheng He, Kenton Lee, Mike Lewis, and Luke Zettlemoyer. 2017. Deep semantic role labeling: What works and whats next. In *Proceedings of the Annual Meeting of the Association for Computational Linguistics*.

Sepp Hochreiter and Jürgen Schmidhuber. 1997. Long short-term memory. *Neural Comput.*, 9(8):1735–1780.

Andrej Karpathy and Fei-Fei Li. 2015. Deep visual-semantic alignments for generating image descriptions. pages 3128–3137. IEEE Computer Society.

Diederik P. Kingma and Jimmy Ba. 2014. Adam: A method for stochastic optimization. *CoRR*, abs/1412.6980.

Ioannis Konstas, Srinivasan Iyer, Mark Yatskar, Yejin Choi, and Luke Zettlemoyer. 2017. Neural amr: Sequence-to-sequence models for parsing and generation. pages 146–157.

Thang Luong, Hieu Pham, and Christopher D. Manning. 2015. Effective approaches to attention-based neural machine translation. In *Proceedings of the 2015 Conference on Empirical Methods in Natural Language Processing, EMNLP 2015, Lisbon, Portugal, September 17-21, 2015*, pages 1412–1421.

Diego Marcheggiani, Anton Frolov, and Ivan Titov. 2017. A simple and accurate syntax-agnostic neural model for dependency-based semantic role labeling. In *Proceedings of the 21st Conference on Computational Natural Language Learning (CoNLL 2017)*, pages 411–420, Vancouver, Canada. Association for Computational Linguistics.

Diego Marcheggiani and Ivan Titov. 2017. Encoding sentences with graph convolutional networks for semantic role labeling. In *Proceedings of the 2017 Conference on Empirical Methods in Natural Language Processing*, pages 1506–1515, Copenhagen, Denmark. Association for Computational Linguistics.

Tomas Mikolov, Ilya Sutskever, Kai Chen, Greg Corrado, and Jeffrey Dean. 2013. Distributed representations of words and phrases and their compositionality. In *Proceedings of the 26th International Conference on Neural Information Processing Systems - Volume 2*, NIPS'13, pages 3111–3119, USA. Curran Associates Inc.

Martha Palmer, Paul Kingsbury, and Daniel Gildea. 2005. The proposition bank: An annotated corpus of semantic roles. *Computational Linguistics*, 31.

Jeffrey Pennington, Richard Socher, and Christopher D. Manning. 2014. Glove: Global vectors for word representation. In *Empirical Methods in Natural Language Processing (EMNLP)*, pages 1532–1543.

Vasin Punyakanok, Dan Roth, and Wen-tau Yih. 2008. The importance of syntactic parsing and inference in semantic role labeling. *Comput. Linguist.*, 34(2):257–287.

Michael Roth and Mirella Lapata. 2016. Neural semantic role labeling with dependency path embeddings. In *Proceedings of the 54th Annual Meeting of the Association for Computational Linguistics (Volume 1: Long Papers)*, pages 1192–1202, Berlin, Germany. Association for Computational Linguistics.

Nitish Srivastava, Geoffrey Hinton, Alex Krizhevsky, Ilya Sutskever, and Ruslan Salakhutdinov. 2014. Dropout: A simple way to prevent neural networks from overfitting. *J. Mach. Learn. Res.*, 15(1):1929–1958.

Ilya Sutskever, Oriol Vinyals, and Quoc V Le. 2014. Sequence to sequence learning with neural networks. pages 3104–3112.

Oscar Täckström, Kuzman Ganchev, and Dipanjan Das. 2015. Efficient inference and structured learning for semantic role labeling. *Transactions of the Association for Computational Linguistics*, 3:29–41.

Oriol Vinyals, Ł ukasz Kaiser, Terry Koo, Slav Petrov, Ilya Sutskever, and Geoffrey Hinton. 2015. Grammar as a foreign language. pages 2773–2781.

Sheng Zhang, Kevin Duh, and Benjamin Van Durme. 2017. Mt/ie: Cross-lingual open information extraction with neural sequence-to-sequence models. In *Proceedings of the 15th Conference of the European Chapter of the Association for Computational Linguistics: Volume 2, Short Papers*, pages 64–70. Association for Computational Linguistics.

Jie Zhou and Wei Xu. 2015. End-to-end learning of semantic role labeling using recurrent neural networks. In *Proceedings of the 53rd Annual Meeting of the Association for Computational Linguistics and the 7th International Joint Conference on Natural Language Processing (Volume 1: Long Papers)*, pages 1127–1137, Beijing, China. Association for Computational Linguistics.

Predicting Concreteness and Imageability of Words Within and Across Languages via Word Embeddings

Nikola Ljubešić
Dept. of Knowledge Technologies
Jožef Stefan Institute
Jamova cesta 39, SI-1000 Ljubljana
`nikola.ljubesic@ijs.si`

Darja Fišer
Dept. of Translation, Faculty of Arts
University of Ljubljana
Aškerčeva 2, SI-1000 Ljubljana
`darja.fiser@ff.uni-lj.si`

Anita Peti-Stantić
Faculty of Humanities and Social Sciences
University of Zagreb
Ivana Lučića 3, HR-10000 Zagreb
`anita.peti-stantic@ffzg.hr`

Abstract

The notions of concreteness and imageability, traditionally important in psycholinguistics, are gaining significance in semantic-oriented natural language processing tasks. In this paper we investigate the predictability of these two concepts via supervised learning, using word embeddings as explanatory variables. We perform predictions both within and across languages by exploiting collections of cross-lingual embeddings aligned to a single vector space. We show that the notions of concreteness and imageability are highly predictable both within and across languages, with a moderate loss of up to 20% in correlation when predicting across languages. We further show that the cross-lingual transfer via word embeddings is more efficient than the simple transfer via bilingual dictionaries.

1 Introduction

Concreteness and imageability are very important notions in psycholinguistic research, building on the theory of the double, verbal and non-verbal, modality of representation of concrete words in the mental lexicon, contrasted to single verbal representation of abstract words (Paivio, 1975, 2010). Although often correlated with concreteness, imageability is not a redundant property. While most abstract things are hard to visualize, some call up images, e.g., *torture* calls up an emotional and even visual image. There are concrete things that are hard to visualize too, for example, *abbey* is harder to visualize than *banana* (Tsvetkov et al., 2014).

Both notions have proven to be useful in computational linguistics as well. Turney et al. (2011) present a supervised model that exploits concreteness to correctly classify 79% of adjective-noun pairs as having literal or non-literal meaning. Tsvetkov et al. (2014) exploit both the notions of concreteness and imageability to perform metaphor detection on subject-verb-object and adjective-noun relations, correctly classifying 82% and 86% instances, respectively.

The aim of this paper is to investigate the predictability of concreteness and imageability within a language, as well as across languages, by exploiting cross-lingual word embeddings as our available signal.

2 Related Work

While much work has been done on exploiting word embeddings in expanding sentiment lexicons (Tang et al., 2014; Amir et al., 2015; Hamilton et al., 2016), there is little work on predicting other lexical variables, concreteness and imageability included.

Tsvetkov et al. (2014) performed metaphor detection, using, among others, concreteness and imageability as their features. To propagate these features, obtained from the MRC psycholinguistic database (Wilson, 1988) to the entire lexicon, they used a supervised learning algorithm on vector space representations, where each vector element represented a feature. Performance of these classifiers was 0.94 for concreteness and 0.85 for imageability. They also applied the concreteness and imageability features to other languages by projecting features with bilingual dictionaries.

Broadwell et al. (2013) extended imageability scores to the whole lexicon by using the MRC

Proceedings of the 3rd Workshop on Representation Learning for NLP, pages 217–222
Melbourne, Australia, July 20, 2018. ©2018 Association for Computational Linguistics

imageability scores and hyponym and hyperonym links from WordNet.

Rothe et al. (2016) trained an orthogonal transformation to reorder word embedding dimensions into one-dimensional ultradense subspaces, the output thereby being a lexicon. They trained the transformations for sentiment, concreteness and frequency. For obtaining training data for concreteness, they used the BWK database (Brysbaert et al., 2014). They showed that concreteness and sentiment can be better extracted from embedding spaces than frequency, with a Kendall τ correlation coefficient of 0.623 for concreteness. Rothe and Schütze (2016) further exploited this method to perform operations over the extracted dimensions, such as given a concrete word like *friend*, find the related, but abstract word *friendship*.

Contributions In this paper we perform a systematic investigation of transfer of two lexical notions, concreteness and imageability, (1) to the remainder of the lexicon not covered in an annotation campaign, and (2) to other languages.

While there were already successful transfers within a language based on word embeddings (Tsvetkov et al., 2014; Rothe and Schütze, 2016), the only cross-lingual transfer was based on transfer via bilingual dictionaries (Tsvetkov et al., 2014). In this paper we compare the effectiveness of cross-lingual transfer via word embeddings and via bilingual dictionaries.

A byproduct of this research is a lexical resource in 77 languages containing per-word estimates for concreteness and imageability.

3 Data

3.1 Lexicons

In our experiments we use two existing English and one Croatian lexicon with concreteness and imageability ratings.

For English we use the MRC database (Wilson, 1988) (MRC onwards), consisting of 4,293 words with ratings for concreteness and imageability. The ratings range from 100 to 700 and were obtained by merging three different resources (Wilson, 1988).

We also use the BWK database consisting of 39,954 English words (Brysbaert et al., 2014) (BWK onwards) with concreteness ratings summarized through arithmetic mean and standard deviation. The ratings were collected in a crowdsourc-

ing campaign in which each word was labeled by 20 annotators on a 1–5 scale.

For Croatian we use the MEGAHR database (MEGA onwards), consisting of 3,000 words, with concreteness and imageability ratings summarized through arithmetic mean and standard deviation. The ratings were collected in an annotation campaign among university students, with each word obtaining 30 annotations per variable on a 1–5 scale.

For performing cross-lingual transfer via a dictionary, we use data from a large popular online Croatian-English dictionary[1] containing around 100 thousand entries.

3.2 Embeddings

For both in-language and cross-lingual experiments we use the aligned Facebook collection of embeddings[2], trained with fastText (Bojanowski et al., 2016) on Wikipedia dumps, with embedding spaces aligned between languages with a linear transformation learned via SVD (Smith et al., 2017) on a bilingual dictionary of 500 out of the 1000 most frequent English words, obtained via the Google Translate API[3].

We also experimented with another cross-lingual embedding collection (Conneau et al., 2017), obtaining similar results and backing all our conclusions. This is in line with recent work on comparing cross-lingual embedding models which suggests that the actual choice of monolingual and bilingual signal is more important for the final model performance than the actual underlying architecture (Levy et al., 2017; Ruder et al., 2017). Given that one of our goals is to transfer concreteness and imageability annotations to as many languages as possible, using cross-lingual word embeddings based on Wikipedia dumps and dictionaries obtained through a translation API is the most plausible option.

4 Experiments

4.1 Setup

We perform two sets of experiments: one within each language, and another across languages.

---

[1] http://www.taktikanova.hr/eh/
[2] https://github.com/facebookresearch/
fastText/blob/master/pretrained-vectors.
md
[3] https://github.com/Babylonpartners/
fastText_multilingual

While in-language experiments are always based on supervised learning, in cross-lingual experiments we compare two transfer approaches: one based on a simple dictionary transfer, and another on supervised learning on the word embeddings in the source language, and performing predictions on word embeddings in the target language, with the two embedding spaces being aligned.

We perform our prediction experiments by training SVM regression models (SVR) and deep feedforward neural networks (FFN) over standardized (zero mean, unit variance) embeddings and each specific response variable. We experiment with all available gold annotations as our response variables, namely both the arithmetic mean and standard deviation of concreteness and imageability.

We tuned the hyperparameters of each of the regressors on a subset of the Croatian, MEGA dataset in the case of the in-language experiments, and another subset of the BWK dataset for the cross-lingual experiments. Given that we perform the final experiments on the whole datasets, and that we have two additional English datasets at our disposal for the in-language experiments and three additional dataset pairs for the cross-lingual experiments, we consider our approach to be resistant to the overfitting of the hyperparameters going unnoticed.

While the SVR proved to work well with the RBF kernel, the C hyperparameter of 1.0 and the γ hyperparameter of 0.003, the feedforward network obtained strong results with two fully-connected hidden layers, consisting of 128 and 32 units each and ReLU activation functions, with a dropout layer after each of the hidden layers, and an output layer with a linear activation function. We optimized for the mean squared error loss function and ran 50 epochs on each of the datasets, with a batch size of 32.

While we used the same regressor setup for the SVR system for both the in-language and cross-lingual experiments, for the FFN system the dropout probability in the in-language experiments was 0.5, while in the cross-lingual setting the dropout probability was set to 0.8, obtaining thereby a more general model which transfers better to the other language.

We perform in-language experiments via 3-fold cross-validation, while we train models on our source language dataset and evaluate the models on our target language dataset for cross-lingual experiments. We evaluate each approach via the Spearman rank and Pearson linear correlation coefficients. In the paper we report the Spearman correlation coefficient only as the relationships across both metrics in all the experiments are identical. We perform our experiments with the `scikit-learn` (Pedregosa et al., 2011) and `keras` (Chollet et al., 2015) toolkits.

4.2   In-language Experiments

We start our experiments in the in-language setting, running cross-validation experiments over each of our three datasets on all available variables. The results of these experiments, with some basic information on the size of the datasets, are given in Table 1. Aside from the three lexicons introduced in Section 3.1, we experiment with another lexicon, BWK.3K, which is a randomly downsampled version of the BWK lexicon to the size of the two remaining lexicons. We introduce this additional resource (1) to control for dataset size when comparing results on our different datasets and (2) to measure the impact of training data size by comparing the results on the two flavours of the BWK dataset.

The results in Table 1 show that the support vector regressor consistently performs better than the feedforward neural network at predicting almost all values, with relative error reduction lying between 7% and 12%. The bold results are statistically significantly better than the corresponding non-bold ones given the approximate randomization test (Edgington, 1969) with $p < 0.05$. Our assumption is that the stronger FFN model does not show a positive impact primarily due to the small size of the datasets and the simplicity of the modeling problem.

We can further observe that the arithmetic mean is much easier to predict than standard deviation on both variables in all the datasets. This can be explained by the fact that standard deviation on the two phenomena can partially be explained with the level of ambiguity of a specific word, and this type of information is at least not directly available in context-based word embeddings.

Furthermore, imageability seems to be consistently slightly harder to predict than concreteness. Our initial assumption regarding this difference was that imageability is a more vague notion for

dataset	MEGA		BWK		BWK.3K		MRC	
lang	hr		en		en		en	
size	2,682		22,797		3,000		4,061	
method	SVR	FFN	SVR	FFN	SVR	FFN	SVR	FFN
C.M	**0.760**	0.742	**0.887**	0.879	**0.848**	0.834	**0.872**	0.863
C.STD	**0.265**	**0.274**	**0.484**	0.461	**0.376**	**0.364**	-	-
I.M	**0.645**	0.602	-	-	-	-	**0.803**	0.787
I.STD	**0.439**	**0.415**	-	-	-	-	-	-

Table 1: Results of the in-language experiments on predicting mean (.M) and standard deviation (.STD) of concreteness (C) and imageability (I), either using a support vector regressor (SVR) or feed-forward network (FFN). Evaluation metric is the Spearman correlation coefficient.

human subjects, and therefore their responses are more dispersed, adding to the complexity of the prediction. However, analyzing standard deviations over concreteness and imageability showed that these are rather the same. We leave this open question for future research.

When comparing the results on predicting mean concreteness on the full BWK and the trimmed BWK.3K datasets, we see a significant improvement of the predictions of the on the larger dataset, showing that having 10 times more data for learning can produce significant improvements in the prediction quality.

4.3 Cross-lingual Experiments

In cross-lingual experiments we compare our two approaches to cross-lingual transfer: dictionary lookup (DIC onwards) and supervised learning on aligned word embedding spaces via the two methods introduced in Section 4.2, SVR and FFN.

The DIC method simply looks up for each word in the source language resource all possible translations to the target language and directly transfers the concreteness and imageability ratings to the target language words. In case of collisions in the target language (two source language words being translated to the same word in the target language), we perform averaging over the transfered ratings. In our experiments, the arithmetic mean showed to be a better averaging method than the median, we therefore report the results on that averaging method.

The SVR and FFN methods use supervised learning in a very similar fashion to the in-language experiments described in Section 4.2. We train a supervised regression model on the whole source language dataset, using word embedding dimen-

sions as features and the variable of choice as our target. We obtain estimates of our variable of choice in the target language by applying the source-language model on the target-language word embeddings since the two embedding spaces are aligned.

For both approaches we compare the target-language estimates with the gold data available from our lexicons.

We present the results of the cross-lingual experiments in Table 2. Our first observation is that, while in the in-language setting the SVR method has regularly outperformed the FFN method, in the cross-lingual setting this is not the case any more, with SVR and FFN obtaining very similar results, in five out of six cases in the range of no statistically significant difference. Our explanation for the loss of the positive impact in using the weaker, support vector regression model, is that with the noisy alignment of the two embedding spaces the prediction problem became harder, now both models performing similarly. While the strong point of SVR is that it performs very well on small datasets, the strong point of the FFN method is that it generalizes better.

That higher generalization is beneficial in case of the cross-lingual problem is observable in the difference in the hyperparameter tuning results on the FFN method, where in the in-language setting the optimal dropout was 0.5, while in the cross-lingual setting it is 0.8.

Our second observation is that all the predicted ratings suffer in the cross-lingual setting, when compared to the in-language results presented in Table 1, observing for the SVR method a drop of around 5 to 15%. While standard deviation was already poorly predicted in the in-language set-

| source | MEGA (hr) | | | BWK (en) | | | MEGA (hr) | | | MRC (en) | | |
| target | BWK (en) | | | MEGA (hr) | | | MRC (en) | | | MEGA (hr) | | |
	SVR	FFN	DIC	SVR	FFN	DIC	SVR	FFN	DIC	SVR	FFN	DIC
C.M	**0.791**	**0.793**	0.728	**0.724**	**0.719**	0.641	**0.797**	**0.794**	0.611	**0.651**	**0.644**	0.638
C.STD	0.178	0.141	0.224	0.185	0.145	0.137	-	-	-	-		
I.M	-	-	-	-	-	-	**0.694**	**0.683**	0.523	**0.548**	0.531	0.503

Table 2: Results of the cross-lingual experiments, either using supervised learning (SVR, FFN), or simple dictionary lookup (DIC). Evaluation metric is the Spearman correlation coefficient. Results in bold are best results per problem with no statistically significant difference.

ting, in the cross-lingual setting it drops even further to a non-useful level, below 0.2. This is the reason why we do not calculate statistical significance of the differences in these results and do not include their estimates in our final 77-languages-strong resource. In the final cross-lingual resource we include only the mean of concreteness and imageability, the notions for which we have obtained strong correlation in our cross-lingual experiments.

Finally, when comparing the cross-lingual transfer via embeddings (SVR and FFN) and via a dictionary (DIC), the learning-on-embeddings approach outperforms the dictionary method in each instance, with the relative loss in correlation when moving from the EMB to the DIC approach of 5% to 25%.

4.4 Regressor Coefficient Analysis

Our final analysis concerns the question of how many of the embedding dimensions are crucial for our regressors to predict the notions of concreteness and imageability. We consider two potential scenarios: (1) each of the notions are encoded in one or a few of the embedding dimensions and (2) the notions are encoded in many embedding dimensions.

The analysis is performed by calculating the cumulative distribution of absolute and normalized (sum to 1), reversely sorted coefficients of the SVM regressor with a linear kernel. For both phenomena, concreteness and imageability, the distributions show that the predictions are based on a significant number of embedding dimensions. Namely, while 80 most informative dimensions cover 50% of the coefficients' mass, half of the dimensions (150) cover 80% of that mass. This shows for the second scenario – concreteness and imageability are encoded in a significant number of embedding dimensions – to be true.

5 Conclusion

In this paper we have shown that concreteness and imageability ratings can be successfully transfered both to non-covered portions of the lexicon and to other languages via (cross-lingual) word embeddings.

With the in-language experiments we have shown that the arithmetic mean of both notions is much easier to predict than their standard deviation, the latter probably encoding word ambiguity, type of information not directly present in word embeddings.

Our experiments across languages have shown that the loss in comparison to in-language experiments on predicting the means of both concreteness and imageability are around 15%, a reasonable price to pay given the applicability of the method to all of the 77 languages present in the word embedding collection. The predictions of concreteness and imageabililty obtained in the 77 languages are available at `http://hdl.handle.net/11356/1187`.[4]

Comparing the two methods of transfer – dictionary vs. cross-lingual embeddings, shows regularly better (5%–15%) results of the latter, proving once more the usefulness of word embeddings, especially in the currently expanding cross-lingual setup.

Acknowledgements

The work described in this paper has been funded by the Croatian National Foundation project HRZZ-IP-2016-06-1210, the Slovenian Research Agency project ARRS J7-8280, and by the Slovenian research infrastructure CLARIN.SI.

---

[4]Ongoing developments are stored at `https://github.com/clarinsi/megahr-crossling/`.

References

Silvio Amir, Ramón Astudillo, Wang Ling, Bruno Martins, Mario J Silva, and Isabel Trancoso. 2015. Inesc-id: A regression model for large scale twitter sentiment lexicon induction. In *Proceedings of the 9th International Workshop on Semantic Evaluation (SemEval 2015)*. pages 613–618.

Piotr Bojanowski, Edouard Grave, Armand Joulin, and Tomas Mikolov. 2016. Enriching word vectors with subword information. *arXiv preprint arXiv:1607.04606* .

George Aaron Broadwell, Umit Boz, Ignacio Cases, Tomek Strzalkowski, Laurie Feldman, Sarah Taylor, Samira Shaikh, Ting Liu, Kit Cho, and Nick Webb. 2013. Using imageability and topic chaining to locate metaphors in linguistic corpora. In Ariel M. Greenberg, William G. Kennedy, and Nathan D. Bos, editors, *Social Computing, Behavioral-Cultural Modeling and Prediction*. Springer Berlin Heidelberg, Berlin, Heidelberg, pages 102–110.

Marc Brysbaert, AB Warriner, and V Kuperman. 2014. Concreteness ratings for 40 thousand generally known english word lemmas. *BEHAVIOR RESEARCH METHODS* 46(3):904–911.

François Chollet et al. 2015. Keras. `https://keras.io`.

Alexis Conneau, Guillaume Lample, Marc'Aurelio Ranzato, Ludovic Denoyer, and Hervé Jégou. 2017. Word translation without parallel data. *arXiv preprint arXiv:1710.04087* .

Eugene S. Edgington. 1969. Approximate randomization tests. *The Journal of Psychology* 72(2):143–149. https://doi.org/10.1080/00223980.1969.10543491.

William L. Hamilton, Kevin Clark, Jure Leskovec, and Dan Jurafsky. 2016. Inducing domain-specific sentiment lexicons from unlabeled corpora. In *Proceedings of the 2016 Conference on Empirical Methods in Natural Language Processing, EMNLP 2016, Austin, Texas, USA, November 1-4, 2016*. pages 595–605. http://aclweb.org/anthology/D/D16/D16-1057.pdf.

Omer Levy, Anders Søgaard, and Yoav Goldberg. 2017. A strong baseline for learning cross-lingual word embeddings from sentence alignments. In *Proceedings of the 15th Conference of the European Chapter of the Association for Computational Linguistics: Volume 1, Long Papers*. Association for Computational Linguistics, pages 765–774. http://aclweb.org/anthology/E17-1072.

A. Paivio. 1975. *Coding Distinctions and Repetition Effects in Memory*. Research bulletin. Department of Psychology, University of Western Ontario.

Allan Paivio. 2010. Dual coding theory and the mental lexicon. *The Mental Lexicon* 5(2):205–230.

F. Pedregosa, G. Varoquaux, A. Gramfort, V. Michel, B. Thirion, O. Grisel, M. Blondel, P. Prettenhofer, R. Weiss, V. Dubourg, J. Vanderplas, A. Passos, D. Cournapeau, M. Brucher, M. Perrot, and E. Duchesnay. 2011. Scikit-learn: Machine learning in Python. *Journal of Machine Learning Research* 12:2825–2830.

Sascha Rothe, Sebastian Ebert, and Hinrich Schütze. 2016. Ultradense word embeddings by orthogonal transformation. *CoRR* abs/1602.07572.

Sascha Rothe and Hinrich Schütze. 2016. Word embedding calculus in meaningful ultradense subspaces. In *Proceedings of the 54th Annual Meeting of the Association for Computational Linguistics (Volume 2: Short Papers)*. volume 2, pages 512–517.

Sebastian Ruder, Ivan Vulić, and Anders Søgaard. 2017. A survey of cross-lingual embedding models. *CoRR* abs/1706.04902. http://arxiv.org/abs/1706.04902.

Samuel L. Smith, David H. P. Turban, Steven Hamblin, and Nils Y. Hammerla. 2017. Offline bilingual word vectors, orthogonal transformations and the inverted softmax. *CoRR* abs/1702.03859. http://arxiv.org/abs/1702.03859.

Duyu Tang, Furu Wei, Bing Qin, Ming Zhou, and Ting Liu. 2014. Building large-scale twitter-specific sentiment lexicon: A representation learning approach. In *Proceedings of COLING 2014, the 25th International Conference on Computational Linguistics: Technical Papers*. pages 172–182.

Yulia Tsvetkov, Leonid Boytsov, Anatole Gershman, Eric Nyberg, and Chris Dyer. 2014. Metaphor detection with cross-lingual model transfer. In *ACL*.

Peter D. Turney, Yair Neuman, Dan Assaf, and Yohai Cohen. 2011. Literal and metaphorical sense identification through concrete and abstract context. In *Proceedings of the Conference on Empirical Methods in Natural Language Processing*. Association for Computational Linguistics, Stroudsburg, PA, USA, EMNLP '11, pages 680–690.

Michael Wilson. 1988. Mrc psycholinguistic database: Machine-usable dictionary, version 2.00. *Behavior Research Methods, Instruments, & Computers* 20(1):6–10.

Author Index